Numbers

Pentecostal Commentary Series

Editor-in-Chief

John Christopher Thomas (*Pentecostal Theological Seminary, Cleveland, and Centre for Pentecostal and Charismatic Studies, Bangor University*)

Associate Editor

Lee Roy Martin (*Pentecostal Theological Seminary, Cleveland*)

VOLUME 09

The titles published in this series are listed at *brill.com/pcs*

Numbers

A Pentecostal Commentary

By

Wilfred Hildebrandt

BRILL

LEIDEN | BOSTON

Library of Congress Cataloging-in-Publication Data

Names: Hildebrandt, Wilfred, author.
Title: Numbers : a Pentecostal commentary / by Wilfred Hildebrandt.
Description: Leiden : Brill, [2024] | Series: Pentecostal commentary series, 2589-9902 ; volume 09 | Includes bibliographical references and index.
Identifiers: LCCN 2024037762 (print) | LCCN 2024037763 (ebook) | ISBN 9789004711327 (paperback) | ISBN 9789004711341 (ebook)
Subjects: LCSH: Bible. Numbers–Commentaries.
Classification: LCC BS1265.53 .H55 2024 (print) | LCC BS1265.53 (ebook) | DDC 222/.1407–dc23/eng/20240903
LC record available at https://lccn.loc.gov/2024037762
LC ebook record available at https://lccn.loc.gov/2024037763

Typeface for the Latin, Greek, and Cyrillic scripts: "Brill". See and download: brill.com/brill-typeface.

ISSN 2589-9902
ISBN 978-90-04-71132-7 (paperback)
ISBN 978-90-04-71134-1 (e-book)
DOI 10.1163/9789004711341

Copyright 2025 by Wilfred Hildebrandt. Published by Koninklijke Brill BV, Leiden, The Netherlands.
Koninklijke Brill BV incorporates the imprints Brill, Brill Nijhoff, Brill Schöningh, Brill Fink, Brill mentis, Brill Wageningen Academic, Vandenhoeck & Ruprecht, Böhlau and V&R unipress.
Koninklijke Brill BV reserves the right to protect this publication against unauthorized use. Requests for re-use and/or translations must be addressed to Koninklijke Brill BV via brill.com or copyright.com.

This book is printed on acid-free paper and produced in a sustainable manner.

Contents

Series Preface   IX
Acknowledgements   XIII

Introduction   1
1   Method and Approach for a Pentecostal Commentary   2
2   Name of the Book   4
3   The Hebrew Text and Translation   5
4   Literary Genres and Structure   6
5   Structure and Organizational Layout   7
6   Chronology and Audience   13
7   The Place of Numbers in the Pentateuch   17
8   The Primary Theme of the Torah   18
9   The Unity of the Pentateuch   22
10 The Life and Leadership of Moses   23
11 Torah Composition and the Question of Mosaic Authorship   29
12 A Selection of Seven Predominate Themes in Numbers   39

Commentary

PART 1
The Exodus (First) Generation in the Wilderness (Numbers 1–25)

1.1–10.36   Administration and Organization for Israel's Journey to the Promised Land   63
    1.1–54   Taking a Census and Mustering the Military   63
        Reflection and Response, Numbers 1: Order and Documentation   73
    2.1–34   The Israelite Camp   75
        Reflection and Response, Numbers 2: Countless People Camping with Yahweh   81
    3.1–51   The Levites and the Aaronides   83
    4.1–49   Census of the Levites   91
    5.1–31   Physical and Spiritual Conditions   95
    6.1–27   The Nazirite Vow   103
        Reflection and Response, Numbers 3–6: Levites and Priests Serving as Clergy   112

7.1–89	The Tabernacle and Altar Dedication	113
8.1–26	Consecration of the Levites	118
	Reflection and Response, Numbers 7–8: The Lord Communicates 123	
9.1–23	The Passover and the Cloud	125
10.1–36	Moving Forward to a Promised Land	132
	Reflection and Response, Numbers 9–10: Shepherds for the Wilderness Itinerary 139	
11.1–25.18	**Hardships, Conflicts, Rebellion and Judgment**	**142**
11.1–35	Prophetic Leadership	142
12.1–16	Family and Leadership Conflict	152
	Reflection and Response, Numbers 11–12: Prophetic Leadership in the Wilderness 160	
13.1–14.45	The Reconnaissance Mission	163
	Reflection and Response, Numbers 13–14: Shepherds and Spies for the Wilderness Itinerary 182	
15.1–41	Cultus Offerings and Sacrifices	185
16.1–17.13	Leadership Ambitions	194
	Reflection and Response, Numbers 16–17: Yahweh Determines Leaders 206	
18.1–32	Protecting Sanctuary, Clergy and People	208
19.1–22	Ritual Purification Rites	215
	Reflection and Response, Numbers 15–18: Attending to Spiritual Matters 220	
20.1–22.1	Conflicts Escalate and Infuriate	221
	Reflection and Response, Numbers 11–21: Wandering in a Wilderness 235	
22.2–24.25	External Conflicts: Israel and Moab	238
	Reflection and Response, Numbers 22–24: Yahweh's Blessing and Prophecy 253	
25.1–18	Israel's Religious Failure	256
	Reflection and Response, Numbers 11–25: Severe Warnings before the Second Census 262	

CONTENTS

PART 2
The Second Generation Anticipates Entry into the Land of Promise (Numbers 26–36)

26.1–32.42   From Moab to Canaan: Preparing to Receive Their 'Inheritance'   267
- 26.1–65   Second Generation Census   268
- 27.1–23   Land Issues and Leadership Transitions   273
   Reflection and Response, Numbers 26–27: Second Chances and Transitions in Life   282
- 28.1–29.40   Offerings and Sacrifices   284
- 30.1–16   Making Vows   296
   Reflection and Response, Numbers 28–30: Spiritual Discipline and Personal Responsibility for Words   299
- 31.1–54   Vengeance on the Midianites   301
- 32.1–42   Land Allocations   306

33.1–56   A Synopsis of the Wilderness Expedition   313
- 33.1–2   Moses' Records   314
- 33.3–15   Departing Egypt   315
- 33.16–36   Sites of Wandering   317
- 33.37–49   From Mount Hor to the Abarim Mountains   318
- 33.50–56   Poised for Conquest   320

34.1–36.13   Anticipation of the Promised Land   323
- 34.1–15   The Covenantal Borders   324
- 34.16–29   Leaders for Land Allocations   326
- 35.1–5   The Levitical Towns   327
- 35.6–15   Designated Towns of Refuge   329
- 35.16–29   Premeditated Murder   332
- 35.30–34   Legal Summation   333
   Reflection and Response, Numbers 33–35: The Promise of Land   335
- 36.1–4   Inheritance Security   337
- 36.5–12   Marriage   339
- 36.13   The Reliable Leadership of Moses   340
   Reflection and Response, Numbers 26–36: Anticipating the Inheritance   341

Select Bibliography   345
Index of Modern Authors   347
Index of Scriptures   349
Index of Subjects   360

Series Preface

The purpose of this commentary series is to provide reasonably priced commentaries written from a distinctively Pentecostal perspective primarily for pastors, lay persons, and Bible students. Therefore, while the works are based upon the best of scholarship, they are written in popular language. The aim is to communicate the meaning of the text, with minimal technical distractions.

In order to explain the need for such an attempt to read the biblical text, it is necessary to understand something of the ethos of Pentecostalism.

Pentecostalism is a relatively recent phenomenon in comparison to its Christian siblings, given that its formal origins go back about a hundred years. By any means of calculation, it continues to grow very rapidly in many places around the globe and accounts for a not insignificant percentage of the world's Christians. Current estimates of those who would identify themselves as part of the Pentecostal-Charismatic movements range from 380,000,000 to 683,000,000. According to David Barrett, the global profile of Pentecostalism is as follows:

> Some 29 percent of all members worldwide are white, 71 percent are non-white. Members are more urban than rural, more female than male, more children (under eighteen years) than adults, more third world (66 per cent) than western world (32 per cent), more living in poverty (87 per cent) than affluence (13 per cent), more family-related than individualist.[1]

Yet, despite its demographic significance, Pentecostalism continues to be largely misunderstood by many outside the movement. For example, there are those who '... see Pentecostalism as essentially fundamentalist Christianity with a doctrine of Spirit baptism and gifts added on' and others who view it '... as an experience which fits equally well in any spirituality or theological system—perhaps adding some needed zest or interest'.[2] Yet, those who know the tradition well are aware how far from the truth such assessments are. As Donald

---

1 D. Barrett, 'Statistics, Global', *Dictionary of the Pentecostal and Charismatic Movements* (ed. S.M. Burgess and G.B. McGee; Grand Rapids: Zondervan, 1988), p. 811.
2 Steven J. Land, *Pentecostal Spirituality: A Passion for the Kingdom* (JPTSup 1; Sheffield: Sheffield Academic Press, 1993), p. 29.

W. Dayton[3] and Steven J. Land[4] have demonstrated, standing at the theological heart of Pentecostalism is the message of the five-fold gospel: Jesus is Savior, Sanctifier, Holy Spirit Baptizer, Healer, and Coming King. This paradigm not only identifies the theological heart of the tradition, but also immediately reveals the ways in which Pentecostalism as a movement is both similar to and dissimilar from others within Christendom. When the five-fold gospel paradigm is used as the main point of reference Pentecostalism's near kinship to the holiness tradition is obvious, as is the fundamental difference with many of those within the more reformed evangelical tradition. It also reveals the surprising similarities between Pentecostalism and the Roman Catholic and Orthodox traditions.

Therefore, the production of a Pentecostal Commentary Series representative of the tradition's ethos requires more than simply selecting contributors who have had a glossolalic experience. Rather, the process of composition as well as the physical format of the commentary should be in keeping with the ethos and spirituality of the tradition.

In the attempt to ensure a writing process representative of the tradition, each contributor has been urged to incorporate the following disciplines in the writing of the commentary on a particular biblical book.

Writers have been encouraged to engage in prayer for this project, both as individuals and as members of a community of believers. Specifically, the guidance of the Holy Spirit has been sought in these times of prayer, for the leadership of the Spirit in interpretation is essential. Specific times of prayer where the body intercedes on the writer's behalf and seeks to hear from the Lord have been encouraged.

Given the Pentecostal commitment to body ministry, where various members of the body have specific calls and responsibilities, writers have been asked to explore ways in which their scholarship might be contextualized within their own local church body and thereby be strengthened by the dynamic interaction between the Holy Spirit, the body of Christ, and the Word of God. Writers were encouraged to covenant with their churches concerning this writing project in order to seek out their spiritual support. Where possible, writers were asked to explore the possibility of leading a group Bible study on the given biblical book. Ideally, such groups included representatives from each group of the target readership.

Writers were also encouraged to seek out the advice and critique of gifted colleagues who would join with them in this project so as not to work in isola-

---

3   Donald W. Dayton, *The Theological Roots of Pentecostalism* (Peabody, MA: Hendrickson, 1991).
4   Land, *Pentecostal Spirituality*.

tion. This endeavor was conceived as too difficult and far reaching to go alone. Rather it is conceived of as part of the ministry of the body of Christ, for the glory of God.

The commentary attempts to be in keeping with the ethos and spirituality of the tradition in its physical format as well. Specifically, the commentaries seek to reflect the dialogical way in which the tradition tends to approach the biblical text. Thus, each commentary begins with a series of questions designed to lift up corporate and individual issues that are illuminated in the biblical book under examination. This section identifies those key issues that are taken up in the commentary which follows. As a hermeneutical task, this section invites the reader to interpret his/her life context in a confessional-critical manner, revealing the need(s) to be addressed by the text. Such an opening serves to contextualize the commentary in the life of the church from the very beginning and serves to teach the reader how the Bible can legitimately be used in contemporary life.

Flowing out of this initial section, the introduction proper seeks to inform the reader as to the need, process, purpose, time, and place of composition. As a trajectory of the initial section, the introduction proper seeks be a necessity for the reader and seeks to avoid the strange and irrelevant discussions that introductions often pursue. The introductions normally include topics of special interest to Pentecostals along with the normal introductory matters of authorship, place of composition, destination, audience, date, and theological emphases. A rather detailed discussion of the genre and structure of the book forms the basis of organization for the exposition that follows. In addition, a section devoted to the book's teaching about the Holy Spirit is included in the introduction.

The commentary proper provides a running exposition on the text, provides extended comments on texts of special significance for Pentecostals, and acknowledges and interacts with major options in interpreting individual passages. It also provides periodic opportunities for reflection upon and personal response to the biblical text. The reflection and response components normally occur at the end of a major section of the book. Here, a theme prominent in a specific passage is summarized in the light of the reading offered in the commentary. Next, the readers encounter a series of questions designed to lead them in corporate and personal reflection about this dimension of the text. Finally, the readers are encouraged to respond to the biblical text in specific ways. Such reflection and response is consistent with the tradition's practice of not simply hearing the words of Scripture but responding to them in concrete ways. It is the literary equivalent to the altar call.

In the attempt not to overtax the popular reader footnotes have been used *carefully* and *sparingly*. However, when additional, more technical discussions are deemed necessary, they are placed in the footnotes.

In addition, Greek and Hebrew words are ordinarily found only within parentheses or in the footnotes. Every attempt has been made to ensure that the constituency of the movement are represented in some way among the contributors. It is my hope and prayer that the work of these women and men, from a variety of continents, races, and communities, will aid the Pentecostal community (and other interested individuals and communities) in hearing the biblical text in new and authentic ways.

Editor in Chief
John Christopher Thomas

Old Testament Editor
Lee Roy Martin

New Testament Editor
John Christopher Thomas

Acknowledgements

I am grateful to the visionaries who launched the Pentecostal Series of Commentaries with their criteria of careful exposition and practical applications. The word of God is so valuable and powerful that it is always a pleasure to study any portion of it. Numbers has proven to be a delightful book to exegete. During this project I have experienced the fresh inspiration, constant motivation, and keen instruction that only the Spirit of God can give.

I appreciate the encouragement of my wife Lillian throughout the years of research and writing for this commentary. She read the manuscript, suggested several edits and offered valuable insights. I am grateful for the support and affirmations of my parents, Edward and Emma, who were thrilled with my calling to theological studies. After their suffering during the second world war, they longed for peace and named their first son Wilfred. Literally "friedenstifter" means peacemaker which gave me the vision and desire to live up to their expectations. The importance of names is unmistakable in the Book of Numbers and in Hebrew culture, which will be evident in this commentary.

I am indebted to many professors who taught and mentored me in my own theological formation at Western Pentecostal Bible College and Regent College. Many of them are referenced in this commentary due to their writings, including Roger Stronstad, William Dumbrell, Carl Armerding, James Houston, Gordon D. Fee, Sven Soderlund, and Bruce K. Waltke. Professor Willem Boshoff at the University of South Africa was influential in my Old Testament research.

I am grateful to Lee Roy Martin for his untiring work on this series and the Numbers commentary in preparation for publication. May this work prove to be inspirational and helpful for all those who worship Yahweh and aspire to be influential leaders.

Wilfred Hildebrandt

Introduction

Numbers is the fourth book in the Pentateuch and presents several narratives, lists of leaders, itemised sacred materials, offerings, and sacrifices. It includes many legislative instructions, but mainly records events pertaining to the journey of a very large population of people who migrate from Egypt to Canaan. This commentary is an exposition of the details of the thirty-six chapters of Numbers, in a theological narration of the various contents, details and genres.

For readers of the book of Numbers, many questions may arise when observing the contents and stories. Does God allocate land to people and nations? Does God actually punish oppressive regimes, rulers, and nations for certain behaviours? In our contemporary settings are we to expect God to supernaturally provide resources like food and water for huge populations that are in need? What roles are political leaders responsible for when it comes to the social, physical, and religious aspects of nationhood? Is warfare mandated by God on behalf of one nation against others? Is a blend of political and religious leadership the best approach for leading people? Are the leadership roles presented in Numbers still valid forms for application in a modern context? Does God raise up prophetic leaders in order to guide nations in their development? Are some of the calamities that affect the world today, such as plagues, earthquakes, famine, drought, and war caused by God? Does God show preferential treatment to some people and nations over against other people? Is there a way of living on earth that will bring divine blessing and favor on individuals, leaders, and people groups?

These are legitimate queries which suggest that the book of Numbers may be a complicated document. Even so, the book is worthy of careful exposition to determine important events and principles in Israel's history. The wilderness wandering episodes are often referred to in the OT as a period of conflict that God's people should learn from (cf. Psalms 68; 78; 95; 106; Ezekiel 20). Not only so, but the themes and motifs of Numbers continue to have much relevance in every generation since the materials were recorded. This includes Israel's national goals, leadership structure, prophetic leadership, land acquisition, resource management, religion, cultus and worship, war, plagues, health care and more! The significance of these themes for the current conflicts in the world cannot be overstated. Most of the conflicts are rooted in the dearth of effective leadership where greed, power, and pride are so pervasive. The clamour of the nations for resources, land, and prosperity is vociferous. The problems that nations are facing in providing health care, security, food, and water supplies are intensifying rapidly. Interestingly, the ancient book of Numbers has many perceptive narratives and insights for contemporary challenges.

1 Method and Approach for a Pentecostal Commentary

There are several excellent commentaries on Numbers, written from diverse theological perspectives and readily available to readers—so why write another one? This commentary purports to be written from a Pentecostal perspective that emulates a careful reading of the Hebrew text from a perspective that includes specific characteristics. Many of these are common for evangelical scholarship and may not be unique. They may simply be a reiteration of what many readers already apply when approaching Scripture. This includes a reverential reading of the final documents that were received in Judaism and Christianity as authoritative. Pentecostals affirm a high valuation of the Spirit's inspiration of the original text for theological and practical application to contemporary life. They also affirm that the Holy Spirit continues to illumine the words of scripture to the believer's heart and mind. Additionally, Pentecostals admit that their personal experiences have a considerable impact on the reading and interpretation. This primarily has to do with the reading of scripture from the NT 'vantage of Pentecost' where readers have had a similar experience as Early Church Christians according to several passages in Acts (cf. Acts 2.1–4; 8.15–19; 10.44–46; 19.1–7).[1] Therefore, the spiritual, cultural, and historical experiences of the reader have a bearing on how they interpret the inspired scriptures.[2] However, although the texts are approached with open hearts and minds, Pentecostals affirm the Scriptures must be studied in accordance with historical, grammatical readings, preferably in the original languages. This level of study restrains the reader from allegorical interpretations or eisegesis which imports the reader's ideas into the text. Furthermore,

---

1 The import of what a Pentecostal perspective entails is succinctly presented in C.S. Keener, *Spirit Hermeneutics: Reading Scripture in Light of Pentecost* (Grand Rapids, Eerdmans, 2016), pp. 19–56.
2 In my private reading and study in the Book of Numbers I have become aware of how much my personal journey and experiences have impacted my understanding of certain texts. This includes my butchering skills in a former career (i.e. sacrificial system!), Spirit baptism with speaking in tongues and prophesying, global mission service in Africa with several diverse people groups and cultures, extensive travel, an intercultural teaching career, and helping my grandsons with their quail farm. Additionally, like most pilgrims on this earth I have had my own personal 'wilderness experiences'. In recognizing this I hope that my presuppositions and encounters have not clouded my understanding and interpretation in a negative way!

INTRODUCTION   3

it acknowledges the intertextual nature of Scripture in the Pentateuch, which call for readings that observe narratives which have similar historical events, connections, repetition, or direct parallel passages.

With these perspectives in mind, the Hebrew text, as well as several English translations, are used to exposit the meaning of passages, narratives, and records. Several commentaries were chosen for insights and comparison to include views from different theological perspectives. Some of these are considered the best for various reasons. J. Milgrom and rabbinic resources are appreciated for their expertise in biblical Hebrew, Hebrew literary structure, cultural practices, sacrificial cultus language, and religious knowledge.³ J. Milgrom's, B. Levine's, and G. Gray's commentaries are very detailed and exhaustive literary works rooted in exegetical, grammatical, critical, and theological analysis. Levine and Gray stand out for their source critical analysis, documentary compositional theories and interpretations.⁴ R. Allen, and T. Ashley offer careful exposition of texts in a balanced way, along with practical application and insights in particular sections.⁵ D. Hymes offers significant insights and scholarship from a Pentecostal perspective in his articles and thesis on Numbers.⁶

The Hebrew word studies in the *Theological Dictionary of the Old Testament* (15 volumes; abbreviated as *TDOT*) are a 'gold mine' of valuable articles on word etymology, Hebrew terms, biblical, and theological usage. Although the authors generally come from diverse, and critical perspectives with significant presuppositions of literary composition, the articles present very important scholarly content for consideration.⁷ This will be evident in the word study references throughout the commentary. To assist readers who desire to engage in further theological word studies, the author has referenced key Hebrew words in brackets which identify the word used in the text. The translation of the word precedes the Hebrew in quotation marks. An online tool that the author appreciates very much for OT study and research is *Sefaria.org*. It presents the Jewish

---

3   J. Milgrom, *Numbers: The JPS Torah Commentary* (The Jewish Publication Society, 1990).
4   B.A. Levine, *Numbers 1–20: A New Translation with Introduction and Commentary* (Anchor Bible; New York: Doubleday, 1993). B.A. Levine, *Numbers 21–36: A New Translation with Introduction and Commentary* (Anchor Bible; New York: Doubleday, 2000). G.B. Gray, *A Critical and Exegetical Commentary on Numbers* (ICC; Edinburgh: T & T Clark, 1903).
5   R.B. Allen, *Numbers* (Expositor's Bible Commentary, ed. F.E. Gaebelein, Vol. 2.; Grand Rapids: Zondervan, 1990). T.R. Ashley, *The Book of Numbers* (NICOT; Grand Rapids: Eerdmans, 1993).
6   D.C. Hymes, 'A Pluriform Analysis of Numbers 10.11–14.45' (PhD Thesis: University of Wales, Bangor, 2010).
7   This means that many of the articles assume the documentary hypothesis which features a heavier hand in the Torah's composition by the 'Priestly' sources which were assumed to be finalized hundreds of years after the Mosaic period.

Publication Society's (JPS) translation which is based on the Hebrew Masoretic text of Biblia Hebraica Stuttgartensia (BHS), and provides significant research tools for the Hebrew text, word definitions and usage, grammar and numerous rabbinic commentaries. Additionally, the standard research tools for word studies, lexicons, concordances, and digital tools were employed as essential and valuable for any serious Bible study.

Being a book on 'numbers', word usage will often be noted with the number of times key words are used in the documents. The statistics of the number of times words are used often indicate important emphases, primary themes, motifs, and elements to consider. On the other hand, the dearth of expected word usage may also indicate important theological matters to consider—especially in the development of ancient writings like the Torah. This means that some concepts are introduced in basic ways but are not fully developed. In other words, several important themes are introduced in the Torah which are then fleshed out in progressively disclosed ways in other OT documents.

A Pentecostal commentary may be from a unique perspective but for the most part it simply means that the reader is open to pneumatic influences in prayer, Scripture reading, interpretation, and community affirmations. However, like all exegetes, Pentecostals are also dependent on the community of faith from all theological perspectives—and especially on the scholars who understand the original languages and texts of Scripture and offer their carefully reasoned insights.

2   Name of the Book

Various names are given to this document and 'Numbers' is a common title based on the census lists of Numbers One and Twenty-six. Moreover, many numbers are recorded which tabulate people, tribes, leaders as well as offerings and gifts. In fact, in the thirty-six chapters of the book there are over 590 numeric references. English versions hold to the name of Numbers based on the term '*numeri*' in Latin which took the lead from the Septuagint '*arithmoi*' in Greek. The Hebrews, however, typically name a book after an evocative word in the opening stanza. In the case of Numbers, the fourth term (מדבר; '*bemidbar*') meaning 'in the wilderness', has been selected—primarily because this sets the main background for the events which follow. Namely, Israel sojourns in several wilderness contexts for an extensive forty-year period. Also notable is the first word of the scroll, 'And He spoke', (דבר). This is a very appropriate term in the case of Numbers because the book is characterized by God's continual and frequent communication with Moses and the Israelites.

INTRODUCTION

This commentary will refer to the book of Numbers as the main title but features the core themes that are presented during the forty-year period which is characterized by Israel's wilderness experience. It is in the wilderness where Yahweh communicates with selected leaders and reveals his presence and care for the people of Israel as he leads them towards the covenantal land of promise. The journey encompasses the trek from Mount Sinai to the border of a special place for a new generation of Israelites.

3 The Hebrew Text and Translation

The Masoretic text of Numbers is in an excellent state of preservation with few and insignificant variations between manuscripts. However, the Septuagint and Samaritan versions record a few differences and occasionally incorporate material from other parallel passages which harmonize certain details.[8]

In this commentary most quotations of Scripture are taken from the New International Version (NIV), based on the 2011 updated text.[9] Comparison of the NIV translation with other translations may be evident in some of the commentary. The author has also taken considerable consideration of the Jewish Publication Society's translation which is used by *Sefaria.org*. The JPS *Tanakh* is based on the Hebrew Masoretic text of Biblia Hebraica Stuttgartensia, the famed Leningrad Codex (traceable to Aaron ben Moses ben Asher ca. 930 and revised in 1010 by Samuel ben Jacob, a scribe who worked in Egypt).

One of the most distinctive components in the book of Numbers is the extraordinary amount of numbers. Literally, there are hundreds of words used to specify the number of people in a family, clan, or group, and two lengthy census lists which specify names with leaders (about 590 numerals). Certain offerings, sacrifices, products, animals, deaths, and cultic utensils are quantified and measured. These numbers take up a considerable amount of text in the book but provide evidence of a very structured, detailed, and orderly society. It should also be noted that the recording and translation of the numerous numbers involved meticulous work for the scribes who included their accounting for the book in the *masorah finalis* (at the end of the text). For Numbers, at the end of the manuscript, the scribes recorded that there were 1288 verses with

---

8 Cf. Milgrom, *Numbers*, p. xi; Allen, *Numbers*, p. 661; Hymes, 'A Pluriform Analysis of Numbers 10.11–14.45'.

9 Holy Bible: New International Version, 2011, International Bible Society. When the Jewish Publication Society (JPS), or other translations are used, it will be noted.

the mid-point being Numbers 17.20. Before the BHS was divided into chapters, the scribes identified 452 'sedarim' (orders; divisions) in the OT for their weekly lessons to be read over a 3-year lectionary cycle in the Palestinian usage.[10] For the book of Numbers there are 33 'sedarim', as there are for Exodus.[11]

4   Literary Genres and Structure

A great variety of genres are utilized in the book of Numbers, which makes it interesting to read. For this reason, many writers despair in finding an organizational premise to the book. In the end it may be fruitful to think of Numbers as carefully assembled documents. These include census lists, stories, travel logs, prophecies (and ecstatic utterances), offering inventories, poetry, supplications, legislative materials, and a multitude of instructions! Additionally, it is appropriate to consider the book of Numbers as a type of 'community obituary'. It is a morbid thought but at the end of the second census the summation affirms a staggering outcome. 'For the LORD had told those Israelites they would surely die in the wilderness, and not one of them was left except Caleb son of Jephunneh and Joshua son of Nun' (Num. 26.65). Notable examples of death include the burial at *Kibroth Hattavath* (Num. 11.34), the decree that a generation will die in the wilderness (Num. 14.29–35), the ten negative spies (Num. 14.37), the 250 Korahites and 14,700 people (Num. 16.35), Miriam (Num. 20.1), Aaron (Num. 20.22–29), death by snake bites (Num. 21.6), 24,000 by plague (Num. 25.9), Zelophehad (Num. 27.3), Moses (Num. 27.12), the Midianites and Balaam (Num. 31.7–20). These are some of the numerous accounts of judgment where scores of people perish in a variety of ways including by fire, plague, sinkhole or earthquake, and food poisoning. The deaths of Miriam, Aaron, and Moses are also notable events in the wilderness, although Moses' death is more of an announcement which is finally described in Deuteronomy (cf. Deut. 32.48–52; 34.5–12). Death and burials were a constant reality for the Israelite nation. Numbers provides the written obituary with numerous names as a record of one generation of people who perished in the wilderness. References to death (ca. 25 times) and die or died (ca. 46 times) occur often in Numbers. However, explanations or details on preparations for burial and interment are strangely silent.

---

10   E. Wurthwein, *The Text of the Old Testament: An Introduction to the Biblia Hebraica* (trans. E.F. Rhodes; Grand Rapids: Eerdmans, 1979), p. 21.
11   The scribes also counted 400,945 consonantal letters in the Torah to ensure accuracy. This amounts to 970,856 Hebrew words and 5,845 verses.

Milgrom provides a technical summation of other literary genres used in Numbers: narrative (4.1–3), poetry (21.17–18), prophecy (24.3–9), victory song (21.27–30, pre-Israelite), prayer (12.13), blessing (6.24–26), lampoon (22.22–35), diplomatic letter (21.14–19), civil law (27.1–11), cultic law (15.17–21), oracular decision (15.32–36), census list (26.1–51), temple archive (7.10–88), and itinerary (33.1–49).[12] Furthermore, there is a fluctuation of the main genre materials between legislative material and narration of significant events, which lends itself to the perspective of many who claim there is no organizational structure to the document. Milgrom notes that the narrative portions are focused on the wilderness trek whereas the legal materials concern the three main stations of the march: Sinai (1–10.10), Kadesh (chapters 15, 18–19), and the steppes of Moab (chapters 28–30, 34–36). However, there are a few exceptions to the fluctuation. The mixing of genres appears to be typical of ancient Near Eastern vassal treaties where the suzerain presents benefits offered in narrative form followed by stipulations to be obeyed in legislative statements. Thus, 'The book of Numbers also operates in the shadow of Sinai: Israel has accepted the suzerainty of its God and is bound to His law, while the narratives continue to manifest divine Providence (and Israel's backsliding)'.[13]

5 Structure and Organizational Layout

Due to the complex assembling of literary materials in Numbers, a considerable variety of outlines have been offered by commentators. Some of them are very detailed and organize the material according to the generational emphasis of people or the diverse genres. Others prefer the geographic notices, or the thematic highlights. For the purposes of this commentary the author has adapted two concise summations that should serve as a compass for reading Numbers. The modest and concise summary of W. Dumbrell features the three main geographical locations in Numbers. The second outline from Allen provides a more detailed overview of the main contents which are organized according to the two generational emphases. Allen modified the outline of Olsen with more detail and structures the two major sections with several sub-themes.[14]

---

12 Milgrom, *Numbers*, p. xiii.
13 Milgrom, *Numbers*, p. xvi.
14 W.J. Dumbrell, *The Faith of Israel: Its Expression in the Books of the Old Testament* (Grand Rapids: Baker Book House, 1988), p. 48. Cf. Allen, *Numbers*, pp. 668–675. Cf. D.T. Olsen, *The Death of the Old and the Birth of the New: The Framework of the Book of Numbers and the Pentateuch* (Brown Judaic Studies; Chico, CA.: Scholars Press, 1985), pp. 118–120.

This commentary adapts the outlines of Olsen and Allen, taking into consideration the genre variations of lists, laws, and narratives, with observations of significant thematic developments, but adds my own detailed headings.

Part 1		The Exodus (First) Generation in the Wilderness (Numbers 1–25)
1.1–10.36		Administration and Organization for Israel's Journey to the Promised Land
	1.1–54	Taking a Census and Mustering the Military
	1.1	Yahweh's Instruction
	1.2–14	The Census Undertaking
	1.15–16	Chosen Leaders
	1.17–46	Counting the Males
	1.47–54	The Levites
	2.1–34	The Israelite Camp
	2.1–2	Organization of the Camp
	2.3–16	Tribal Allotments
	2.17–31	Preparations for Embarkment
	2.32–34	The Israelite Population
	3.1–51	The Levites and The Aaronides
	3.1–4	Levitical Families
	3.5–10	The Aaronides
	3.11–13	The Firstborn
	3.14–39	Counting the Levites
	3.40–51	Redemption Fees
	4.1–49	Census of The Levites
	4.1–20	The Levitical Census and the Kohathites
	4.21–28	The Gershonites
	4.29–33	The Merarites
	4.34–49	Counting the Servants of the Cultus
	5.1–31	Physical and Spiritual Conditions
	5.1–4	Maintaining Purity in the Camp
	5.5–10	Relational Restitution
	5.11–31	A Marital Conflict
	6.1–27	The Nazirite Vow
	6.1–12	The Nazirite and the Vow
	6.13–21	Finalizing the Vow
	6.22–27	The Divine Blessing
	7.1–89	The Tabernacle and Altar Dedication
	7.1	Consecrating the Tabernacle
	7.2–11	Bringing the Offerings
	7.12–83	Leader's Contributions

INTRODUCTION

	7.84–88	The Altar
	7.89	Moses Before the Lord
	8.1–26	Consecration of the Levites
	8.1–4	The Seven-Branched Lampstand
	8.5–7	Consecration of the Levites
	8.8–13	Sacrifices
	8.14–19	Set Apart for Yahweh
	8.20–22	Applying Instructions
	8.23–26	Retirement Option
	9.1–23	The Passover and the Cloud
	9.1–5	The Passover
	9.6–13	Passover for the Unclean
	9.14	Passover for Foreigners
	9.15–23	The Guidance and Presence of the Lord
	10.1–36	Moving Forward to a Promised Land
	10.1–7	Trumpet Signals and Departure
	10.8–10	Priestly Privilege
	10.11–28	Preparing for Departure from Mount Sinai
	10.29–32	Guidance on the Journey
	10.33–36	The Ark of the Covenant
11.1–25.18		Hardships, Conflicts, Rebellion and Judgment
	11.1–35	Prophetic Leadership
	11.1–3	The Complaint
	11.4–9	The Provisions
	11.10–15	Moses Protests
	11.16–23	Yahweh's Response and Moses' Negotiation
	11.24–30	Sharing of the Spirit
	11.31–35	An Abundance of Quail
	12.1–16	Family and Leadership Conflict
	12.1–2	Family Tensions
	12.3–5	Moses' Humility
	12.6–8	The Prophetic Blessing
	12.9–16	Divine Judgment
	13.1–14.45	The Reconnaissance Mission
	13.1–3	Selecting Leaders for the Exploration
	13.4–16	Selected Explorers
	13.17–24	The Commission
	13.25–29	Forty Days in the Promised Land!
	13.30–33	The Exhortation
	14.1–10a	The People Protest

14.10–12	Yahweh Responds with A Devastating Change in Itinerary
14.13–19	Moses Intercedes
14.20–25	Yahweh Relents
14.26–35	Yahweh Pronounces the Judgment
14.36–45	A Death Sentence and Further Repudiation
15.1–41	Cultus Offerings and Sacrifices
15.1–16	Cultic Requirements
15.17–21	Aspiration
15.22–31	Personal Responsibility
15.32–36	Sabbath Observance
15.37–41	Remembering Commandments
16.1–17.13	Leadership Ambitions
16.1–2	Confrontation
16.3–11	Leadership Conflicts
16.12–17	A Summons and A Repudiation
16.18–34	The Contest
16.35–40	Sacred Office
16.41–50	Sacred Offering
17.1–13	Aaron is Upheld
18.1–32	Protecting Sanctuary, Clergy, and People
18.1–7	Instructions for the Priests
18.8–19	Benefits for the Priest and Levites
18.20–24	God Will Provide
18.25–32	Tithe Instructions
19.1–22	Ritual Purification Rites
19.1–10	Ritual Instructions
19.11–13	Cleansing Rituals
19.14–22	Further Lessons on Defiling Circumstances
20.1–22.1	Conflicts Escalate and Infuriate
20.1–5	Death of Miriam
20.6–13	Moses Will Not Enter the Promised Land
20.14–21	External Threats
20.22–29	Death of Aaron
21.1–3	External Threats of the Canaanites
21.4–9	Complaints and Judgment
21.10–20	Yahweh Will Bless
21.21–22.1	Victories in Battle
22.1	Camp on the Jordan
22.2–24.25	External Conflicts: Israel and Moab

INTRODUCTION

22.2–6	Balak, Moabites, and Midianites
22.7–12	The First Invitation from the Elders of Moab and Midian
22.13–20	The Second Invitation from Distinguished Messengers
22.21–35	Balaam's Journey and the Divine Messenger
22.36–23.12	Balak and Balaam
23.13–26	Balaam's Second Oracle
23.27–24.9	Balaam's Third Oracle
24.10–14	Balak's Anger
24.15–19	Balaam's Fourth Oracle
24.20–25	Three Brief Oracles and Balaam's Departure
25.1–18	Israel's Religious Failure
25.1–3	Another Apostasy
25.4–9	The Judgment
25.10–18	A Covenant of Peace for Phinehas

Part 2   The Second Generation Anticipates Entry into the Land of Promise (Numbers 26–36)

26.1–32.42	From Moab to Canaan: Preparing to Receive Their 'Inheritance'
26.1–65	Second Generation Census
26.1–51	The Census
26.52–56	Land Allotments
26.57–62	Census for the Levites
26.63–65	Summation
27.1–23	Land Issues and Leadership Transitions
27.1–11	Inheritance Regulations
27.12–14	Moses' Final Days
27.15–17	Moses' Leadership Succession Prayer
27.18–21	Joshua's Commissioning
27.22–23	Moses Publicly Lays Hands on Joshua
28.1–29.40	Offerings and Sacrifices
28.1–8	The Daily Offerings
28.9–10	Sabbath Offerings
28.11–15	The Monthly Offerings
28.16–25	The Passover and Festival of Unleavened Bread
28.26–31	The Feast of Weeks
29.1–7	Annual Congregation in the Seventh Month
29.8–11	Day of Atonement
29.12–34	Week Three in the Seventh Month
29.35–40	Final Day Offerings and Summation

	30.1–16	Making Vows
	30.1–2	A Man's Word
	30.3–5	A Woman's Pledge
	30.6–16	A Married Woman's Vow
	31.1–54	Vengeance on the Midianites
	31.1–6	Carrying out Yahweh's Sentence
	31.7–12	Death and Plunder
	31.13–18	Breach of Instruction and Punishment
	31.19–24	Ceremonial Cleansing
	31.25–47	Allocating the Plunder
	31.48–54	Impressive Results
	32.1–42	Land Allocations
	32.1–5	A Special Request from the Reubenites and Gadites
	32.6–15	Moses Fears Another Reversion
	32.16–27	Negotiations
	32.28–32	Finalizing the Appeal
	32.33–38	Land Inheritance in the Transjordan
	32.39–42	Manasseh
33.1–56		A Synopsis of the Wilderness Expedition
	33.1–2	Moses' Records
	33.3–15	Departing Egypt
	33.16–36	Sites of Wandering
	33.37–49	From Mount Hor to the Abarim Mountains
	33.50–56	Poised for Conquest
34.1–36.13		Anticipation of the Promised Land
	34.1–15	The Covenantal Borders
	34.16–29	Leaders for Land Allocations
	35.1–5	The Levitical Towns
	35.6–15	Designated Towns of Refuge
	35.16–29	Premeditated Murder
	35.30–34	Legal Summation
	36.1–4	Inheritance Security
	36.5–12	Marriage
	36.13	The Reliable Leadership of Moses

6 Chronology and Audience

6.1 *Chronology*

The events recorded in the book of Numbers continues to narrate the pilgrimage of Israel which began in Egypt (cf. Exodus 14).[15] The beginning of this trek from Egypt to a place of worship designated by Yahweh could have conceptually been reached by Israel in a three day walk from the Egyptian border (Exod. 3.18). When the people arrived at Mount Sinai the people camped there for one year before they were instructed to prepare for departure. The first ten chapters of the fourth book in the Torah depict significant, orderly, focused activity—especially concerning the leadership formation and camp arrangements.[16] Numbers includes a detailed travel itinerary which begins with a reflection on the beginning of their epic journey from Egypt.

> At the LORD's command Moses recorded the stages in their journey. This is their journey by stages: The Israelites set out from Rameses on the fifteenth day of the first month, the day after the Passover. They marched out defiantly in full view of all the Egyptians, who were burying all their firstborn, whom the LORD had struck down among them; for the LORD had brought judgment on their gods. (Num. 33.3–4)

The people received instructions from Moses which were designed to prepare them for the next phase in their journey to Canaan. The narration of the trek includes geographical locations, events and a variety of instructions concerning regulations for worship, encampment, and organization.

Although the time interval covered in the book of Numbers is forty-years, the events and circumstances are a limited selection of important material. This means that there are many years of Israel's experiences during their wilderness habitation which are basically periods of silence, indicating that some things were just too mundane or painful to record! What Numbers does reveal is that the nation was on location at Mount Sinai with a tabernacle erected. There, 'The LORD spoke to Moses in the tent of meeting in the Desert of Sinai on the first day of the second month of the second year after the Israelites came out

---

15 Watts states that 'The Pentateuchal story describes the law's audience quite explicitly: Israel in the wilderness (Exodus, Leviticus, and Numbers) and on the plains of Moab (Deuteronomy)'. Cf. J.W. Watts, 'Reader Identification and Alienation in the Legal Rhetoric of the Pentateuch', *Biblical Interpretation* 7.1 (1999), p. 106.

16 In fact, Gray comments that these chapters could have been included in the Book of Exodus since the material is so inter-connected. Gray, *Numbers*, p. xxiv.

of Egypt' (Num. 1.1). Consequent date references in Numbers indicate that the events which occur in the first ten chapters, take place from the first day of the second month in Israel's second calendar year, and that the episodes recorded from chs. 1–10, take place in a mere nineteen days!

Therefore, the wilderness phase for Israel is presented according to two main segments of time with very unequal periods and significance. The first stage is a positive one-year stretch beginning with the pinnacle of Israel's exodus experience when the people are gathered at Mount Sinai. There the Mosaic covenant was revealed and ratified, and laws were given. From this setting, the Israelites finally move forward. 'On the twentieth day of the second month of the second year, the cloud lifted from above the tabernacle of the covenant law. Then the Israelites set out from the Desert of Sinai and traveled from place to place until the cloud came to rest in the Desert of Paran' (Num. 10.11–12). At this point the Exodus and Mount Sinai experience was thirteen months behind them.

The second stage in Numbers involves a thirty-eight-year sojourn from the wilderness of Sinai to the Wilderness of Paran. Beginning in the second year after Sinai, on the twentieth day of the second month, this period comes to an end after a battle with the Midianites (Numbers 31). This event brings the second phase of Israel's testing in the wilderness to a conclusion of sorts. The nation moves out of the wilderness into the Transjordanian lands. The itinerary of Israel's epic forty-year sojourn is presented in Numbers 33 as a retrospective of the whole period during which a generation of warriors died 'because of their lack of faith' (cf. Deut. 2.14–16). S. Talmon refers to Numbers 11.1 to 31.5 as 'the book of Israel's failings' due to the numerous disappointments narrated there.[17]

What we read in Numbers is a summation of a forty-year period that illustrates the consequences of Israel's approach to the covenantal agreement with Yahweh—a blend of positive but mainly negative experiences. The wilderness wanderings depicted in Numbers reflect the results of their covenantal failures. This period of testing also serves as an example to the generation of the second census, to not follow in the steps of the forefathers. Chapters 21 to 36 are mostly limited to a five-month period in the fortieth year after leaving Sinai.

Finally, at the end of Numbers, Israel is in position to see and take the promised land. A new generation is on the brink of entering the covenantal inheritance. Their instructions are clear, and concise, but monumental in scope:

---

17 S. Talmon, 'מדבר', TDOT, VIII, p. 113.

> On the plains of Moab by the Jordan across from Jericho the LORD said to Moses, 'Speak to the Israelites and say to them: "When you cross the Jordan into Canaan, drive out all the inhabitants of the land before you. Destroy all their carved images and their cast idols and demolish all their high places. Take possession of the land and settle in it, for I have given you the land to possess. Distribute the land by lot, according to your clans. To a larger group give a larger inheritance, and to a smaller group a smaller one. Whatever falls to them by lot will be theirs. Distribute it according to your ancestral tribes."' (Num. 33.50–54)

With an emphasis on the beginning and the end of the wilderness period, the book seems to feature the positive opportunities before the nation. This makes the response of Israel to not enter the promised land as intended by Yahweh early in the journey all the more disappointing (Numbers 13–16). It accentuates the immense waste of time spent in the wilderness. However, there are notable events recorded in Numbers 10–21 that have a significant bearing on Israel's future and eventual conquest of the promised land.

Although the idea of wandering the wilderness for forty years may seem like a life sentence (indeed for some it was), Talmon reminds us that this period is still subordinate to other periods of history where Israel was outside of the promised land. After all, their apparent exile in Egypt lasted about ten times that phase, or ten generations (400 years according to Gen. 15.13, and 430 years according to Exod. 12.41).[18]

6.2 *Audience*

The book of Numbers narrates the events of one of the most difficult periods in Israel's history. During a forty-year period, the record claims that a whole generation of individuals lived and died in the wilderness. The primary audience for the narration appears to be the second generation of people who lived to witness the second census in preparation for entry into Canaan. The narratives and events serve as a reminder of significant failures in the nation that were not to be repeated. These include the lack of faith and trust in the promises and provisions of Yahweh. A robust obedience to the instructions of Yahweh given through designated leaders was prerequisite. A reverential awareness in the presence of Yahweh was expected with careful implementation of restrictions in approaching sacred things. A forward perspective in following Yahweh to the land of promise in accordance with his faithful provisions was expected.

---

18 Cf. Talmon, 'מדבר', pp. 105–107.

Ultimately, the primary audience for the book of Numbers is every living generation in the nation of Israel which valued the written words of the Torah since they were recorded and preserved. The history of transmission of the scrolls and documents reveals a meticulous preservation and record. Each generation was to keep and obey the words of the Torah. This means, the book was intended for all believers in Yahweh. It was a record to be mined for its warnings, exhortations, and patterns of divine human interaction as lessons to keep people on the path of righteousness—in every generation. Moreover, it is particularly relevant for those who experience 'wilderness' type seasons in life—whether they are caused by a lack of resources, disgruntled people (whether friends, relatives, or enemies), misdirected leaders who inspire conflict, disorder and even chaos, plagues, or curses. Seasons of despair in the valley of the shadow of death would arise and often required the Good Shepherd to lead people through the valley back up the mountain of victory. For this, the leadership of Yahweh was essential (Psalm 23). However, the Lord chooses to lead in partnership with the leadership of human shepherds who are commissioned to guide the people of God in appropriate ways (Num. 27.15–21).

These theological contributions from the book of Numbers continued to find respect and value in the community of faith through many generations. The apostle Paul noted the impact for his audience at Corinth and exhorted them not to be ignorant of Israel's trials and experiences in the wilderness because there were relevant lessons to be learned for all believers.

> For I do not want you to be ignorant of the fact, brothers and sisters, that our ancestors were all under the cloud and that they all passed through the sea. They were all baptized into Moses in the cloud and in the sea. They all ate the same spiritual food and drank the same spiritual drink; for they drank from the spiritual rock that accompanied them, and that rock was Christ. Nevertheless, God was not pleased with most of them; their bodies were scattered in the wilderness. Now these things occurred as examples to keep us from setting our hearts on evil things as they did. (1 Cor. 10.1–6)

Paul applied certain events from Exodus and Numbers as warnings not to be idolaters, immoral, grumblers or those who test the Lord. Rather, lessons learned were meant to strengthen believers and equip them to conquer temptations that may come in difficult seasons of life.

7 The Place of Numbers in the Pentateuch

The book of Numbers is the fourth book of the Torah or Pentateuch in the English Bible. In Judaism, 'torah' (תורה) refers to the laws or instructions that form a significant part of the five books. The Greek term 'Pentateuch' is used to refer to the first five books of the OT which include Genesis, Exodus, Leviticus, Numbers and Deuteronomy. The Torah has been the most influential document of the OT books for many generations of readers. Its claims and epic narratives have pierced the imagination and hearts of sacred and secular bibliophiles alike. Its worldview regarding creation, origins, human depravity, eternal prospects, and supernatural activity demand analysis with serious reflection. The contents of Scripture are not just ancient speculations but claim to reveal real foundational spiritual truths. Each book in the Torah is an essential part of the whole and deserves careful analysis and exposition. However, some commentators in the last century have often diminished the value and influence of Numbers due to the seemingly random structure and diverse genres. Others have lamented the lack of coherence in content, the primary focus, as well as the fluctuation of narrative and legal materials. Nevertheless, commentators and scholars in the last few decades have been successful in elucidating the valuable thematic emphases which Numbers presents. D.J.A. Clines is one of the authors who shows that 'Numbers establishes from its very beginning the thematic element of the land as the end to which everything drives, and its matter and movement are consistently oriented toward that goal'.[19] With the land motif and other thematic features, Numbers is an essential part of the Torah and develops the over-arching narrative to an epic conclusion.

Ultimately, the five books of the Pentateuch have been received and read for well over two thousand years and continue to be a source of inspiration to several communities of faith. To effectively comprehend the books of the Pentateuch, they must be read within the integrated whole of the Torah. In doing so, the unity and intention of the books become clearer and comprehensible. Therefore, this commentary will often refer back to events and texts in Genesis, Exodus, and Leviticus, which inform considerable material in Numbers. At times parallel passages in Deuteronomy will be referred to for important insights, as well as the Book of Joshua for its relevant content.[20] Due to the

---

19 D.J.A. Clines, The *Theme of the Pentateuch* (Sheffield: JSOT Press, 1986), p. 86.
20 In fact, scholars often view the major themes of the first part of the OT, within the Hexateuch—the Torah plus the Book of Joshua. The main reason for this is that the conquest and taking of the promised land brings the fulfillment of the covenantal promises into perspective. An excellent synopsis of what this entails in diagram form is presented

limitations of space, the commentary will only refer to other Scriptures when necessary. To grasp the thematic development which flows through the Torah, the following narrative insights must be understood to navigate Numbers effectively. It provides an overview of essential OT covenantal theology which is foundational to the Pentateuch. Although there are numerous scholars who have elucidated these themes in various contexts, the work of Clines is the main source of the following adapted thoughts.

8   The Primary Theme of the Torah

Many motifs and themes are evident in the Pentateuch. However, the predominate and overarching theme is succinctly and accurately stated by Clines: 'The theme of the Pentateuch is the partial fulfilment—which implies also the partial non-fulfilment—of the promise to or blessing of the patriarchs. The promise or blessing is both the divine initiative in a world where human initiatives always lead to disaster, and a re-affirmation of the primal divine intentions for man'.[21] The main contours of this assertion are evident in the thematic development which presents the promise of blessing as God's initiative. Human initiatives taken by the patriarchs usually lead to trouble, threat, or disaster. However, the primal intentions of God for man are reaffirmed throughout the Pentateuch from the three-fold covenantal promises stated in Genesis 12.1–3.[22]

Three core promises are specified in Genesis and then reiterated in numerous texts. The first promise is that of descendants (Gen. 12.2; 13.15; 15.4 f.; 17.2, 4–7; 22.16 ff.; Deut. 1.10 f.). The Lord will provide a son and posterity that will develop into a nation. This then is focalized in the narratives of Genesis 12–50 which are mainly concerned with Abraham, Isaac, Jacob, and Joseph. This

---

by Milgrom showing the Hexateuch's dominant structure in the form of a grand introversion pattern which highlights the main themes. The central theme is the theophany of Yahweh's presence (Exodus 33) and the covenantal arrangement with Israel. Cf. Milgrom, *Numbers*, p. xviii.

[21] Clines, *The Theme of the Pentateuch*, p. 29. Also cf. W.C. Kaiser, Jr. *Toward an Old Testament Theology* (Grand Rapids: Zondervan, 1978), which is thoroughly based on the theme of promise as found in Genesis 12 and developed in the OT.

[22] The promises are enshrined in the covenants of the OT which form the main theme and structure of OT theology. This is how W. Eichrodt presents his comprehensive theology in a two-volume exposition with 'covenant' as the central unifying concept in structure and theme. Cf. W. Eichrodt, *Theology of the Old Testament* (Vol. 1; trans. J.A. Baker; Philadelphia: Westminster, 1961).

is the lineage of successors through whom the promise of posterity was fulfilled. However, the promise of posterity is continually threatened in various ways. Is it really possible for the aged Abraham to have a son with Sarah? After twenty-five years of patience will Isaac survive and be a productive patriarch? The testing of Abraham puts this prospect in danger when Abraham takes Isaac to Moriah as a burnt offering (Gen. 22.1–19). Moreover, the patriarchal ancestress is often in danger (Genesis 12; 20; 26) in addition to the barrenness of the patriarchal wives (Sarah, Rebekah, Rachel; cf. Gen. 11.30; 17.36; 18.10–11; 22.12). Several narratives describe the fraternal rivalries which endangered the lives of heirs to the promises (Ishmael; Jacob; Joseph). Finally, the famines that occurred in Canaan threatened the survival of the patriarchal family and eventually forced them out of the land (Gen. 12.10; 26.1; 41.54). This pattern of selection, separation and contention informs the content of Genesis. This pattern clearly threatens the realization of God's promises which brings about the forward anticipation of a future fulfilment. It is the pattern that affects Israel in Numbers 13–14 when the nation fails to follow through with the Lord's guidance into the promised land.

At the end of Gen. 46.27, the promised family is established although the descendants did not amount to the stars of heaven (Gen. 15.5), nor the sand of the sea (Gen. 22.17), and Abraham's status as the father of the nations is yet to be realized (Gen. 17.5). In Genesis, the patriarchal family of Jacob and sons amounts to about seventy and the group doesn't flourish until they are in Egypt (Exod. 1.7, 9, 12, 20). Thus, Genesis closes with a forward perspective on the realization of the covenantal promises.

The second key element in the covenantal promise concerns God's relationship with the descendants of Abraham. Two primary points of focus, which firmly establish relationship, are the Exodus event and the Sinai revelation. Key recurring words emphasize the Lord's intentions: 'I will bless you'; 'I will make my covenant between me and you'; 'I will be your God'. These phrases indicate the meaning of the promise. Because God wants a relationship with Israel, he initiates this relationship by delivering Israel from Egypt. The contours of the relationship are developed in the Book of Exodus and Leviticus where the blessings of God are experienced in a Divine-human relationship (cf. Gen. 12.2 f.; 17.1–11; 26.24; 28.13–15; Exod. 3.12; 6.6 ff.; Lev. 26.12).

In Exod. 2.24, God remembers his covenant with the patriarchs. His care and concern for Israel is evidenced in the great deliverance of Israel, a primary action which establishes the covenantal relationship (Exod. 6.3–6). The covenant confirms that Israel belongs to God (Exod. 7.4, 16; 8.1; 3.10; 4.22) and should worship God alone in appreciation for deliverance (Exod. 7.16; 8.1, 21). Yahweh is to be the only God of the Hebrews (Exod. 9.1; 10.3). The conflict between Pharaoh and Moses concerns permission for the Hebrews to formalize their relationship with Yahweh by offering sacrifices and worshipping him. Therefore, the Exodus event signifies that the promise 'I will be your God' is fulfilled (Exod. 15.2). With the deliverance of Israel from Egypt, a new relationship and understanding of Yahweh as redeemer is initiated (Exodus 6). Although God keeps his promise, the question remains whether Israel will reciprocate and obey Yahweh alone. Threats to the covenantal relationship are real and persistent as Israel murmurs against God (Exod. 16.8). The people question God's presence (Exod. 17.7), even when God consistently provides for daily needs (water; manna; quail; cf. Exod. 16.12). God also gives victory in battle (Exod. 17.8–16), but Israel still complains.

At Sinai, Yahweh affirms his love and selection of Israel to solidify the covenantal relationship. Israel is God's own possession, a kingdom of priests, and a holy nation (Exod. 19.17). Relationship is evidenced in the peoples' meeting with God (Exod. 19.17), talking with God (Exod. 20.22), witnessing God's presence (Exod. 24.10) and in sharing a communal meal (Exod. 24.11).

Israel's appropriate response to God is hearing and obeying. However, the worship of other gods threatens to destroy their relationship with Yahweh as other gods often claim Israel's allegiance (Exod. 32.4; the calf episode is a disastrous event). With the promise in jeopardy, God threatens to destroy the nation but is reminded of his promise (Exod. 32.11–13). The definition and characteristics of the relationship become clearer through God's revelation to Moses in Exodus 33, and in the Book of Leviticus where Yahweh clarifies how the established relationship is to be maintained. The focus is on the regulation of ritual worship for the offering of gifts and dealing with sins that must be removed, in order to remain in relationship with a holy God. God gives statutes and ordinances that when implemented will preserve their relationship with a holy God by calling them to obedience (Lev. 26.46; 27.34; cf. Exod. 19.17). The conditional parameters of obedience and adherence to God's ways (Lev. 26.3–11) result in the realization of the promise, 'I will walk among you and be your God, and you will be my people' (Lev. 26:12).

Finally, the third promise made to the patriarchs concerns the gift of the land (Gen. 12.1–3, 7), which is given as a grant, and explored by Abraham to a significant degree (Gen. 12.5–9; 13.17).[23] The Patriarch, with family and servants, live in the land by faith since it belongs to the Canaanites (Gen. 12.6). All that is owned by Abraham is a burial plot (Gen. 23.17–20) and a place for an altar

---

23 The land of promise to Abraham 'runs through the patriarchal narratives like a red thread (Gen. 12.7; 13.15, 17; 15.18; 17.8; 24.7; 26.3 f.; 28.13 f.; 35.12; 48.4; 50.24)' (cf. M. Ottosson, 'ארץ', *TDOT*, I, p. 403).

(Gen. 33.19 f.). Abraham walks and dwells in Canaan but for the most part, the patriarchal narratives take place outside of the promised land. The Pentateuch narratives present God's people as sojourners who seem to always be travelling somewhere! In the final chapters of Genesis, the people of the promise are in Egypt and the reality of land ownership is only a dream (cf. Gen. 12.1, 7; 13.14 f.; 15.18; 35.12; Exod. 3.8; 6; Deut. 1.8). Realization of the land will finally be addressed in Numbers and Deuteronomy, after hundreds of years.

At the beginning of Numbers, the taking of the land is ultimately in focus. Young Israelite men are counted and prepared for military operations. Even though the land is promised, it must be fought for. Israel obediently moves from Sinai towards the land (Num. 1.1–10.10), to which Yahweh said, 'I will give it to you' (Num. 10.11, 29). Just as Abraham reconnoitred the promised land, so too must the land be explored before Canaan can be conquered. The twelve spies are sent into Canaan with the fulfilment of the promise in view (Numbers 13–14). However, many threats arise to thwart the realization of an easy victory in taking possession of Canaan. The people forfeit their chance by listening to negative reports and by refusing to proceed in faith. Resources are necessary and as the difficulties in procurement arise, Israel craves for the food staples they were used to in Egypt (Num. 11.4, 13). Several challenges inspire rebellion against the leadership of Moses (Num. 11.26–29; 12; 13–14; 16) and evoke fear of entry to Canaan due to the formidable enemies in the land (Num. 13.32; 20). At times, Israel wants to forget about God's promises, but Moses appeals to Yahweh's 'promise on oath', thereby halting divine judgment (Num. 14.16; cf. Exod. 32.13). In the end, only Joshua and Caleb of their generation will enter the land (Num. 14.23, 30 f.). In Numbers 20–22 the people get closer to the land, but it is only in the last ten chapters of Numbers where they are finally in a position to realize entry.

In Moses' final covenantal exhortation, the Book of Deuteronomy focuses on the land and the required lifestyle in the land. The Lord's commitment is to bless the people of God for living in covenant relationship, but also to curse when rebellion and persistent apostasy is evident (Deuteronomy 28–29). The phrase 'land you are to possess' occurs twenty-two times, and terms for 'land, ground, cities which God gives you', about thirty-four times.[24] Moses affirms that the land remains before the people for the taking (Deut. 1.8; 4.1), and that the promises still stand (Deut. 6.3, 19; 9.28; 6.10, 18, 23; 7.8). The covenantal exhortation is completely oriented to the land that remains to be entered

---

24   Cf. Clines, *Theme of the Pentateuch*, pp. 40–43.

and considers entry into the land as a fulfilment of the patriarchal promise. In the end, Deuteronomy 34 presents the leadership role of Joshua who will be responsible for the conquest of the land and ushering in Yahweh's inheritance for his people.

In many ways, the book of Numbers is the bridge which brings Israel over incredible obstacles into the promised land. The covenantal people have expanded in population to incredible numbers. Although their relationship with Yahweh was often impudent, the Lord remained with the people and kept his promises to bring them to the land of promise. At the end of Numbers, the people are poised for entry to their new home and life looks promising. The Lord's faithfulness to his covenant is clear and Israel is ready for the period of conquest. These are the binding motifs that flow through the Pentateuch and are eventually realized in the period of conquest.

9   The Unity of the Pentateuch

Although there are differing views about the Pentateuch's primary focus, whether it is the covenant, Israel, the cultus institutions or Moses, the survey above provides an accurate summation of how these important themes fit together.[25] With the thread of covenantal promise permeating the Pentateuch, the unity and dependence of the individual books within the whole, becomes clearer. There is a forward anticipation of thematic development and a steady progression towards the fulfilment of the covenantal promises. The conclusion of each book provides a unifying connection with a chronological, theological, and geographical element. Thus, the Book of Genesis ends with the death of Joseph who prophesies that God will fulfil the patriarchal promises and requests for his descendants to return his bones to the land of promise in the future (Gen. 50.22–26). Exodus begins with an exponential population growth among the Hebrews and ends with the glory of the Lord filling the freshly built Tabernacle. The sanctuary is prepared for its journey to the land where it will finally have a permanent place of rest (Exod. 40.34–38). Leviticus is the record of instructions and commands which God revealed to Israel through Moses during several excursions on Mount Sinai. These detailed instructions are an

---

25   For example, R. Knierim states that 'the Pentateuch is not the story or history of Israel's beginnings but the story of the life of Moses which is fundamental for the beginnings of Israel's history: that it is the vita, or the biography of Moses'. Cf. R.P. Knierim, 'The Composition of the Pentateuch', in *The Task of Old Testament Theology* (Grand Rapids: Eerdmans, 1995), p. 372.

INTRODUCTION

essential revelation for the nation so that they know Yahweh's expectation for relating to him in all his holiness and majesty (Lev. 27.34; cf. 26.46).

The book of Numbers continues with the record of revealed laws and instructions to Moses for the nation in preparation for their entry into Canaan, their covenantal inheritance (Num. 36.13). The narration of lists, leaders, offerings, and events are recorded with the ever-present focalization on the forward movement to the land—even though progress was protracted. Finally, Deuteronomy summarizes Yahweh's faithfulness to Israel in implementing the covenantal promises during their wilderness journeys. Moreover, Yahweh warns the nation of potential curses that will be implemented for covenantal disobedience and blessings that will be bestowed for obedience. Although Deuteronomy ends with the death of a great leader, the Lord provides Joshua who will be the shepherd to lead the nation into the promised land. With Joshua and Eleazar in places of leadership, the future looks bright for Israel's prospects.

10   The Life and Leadership of Moses

The scriptures present a captivating story about a child born in Egypt who was named Moses. Born into a Levitical family, the birth and rescue of Moses is briefly narrated in Exod. 2.1–10 as occurring during the pogrom against Hebrew male children by the Pharaoh. The whole synopsis is shrouded in the providence of God with arrangements that brought Moses into the Pharaoh's palace in the care of his daughter. According to Acts 7.20–44 Moses was raised in the educational institutions of Egypt and acquired skills that would serve him well in life.[26] According to this synopsis from Kitchen, life for Moses could have

---

26   Extended commentary is given in Stephen's sermon (Acts 7.20–44) and in the Book of Hebrews. The Hebrew's writer highlights the faith of Moses' parents and their protective care for the infant even though their lives were endangered. This same profound faith became part of Moses' spiritual heritage when he was a mature man of standing in the Pharaoh's court. At some point in his life, he became very aware of his Hebrew heritage and based on his conviction, chose to relinquish his privileges in the courts of Egypt. The author of Hebrews claims,

   He chose to be mistreated along with the people of God rather than to enjoy the fleeting pleasures of sin. He regarded disgrace for the sake of Christ as of greater value than the treasures of Egypt, because he was looking ahead to his reward. By faith he left Egypt, not fearing the king's anger; he persevered because he saw him who is invisible. By faith he kept the Passover and the application of blood, so that the destroyer of the firstborn would not touch the firstborn of Israel. (Heb. 11.23–28)

included his adoption into the Egyptian harem and royal court of the East Delta region after being found by a princess. There he grew to adulthood in the Egyptian court as a Semite.[27] However, his influence in the Pharaoh's court was thwarted by the murder of an Egyptian which brought about his exile in Midian where he found a new life, a wife and basically looked after the flocks of his father-in-law Jethro (Exodus 18; cf. also called Hobab, a Kenite; cf. Num. 10.29).

After an extensive period of family life in Midian, Moses was in the wilderness at Mount Horeb when he encountered the burning bush theophany. There he was called by God and commissioned to lead in a deliverance mission: 'So now, go. I am sending you to bring my people the Israelites out of Egypt' (Exod. 3.10). The 'call narrative' of Moses by God presents motifs that will become a pattern for other prophets (cf. Exodus 3).[28] At Horeb, Moses was confronted by the angel of the Lord who appeared in the form of a burning bush. Once the attention of Moses was obtained, God called to him, 'Moses, Moses', to which he responded, 'Here I am' (Exod. 3.2–4). The presence of God marks off the site as sacred ground. Moses responded with reverence, fear (Exod. 3.5–6, 11), and objections to the call due to feelings of inadequacy. Moses was very reluctant to accept his assignment. To his human responses, God insisted on compliance, affirms the commission, and assures Moses of his divine presence. Additionally, God provided several signs as confirmations to encourage him in his mandated tasks (Exod. 3.12; 4.1–10).

The Horeb event was the climactic occasion for Moses which took him from the pastures of Midian back to Egypt for his prophetic role in Israel's deliverance. There he contended with the new Pharaoh and eventually escorted several clans of people to Mount Sinai. The Exodus narratives detail Moses' confrontations with the Pharaoh until the Israelites are finally released to worship Yahweh. The great Exodus event becomes the watershed narrative of deliverance which allowed the people to forge their way to Mount Sinai for the covenant that shaped Israel into a nation. During the Sinai encampment, Moses uses his academic training and knowledge to mediate a contem-

---

27 K.A. Kitchen, *On the Reliability of the Old Testament* (Grand Rapids: Eerdmans, 2003), pp. 295–296.
28 Notable examples include Samuel (1 Samuel 3), Elisha (1 Kgs 19.16–21), Isaiah (Isaiah 6), Jeremiah (Jeremiah 1), Ezekiel (Ezekiel 1–3), and the servant of the Lord in Isaiah 42–61. The pattern of Moses' call will also be observed in the book of Judges where Israel falls into apostasy, cries out to Yahweh for deliverance, repents of sin and experiences deliverance through a charismatic judge raised up by Yahweh. Moses serves in a similar pattern when he answers the call, returns to Egypt, and confronts the Pharaoh in Egypt.

porary covenant with long-standing Semitic legal background and constructs a wooden-framed tent shrine based on proven Egyptian technology.[29] Moses then received revelation regarding the instructions for the holy sanctuary as well as the prescriptions for priestly functions.

The Lord's call upon Moses' life is the summons to prophetic leadership. This is not a secular form of leadership involving power and military force but a subjugated obedience to the will of Yahweh. Moses must hear and lead according to God's instructions. Although the title of 'prophet' (נביא) is seldom used in reference to Moses (cf. Numbers 11; 12), his whole leadership function during the last forty years of his life emulated what prophets were meant to be. In Exodus 7 it is explained that Aaron will be Moses' prophet while Moses will be like God to Pharaoh. God will use great acts of judgment to bring his intentions to bear. Moses declares that both Israel and Egypt will witness the miraculous exodus (Exod. 14.13–18), with positive outcomes: 'And when the Israelites saw the mighty hand of the LORD displayed against the Egyptians, the people feared the LORD and put their trust in him and in Moses his servant' (Exod. 14.31).

The characteristic phrase, 'the LORD spoke to Moses' highlights the relational reality of God's presence with the redeemed people of Israel. This reality is expressed in a variety of phrases which feature the truth that God is not silent. In fact, God communicates vociferously, and his audible speech can be frightening! The narratives in Numbers reflect the arrangement requested by the people and accepted by Yahweh whereby the selected mediator would share God's words received in private, with the nation in public—God speaks through prophets and the people must listen (Exodus 18–19; Deut. 5.23–29; 18.15–17).[30] In the book of Numbers alone there are about one hundred and fifty expressions of Yahweh communicating with Moses. This is a primary element in prophetic leadership.[31] Additionally, the fulfilment of carrying out the instructions of Yahweh is an essential part of the prophet's role. In Numbers the characteristic phrase 'just as the LORD commanded Moses', is utilized 28 times to affirm the prophet's compliance with the Lord's commands.

---

29   Kitchen, *On the Reliability of the Old Testament*, pp. 295–296.
30   God's speech may be evident in explicit instruction (Numbers 1; 4), warning (Num. 1.51–53; 4.17–20), explanation (Num. 3.11ff.), testing (Numbers 5), and blessing (Num. 6.22–27). The favorite place of communication was Sinai but on a regular basis, the tent of meeting. 'When Moses entered the tent of meeting to speak with the LORD, he heard the voice speaking to him from between the two cherubim above the atonement cover on the ark of the covenant law. In this way the LORD spoke to him' (Num. 7.89).
31   Cf. Allen, *Numbers*, p. 702.

According to Scripture, Moses is one of the greatest leaders in the OT history. Not only is he lauded the greatest prophet, but he is the one to be emulated by all other prophets. Deuteronomy 34.10 claims that since his lifespan of 120 years, 'no prophet has risen in Israel like Moses whom the LORD knew face to face'. The prophetic role for Israel is essential. 'I will raise up for them a prophet like you from among their fellow Israelites, and I will put my words in his mouth. He will tell them everything I command him. I myself will call to account anyone who does not listen to my words that the prophet speaks in my name' (Deut. 18.18–19). Illustrating these texts, Num. 11.17 shows how Yahweh related to Moses and empowered him. 'I will come down and speak with you there, and I will draw upon the spirit that is on you and put it upon them. They will share the burden of the people with you so that you will not have to carry it alone'. Of all the amazing characters in the OT, Moses towers over them in the number of roles he exemplified. In addition to prophet, he was a scribe, poet, priest, author, hero deliverer, law giver, miracle worker, intercessor, and servant of the Lord. The importance of Moses' life in the Pentateuch may be garnered to a certain extent by the number of times his name is cited in the texts. 'Moses' is mentioned 285 times in Exodus, 82 in Leviticus, 231 in Numbers and 36 in Deuteronomy.[32] His name appears about 720 times in the OT and 85 times in the NT. Additionally, there are numerous allusions to Moses as the great law giver and prophet. Hosea 12.13 declares, 'The LORD used a prophet to bring Israel up from Egypt, by a prophet he cared for him'. The OT ends with a reference to him in Malachi 4.4, 'Remember the law of my servant Moses'. The NT presents him in conversation with Jesus at the transfiguration event noted in all three synoptic gospels (Mt. 17.3; Mk. 9.4; Lk. 9.30).

Moses has the most intimate and incredible experiences with God of any other OT person (although David is mentioned more often). He spends many extended times with God on Mount Sinai and receives laws with detailed instructions as well as specifications for the tabernacle and cultic calendar (perhaps eight sessions according to Exodus). Scripture provides a realistic and consistent presentation of his stature as well as his flaws. This feature is another indicator of the Scripture's veracity in depicting Moses' character, nature, and behaviour without polishing, explaining, or embellishing the record. He is presented with several failures, limitations, anger, fatigue, and frustration. He even required help from Aaron with the communication functions that God called

---

[32] In Joshua his name is mentioned 53 times. Moses is cited in the NT about 85 times, an indicator of his enduring legacy and historical impact (38 times in the Gospels, 23 in Acts, and 12 in Hebrews).

him to. In tandem with Aaron, Moses also depended on the elders of Israel to work with the Israelites (Exod. 3.16, 18; 12.21; Numbers 11).

Most of the events and details in the Pentateuch pertain to the forty years of Israel's pilgrimage from Sinai to the promised land. Although the challenges of leadership are rigorous, burdensome, and persistent, Moses as a reluctant leader, remains a humble servant (Num. 12.3). He 'prays' (פלל) and negotiates for the people, often standing as mediator between them and God (Num. 11.2; 21.7). On a few occasions when God's anger is very 'hot', due to the persistent rebellious acts of some people, he resolves to destroy the nation (Exod. 32.10; Num. 14.12–19). In such cases Moses is quick to intervene, often falling prostrate before the Lord to ask for another chance for the people (cf. Num. 11.2; 12.13; 14.13–20; 16.22; 21.7). This characteristic is exemplified in the golden calf incident where Moses pleads forgiveness on behalf of Israel: "So Moses went back to the LORD and said, 'Oh, what a great sin these people have committed! They have made themselves gods of gold. But now, please forgive their sin— but if not, then blot me out of the book you have written'. The LORD replied to Moses, 'Whoever has sinned against me I will blot out of my book. Now go, lead the people to the place I spoke of, and my angel will go before you. However, when the time comes for me to punish, I will punish them for their sin'" (Exod. 32.31–34). Yahweh listened to the intercession of Moses and relented on his initial judgment with a mitigation of his response due to the prophet's appeal.

It appears from these examples that Yahweh expected the prophet to intercede on behalf of Israel and he took Moses' prayers seriously. Intercession causes Yahweh to pause, listen to Moses, and after the prophet's petition, say 'I pardon (סלח) as you have asked' (Num. 14.20; cf. Exod. 33.13). Moses' prayer changes God's determination to destroy and mitigates his response to punish. The Psalmist's reflection on this historical event recognizes Moses' impressive intercessory role: 'So he said he would destroy them—had not Moses, his chosen one, stood in the breach before him to keep his wrath from destroying them' (cf. Ps. 106.23).[33] In the matter of intercession, Moses is not only the standard by which other prophets will be measured, but is a prophet that will be emulated and respected by many others ... 'God will raise up for you a prophet like me from your brothers' (Deut. 18.15–18).

This is why the heroic summaries of his legacy in Deuteronomy 18 and 34 hold him up as the pinnacle of OT prophetic leadership.[34] In fact, prophets in

---

33 Milgrom, *Numbers*, p. xxxix.
34 G.W. Coats, 'Legendary Motifs in the Moses Death Reports', in D.L. Christensen (ed.), *A Song of Power and the Power of Song: Essays on the Book of Deuteronomy* (Winona Lake,

Israel ultimately had the more powerful leadership roles in that they depended on divine revelation of laws, regulations, and explicit directions from Yahweh for the covenantal community. Moses emulated every aspect of this from each Sinaitic revelation down to the application of legislation. Furthermore, one of the main roles for prophetic leadership in the early stages of development, was for the prophet to move the nation forward in accordance with the divine plans and purposes of Yahweh. In this function, the prophet had to hear the divine instructions accurately in order to implement them flawlessly with the right timing. In this sense, the prophet was a visionary due to the clear revelations given by Yahweh, and his strength to implement the divine agenda.

> Listen to my words: When there is a prophet among you, I, the LORD, reveal myself to them in visions, I speak to them in dreams. But this is not true of my servant Moses; he is faithful in all my house. With him I speak face to face, clearly and not in riddles; he sees the form of the LORD. Why then were you not afraid to speak against my servant Moses? (Num. 12.6–8)

Even when there were failures, setbacks, and conflicts, the prophet had to keep making progress in moving the nation forward to fulfil their purpose as a kingdom of priests and a holy nation. Even when Moses had personal failures, he still was faithful in bringing Israel to the precipice of the promised land so that they could realize their promised inheritance. Although scholarship often questions the veracity of Moses' historical life and legacy, the divine perspective of his leadership is astounding.[35] Not only was Moses a powerful prophet in every dimension, but his legacy that he was the Lord's special servant who set the standard for all the prophets who would succeed him, is assured. 'He is

---

IN: Eisenbrauns, 1993), pp. 181–194. Coats points out the three key motifs whose 'primary intention is to describe outstanding virtues and feats, either moral or physical, not in God, but in man'. The motifs are the amazing vitality of Moses' still at the end of his life (Deut. 34.7), the incredible weight of authority that he carried above all other leaders, and the special intimate relationship that Moses had with God in 'face to face' communication (pp. 182–185).

35 After surveying the many qualities and functions of a leader that Moses embodies, Whybray, *Introduction to the Pentateuch* (Grand Rapids: Eerdmans, 1995), p. 65, notes,
> It is obvious that this picture of such an all-embracing authority figure cannot be a homogeneous one, incorporating as it does all the functions of rulers and of holy men that later Israel was to encounter during its history. It would seem rather that, whatever historical reality may lie behind this figure, there has been a legendary development, perhaps of tremendous proportions.

INTRODUCTION

the archetypal prophet whose mission epitomizes the distinguishing features of later classical apostolic prophecy'.[36]

11 Torah Composition and the Question of Mosaic Authorship

The pendulum of views regarding the authorship of the book of Numbers has swung from traditional acceptance of Mosaic composition to more critical perspectives of documentary theories through vast periods of time, then back to the potential of Moses as the primary scribe. Reasons for this will be noted below but it is appropriate to begin with a summary of what the Scriptures claim. This perspective is necessary due to numerous scriptural claims that attribute some level of authorship to Moses. While it is impossible to resolve the authorship debate to any degree in this brief opinion, it is important to affirm the amazing authority of Moses' contribution as well as the scribes who were influential in preserving and completing the final document as it stands in Numbers 1–36. Realistically, it is inconceivable to discover the whole process that took place over a thousand years of history to bring the scriptures to their present state. My own perspective has developed over time but remains confident that a historical person named Moses provided a considerable amount of the Torah's content. This includes legislative material, narratives, chronicle lists of names, itinerary details and poetic material for the scribal undertakings that eventually brought the contents to the present compositional form. This also includes oral transmission of content as well as some written records.

11.1 Moses' Contribution

Several scriptures assume that Moses had writing capabilities to fulfil the divine directives to record instructions, words, laws, covenantal history, statutes, and itinerary locations (cf. Exod. 17.14; 24.3–4, 27–28; Num. 33.2). He was instructed by Yahweh to record the ten commandments (Exod. 34.4, 27–29) which included the book of the covenant (Exod. 20.22–23.33). While these references indicate that writing and record keeping was a fact of life in Moses' experience, the scriptures do not provide many details on the authorship practices in the ancient near east. However, historical data and archaeological discoveries provide much evidence regarding ancient libraries in royal courts that were

---

36   N.M. Sarna, *Exodus: The JPS Torah Commentary* (Philadelphia: The Jewish Publication Society, 1991), p. xiii.

written, maintained, and preserved by scribes. Many biblical documents were finalized by scribes and editors who remain anonymous. Primarily, priests and prophets become responsible for the nation's records and documents.

At the end of his one hundred and twenty-year lifespan, the witness of the Torah verifies that Moses wrote the 'law' and deposited it with the Levitical priests who were responsible for the sacred Tabernacle. To the priests and the elders was given the responsibility of reading the written law so that it would be revered and obeyed in Israel. 'So Moses wrote down this law and gave it to the Levitical priests, who carried the ark of the covenant of the LORD, and to all the elders of Israel'. Then Moses commanded them:

> At the end of every seven years, in the year for cancelling debts, during the Festival of Tabernacles, when all Israel comes to appear before the LORD your God at the place he will choose, you shall read this law before them in their hearing. Assemble the people—men, women and children, and the foreigners residing in your towns—so they can listen and learn to fear the LORD your God and follow carefully all the words of this law. Their children, who do not know this law, must hear it and learn to fear the LORD your God as long as you live in the land you are crossing the Jordan to possess. (Deut. 31.9–13).

This text continues with Moses' instruction to the Levites regarding the deposition of the Book of the Law: 'After Moses finished writing in a book the words of this law from beginning to end, he gave this command to the Levites who carried the ark of the covenant of the LORD: "Take this Book of the Law and place it beside the ark of the covenant of the LORD your God. There it will remain as a witness against you"' (Deut. 31.22–26). While these attributions are clear, the extent of the 'law' that was penned and deposited by Moses is still in question.[37]

References to Moses actually writing or being instructed to write include the following: "Then the LORD said to Moses, 'Write this on a scroll as something to be remembered and make sure that Joshua hears it, because I will completely blot out the name of Amalek from under heaven'" (Exod. 17.14). After the Mount Sinai episode: 'When Moses went and told the people all the LORD's words and laws, they responded with one voice, "Everything the LORD has said we will do". Moses then wrote down everything the LORD had said' (Exod. 24.3–4).

---

37   It is appropriate to assume that the main foundational documents were the ten commandments (Exod. 34.1; cf. Deut. 5.22–27), and 'the book of the covenant' (Exod. 20.22–23.33).

> Then the LORD said to Moses, 'Write down these words, for in accordance with these words I have made a covenant with you and with Israel'. Moses was there with the LORD forty days and forty nights without eating bread or drinking water. And he wrote on the tablets the words of the covenant—the Ten Commandments. (Exod. 34.27–28)

Although these statements are clear, typically in the Semitic Near East laws were transmitted in oral form.[38]

The primary attribution of Moses writing in Numbers occurs in chapter 33 which is the summary of Israel's epic sojourn in the wilderness. It purports to be the stages in the journey of the Israelites and 'At the LORD's command Moses "recorded" (כתב) the stages in their journey' (Num. 33.2). The itinerary list from Egypt to the Plains of Moab, claims to be an intimate reflection on the various places that Israel traversed and camped on the way to Canaan. One other reference is notable regarding a test for the selection of the Aaronides: 'The LORD said to Moses, "Speak to the Israelites and get twelve staffs from them, one from the leader of each of their ancestral tribes. Write the name of each man on his staff. On the staff of Levi write Aaron's name, for there must be one staff for the head of each ancestral tribe"' (Num. 17.2–3). In another passage (Num. 21.14), the 'Book of the Wars of the Lord' is footnoted, indicating recorded material in some form that is no longer extant.

In Deuteronomy 32, the Song of Moses is a lengthy summation of God's forbearance and care for the Israelites who did not return Yahweh's affections and deserted the Lord's ways. The song is forty-three verses long and Moses was instructed to record the song, to recite and teach it for Israel to remember and obey it. 'So Moses wrote down this song that day and taught it to the Israelites' (Deut. 31.22, cf. 31.19, 30; 32.44–47).[39]

---

38   J.A. Sanders, *Torah and Canon* (Philadelphia: Fortress Press, 1972), p. 31. The corpus of laws that are in Deuteronomy 12 to 26 are part of the ancient record attributed to Moses in his final words to the nation. Sanders notes that scholarship is virtually unanimous that these chapters 'made up the contents of the scroll found in the Jerusalem Temple during the repairs being made on it in the eighteenth year of King Josiah (621 B.C.), as it is reported in 2 Kings 22' (cf. pp. 36–37).

39   Several other references in scripture are made where writers attribute material to the law of Moses (cf. Josh. 8.31–32; 23.6; 1 Kgs 2.3; 2 Kgs 14.6; 23.25; Ezra 3.2; 7.6; Neh. 1.7–9; 13.1; Dan. 9.1, 13; 2 Chron. 23.18; 34.16; also NT references, cf. Mk 10.5; 12.19–27; Lk. 2.22; 24.44; Jn 1.45). Cf. J.H. Tigay, *Deuteronomy: The JPS Torah Commentary* (The Jewish Publication Society, 1996), pp. 298–299; 508–513.

11.2 *Moses' Revelation*

The time and place for his inspiration appears to have begun at Mount Sinai and continued during the wilderness journey at the Tent of Meeting. His marathon experience in the presence of God on Sinai for forty days and nights occurs twice followed by several trips up the mountain for the further unveiling of divine oracles. From Moses' first trek up Mount Sinai to the last, he mainly ascends the mountain to be in the presence of Yahweh in order to receive instruction and revelation at the Lord's invitation. The Sinaitic pilgrimages include three which are recorded in Exodus 19. The first is at the Lord's invitation and includes the covenantal purposes for Israel (Exod. 19.3–8). In the second, Moses is to prepare the people for the Lord's appearance on Mount Sinai for the revelation of the theophany (Exod. 19.7–14). Another ascent is evident together with Aaron (Exod. 19.24; 24.1–8; cf. Deut. 24.1–3). It appears that the ten commandments were revealed during another period on the mountain (Exod. 20.18–26) with additional instructions. Moses is summoned again for an extensive forty-day period where he receives the tablets of stone inscribed with the law (Exod. 24.12–18). Another intriguing episode of Moses' communication with God on the mountain is revealed in Exod. 32–33.23. There Moses pleads for Yahweh's presence on the journey to the land of promise. Finally, Moses receives tablets for the second time and has another intimate encounter with God (Exod. 34.1–9).

This documentation of Moses ascending Mount Sinai to receive divine revelation has been the cornerstone of authority for Mosaic authorship. Additional experiences at the tent of meeting over the forty-year period of his prophetic leadership provided ample opportunity to receive instruction, covenant, and legal advice. Moreover, it provided Moses the opportunity to record the events, itinerary and inspired words as directed by Yahweh.

A comparison of the Mosaic law codes indicates knowledge of other ancient near eastern documents like Hammurabi's law code (cf. Exod. 21.24; Lev. 24.20; Deut. 19.21). Knowledge of such documentation would be expected of those who served and were trained in the Pharaoh's court according to customary educational practice and diplomacy between foreign courts and nations (cf. Acts 7). According to Kitchen there is no factual evidence to exclude such a person from having the skills to write some of the materials in the Pentateuch in the late second millennium. In fact, the biblical story provides ample viability on how a foreigner in Egypt could acquire the skills to formulate treaty documentation, laws, and content which was typical of learned scribes in royal courts. It was Moses' upbringing in the Egyptian court that implies his membership in the ruling body of courtiers, officials, and attendants—trained to serve the government. Furthermore, training required fluency in language and the learning of hieratic and hieroglyphic script.[40] Moses was just one of many but according to the biblical record, he was a man of exceptional skill, learning, and leadership proficiency.

Evidence of ancient legal traditions as well as poetic and narrative devices serve to undergird the traditional theory of Mosaic scribal skill.[41] His unique training in the Pharaoh's court where the study of religion, math, ancient laws, creation myths and other literature was common, provides a reasonable background for this assertion. This context may also have afforded him with court records and materials in the Egyptian royal library. Furthermore, the consensus of final documentary compilation indicates that editors were convinced of Moses' primary function as authoritative law giver by recording his name six-hundred times in the third person as speaking and doing what Yahweh instructed. This is an unusual way to write but it may reflect an ancient form whereby authoritative involvement with the record is asserted. The excessive repetition of name and expressions of God speaking with Moses listening and recording are a primary feature of authoritative documentation.

11.3   *Contemporary Views*

For most of church history the traditional biblical view of Moses described above has been endorsed and upheld as credible and authoritative. However, with the rise of critical re-evaluation of scripture's composition and canonical formation, many elements of Moses' life and contribution have been questioned. In fact, some scholars even query whether Moses was a historical figure at all, let alone the composer of the Torah! In the article about Moses in the *Theological Dictionary of the Old Testament*, H. Cazelles and H.J. Fabry include four pages of bibliography pertaining to Moses. The scholarship indicated by the numerous resources verifies the importance of Moses and for some authors, authenticates the views set forth in scripture. However, for many scholars with diverse presuppositions and higher critical assumptions, the perspectives may be very different:

> There is Martin Noth's Moses of whom nothing is known except the site of his burial outside of Israel. There is Julius Wellhausen's Moses, the liberator who led the Israelites to the oasis of Kadesh. There is Moses the priest

---

40 Kitchen, *On the Reliability of the Old Testament*, p. 287.
41 In addition to scribal functions by prophets and priests, the wise man or 'sage' also had literary skills that were used in royal courts and recorded the didactic materials that are in the books of wisdom literature (cf. Sanders, *Torah and Canon*, p. 41).

of Eduard Meyer, Moses the prophet of Andre Neher and Martin Buber, Moses the Egyptian of Sigmund Freund and A. Slosman, Moses the lawgiver of Jewish tradition, Moses the theologian of the Koran, Moses the mystic of Gregory of Nyssa, and many more.[42]

It is fairly evident from this survey, the TDOT articles, and OT studies in general, that Mosaic authorship is a theory but not considered probable. In fact, some commentators do not even discuss him as a viable option or a historical figure, and instead, focus their attention on source criticism with documentary theories which analyze the 'strands' of material to determine the editors or redactors and the schools of thought they represent.

Traditionally Judaism and Christianity assumed Mosaic authorship for Pentateuchal material that was viewed as unified and datable.[43] Scholarship began to dismantle the Pentateuch into documents based on critical criteria which applied literary critical methods to texts primarily from the eighteenth century onwards. These theories have proven difficult to displace. Although the proposals which postulate various strands of materials may aid in the understanding of complex elements in the text, they do not adequately answer key questions concerning the variation in use of divine names, repetition, terminology, doublets, style, cohesiveness, and apparent contradictions in the final version. However, some of the theories on the final compilation of materials may shed light on the process of writing that began with Moses and were handed on to respective editors. Such 'documents' were then finalized by editors or tradents that reflected different schools of thought or theological perspectives.[44] Generally, the core traditions include the following titles but there are many additional sub-categories also mentioned in commentaries. Primary 'schools' or 'traditions' are the 'Yahwist' labelled 'J' (ca. 950–850 BC); the 'Elohist' labelled 'E' (ca. 850–750 BC); the 'Priestly' labelled 'P' (ca. 500–540 BC); and

---

[42] Cf. H. Cazelles and H.J. Fabry, 'משה', TDOT, IX, pp. 30–31. P.D. Miller, '"Moses My Servant": The Deuteronomic Portrait of Moses' in D.L. Christensen (ed.), *A Song of Power and the Power of Song: Essays on the Book of Deuteronomy* (Winona Lake, IN: Eisenbrauns, 1993), pp. 301–312.

[43] B.S. Childs, *Introduction to the Old Testament as Scripture* (Fortress Press: Philadelphia, 1979), pp. 112 ff.

[44] For an historical overview of the critical views of the Pentateuch's composition and how they developed, see the helpful but inconclusive chapter by Whybray, *Introduction to the Pentateuch*, pp. 12–28. Also, consider Alexander's extensive details in T.D. Alexander, *From Paradise to the Promised Land: An Introduction to the Pentateuch* (Grand Rapids: Baker Academic, 3rd edn, 2012), pp. 3–62.

the 'Deuteronomistic' labelled 'D' (ca. 561–520 BC).[45] To elucidate the meaning, views and interpretation of these different groups, scholars have developed many different critical tools to apply to the OT records.

The amount of writing on the subject and available texts is staggering. For space considerations, only a few methods that contemporary commentators employ in their work are noted. In source criticism, scholars diligently work to dissect specific content that may be attributed to certain writers or tradents. The focus is on determining what sources were used to thread together the materials that ultimately were used to compose a narrative, a section or book. In tradition criticism, the traditions noted as Yahwist, Elohist, Deuteronomistic and Priestly are compared in order to determine the different interpretations or understandings of events, or ideas that were narrated. This type of analysis helps to determine how a particular tradition achieves canonical value for communities of faith and informs their identity.[46]

Form critics seek to discover the probable oral phases of speeches and events with the subsequent narrative transmission from one generation to another. 'Form criticism is an attempt to make precise observations about the kinds of literature out of which the various units of the Bible are composed'.[47] Here the scholar seeks to determine the initial contexts (*Sitz im Leben*) of the various materials that exist. Original forms of content which contained the material or narrative are proposed and determined before they were recorded. Those who apply the traditio-historical methods analyze how probable historical settings and cultic practices at the time of composition may have influenced the material. Redactors focus on the various source materials and narratives to discern how content may have been stitched together in the final stages of composition. More importantly, Sanders observes that redaction criticism seeks to recover the main ideas of those people who give new shape to earlier materials and narratives. Redactors actually have things to say as they edit former materials for new purposes, new contexts and communities, in order to address contemporary situations.[48]

Due to the complexity of determining the details of the compositional process, several commentators have mainly focused on the literary analysis of the

---

45 W. Boshoff, E. Scheffler, and I. Spangenberg, *Ancient Israelite Literature in Context* (Pretoria: PROTEA Book House, 2000), pp. 87–163. The value of this text is the analysis of the sections of material and summary of contents that are attributed to the proposed traditions and documents.
46 Sanders, *Torah and Canon*, pp. xii–xiv.
47 Sanders, *Torah and Canon*, p. xi.
48 Sanders, *Torah and Canon*, p. xii.

final documents as they currently stand. Tradition and history are taken seriously to discover the probable process used by redactors who carefully knit together certain materials, presumably without changing the content or intentions of primary authors. Editorial comments may be observed, and composite traditions analyzed for linguistic techniques that were used to stitch materials together to complete the narrative (cf. Numbers 16 for example). One of the greatest issues with some of the documentary theories is the inordinate amount of discussion given to the theoretical speculation on different 'authors' and their assumed reasons for selecting, redacting, and finalizing materials. Often these sections in commentaries are longer than the actual comments on text and meaning. Although the assumed audience and context of final editorial work is important, the conclusions can supplant the accurate interpretation of the narrative. This occurs often with reference to the Pentateuch which critical scholarship often relegates to very late priestly work. This brief summary serves to echo what many scholars have stated in recent years, namely, that theories of the Pentateuch's authorial process continue to be inconclusive.

It is evident from some scholarship that different critical tools have made considerable contributions to the understanding of texts and how scripture may have been composed over the course of several hundred years before being adopted as canonical. Therefore, the conclusion by Kitchen indicating the great divide in OT scholarship is too ardent. He notes two extremes in his judgment concerning composition: "A large amount of inconclusive discussion by biblical scholars in almost two hundred years has established next to nothing with any surety and has vacillated all the way between extreme conservatism ('Moses wrote all the Pentateuch') and total nihilism ('There was no Moses, and he left nothing')".[49]

The value of critical scholarship lies in the careful scrutiny of texts and the discussion of canonical finalization. This focus provides some realistic insights into the process and explains why the OT documents were so carefully preserved. It is the narrative of the nation's past and historical experience of God that become so essential to the life of the nation that these records are ultimately canonized. Sanders provides key insights into the process in that, 'The Torah as we have it was shaped by the experience of Israel's destitution and transformation …. It was that experience which determined the shape of the preexilic traditions, of ancient Israel and Judah, which answered the existential questions put to them because of that experience'.[50] Torah becomes indispens-

---

[49] Kitchen, *On the Reliability of the Old Testament*, p. 299.
[50] Sanders, *Torah and Canon*, p. 118.

able to every generation of Israel that looks to God's acts in the past for an indicator of how he may give the community new life, essence, and identity in contemporary contexts of conflict. The narratives of God's interventions and actions in history become treasures of hope for the people of faith. They are preserved, narrated, and trusted for new situations requiring fresh interventions. They confirm the nation's identity as well as lifestyle requirements in the community of faith. They become fresh, authoritative, scriptural requirements for the believing community to observe.

11.4 *Mosaic Authority*

Former claims denying the possibility of Mosaic scribal activity have required revision since discoveries in archaeology as well as philology continue to point to the amazing scribal ability of ancient writers. For sure the purpose of biblical assertions for Mosaic authorship and Pentateuchal claims of divine inspiration for the words, events, instructions, and details recorded in the book serve to elevate the authority of Moses as Israel's great leader. This is the core function of the affirmations for Mosaic authorship. Another way that Mosaic authority is conveyed is through the Pentateuch's presentation of the content through three primary voices, namely, God, Moses and the 'omniscient narrator'. This provides a divine perspective to the content through the narrator's authorial control of what is said and what it means. 'Thus, the Pentateuch's use of a third-person omniscient and impersonal narrator resists the unifying rhetoric of the divine and human speeches which it contains'.[51] The effect of this method in narrating the content is to affirm the divine revelation through Moses to the reader/audience for acceptance and application in every generation.

Of course, the details regarding composition and development to the finalization of the canonical shape of the Pentateuch are complex. However, the problem is often exacerbated with an imposition of modern concepts of authorship without due respect for ancient systems. Neither the focus on historical problems nor the appeals to religious tradition can do 'justice to the canonical understanding of Moses' relationship to the Pentateuch'.[52] Therefore,

---

51 Watts, 'Reader Identification and Alienation', p. 101. Watts (p. 112) summarizes how this functions and affects authoritative interpretation:
   These three dominant voices of the Pentateuch are interdependent and almost interchangeable: the anonymous narrator, like Moses the scribe, requires both divine inspiration and reader acceptance for authorization of the story; the divine lawgiver requires reader acceptance of human mediation of the commandments; the prophetic scribe depends on authority delegated by both God and readers to interpret the stories, the laws, and the sanctions.

52 Childs, *Introduction to the Old Testament as Scripture*, p. 133.

we must acknowledge the primary roles of Moses according to the witness of scripture in his mediatorial role in receiving the divine law at Sinai. For this mediation he was spared at birth, trained, called, and commissioned to write and teach the Torah to Israel (Exodus 2–3; 24.3–4; 34.27). B. Childs highlights the instructions of Deut. 31.9–13 which requires the giving of the law to successive generations and the penultimate legacy of Moses to provide the laws of God for Israel's shalom in the land. 'In this way the authorship role of Moses performs a normative role within a canonical context from a very early period. Thus, laws attributed to Moses were deemed authoritative, and conversely authoritative laws were attributed to Moses'.[53] The importance and role of Moses' authority as author is clear but the timing of the Torah's finalization is the undetermined issue.[54]

The reality is that although much scholarship and effort has gone into the compositional origins, the literary history and process of final adoption as canon is still under deliberation. This is natural for ancient documentation—the main concern was for preservation of the text as it was transmitted and scrutinized by the community. The materials and documents were still considered 'in process' with the goal of canon yet before the community (if it was even a concept at the time). Meanwhile, it was the responsibility of the prophets who continued to be inspired with the role of expanding and applying the texts to issues of community life. B. Waltke claims that Moses provided for successive prophets to supplement and add to earlier canonical materials. 'In Deuteronomy 18.14–22, Moses provides for prophets after him to be his surrogates and to add new revelation to his Book of the Law' (cf. Deut. 5.25–29).[55] In other words, the Lord will continue to appoint prophets like Moses to carry on the task of mediating the divine words (Deuteronomy 18–19), but they would do so based on the authority of the inspired prophets before them—with Moses being their exemplar (cf. Jer. 7.25; Ezek. 38.17). An example of this may be seen in B. Lee's essay concerning Moses and Second Temple scribal practices concerning prophetic engagement with divine proclamation and the speeches of Moses.[56]

---

53   Childs, *Introduction to the Old Testament as Scripture*. p. 134. Ultimately the writings that are received and canonized by the community are evidence of the authority the true prophets achieved. Those who did not achieve this recognition forfeit the opportunity and authority to speak on behalf of Yahweh.

54   However, the canonical criticism of Childs and Sanders is very valuable in providing insights on the process and timing which led to the reception of authoritative documents.

55   B.K. Waltke, 'How We Got the Old Testament', *CRUX* 30.4 (Dec. 1994), p. 15. Tigay, *Deuteronomy*, pp. 498–502.

56   Lee concludes with an insightful comment concerning Moses' reputation as an exemplary prophet up to the Second Temple period: 'Inherent to this reference is the understand

A helpful way of comprehending the biblical understanding and function of Moses as the transmitter and teacher of the law is summarized by H. Gese. His reminder that contemporary authorship standards are very different from ancient documentation is an important note due to the imposition of foreign criteria on authors. He claimed that it is essential to acknowledge that the events of tradition history occurred in a specific context which connects the teaching or material to certain realms of tradition (*Sitz im Leben*). 'The strands of tradition which were formed in this manner often reveal specific concepts of authorship. In complete contrast to our concept of authorship, the traditional material is not considered "intellectual property". As the transmitters receive and hand on, they are also responsible contributors to the process, but they are not authors. It is in keeping with the nature of the material that the founder of such a school of tradition is regarded as the author. Accordingly, we can understand that the Mosaic Torah must be regarded as revelation given to Moses, even when its formulations and the structure of its content date from a later time. When the Pentateuch says, "Moses spoke", this expresses a real truth which cannot be properly dealt with by the objection, raised by our limited way of thinking, that this is unhistorical'.[57]

In summation, one of Scripture's greatest claims to inspiration has to do with the Sinaitic periods of revelation where Moses was in the presence of God for extended periods of time in a way that no other prophets or leaders could make claim. This assertion along with numerous claims to intimate communication with Yahweh, face to face, in Numbers, verifies the involvement of Moses in the content of Numbers and the authority it holds. Moses laid the foundation of the OT Torah on which the other prophets continued to build.

12   A Selection of Seven Predominate Themes in Numbers

The book of Numbers presents a variety of documents and narratives which reveal the challenges of Israel after the great exodus event from Egypt on their journey towards the promised covenantal land. The journey holds formidable challenges, dangers, and adventures. Although there is great potential for the nation to inherit the covenant land for their habitation, their spiritual failures

---

ing that prophetic activity is a (sometimes-contentious) conversation with voices past, divine or otherwise'. Cf. B. Lee, '"Face to Face": Moses as Prophet in Exodus 11.1–12.28', in M.J. Boda and L.M. Wray Beal (eds.), *Prophets, Prophecy, and Ancient Israelite Historiography* (Winona Lake, IN: Eisenbrauns, 2013), p. 19; cf. pp. 3–21.

57   H. Gese, *Essays on Biblical Theology* (Minneapolis: Augsburg, 1981), p. 21.

hamper the realization of this promise. The wilderness wanderings become an ultimate testing ground for Israel's faith, obedience, and adherence to Yahweh's instructions. Whereas Yahweh proved to be faithful in guiding, providing, and protecting, the nation struggled to reciprocate the divine affections. A generation of exodus participants perished in the desert. Some of the prominent themes in this epic sojourn are briefly introduced here and include the leadership, providence and guidance of Yahweh, societal leadership structures, prophecy and prophetic leadership, worship, the Spirit of God, conflict, testing, judgment, anointing, healing, blessing, and cursing. A brief synopsis of some themes is offered here with more development of thematic emphases provided in commentary sections.

12.1 Theme One: The Leadership of Yahweh

12.1.1 The Lord Reveals Himself

The primary reference to the divine name in Numbers is the covenantal name of 'Yahweh' (יהוה) which appears 358 times in contradistinction to 'Elohim' (אלהים) which is used 32 times.[58] Yahweh is the over-arching presence throughout the book, and he chose to speak mainly to Moses, providing continual direction for the organization, leadership, and movement of the nation. From the beginning of Numbers, the revelation of the character, nature and will of the Lord continues to be disclosed to the Israelites as Yahweh communicates the divine will (approximately 150 times the Lord speaks). The characteristic phrase, 'the LORD spoke to Moses' highlights the relational certainty of the divine presence with the redeemed people of Israel. This reality is expressed in a variety of phrases which feature the truth that Yahweh was not silent. In fact, he was loud, and his audible speech was frightening! This caused the people to request a mediator to share words received in private, to the nation in public. This is prophetic communication at its best: "When the people saw the thunder and lightning and heard the trumpet and saw the mountain in smoke, they trembled with fear. They stayed at a distance and said to Moses, 'Speak to us yourself and we will listen. But do not have God speak to us or we will die'. Moses said to the people, 'Do not be afraid. God has come to test you, so that the fear of God will be with you to keep you from sinning'" (Exod. 20.18–20; cf. Deut. 5. 23–29; 18.15–18).

---

58 References to the divine name in other books of the Pentateuch: 'Yahweh' (יהוה) (translated the LORD, but articulated 'Adonai'), occurs 354 times in Exodus, 281 in Leviticus, and 442 in Deuteronomy. 'Elohim' (אלהים) (translated God) occurs 113 times in Exodus, 47 in Leviticus, and 320 in Deuteronomy.

Yahweh's speech is evident through explicit instruction (Numbers 1; 4), warning (Num. 1.51–53; 4.17–20), explanation (Num. 3.11 ff.), testing (Numbers 5), and in blessing (Num. 6.22–27). In Exodus the favoured place of communication was on Mount Sinai but also in the Tent of Meeting. In Numbers, Yahweh usually meets Moses and leaders at the Tabernacle but also in the Tent of Meeting. 'When Moses entered the Tent of Meeting to speak with the LORD, he heard the voice speaking to him from between the two cherubim above the atonement cover on the ark of the covenant law. In this way the LORD spoke to him' (Num. 7.89). The import of this theme where Yahweh communicates frequently and clearly, affirms that mankind cannot live on bread alone with physical comforts, but needs the very word and instruction of the Lord.

This theological principle undergirds the prophetic leadership theme in Numbers—namely, Moses is dependent on hearing from the Lord regarding major and some minor issues. The Lord's perspective is crucial to facilitating and implementing instructions for the nation. Moses' role is to effectively communicate the divine words. From Exodus to Deuteronomy, the laws of the Lord are prominently presented to reveal the divine expectations for Israel's domestic life, culture, and lifestyle. These are exacting requirements and primarily reflect the social conditions and context of the wilderness environment.

12.1.2   The Lord Guides, Sustains, and Provides

Just as Yahweh reveals himself to Israel in tangible ways in Exodus, so he continues to guide the nation in visible ways. The main role of the pillar of cloud and of fire is to give guidance and protection. This is the dominant theme in Exod. 13.17–14.31. 'By day the LORD went ahead of them in a pillar of cloud to guide them on their way and by night in a pillar of fire to give them light, so that they could travel by day or night. Neither the pillar of cloud by day nor the pillar of fire by night left its place in front of the people' (Exod. 13.21–22). As the nation embarks on their pilgrimage under threatening conditions, God gives a visible beacon for the people to follow (cf. Exod. 40.38). This theme of guidance continues in Numbers as the people prepare for travel and battle. The presence of Yahweh is in their midst, symbolized by the cloud which led the people during the day and night, but also regulated times of travel and times of rest (cf. Num. 9.15–23). 'Whenever the cloud lifted from above the tent, the Israelites set out; wherever the cloud settled, the Israelites encamped' (Num. 9.17; cf. Exod. 40.34–38; Neh. 9.12–19; Ps. 99.7).

The visible pillar of cloud and fire functions to assure Israel of the divine presence during their wilderness journey to the land of promise. The cloud hides the 'face of God' but visibly indicates the presence of God among his people. It is noteworthy that the pillar of cloud and fire begins leading Israel before the exodus event, continues through the wilderness trial, and up to the point of resting on the Tabernacle. At the Tabernacle, the goal of God's redemptive work, the worship of God, appears to be achieved. The presence of God rests on the earthly dwelling which Moses was inspired to build and consecrate. The symbols of Yahweh's presence are transferred to the tabernacle (cf. Num. 9.22). Through the cloud, the glory and presence of Yahweh are imparted. When the tabernacle is completed 'the cloud covered the Tent of Meeting, and the glory of the LORD filled the tabernacle' (Exod. 40.34ff.). At the end of the book of Exodus, the narrative features the presence of God in the midst of the people at worship. It is anticipated that the mode of transport for the Tabernacle will be communicated in the book of Numbers.

Furthermore, the care of the nation in the wilderness is an essential theme in Numbers. This involves not only the organizational elements of the nation's needs, but the provision of daily resources required to nourish and hydrate the massive population. Although the people often desire a menu with diverse staples that they may have been used to in Egypt, the Lord made sure that their physical needs were met (Numbers 11). Even in challenging incidents where the people of God complained, Yahweh continued to provide for daily needs. When necessary, he also brought about punishment for excessive murmuring and rebellion. The Lord's care and discipline was part of the covenantal assurances given to the people to encourage their faithfulness: 'Worship the LORD your God, and his blessing will be on your food and water. I will take away sickness from among you, and none will miscarry or be barren in your land. I will give you a full life span' (Exod. 23.25–26). Worship the Lord (יהוה) your God (אלהים).

12.2 Theme Two: Yahweh's Holiness Compels Sanctified Worship

The revelation of Yahweh through intimate communication with Abraham and Moses followed by theophany made clear that his enduring characteristic was absolute holiness. Yahweh's presence made locations of revelation and communication sacred. Humans were on holy ground (Gen. 17.3, 17; Exod. 3.5; 19.12–13, 20–22). In some facets the Pentateuch is a manual for Israel on how to approach God. It contains detailed instructions which specify required offerings and sacrifices. It also outlines the authorized functionaries who are permitted to have access to the sanctuary, altar, and most holy place. Therefore, much of the book of Numbers has to do with the ministry of priests and Levites.

According to the book of Exodus, the divine purpose in moving Israel out of Egypt is for the nation to be 'gathered together' in worship of Yahweh. The Lord's primary act of deliverance and redemption serves to motivate Israel's response of gratitude, love, and reverence for divine intervention. Not only did Yahweh elect Israel but he brought them to Mount Sinai for the Mosaic covenant, for the revelation of covenantal laws and theophany (Exodus 19). It is also the place where over an extended period of time the Tabernacle was constructed as the central place of worship.[59] In all of this the Lord's presence is with his people. As they prepare for their epic journey, Yahweh travelled with them in the glory cloud and continued to meet with them at the Tent of Meeting and Tabernacle (Exodus 40; Numbers 7). The worship of Yahweh is mainly featured in the Book of Leviticus which prescribes the procedures that must be implemented in approaching Yahweh at the sanctuary. For the Lord's presence to be manifested, specifications for approaching him are made clear to instil reverence and devotion. An appropriate approach is also necessary to provide prepare for people's needs to be presented to God so that his beneficence may be experienced. Levine makes this objective for worship clear in that it must 'create an environment conducive to establishing a relationship that allows humans, individually and collectively, to bring their needs to the attention of God, the source of power and blessings'.[60]

In Numbers these themes of worship continue and are central to demonstrate several principles. Yahweh communicates with Moses and Israel's leaders at the sanctuary. To approach Yahweh appropriate sacrifices and offerings are required and are specified for daily and periodic administration (Numbers 15; 18–19; 28). Priests and Levites are trained, commissioned, and ordained for their work (Numbers 3–4; 8.5 ff.). They were commissioned to protect the sacred areas and to officiate the required sacrifices. The sanctuary area and materials are prepared for a nomadic journey with Yahweh centrally located among the people. The sanctity of the Tabernacle area is made very clear so that no encroachment on the place of worship is made.

Detailed instructions reveal how the nation must worship, emphasizing the holiness of God. A wholistic approach to life is presented for Israel to live an abundant, culturally sound, and law-abiding lifestyle. However, due to the depravity of humankind, sin and tragic consequences were inevitable—

---

59 Sarna, *Exodus*, p. xiii, affirms that

> two of the most important institutions of biblical Israel find their origins in Exodus: about one third of it deals with the organization of the cult around the central place of worship with a hereditary priesthood (13 of 40 chapters). And the prophetic office, of seminal importance for the national history and faith and later also for some of the world's other major religions is initiated through the person of Moses.

60 Cf. B.A. Levine, *Leviticus: The JPS Torah Commentary* (Philadelphia: The Jewish Publication Society, 1989), p. 216.

especially during the challenge of life in the wilderness. To mitigate punishment, defilement and segregation, a system of sacrifice for purification was set in place for individual and community failure (cf. Numbers 5; 9; 15; 19). Although the cultus regulations appear onerous and demanding, Yahweh's intentions for the people are always affirmative. He desires to bless the nation and empower the Israelites to fulfil their covenantal ministry to the nations as priests (Exod. 19.6). With this in mind, the divine blessing is administered by the Aaronides as the pinnacle of their priestly ministry: 'The LORD bless you and keep you; the LORD make his face shine on you and be gracious to you; the LORD turn his face toward you and give you peace. So they will put my name on the Israelites, and I will bless them' (Num. 6.24–27). The Lord's intention for his people is blessing, peace and contentment through his presence in Israel's midst. The achievement of this reality comes through their genuine relationship and approach of a holy God through sacrifice, offering, and prayer.

12.3 Theme Three: Appointed Leadership (Prophet; Priests; Levites; Elders; Military)

From the opening words of Numbers, it becomes very evident that Yahweh chooses to lead Israel through a carefully selected network of leaders. All the leaders are appointed and given the authority and instructions concerning their responsibilities. One of the leadership terms that is used to emphasize the organization of the nation conveys the meaning to be 'lifted up' (נשׂיא). Translated 'prince, leader, or chief', it occurs 56 times in Numbers—more than in any other OT book. Other terms for heads of clans and elders with distinctive roles are also used to delineate important leadership functions for the well-being of the community (and are discussed as they arise in the commentary). Leaders are essential for the wilderness challenges before the nation. The appointing and commissioning of leaders provides the necessary structure that is needed not only to lead a vast group of people, but to nurture them in accordance with the requirements of relationship with a holy God.

An important observation in reading Numbers is the meticulous and regular interweaving of lists regarding the numbering of clans, leaders, offerings, gifts, and materials. The import of this format, which is presented in accordance with obedience to Yahweh's instructions, is that God loves order. There is a way of organizing life in the community which brings structure, meaning and direction that is crucial for the nation. Leaders are accountable to superintend the development and organizational elements of community life. Therefore, the instructions provided are expected to be adhered to by the whole community. Yahweh brings about order by selecting and guiding individual leaders for specific tasks.⁶¹ Just as Elohim brought order out of the primordial chaos and structured the creation of earth, so now does he work through the administration of leaders in Israel to bring order and structure in Israel.

As will be evident from the commentary, the primary leadership role is given to Moses who exemplifies what prophetic leadership is all about. Although there are several occasions in Numbers where Moses would like to give up his role, he serves faithfully until his transition is immanent. A text which captures the prominence of the leadership theme comes when Moses is looking for his successor to be placed. 'May the LORD, the God who gives breath to all living things, appoint someone over this community to go out and come in before them, one who will lead them out and bring them in, so the LORD's people will not be like sheep without a shepherd' (Num. 27.16–17). The prayer of Moses reveals several dynamic truths. Firstly, it is in the providence of God to make the selection and appointment of leaders. Secondly, good leaders are always looking for their successor to take over the responsibilities for the care of people. Leaders are integral to the way God chooses to look after people who are 'like sheep', needing the care and guidance of the shepherd.

Beginning with the selection of Moses, a primary theme in Numbers involves his prophetic leadership. Prophecy is the chosen method of communication with the nation and Yahweh primarily speaks to his servant Moses through whom he shepherds Israel (cf. Num. 11.25; 12.6–8). The characteristic phrase, 'the LORD spoke to Moses' highlights the relational reality of God's presence with the redeemed people of Israel. The theme is rooted in the character of God which is often characterized by order, wisdom, and creative skill. This is how Scripture begins to reveal Elohim and his sovereign creation of the heavens and the earth. He speaks forth his will and by the Spirit of God it materializes in an orderly, creative, and magnificent world (Genesis 1). What begins in an uninhabitable chaotic void becomes a masterpiece of paradisical order. Through prophetic leadership, Yahweh brings about dominion for the sake of his people.

Several times in Numbers there are chaotic situations that occur, and in those episodes, leaders jump into action to bring order out of chaos. Some of

---

61 D.C. Hymes, 'Heroic Leadership in the Wilderness, Part 1', AJPS 9.2 (2006), p. 300, writes, Leadership in the book of Numbers is not vested in just crisis-based assemblies, nor monopolized by Moses or even a Moses-Aaron-Miriam triumvirate. It is a rich and variegated hierarchy that is both institutional and charismatic, legitimate and at times illegitimate. The tribal leadership infrastructure was both institutional and legitimate.

the challenges described in Numbers are demanding, including the preparation of young men for military assignments, training the Levites for risky work around the most sacred duties of the cultus, confronting conflicts in leadership challenges concerning competency, and moving the nation forward to realize the divine vision. In addition to internal conflicts, several external security threats arise from other nations. Furthermore, the acquisition of supplies to meet the daily needs of the people, are massive. *But this is what leadership is all about: leading people through a myriad of difficulties to a desirable goal for the benefit of the whole community in accordance with the divine design for kingdom and dominion.*

Although Moses is the primary leader, he serves closely with the Aaronides who provide leadership in the institutions of the cultus. Aaron serves in tandem with Moses and is frequently involved in major events. Servants with tremendous responsibilities are the Levites, whose work duties are presented in several chapters (Numbers 3–4). Clan leaders look after the tribal needs of individual families but also contribute to the well-being of the community. Military assignments are given to selected men from every tribe who become responsible for the security needs of the nation.

The book of Numbers has much to contribute concerning these leadership themes and provides insights into the principles required for leading God's people in dignified and wise ways to achieve the divine purposes. This is crucial due to the very difficult matters which arise in human experience involving significant suffering, death, punishment, conflict, curses, and power struggles. Numbers provides both human and divine dimensions that are often in tension to reveal insights for both ancient and contemporary life issues. In a significant development which illustrates this reality, Moses is instructed to assemble seventy elders who are also empowered and authorized to serve in the domestic needs of the nation. On this occasion, Yahweh shares the Spirit that empowered Moses with the seventy elders (Num. 11.25). In chapter 11, themes of leadership, inspiration, prophetic speech, judgment, provision, and guidance provide instruction on how the Spirit of God works among the advancing people of God. It is this chapter in the Pentateuch that features the empowerment for leadership by the Spirit of God and explains how Moses is able to accomplish so much in his forty years of ministry.

The implication of the focalization of Numbers on leadership is that many leaders are needed, with significant diversification of skills, in order to effectively serve and care for the needs of the population. However, all selected leaders receive their instructions through the leadership of Moses, the servant of the Lord.

12.4 Theme Four: God's People and the Nations

The whole premise of Numbers concerns an epic journey of the Israelites from Mount Sinai to a 'promised land'. This is an exciting and desirable goal for landless people who look forward with great expectations to entering a place described as 'a land flowing with milk and honey'. The biblical land of Palestine was considered a holy place where Abraham set up altars and worshipped God (cf. Gen. 12.6–8; 13.18; 22.31–33). For Israel it was a mysterious place promised by Yahweh who allocated Canaan to the people as an inheritance where they should live in accordance with the covenantal stipulations. It was a place of grace where they would work out their faith, but it was also a 'geographical sphere in which the people of Israel were to be loyal in their covenant with God and as a 'holy' people were to be set apart from the idolatrous practices of their pagan neighbours (Leviticus 26)'.[62]

The premise of land ownership for the nation is rooted in Israel's covenant with Yahweh which affirms an amazing theological tenet of election. Beginning with the selection of Noah and Abraham, God selects people to address the challenges of humanity. Abraham would become the father of the 'chosen' nation, but he too had to leave his family home in Ur to settle among the peoples of Canaan as a resident alien. To survive, he exercised friendly cooperation with the people even though he had faith that one day the land would be his. However, the context in Canaan included conflict with foreigners and inhabitants who were often in discord with one another. War, plundering, rivalry, and revenge were common activities (Gen. 14.1–12). In such cases, Israel took a defensive or offensive position depending on the situation. God brought blessing or cursing on nations for their treatment of Abraham and Israel (Gen. 12.1–3; 18.16–21). During times of famine and strife, God's people sought refuge in foreign lands like Egypt.

The concise summation of what Yahweh's election means for Israel occurs at Mount Sinai: 'Now if you obey me fully and keep my covenant, then out of all nations you will be my treasured possession. Although the whole earth is mine, you will be for me a kingdom of priests and a holy nation. These are the words you are to speak to the Israelites' (Exod. 19.5–6). The chosen people are a 'treasured possession' (סגלה), which is the clearest affirmation of God's special covenantal relationship with Israel (Exod. 19.5; cf. Deut. 7.6; 14.2; 26.18–19). As a 'kingdom' (ממלכה) of 'priests' (כהן), they will be a sovereign nation in

---

[62] J.M. Houston, 'The Geographical Setting of the Bible', in F.E. Gaebelein (ed.), *The Expositor's Bible Commentary: Introductory Articles* (Vol. 1; Grand Rapids: Zondervan, 1979), p. 93.

order to have the capacity to fulfil their mission as priests, set apart for ministry to other nations.⁶³ As a special people with an incredible commission, an essential requirement for the nation is their call to 'holiness' (קדוש) (cf. Lev. 19.1). They are the 'people' (עם), the 'nation' (גוי) of God through whom he will reach out to foreign nations. To be sure, this status often led to pride and Israel soon forgot about the divine purpose to serve the nations as a royal priesthood. Mediation implied that they should bring blessing, knowledge of Yahweh, and wisdom for societal life to the nations. Moreover, a glaring paradox is evident in Israel's relationship with the nations. Yahweh's intention was to set them apart for influence and to bring them into the promised land as Israel's inheritance. However, on several occasions the people want to return to Egypt! (cf. Num. 11.5, 18–20; 14.3–4; 20.5; 21.5). Additionally, Israel was always attracted to the religious beliefs and practices of other nations.

Early in Israel's history, foreigners were attracted to the nation (Exod. 12.35–38). In fact, Israel included many foreigners who attached themselves to the nation during and after the Exodus. A variety of terms are used such as the 'rabble' or a mixed multitude, aliens, and 'foreigner or stranger' (גר) among the Israelites. Quite often foreigners make positive contributions in the life of the nation and are valued community participants (i.e., Hobab, Jethro, Zipporah, a Cushite wife, Caleb, etc.). Foreigners who desired to live among the Israelites were to be treated in a neighbourly fashion and 'loved' (Lev. 19.33–34; 23.22; Deut. 10.17–19; 14.29), and also 'taught' (Deut. 31.12–13; 24.14–22; 27.19). In fact, marriage to foreigners was permitted so long as the marriage partner chose Yahwism. Sometimes foreigners to the covenant exhibit more faith than people in Israel and are examples of what God desired! This is exemplified in Jethro's declaration: 'Praise be to the LORD who rescued you from Egypt … Now I know that the LORD is greater than all other gods for he did this to those who had treated Israel arrogantly' (cf. Exod. 18.9–12).

While these truths are great ideals for Israel, the premise also infers that since the land of promise is already occupied, it will take war to remove the landholders. Sure enough, when Israel's spies investigate the quality of land and estimate the forces holding Canaan, they soon realize that the inhabitants pose a formidable challenge. Skirmishes and battles begin with the Canaanites, Moabites, Midianites, Amorites, and the Transjordanian tribes (cf. Numbers 21; 31–32). These battles prepare Israel for the major conquest to come under the leadership of Joshua. The threatening presence of Israel made the nation's relationship with the inhabitants tenuous at best and brought into

---

63 Sarna, *Exodus*, p. 104.

question their ability to be instruments of judgment on one hand, and instruments of peace on the other.

God's sovereignty in dealing with Israel and the nations is evident in the Pentateuch and specifically illustrated in the Balaam section (Numbers 22–24). Numbers provides keen insights into several issues that all nations desire: fertile land with water and food resources, security, and equitable trade with neighbours. However, where there is deficient, self-seeking leadership and false religious practice, nations will often have challenging 'wilderness' experiences, with negative consequences that can last for decades and generations. Many lessons are presented for Israel and the nations to seek blessing and well-being from the Lord who is able to provide it for his people.

12.5   Theme Five: The Wilderness Wandering Theme of Testing

Although God chooses Israel and establishes a covenant with his people, it does not give them an automatic easy life. They are prone to the same problems and challenges of forging out their culture and lifestyle as are the other nations. In fact, they are often more challenged than other people due to the high standards of the covenantal relationship. Concerning this relational context, an important theme in scripture concerns the role of 'testing' the covenantal partner. A prime example is Abraham who was tested regarding his son Isaac (Genesis 22). Other examples include Adam and Eve in the garden of Eden, as well as Noah who is instructed to build an ark. For Israel, the test concerns trust in the faithful care of Yahweh to meet primary needs in the wilderness. After the Exodus experience God led Israel through the wilderness (Exod. 13.17–18) which included very difficult terrain (Deut. 1.19). This initial trek was a preliminary test for Israel to see how they would respond to God's leading, provision and instructions. This is illustrated with the provision of manna: 'Then the LORD said to Moses, "I will rain down bread from heaven for you. The people are to go out each day and gather enough for that day. In this way I will test them and see whether they will follow my instructions"' (Exod. 16.4). During this time Israel also tested the Lord, showing their dissatisfaction with Yahweh as well as with the leadership of Moses (cf. Exod. 5.19–23; 14.10–12; 17.2). Israel was a difficult people to lead as these few examples show.

Right after the victory song in Exod. 15.1–21, the people came to *Marah* where the water was bitter, and people grumbled against Moses. God responded by showing Moses a tree that made the waters drinkable (Exod. 15.22–27). God then brought them to an oasis called Elim. The water resources needed by the nation were enormous, but Psalm 69.7–9 also affirms the Lord's adequate provisions in rainfall: 'When you, God, went out before your people, when you marched through the wilderness, the earth shook, the heavens poured down rain, before God, the One of Sinai, before God, the God of Israel. You gave abundant showers, O God; you refreshed your weary inheritance'. Again, in the wilderness of Sin the people cried out for food and lamented the loss of Egypt's menu items (Exod. 16.1–3). God answered with provisions of quail and manna (Exod. 16.13–15; 31, 35). Also, at *Massah* and *Meribah*, the need arose for water supplies (Exod. 17.1), so Moses was instructed by God to strike the rock (Exod. 7.1–7). However, the most serious incident occurred with the golden calf while Moses was on Mount Sinai. The people quickly forgot about their covenantal commitments and worshipped the calf idol. In that episode the Lord was prepared to severely punish the 'stiff-necked' people and only relented through Moses' intercessory prayers (Exod. 32.7–10).

The theme of testing is even more prominent in the book of Numbers, where a typical pattern is observed in several narratives (a need; response; provision and often judgment). The pattern usually follows the need like at Taberah (Num. 11.1–3) where the people strongly complained, and God consequently reacted in judgment. In this example there is no provision noted. At *Kibroth-Hattavah* the people complained about the lack of variety in their diet (Num. 11.4–34) although they had food. The Lord provided meat and quail, but he also brought judgment on some who died in a plague.

The most serious incident occurs when the twelve spies are sent out to survey the promised land. The land proved to be very productive with excellent produce characterized as 'milk and honey' (Num. 13.27), but they were deterred by the people who lived in fortified cities (Num. 13.28). People grumbled against Moses and accused God of wanting to slay them—they desired a return to Egypt (Num. 14.3–4). In this case, provision was not evident but judgment by pestilence came upon many (Num. 14.12). God promised further judgment for those who saw his glory and signs yet 'tested' (נסה) him ten times—they would not be permitted to see the promised land. Moses interceded and the Lord replied with a mitigated verdict.

> I have forgiven them, as you asked. Nevertheless, as surely as I live and as surely as the glory of the LORD fills the whole earth, not one of those who saw my glory and the signs I performed in Egypt and in the wilderness but who disobeyed me and tested me ten times—not one of them will ever see the land I promised on oath to their ancestors. No one who has treated me with contempt will ever see it. (Num. 14.20–23)

Joshua and Caleb were an exception to this judgment but the ten spies with the negative report died by plague.

INTRODUCTION

The wilderness testing era will frequently be returned to in scripture as a theological lesson for Israel to learn from. This is evident in several passages in both the Old and New Testaments (cf. Num. 33.1–53; Deut. 1.6–3.29; Pss. 78.17 ff.; 95.7–11; 1 Cor. 10.1–11; Heb. 3.15–19). These passages often characterize Israel as a stubborn lot who failed to recognize the provisions and care of Yahweh.

12.6 Theme Six: *The Spirit of God*

Several themes noted above have content or elements which could be referred to as important 'Pentecostal' themes—that is, content with 'Spirit' associations. Prophetic leadership, inspiration, divine presence and guidance, holiness, miraculous provisions, and worship are just a few. References to the Spirit of God in the Pentateuch are limited but Numbers includes the most citations of 'Spirit' (רוח)—primarily to the Spirit's role in chapter 11. The term 'רוח' occurs 38 times in the Pentateuch but only some of the references are to be translated as the 'Spirit' of God. Typically, 'רוח' refers to wind, breath, or spirit in mankind with some kind of anthropological meaning.[64] However, in the book of Numbers with 14 occurrences of רוח, six references in chapter 11 begin to develop core elements in the Spirit's role. In the OT the motifs where the Spirit of God has an active role, are related to creation, the establishment and preservation of God's people, most leadership functions and in relationship to prophets and prophetic expression.

With the limited number of specific references to the Spirit of God in Numbers, we want to be careful in jumping to certain conclusions. However, the Spirit of God appears to be a humble but pervasive presence in Numbers—not referred to much and often hidden, but tangibly present and powerful. The Spirit of God is the unseen force which keeps moving the nation and leaders in a forward trajectory. A broader study of the Spirit's role in the nation demonstrates the Spirit's vital presence in the establishment, preservation, judgment, and restoration of God's people.[65] In our reading of the book of Numbers, a discerning attempt is made to observe how the presence and work of the Spirit of God leads Israel during the wilderness trek and also facilitates the prophetic leadership of Moses. There are two primary aspects to the Spirit's role at a 'macrolevel' that will be briefly observed here, and the main one is how Yahweh's presence is revealed.

---

64 Cf. Hildebrandt, *An Old Testament Theology of the Spirit of God* (Peabody, MA: Hendrickson, 1995), for a detailed study of the 389 references to the term in key categories. Cf. S. Tengström, 'רוח', *TDOT*, XIII, pp. 378–391.

65 Cf. Hildebrandt, *An Old Testament Theology of the Spirit of God*, pp. 67–103.

The pervasive divine presence of God is evident in theophany on Mount Sinai with thunder, lightning, a dense cloud, smoke with fire—an incredible display of sound and sight (Exod. 19.18–20). This is how God chose to reveal himself and authorize Moses before the people with revelation and the giving of covenant. The event also leads to the endorsement of the prophet's role in mediating the words of Yahweh to the people. The glory cloud becomes the visible representation of the Lord's presence and eventually transitions from the mountain to the Tabernacle with the people. In fact, Israel's experience at Mount Sinai prepares the nation for their worship and approach of God at the Tabernacle. The summit represents the inner sanctum and Holy of Holies where only Moses and the high priest are permitted entry. The mid-point of the mountain is like the outer court which is sanctified for the priest's ministry and the base of the mountain represents the outer court that is the boundary for the people (Exod. 19.12–25).[66]

The theophanic spectacle reveals the presence, power and majesty of the Lord who is invisible, but present. Only Moses has a unique revelation of Yahweh's most intimate presence in an intense encounter where Yahweh proclaims his name, reveals his character, and affirms his covenantal promises (Exod. 33.12–34.14). After the Sinai event, Yahweh's presence is revealed through the glory cloud (כבוד) where the presence of Yahweh was so intense that Moses could not enter the tent of meeting (Exod. 40.34 ff.).

In Numbers 9 the divine presence takes up residence at the Tabernacle, affirming to Israel that Yahweh remains with his people. 'On the day the tabernacle, the tent of the covenant law, was set up, the cloud covered it. From evening till morning the cloud above the tabernacle looked like fire. That is how it continued to be; the cloud covered it, and at night it looked like fire' (Num. 9.15–16). The guidance of the Lord is emphasized by his commands and instruction to either move or stay. Moreover, this passage affirms Yahweh's presence in the 'cloud' (ענן) with eleven references, in order to guide Israel through the wilderness with his seven-fold commands (Num. 9.18–23).[67] This text reiterates the basic content of Exodus 40 but features the presence of Yahweh in the 'cloud' (ענן) and 'fire' (אש) over the tabernacle. The main role of the pillar of cloud and fire was to convey Yahweh's presence for guidance and protection. This was the dominant theme in Exod. 13.17–14.31 when Israel embarked on their journey from Egypt: 'By day the LORD went ahead of them in a pillar

---

66 Cf. Sarna, *Exodus*, p. 105.
67 The other emphases in these few verses are in regard to the divine presence over the Tabernacle (referred to 7 times) and the Tent of Testimony or Meeting (referred to 4 times).

of cloud to guide them on their way and by night in a pillar of fire to give them light, so that they could travel by day or night. Neither the pillar of cloud by day nor the pillar of fire by night left its place in front of the people'. This was the way that God gave a visible beacon for the people to see while on their journey (cf. Exod. 40.38), but also the way he protected Israel and achieved his purposes (Exod. 14.20–24).

A key connection between the cloud and the Spirit of God occurs in Num. 11.25 where they function together. In this episode we learn that the Spirit is upon Moses for vitality in his leadership role. To facilitate the needs of the nation, Yahweh shares the Spirit that was on Moses with the seventy elders. 'Then the LORD came down in the cloud and spoke with him, and he took of the Spirit that was on him and put the Spirit on the seventy elders'. With this connection we are given insight into the way God works through his Spirit and presence in the cloud (cf. Num. 14.20). The empowering of authorized leadership may be evident to some degree in Moses' leadership record as seen in Exodus, but the source of his skill and prophetic power is not specified until Numbers 11 where the Spirit on Moses is shared with seventy elders. Leaders are a vital component in experiencing the divine blessings of God—people require shepherds (Numbers 27), elders, Levites, priests—who bring order out of the chaos so that life in the land of promise is abundant and pleasant. Numbers 11 illustrates early forms and types in the development of prophecy and prophetic leadership. Primarily, Numbers 11, and 22–24, provide insights into the formation of prophetic and charismatic leadership. When the Spirit's presence is 'visible' in the cloud, and in the leadership of Moses, amazing things happen in the life of the nation.

Other observations are in order when reading the book of Numbers and considering the Spirit's roles in scripture. One of the key connections are drawn from the creation account where God brings order out of the chaotic void to bring about his creation of the universe and the garden of Eden. In similar ways, as Israel prepares to enter their promised 'garden', it becomes evident that it takes meticulous preparation and orderly work to bring the instructions of Yahweh into reality. This is accomplished through Moses and leaders who implement the 'commands' of Yahweh throughout their epic journey. Leaders are counted and trained for their roles in moving the people and the Tabernacle forward. Chapters which record the procedures of census taking reveal an amazing orderly tabulation of people and numbers for military service (Numbers 1–2; 26).

Similarly, the utensils for the sanctuary and personnel of the cultus are counted, prepared, and trained. The procedures of the people in worship are strictly regulated and informed by the meticulous details for offerings and sacrifices regarding the reverence required in approaching God. Consecrated leaders and the Tabernacle with its sacred furnishings are anointed and cared for with scrupulous precision and reverence (Numbers 7–9). There are festivals and offerings which require understanding, sacrifice, and orderly respect according to calendar schedule (Numbers 28–29). Issues of health, judgment and plague are also addressed providing a worldview which reflects a wholistic approach to life. Healing and atonement are themes which are illustrated in a number of contexts.

Due to the holiness of the sanctuary and furnishing in the Tabernacle, utmost care and respect is required by Levites and priests for the sanctuary materials which are anointed for the sanctifying of sacred areas.

12.7 Theme Seven: Covenantal Commitments for Blessing or Cursing

There is one more notable theme that needs to be expounded because it quietly develops from the opening chapters of the Pentateuch through to the end. At times the theme is presented in a flurry of vocabulary (Gen. 12.2–3; Numbers 22–24), but generally the divine blessings are silently observed in Israel's advancement. However, 'the blessing' is an important concept that permeates Scripture and is an integral part of the covenant. The blessing trajectory begins from covenantal expressions in passages with Adam, Noah, and Abraham, which are then fleshed out within the Mosaic covenant and the Lord's design for Israel.

The concept of blessing in the OT affirms that God is able to bring about the positive effects of fertility, long life, prosperity, and security for his people who are living in accordance with covenantal terms. From the first chapter of Genesis the ability of humankind to fulfil the divine commission is dependent on God's 'blessing' (ברך). The fundamental mandate of procreation is contingent on the blessing conferred on individuals. The ability to govern and establish dominion on earth is incumbent on the divine blessing (Gen. 1.28, 22; 5.2; 9.1). Only through the beneficent acts of Yahweh, are the divine promises and blessings realized. God is the source of blessing for the gift of fertility and he 'fills' the barren womb (Gen. 17.16, 20; 22.17; 25.11; 28.3). Divine blessing may bring vitality, health, prosperity, and abundance to the covenant people (Deut. 1.11; 7.13–15; 28.1–14).[68]

The terminology of blessing is a frequent and pervasive theme in Genesis with approximately 85 citations. The meaning of the divine blessing for Israel and the nations is developed in Genesis and then illustrated in its partial fulfil-

---

68   Cf. Hildebrandt, *An Old Testament Theology of the Spirit of God*, pp. 60–62.

ment in Exodus and Numbers. The key elements of the blessing are formulated in the Abrahamic covenant which defines the main components of what blessing and curse actually signifies. Although the theme of Yahweh's beneficence is vital in Numbers, the terminology is limited to a few chapters (Numbers 6; 22–24) with 'blessing' (ברך) referred to 17 times. The opposite term is 'curse' which is used 22 times (Numbers 5; 22–24). Two words for 'curse' are employed with basically the same meaning ('ארר' and 'קבב').[69] The curse or 'execration' was perceived to have inherent power to affect a reversal in the state of 'blessing' (ברך) or to set into effect misfortune. Typically, the curse motif is used against enemies or covenant partners who failed in their duties of not paying tribute, but it could also be used in preparation for battle. On the complete opposite scale of the curse is the positive act to bless. The blessing and cursing theme is the focal point in the Balaam section (Numbers 22–24) where both terms are *Leitwörter* in the passage. The fact that Yahweh's blessings are upon Israel becomes a significant threat for the other nations.[70] This is made clear in Joshua where the sovereignty of Yahweh controls the destiny of the nation that is blessed by the Lord. 'But I would not listen to Balaam, so he blessed you again and again, and I delivered you out of his hand' (Josh. 24.10).

The implicit effect of the blessing in Numbers is observed in the outworking of Yahweh's blessing over Israel when obedience to the covenantal expectations are evident. When compliance with divine instructions is in effect, the nation experiences the benefits of the covenantal promises, such as an increase in population, relational growth in the presence of God through worship in cultus institutions, and the forward movement towards the land of inheritance (Deuteronomy 28). Many of these blessings are experienced by Israel as they prepare for their journey to Canaan.

Blessings are often tangible and physical elements, but a primary indicator of God's favour is evidenced in a relational dimension. In Numbers there are two primary functionaries that work together with Yahweh to bring about blessing. The priests and the prophet. This will mainly be apparent from the contours of the high priestly blessing (Num. 6.22–27), which becomes a key element in the priest's regular service in Israel. Although spoken by the priest, the actual implementation of blessing is dependent on God. 'In the Old Testament the blessing is almost always attributed to God or closely connected with him. The godly man knew that the only kind of benedictory wishes he could utter were

---

69 J. Scharbert, 'ארר', *TDOT*, I, pp. 412–425.
70 The term 'bless' (ברך) occurs in a variety of forms approximately 370 times in the OT with about 17 references in Numbers. Cf. J. Scharbert, 'ברך', *TDOT*, II, p. 296.

those which God alone could bring to reality. Since a blessing can be brought to reality by God alone, and since it denotes an attachment with or a strengthening of solidarity, it is necessary that the person uttering the blessing be in fellowship with God, seek it, or be worthy of it'.[71] Therefore, the blessings of God are not activated through just any spoken formula such as the priestly blessing: 'The LORD bless you and keep you; the LORD make his face shine upon you and be gracious to you; the LORD turn his face toward you and give you peace' (Num. 6.24–26). While this blessing calls for God's beneficence to be turned towards his people, the blessing is only as effective as the compliance of the people. Their experience of divine beneficence that bestows happiness, prosperity, success, respect, fertility, security, peace, and contentment, only becomes a reality when they walk in obedience to God's commands. This is illustrated during the wilderness wanderings of Israel. The priestly blessing will be discussed in chapter 6.

The prophetic functions in facilitating blessing are more complicated. The main form of blessing comes through the prophetic leadership of Moses who leads Israel in a competent, humble, and spiritual manner. He is the selected prophet to whom Yahweh speaks and reveals instructions, guidance, and legislation. This is observed in the regular meetings Moses has with Yahweh at the Tabernacle and in the positive resolutions he facilitates to wilderness challenges. Prophetic leadership is evident in the provision of necessary resources for the nation, as well as in the positive outcomes through Moses' intercessory prayer. Moreover, the consistent management of Israel's threats and conflicts which keep the nation moving forward, although slower than expected, are evidence of Moses' governance skills.

Several commentators disparage the addition of the Balaam narrative in Numbers 22–24 and diminish the purposes of the section. However, the narratives and oracles included there have a very important role and essential function, not only in Numbers but in the OT. The chapters provide a mirror for comparing the prophetic leadership of Moses to other types of functionaries who use the manipulation of forces to harm or help nations. Balaam reflects the more negative role of 'seers' in ancient near eastern contexts, who seek control over forces which could restrain the forward movement and blessing of the nation. The episodes serve to contrast the work of diviners in the ancient near east, with the developing services of Yahweh's 'true' prophet, to show how nations are to achieve positive, divine blessing. Disobedience and rebellion bring the opposite effects of blessing on the people and the curse brings into effect the reversal of covenant blessings (Deut. 28.15–68).

---

71   Scharbert, 'ברך', p. 303; cf. pp. 279–308.

The relationship between Spirit and blessing is also evident in the second part of humankind's commission to 'subdue' and to 'rule'. Just as mankind depends on God for the blessing to enable fertility, success, and prosperity, so they depend on the Spirit of God to enable their work of subduing and ruling. This is vividly portrayed in the creation account where God forms Adam, breathes into him the breath of life, and puts him in the garden to cultivate or 'take care of it' (Gen. 2.7–15). Dominion is a royal function and is illustrated in Numbers with the leadership preparations for the taking of the promised land. God works through Moses and leadership representatives to move the people forward in the establishment of the kingdom. The work of the Spirit of God in this endeavour is observed in the prophetic leadership of Moses (Numbers 11), as well as in his successor Joshua: "So the LORD said to Moses, 'Take Joshua son of Nun, a man in whom is the spirit of leadership, and lay your hand on him'" (Num. 27.16).[72]

Therefore, the book of Numbers illustrates how the divine blessing is essential for every positive reality in the life experience of Israel's national life. The opposite realm of experience manifests results of a curse which combat against all that is good and productive in the nation. Blessing and curse prove to be powerful realities in the people's daily experience, as the exhortation from the book of the covenant affirms: 'Worship the LORD your God, and his blessing will be on your food and water. I will take away sickness from among you, and none will miscarry or be barren in your land. I will give you a full life span' (Exod. 23.25–26).

---

[72] The theme of the successful rule and blessing of God regarding kingdom expansion primarily is evident where charismatic leaders are endowed with the Spirit for their royal functions. Cf. W.J. Dumbrell, 'Spirit and Kingdom of God in the Old Testament', *Reformed Theological Review* 33 (1974), pp. 1ff.

Commentary

∴

PART 1

The Exodus (First) Generation in the Wilderness (Numbers 1–25)

∴

1.1–10.36—Administration and Organization for Israel's Journey to the Promised Land

1.1–54—Taking a Census and Mustering the Military

The book of Numbers continues the narration of Israel's migration from Egypt as recorded in the Book of Exodus. The book also expands on some of the legislative material that is presented in Leviticus to describe lifestyle and work requirements for a nomadic people. Numbers demarcates the locations and preparations of the nation for the next phase in their epic journey from Mount Sinai to their promised inheritance and place of rest.

The covenant and focus on worship obligations recorded in Exodus, becomes a more practical emphasis on instruction concerning 'holiness' in Leviticus—all mediated from Yahweh to Moses. With the Exodus event behind them, Yahweh turns the nation's attention to the covenantal promise of land. Just as Abraham was instructed to go to a new place of dwelling so now the nation is pointed in the direction of a new land as their habitation. The four hundred years of exile in Egypt was finally over and the covenantal promises were falling into place. Israel is poised for action and the Lord sets in motion the forward momentum of the nation as they move towards their 'inheritance'.

Two focalizations are now given shape. One features attention on how Israel will actually enter and conquer the land promised by Yahweh. The other focus is on how Israel will be able to maintain a sanctified covenantal relationship with a holy God.

1.1—Yahweh's Instruction

The book of Numbers opens with specific details that set the context for Israel's pilgrimage from Mount Sinai to the promised land. This occasion occurs thirteen months after the nation's departure from Egypt, one month after the completion of the sanctuary. It is the first day of the second month—a day typically set aside for community events and the day of rest. The Lord who spoke with Moses on Mount Sinai, continues to speak from within the 'Tent of Meeting' (אהל מועד), which is literally the appointed place for meeting with God. It represents a sacred place where Yahweh chooses to communicate with Moses during the transient period in the wilderness.[1] The Tent of Meeting becomes

---

[1] The Tent of Meeting (אהל מועד) is the central focal point for Yahweh's presence in Israel and

the focal point for revelation and direction—the Lord meets with Moses in a movable shrine where the prophet hears the divine word and instruction. The Torah makes numerous references to the Tabernacle and the Tent of Meeting. In essence the Tabernacle is the special sanctuary of Yahweh (Exod. 25.8). It is not a residence where Yahweh lives but it represents the place where He may be said to dwell among the people—it is a sanctuary where the presence of Yahweh is revealed to the community in a tangible way. Moreover, it is the place where Yahweh communicates with Moses, as he previously did on the Mount of Sinai.[2]

The people are pilgrims in the wilderness and require guidance for their journey from Yahweh and his appointed leaders. Literally, the 'Wilderness of Sinai' (מדבר סיני) is an arid region with limited vegetation, water and resources for agriculture or human settlements. However, it is not an extreme desert in most of its locations and adequate resources for supporting human existence as well as flocks and herds, are available.[3] In the early phase of Israel's journey towards the promised land, the wilderness of Sinai is the main location of their encampment and sojourn. In Numbers, the wilderness areas covered from Egypt to the southern borders of the promised land include the Wilderness of Shur (Exod. 15.22), the Wilderness of Zin (Num. 13.21; 20.1; 27.14; 31.11; 33.36; 34.3) and the Wilderness of Paran (Num. 12.16; 13.3, 26).

More than a reference to difficult terrain, the wilderness refers to several diverse geographical regions, rife with historical events and theological meaning. S. Talmon describes the theological connotations of the wilderness period in two distinctive but complementary ways. On the one hand, the period shows the immeasurable beneficence of God in looking after Israel for the forty years of habitation in difficult terrain with miracles, covenantal faithfulness, and instruction. On the other hand, the rebellious behaviour of the nation and 'Israel's doubt that God's power would indeed be able to actualize the promise

---

the vital place of connection for sacred matters. In reference to the holy tent consecrated to Yahweh it is used approximately 133 times in the OT (ca. 30 times in Exodus, 41 in Leviticus and over 50 times in Numbers). Cf. K. Koch, 'אהל', TDOT, I, p. 129; cf. pp. 123–124. The Tabernacle (משכן; Num. 1.50–53) is denoted about 111 times in the OT with 58 mentions in Exodus, 4 in Leviticus and 33 in Numbers. Cf. D. Kellermann, 'משכן', TDOT, IX, pp. 58–64. Some lexicons translate 'אהל' as either tent or tabernacle.

2   At times, references to the Tabernacle are in synonymous parallelism with the Tent of Meeting but initially the Tent appears to be a separate place outside of the camp for private meetings with Yahweh.

3   'Wilderness' is the preferable interpretation of 'midbar' rather than the NIV's 'desert'. The importance of the wilderness (מדבר) and its 271 references in the OT (with most occurrences in Numbers at 48 times), are evident in Talmon's 31-page article (Talmon, 'מדבר', pp. 87–118).

of land for them', brought about a disheartening ordeal in the arid land.[4] The wilderness wanderings of Israel become an historical period synonymous with suffering and testing for the nation in its early covenantal relationship with Yahweh.

1.2–14—The Census Undertaking

In accordance with the Book of Exodus where Yahweh instructs Moses regarding community life and direction, the book of Numbers continues to narrate the words and Torah of the Lord. An explicit directive is given for Moses to initiate the undertaking of a census which will tabulate crucial information concerning the adult males over twenty years of age who are part of the Israelite 'community' (עדה).[5] Each family is to count their sons within clans to determine how many males over twenty are qualified for military deployment. The designation of families (literally ancestral houses) and 'clans' (משפחה) or 'tribes' (מטה) defines the closeness of group affiliations. Familial connections are traced back to the patriarchal families and the tribes which developed from them to the clans which are represented through lineage. Together they form the community of Israelites who are called to be unified in their support for the military. As each person contributes to family duties, and tribal unity, national blessing is anticipated. The designations have implications for family structure and organization but mutual cooperation among the clans is observed for the benefit of the whole nation. The divine design for societal order is rooted in family where growth and development are expected. To assist Moses and Aaron with the census undertaking are the 'heads' (ראש) of each 'clan' (משפחה) who represent their 'ancestral house' (לבית אבתם). The clan leaders are responsible for the well-being of the people in their immediate care.[6]

From the onset of this new phase for Israel, the Lord clearly presents a realistic picture of life to come—there will be war. Preparations for battle will be necessary and counting the cost for each clan is to be accomplished in

---

4   This period of Israel's history becomes the main context or 'topos for Israel's sinfulness' (cf. Exod. 16.2; Numbers 14; 16; 20.1–13; 21.4 ff.; 27.14; cf. Talmon, 'מדבר', pp. 105–107).

5   The 'community' (עדה) in this context specifically refers to all the adult males in Israel's community. It is the 'general assembly, congregation', of all free adult men and empowered with making decisions affecting the entire nation (D. Levy, J. Milgrom, 'עדה', *TDOT*, x, p. 470). One of the functions of the community, and specifically the adult males, was to prepare for deployment in military action.

6   However, the term 'head' (ראש) usually refers to the literal head in its 38 occurrences in Numbers. It can mean census or sum (cf. Num. 1.2, 49; 4.2, 22; 26.2), but also 'chief' or 'head of a family' (cf. Num. 1.4, 16; 7.2), depending on the context.

an orderly procedure. Taking the census requires cooperation, as well as the administrative work of counting and recording. Each tribal unit is responsible for supporting and contributing their eligible sons to form the Israelite army.

Taking the census requires competent leadership and involvement from each clan. Family heritage is esteemed, and all twelve tribes are vital participants in the census. Moses and Aaron are made responsible for the recording of the groups but to assist them, leaders are named and authorized to stand with Moses for the census task. Typically, in ancient near eastern cultures, military conscription began around the age of twenty to ensure that the men were able to carry and use weapons.

To assist Moses and Aaron with the census it is the Lord who designates the leaders by name and heritage (Num. 1.5). Twenty-four names are mentioned reaching back into the patriarchal period to Jacob's sons and recorded in order of the listing in Genesis 35.22–26. Most of the names are from the offspring of Jacob and Leah (six), Rachel (two), Bilah (two), and Zilpah (two). Notable in the listing is the absence of Levi due to the specific duties that the Levites are responsible for (as described in Num. 1.47–53). Additionally, Joseph's sons, Manasseh and Ephraim, are included (thus taking the places of Levi and Joseph). In the second list of names, Gad is inserted after Simeon (cf. the tribal camp arrangements that are presented in Numbers 2).

The listing of twelve tribal fathers is vital and reflects the theological importance of the patriarchal promises being fulfilled in the history of descendants. The tribal fathers and descendants will be mentioned again by individual listings in Numbers 2, 7 and 10. Their prominence in the history of Israel is notable in the numerous mentions of their names in the book of Numbers as noted below. Ten of the names in Hebrew take the form of a noun sentence and four are verbal phrases. Later in Israel, names often include references to Yahweh but initially the divine name known to the patriarchs is '*Shaddai*'. '*El*' forms part of ten names while *Shaddai* is in two.[7]

1.15–16—Chosen Leaders

The selected 'leaders' (נשיא) of the tribes are now presented with their ancestral affiliation and family heritage.[8] As mentioned, personal names are meaningful

---

7 Names in Israel are often descriptive and meaningful, providing reference to experiences and family dimensions or relational realities—often including characteristics or values to be instilled in the child. Additionally, these leaders are not only designated for this special task but are appointed by the Lord to their position.

8 This term applied to leaders indicates a reverential tone of a selected individual that is raised to a position of influence. Out of 126 occurrences in the OT, it is used 60 times in Numbers (H. Niehr, 'נשיא', *TDOT*, X, p. 45), and usually refers to the head of a clan.

and the tribal heads whose stories began in Genesis continue to have significance in Israel's historical development. An indicator of their prominence is evident from the number of citations each son of Jacob has in Numbers (noted below). Those who are elevated to serve or 'assist' (NIV) as leaders are named.

> of Reuben (19 times), Elizur the son of Shedeur;
> of Simeon (11 times), Shelumiel the son of Zurishaddai;
> of Judah (12 times), Nahshon the son of Amminadab;
> of Issachar (10 times), Nethanel the son of Zuar;
> of Zebulun (10 times), Eliab the son of Helon;
> of the sons of Joseph (13 times).
> of Ephraim (12 times), Elishama the son of Ammihud;
> of Manasseh (19 times), Gamaliel the son of Pedahzur;
> of Benjamin (10 times), Abidan the son of Gideoni;
> of Dan (10 times), Ahiezer the son of Ammishaddai;
> of Asher (11 times), Pagiel the son of Ochran;
> of Gad (21 times), Eliasaph the son of Deuel;
> of Naphtali (10 times), Ahira the son of Enan.

In Gen. 29.31–30.24, the record of Jacob's sons and their mothers is presented along with the background to their names. The family intrigues not withstanding, the record often indicates the providential element in the child's birth. The names are usually formed from the circumstances that lead to the birth and have a meaning attached through wordplay.[9] Thus, Reuben. 'The LORD has seen my affliction', implying. 'Now my husband will love me' (Gen. 29.32). Simeon. 'This is because the LORD heard that I was unloved and has given me this one also' (Gen. 29.33). Levi. 'This time my husband will become attached to me, for I have borne him three sons' (Gen. 29.34). Judah. 'This time I will praise the LORD' (Gen. 29.35). Dan. 'God has vindicated me; indeed, He has heeded my plea and given me a son' (Gen. 30.6). Naphtali. 'A fateful contest I waged with my sister; yes, and I have prevailed' (Gen. 30.8). Gad. 'What luck!' (good fortune; Gen. 30.11). Asher. 'What fortune!' meaning, 'Women will deem me fortunate' (Gen. 30.13). Issachar. 'God has given me my reward for having given my maid to my husband' (Gen. 30.18). Zebulun. 'God has given me a choice gift; this time my husband will exalt me, for I have borne him six sons' (Gen. 30.20). Joseph. 'May the LORD add another son for me' (Gen. 30.23–24). Benjamin. '[Rachel] named

---

9 The meaning of the words noted in this paragraph are as rendered in the Jewish Publication Society (JPS, 1985) translation.

him Ben-oni ("Son of my trouble"), but his father called him Benjamin ("son of my wealth or good fortune")' (Gen. 35.18). Manasseh. 'God has made me forget completely my hardship and my parental home' (Gen. 41.51). Ephraim. 'God has made me fertile in the land of my affliction' (Gen. 41.52). From these names, the status and importance of progeny and having sons becomes abundantly clear. Moreover, the names indicate significant meaning as they recognize divine provision but also identify the prevalence of some suffering and family rivalry![10]

Verse 16 is a summation and record of the leaders. 'These were the men appointed from the community, the leaders of their ancestral tribes. They were the heads of the clans of Israel'. The more literal translation in the JPS is, 'Those are the elected of the assembly, the chieftains of their ancestral tribes. they are the heads of the contingents of Israel'. Here and in chapter 2, they are the heads of 'thousands' or the divisions of troops, reflecting their military roles—they oversee and lead the mustered men.[11] The choices of twelve men from the tribes are ratified by the community in a democratic process. They represent the tribal interests of each clan within the larger community. They are the 'leaders' who are 'called and chosen' for crucial roles in the nation (cf. Num. 1.44–45).[12] These leaders are crucial to the 'community' (עדה) which they represent because the whole population is not always able to be present at every event. According to the Pentateuch, the community of Israel is a primitive type of democracy that submits their trust or opposition to the broader vision of

---

10   Allen, *Numbers*, pp. 706–707, lists the probable meanings of the leaders as:
     Elizur ('[My] God is a Rock') son of Shedeur ('Shaddai Is a Flame'), chief of Reuben. Shemumiel ('[My] Peace is God') son of Zurishaddai ('[My] Rock is Shaddai'), chief of Simeon. Nahshon ('Serpentine') son of Amminadab ('[My] Kinsman [God] Is Noble'), chief of Judah. Nethanel ('God has Given') the son of Zuar ('Little One'), chief of Issachar. Eliab ('[My] God I Father') the son of Helon ('Rampart-like' [?]), chief of Zebulun. Elishama ('[My] God Has Heard') the son of Ammihud ('[My] Kinsman [God] Is Majesty'), chief of Ephraim. Gamaliel ('Reward of God') the son of Pedahzur ('The Rock [God] Has Ransomed'), chief of Manasseh. Abidan ('My Father [God] Is Judge') the son of Gideoni ('My Hewer'), chief of Benjamin. Ahiezer ('[My] Brother [God] Is Help') the son of Ammishaddai ('[My] Kinsman [God] Is Shaddai'), chief of Dan. Pagiel ('Encountered by God') the son of Ochran ('Troubled'), chief of Asher. Eliasaph ('God Has Added') the son of Deuel; ('Know God!'), chief of Gad. Ahira ('My Brother is Evil') the son of Enan ('Seeing'), chief of Naphtali.
11   Cf. Niehr, 'נשיא', x, p. 48. He goes on to claim that 'The differing functions of the $n^e\acute{s}\hat{\imath}\hat{\imath}m$ in Numbers elucidate the increasing esteem accorded those who bear the title, from census assistants to military leaders to chiefs over the Levite groups. The $n^e\acute{s}\hat{\imath}\hat{\imath}m$ enjoy the highest esteem where they function as representatives of the twelve tribes (Num. 1.4, 2; 7.2f., 10, 12–88; 17.17, 21; 27.2; 31.13)'. The term is applied to tribal leaders, chief of a clan, military leaders and as a title of respect (Niehr, 'נשיא', p. 50).
12   Cf. Levy, Milgrom, 'עדה', p. 474.

leaders. At times, the community is involved with legal functions in decision making or in carrying out the instructions of Moses—specifically when legal interpretation is required in difficult rulings (Num. 15.32–36; 27.2; 35). These examples show the involvement of the community in hearing and implementing instructions for life in Israel which affect the whole society.

1.17–46—Counting the Males

With leaders organized and the census duties established the nation is assembled for the registration to begin in accordance with the instructions of the Lord to Moses. The term for 'registered, counted or recorded' (פקד) suggests the documentation of each male aged twenty and over according to family heritage and clan membership. The census was taken as directed by Yahweh.

Numbers 1.20 and 46–47 confirms the tallying of each family clan male member over twenty culminates in the grand total of 603,550. The report of each one of the twelve tribes follows an almost identical prescriptive summary with the main variation being the name and total members. The notable emphasis in each statement is the name of the eligible male and their capability for warfare. The first notation serves as an example.

'Now the sons of Reuben, Israel's firstborn, their genealogical registration by their families, by their fathers' households, according to the number of names, head by head, every male from twenty years old and upward, whoever *was able to* go out to war, their numbered men of the tribe of Reuben *were* 46,500' (Num. 1.20–21). With the count taken, the tabulations are recorded as follows.

of Reuben at 46,500;
of Simeon at 59,300;
of Gad at 45,650;
of Judah at 74,600;
of Issachar at 54,400;
of Zebulun at 57,400;
of Ephraim at 40,500;
of Manasseh at 32,200;
of Benjamin at 35,400;
of Dan at 62,700;
of Asher at 41,500; and
of Naphtali at 53,400; with the grand total of 603,550.

In summation, the census is verified as conducted in accordance with the Lord's instruction to number the capable males over twenty years of age, and of all households for military preparation. The census is accomplished through the leadership of Moses, Aaron and twelve designated clan leaders. The population figures recorded here indicate an overall potential minimum populace of about two million people (cf. Num. 11.21; 26.51; Exod. 12.37; 38.26). It is noteworthy that preparation for the census taking is mentioned in Exodus 30.11–16 which includes the payment of a ransom for life to the Lord as an atonement.[13] Gathered funds are to be used in the service of the Tent of Meeting. The total count of men over twenty years of age is repeated in Numbers 2.32 and will receive further commentary there.

1.47–54—The Levites

Levi is not included in the census of males for conscription to army duties. However, the Levites receive special prominence in Numbers and these verses introduce the important functions they have in the nation. In fact, the vast occurrences of 'Levi or Levites' (לוי) in the Pentateuch occur in Numbers with about seventy-five references.[14] The roles, tasks, and challenges of the Levites are featured in several chapters of Numbers with precise details (Num. 1.47–53; 3–4; 8.5–26; 16; 18; 26.57–62; 35). The reasons for omitting the Levites from the census are addressed in Numbers 3–4.

The background details regarding the role and identity of the Levites have ancient historical roots in the Pentateuch. Levites are from the tribe of Levi who is the third son born to Jacob by Leah (Gen. 29.31–35; cf. 34.25–26; 49.5–7). Details from Exodus and Leviticus provide further essentials which inform the choice and duties of what the Levites are called to do in the book of Numbers concerning the cultic aspects of ministry. They are considered substitutes and representatives of the firstborn of other tribes (Exod. 4.22; 13.12–13; 29.9, 44; 40.15; cf. Num. 3.12; 8.10, 16). They are placed in charge of dismantling, carrying, and erecting the Tabernacle (Num. 1.47–54), which they camp around (Num. 1.51–53). Moreover, they support and serve the priesthood (Num. 3.5–10).

Moses is born into a Levite family (Exod. 2.1; 4.14) whose parents are Amran and Jochebed (Exod. 6.20). Moses' special call to lead Israel out of Egypt is the subject matter of a whole chapter in Exodus 3. However, the Levites gain their prominent position in the nation by answering Moses' call for devotion at the golden calf episode. Israel falls into pagan idolatry but the Levites rally to purge

---

[13] Then the LORD said to Moses, 'When you take a census of the Israelites to count them, each one must pay the LORD a ransom for his life at the time he is counted. Then no plague will come on them when you number them' (Exod. 30.11–12). This requirement serves to warn Israel regarding the taking of a census which is not clearly commanded by Yahweh.

[14] Total references to Levi or the Levites in the OT occur 354 times. Cf. D. Kellermann, 'לוי', *TDOT*, VII, p. 486.

the idolaters with the sword and kill about three thousand people. It is this intense fidelity to uphold the covenant by being instruments of judgment that elevates the Levites to the tabernacle service (Exod. 32.25–29; Deut. 10.6–9). Their action against idolatry and sacrilege displays their passionate zeal for the holy things of God. For this act Moses announces their consecration to Yahweh and pronounces the divine blessing upon them (Exod. 32.29).

Just as the Lord instructs Moses to take the initial census, he also tells him to appoint the Levites to sacred duties in the care of the sanctuary. Their roles exempted them from military tasks so that they could look after the Tabernacle. Their duties include the transportation of the Tabernacle and all its furnishings, the take down and setting up. They are responsible for all the associated duties of sanctuary care, maintenance and are to camp nearest to it.

In verses 50 to 53, the focalization on the Tabernacle is elevated by the sevenfold reference to the 'משכן' (a septenary repetitive device which exalts the significance of the sanctuary). Furthermore, it is the 'Tabernacle of the Testimony' (עדות; cf. Exod. 38.21; Num. 1.50–53; 10.11; 16.9)—the 'pact' or covenant—a constant reminder and affirmation of the covenantal promises made by Yahweh at Mount Sinai.[15] There the Lord meets with Israel confirming his covenant in word and in presence. 'You yourselves have seen what I did to Egypt, and how I carried you on eagles' wings and brought you to myself. Now if you obey me fully and keep my covenant, then out of all nations you will be my treasured possession. Although the whole earth is mine, you will be for me a kingdom of priests and a holy nation' (Exod. 19.4–6).[16]

The covenantal agreement is solidified with the theophanic display of fire, smoke, earth tremors and trumpet blasts. Some of these elements continue to be replicated at the Tabernacle during Israel's journey towards the promised land by the pillar of fire and cloud (Exod. 19.17–19). A core purpose for this phenomenon? 'The Lord said to Moses, 'I am going to come to you in a dense cloud, so that the people will hear me speaking with you and will always put their trust in you' (Exod. 9.9)'. Although there is some fluctuation of terminol-

---

15 The term for 'testimony' (עדות) is used 12 times in Numbers, and in the Pentateuch, it often has connections with the term for the 'covenant' (ברית) which occurs only 5 times in Numbers (10.33; 18.19; 25.12–13). The root word signifies 'witness or attestation' (עוד) in the sense of a symbolic record of an agreement or covenantal commitment. The 'Tabernacle of the Testimony' points to the ark where the written document of the covenant is kept as a visible reminder of Israel's covenant with Yahweh (Num. 4.5; 7.89). Cf. H. Simian-Yofre, 'עדות', *TDOT*, x, pp. 497, 512.

16 The 'Tabernacle' (משכן; Num. 1.50–53) is denoted about 111 times in the OT with 58 mentions in Exodus, 4 in Leviticus, and 33 in Numbers. Cf. Kellermann, 'משכן', pp. 58–64.

ogy between the Tent of Meeting and the Tabernacle, the main function of the sanctuary is to focus the communities' attention on the presence of Yahweh in the midst of the people. There, the Lord communicates his will, and the people express their worship. The Tabernacle's visibility functions to promote reverence and holiness among the people. It is the place of offering, sacrifice and blessing when everything is orderly in the nation. References to the Tabernacle and the Tent of Meeting have several variable meanings depending on their context. The terms are primarily relevant for the period of Israel's wilderness journey and conquest until the eventual building of the temple.[17] It is a special place for communication and instruction, primarily for Moses, but also for Israel as a community (Num. 7.89; 11.16–29; 12). It is in the Tent of Meeting where Moses receives instructions for the nation as well as direction in judicial matters. The connection between Tent and Tabernacle seems to develop as the Tabernacle takes the central place in Israel's encampment. In various texts to be considered, it appears that the Tent becomes part of the inner section of the Tabernacle where Moses continues to meet with Yahweh. The 'Tent' becomes the inner sanctum with a 'curtain' (פרכת; a screen or veil; Num. 4.5) which demarcates the ark of the covenant and holiest place from the outer-court and its furnishings. The tangible presence of Yahweh at the sanctuary is an affirmation of the divine instructions to Moses for the nation.

Warnings against the encroachment of laymen or non-authorized persons includes the threat of death (Num. 1.51). Restrictions are placed on all persons who are not authorized to approach sacred things (cf. Num. 3.10, 38) and those who try could be put to death by the Levitical guard. This introductory warning will be elaborated on and reiterated many times in Numbers to highlight the awesome reverence that is required for the sacred spaces and materials that pertain to the sanctuary and cultus. Those who take this warning lightly will experience the wrath of God because, unauthorized encroachment can bring harm upon the whole community. In short, the Levites serve a prominent role in caring for the sacred materials and tabernacle, which they safeguard for the benefit of the whole community. In this introductory passage, the Levite's roles are simply summarized whereas in chapters 3 and 4, their significant responsibilities are outlined and elaborated on.

17　Cf. Koch, 'אהל', p. 129; cf. pp. 118–130. The pattern for the Tent of Meeting was revealed at Mount Sinai (Exod. 25.9). It is often called the 'Tabernacle' (משכן; cf. Exod. 26.1–6). In Exod. 33.7–11 Moses is instructed by Yahweh to pitch a tent outside of the camp where Yahweh will meet with Moses 'face to face' or make his presence known through the pillar of cloud.

The emphatic imperative in verse 49 to not enroll or count the Levites with the other tribes serves to reiterate the differentiation between those who are fit for battle and those who are strictly fit for sacred tabernacle service. The census in Numbers 3–4 tabulates the number of Levites who are responsible for their covenantal duties associated with the sacred materials. In fact, they are given the two-fold assignment of being porters and protectors of the Tabernacle of the Testimony.

To show that things are off to a good beginning in Numbers one, the summation features compliance with the divine instructions and their implementation by Moses. 'The Israelites did all this just as the LORD commanded (צוה) Moses' (Num. 1.54). This will be a recurring theme throughout Moses' epic leadership assignment in the book of Numbers and is a notable refrain in almost thirty texts (cf. Num. 1.19, 54; 2.33–34; 3.51; 4.49; 8.3, 20–22; 10.13; 15.36; 17.26; 20.27; 26.4; 27.22–23; 36.10).

Reflection and Response
Numbers 1: Order and Documentation
Reflection

The book of Numbers is an amazing scroll of ancient literature that has been valued for different reasons for thousands of years. A primary role in the records that are dispersed throughout the document is to feature the essential nature of ancient documentation for Israel. From Numbers, it becomes evident that God values history, character, and people's names. Record keeping and historical reflection are a vital component for the nation. This was not only to preserve information, but to document the words and deeds of Yahweh for all future generations.

Readers may ask why so many names are listed and why verses are often repeated with the same basic summary of almost identical details. Could the writers have saved space and still covered the key information? These are reasonable questions and totally logical for our contemporary context when the economy of words is often regulated. The scribes did not take shortcuts. They had style requirements, protocols, and reasons for their inspired presentation. Furthermore, the oral communication of the materials included several devices which are designed to improve comprehension and remembrance.

The work involved in the process of census taking and writing is a tedious job for leadership. But the records and documents that are written for posterity, serve to guide the mission and remind people of historical events. They enshrine the constitutional terms which give the nation purpose and keep them moving forward. In reflecting on the opening chapter, we must remind ourselves that initially and for long periods of time, the recorded texts were the solitary copy for Israel. The only way people knew the written words was from public reading. Repetition proves to be the best way for people to hear and memorize materials for their own edification. Reiteration of names and words also affirmed the importance of people and proceedings.

The cataloging of the leaders, cultic personnel, roles and duties is the only way of communicating important knowledge for the community. For the people in the wilderness, it keeps them informed of who is looking after the camp, the cultus, the Tabernacle, and the schedule of worship. Names are important for individuals, the community and to God. Names of leaders are repeated to highlight their prominence and accountability. Names often have important meanings attached to them and are given to help guide individual's lives and legacy. Names may remind individuals of their intended relationship and connection with the Lord. In the Psalter the concept of a 'book of life' alludes to the concept that God also keeps a record of the righteous who are listed in it. Alternatively, the wicked may be blotted out (cf. Pss. 9.5; 69.28; cf. Exod. 32.32–33).

The organizational details emphasize that the Lord loves order, clarity, and leadership. Leaders are called, assembled, instructed, and made accountable to fulfil specific responsibilities. The overall purpose in the orderly preparations is to ensure the safety and well-being of the community. The preparations are set in place so that everyone knows the expectations and requirements for the journey ahead. The numbers are also meaningful and symbolic with 'twelve' referring to the community of God's people, as well as to concepts of rule and governance.

Response

How do ancient lists and names inform contemporary life? Do we keep a record of our personal family history for our children's benefit? Do we document some of the events and experiences in our lives that have clear indications of God's providence, rescue, deliverance, and salvation? Are we fulfilling the leadership expectations for home, church, synagogue, and work in a way that will move our institutions forward in positive ways? Do we value each person in our extended relational base and seek ways to affirm their lives?

When we consider the incredible efforts and work of the scribes who toiled to copy the Torah on parchments with primitive materials and tools to preserve the records with meticulous efforts, it should inspire us to consider meaningful ways of doing something similar. Like never before in history, we have amazing tools to record our footprints, images, and lives for posterity, church, and society.

In addition to keeping family records, every business and institution should be reminded of the importance of crucial documents which provide legitimacy for efficient operations. Israel's covenantal, national constitution was foundational for the nation's vision, aspirations, and life. It was essential for keeping the truths of their history of deliverance and salvation before the nation. The recorded legacy provided stability and identity to Israel for thousands of years as the people of God. Many other nations without such records passed from life without a legacy and disappeared in the annals of time. Documentation of history is an important work of skill which provides a legacy for the well-being of families and valued institutions.

2.1–34—The Israelite Camp

After the census instructions are implemented and the military divisions structured, the Lord speaks again to Moses and Aaron concerning the requirements for camp settlement in the community. Although the people are heading to the promised land, there will be many stops and encampments along the way, for periods of rest, renewal, and the acquisition of provisions. Attending to the physical needs of the large population presented here, requires significant leadership organization, cooperation, and order.

The tribal arrangements are detailed in this chapter with a camp structure that is shaped in a square configuration around the Tent of Meeting. Situated closest to the tent are the Levites who have responsibilities for all the sacred duties involving the sanctuary. Some tribal allotments seem to be made in accordance with historical issues and certain characteristics that are recorded in Genesis. The patriarchal narratives feature family dynamics which are at times dysfunctional but mainly show traits of human depravity and cultural adaptation. Additionally, the narratives illustrate themes of blessing and cursing which sometimes have lasting affects in the family legacy, where the sins of individuals may affect family dynamics for several generations (Exod. 20.5). These stories are set in contexts of conflict, trickery, deceit, and suffering. Too often the patriarchs resort to cultural ways of solving societal problems which affect matters of marriage, barrenness, fertility, polygamy, religion, and faith. Some of the consequences from the actions of patriarchal fathers have implications for the leaders and tribal placements which are presented in Numbers Two.

2.1–2—Organization of the Camp

The positioning of each tribe is the subject matter of this chapter. The vicinity of each clan was to be a significant distance from the Tent of Meeting. This is necessary to allow for space at the sacred area around the tent as well as the allocations for Levite families who are camped nearest to the sanctuary. In order to identify the placement and position of each tribe there are banners which provide insignia. Due to the size of the camp, the standards are important visible markers to indicate where members of each clan reside. Some commentators and Jewish traditions suggest that the banners reflect the colours of the precious stones that are on the priestly breast piece. Rabbi Rashi claims, 'Each banner shall have a different sign-a piece of coloured cloth hanging on it, the colour of the one not being the same as the colour of another, but the colour of each tribe shall be like that of his stone that is fixed in the breastplate, and by this means everybody will be able to recognise his banner'.[18] This refers to the Exodus 28 instructions concerning the priest's breast piece and appears to be a logical way of identifying the tribal positions. The breast piece is square with four rows of three precious stones each. 'The first row shall be carnelian, chrysolite and beryl; the second row shall be turquoise, lapis lazuli and emerald; the third row shall be jacinth, agate, and amethyst; the fourth row shall be topaz, onyx and jasper. Mount them in gold filigree settings. There are to be twelve stones, one for each of the names of the sons of Israel, each engraved like a seal with the name of one of the twelve tribes' (Exod. 28.17). Using the colours of the precious stones for the banners would be an effective way to identify each tribe and indicate their location from a distance. The overall effect of the colourful banners that are spread throughout the organized camp would create an impressive sight in the wilderness. Not only so, but the visible markers would assist people in locating their places among the populace.

2.3–16—Tribal Allotments

The desirable position for each clan is specified by the Lord who designates three tribes each to reside in four quadrants around the Tent of Meeting. As in Numbers One there is a stipulated order which designates the geographical location of the tribes, with their standard and leaders. The tribal heads and leader's names are repeated from the census report in Numbers one and then summarized with the total number of army recruits for the three tribal units that are placed on each side. The list of leaders that is recorded here appears

---

18   Cf. Rashi on Num. 2.2; Milgrom, *Numbers*, p. 12.

several times in the primary section of Numbers which is focused on the preparations for an epic journey (cf. Num. 1.5–16; 7.12–88; 10.14–28).

On the east side facing the sunrise are the descendants of Judah, Issachar and Zebulun. The leader of Judah's sons is Nahshon the son of Amminadab with 74,600 men. The leader of Issachar's sons is Nethanel the son of Zuar with a contingent of 54,400 men. The leader of Zebulun's sons is Eliab the son of Helon with 57,400 men.

Together, the males in the camp of Judah total 186,400 in their armies. The divine mandate designates that Judah is to lead the Israelites whenever they depart from places of rest towards the promised land followed by Issachar and Zebulun. It appears that Judah's prominence begins to rise along with the responsibilities in leading the Israelites in their journeys. Judah's descendants are also strong in number and evidently, the historical blessing on Judah begins to be realized (cf. Gen. 49.8–12).[19]

The area south of the Tent of Meeting is designated for Reuben's sons along with the descendants of Gad and Simeon. The leader of Reuben's sons is Elizur the son of Shedeur, with an army of 46,500 men. On his right flank is Simeon's sons with leader Shelumiel the son of Zurishaddai and 59,300 men. On the left side of Reuben is the tribe of Gad, with their leader Eliasaph the son of Deuel and 45,650 men.[20] Together these three tribes amount to an army of 151,450 men and are designated to follow the men of Judah in second place.

2.17–31—*Preparations for Embarkment*

Whenever the camp is directed to move, the Levites are positioned in the middle of the divisions carrying the Tent of Meeting with the various tribal standards providing visible coordinates for the tribes. The processional is carefully orchestrated with every individual and clan in place to move forward as directed.

On the west side of the tent of meeting is the camp of Ephraim with his sons under the leadership of Elishama the son of Ammihud with an army of 40,500

---

19 The proper name of 'Judah' (יהודה) occurs over 800 times in the OT in contexts where it refers to an individual (40 times), the tribe (290 times) and to the land of Judah or political entity (480 times). Cf. H.J. Zobel, 'יהודה', *TDOT*, V, p. 486. In the extensive blessing of Judah, his military prowess and destiny to rule is espoused. 'Judah, your brothers will praise you; your hand will be on the neck of your enemies; your father's sons will bow down to you ... The scepter will not depart from Judah, nor the ruler's staff from between his feet, until he to whom it belongs shall come and the obedience of the nations shall be his' (Gen. 49.8, 10).

20 Most of the Masoretic manuscripts read Reuel instead of Deuel.

men. On his southern flank is the tribe of Manasseh and his sons under the leadership of Gamaliel the son of Pedahzur with an army of 32,200 men. On his northern side is the tribe of Benjamin and his sons led by Abidan the son of Gideoni with 35,400 men. These three tribal units amount to a total of 108,100 numbered men and are designated to set forth in third place.

As noted in the list of tribal heads in Numbers 1, Ephraim and Manasseh, the sons of Joseph are incorporated into the census as tribal heads. Ephraim becomes the head of the western armies with Benjamin and Manasseh. Joseph and Benjamin are the sons of Rachel. The patriarchal narratives are essential background regarding the ancestral families and have implications on certain appointments. Family characteristics often have implications on the dynamics and fortunes of the clan. The blessing of the patriarch on the sons in Genesis 49 illustrates the power of the ancestral blessing.[21] This is evidenced in Jacob's blessing on Joseph which confers positive attributes but also acknowledges the unfortunate intrigues that he is subjected to by his brothers. It also recognizes the blessings of the Lord that are evident on Joseph and are then realized in the legacy for Ephraim and Manasseh who are engrafted into the list of leaders.

North of the Tent of Meeting is an area allocated for Dan's sons along with the descendants of Asher and Naphtali. The leader of Dan's sons is Ahiezer the son of Ammishaddai with an army of 62,700 men. On his right flank is Asher's sons with leader Pagiel the son of Ochran with 41,500 men. On the left side of Dan is the tribe of Naphtali with their leader Ahira the son of Enan and 53,400 men. These three tribes hold an army of 157,600 men and they are designated to follow the other clan armies in last place. Dan has an aggressive military streak (Gen. 49.16–17) while Asher and Naphtali are more passive in nature (Gen. 49.20–21).

With the census taken and the military divisions in place around the sanctuary, the camp is an impressive and orderly sight. Moreover, the Israelite forces and the headcount numbers tabulated here, amount to a sizeable and formidable force.

---

21 Jacob's blessing on Joseph is special. The text summarizes how fruitful and blessed Joseph was and attributes his success and providential care to Yahweh,

> because of the hand of the Mighty One of Jacob, because of the Shepherd, the Rock of Israel, because of your father's God, who helps you, because of the Almighty, who blesses you with blessings of the skies above, blessings of the deep springs below, blessings of the breast and womb. Your father's blessings are greater than the blessings of the ancient mountains, than the bounty of the age-old hills. Let all these rest on the head of Joseph, on the brow of the prince among his brothers. (Gen. 49.22–26)

2.32-34—The Israelite Population

These verses are a reiteration summary of the tabulated numbers in chapter 1 (Num. 1.44–47).

> These are the Israelites, counted according to their families. All the men in the camps, by their divisions, number 603,550. The Levites, however, were not counted along with the other Israelites, as the LORD commanded Moses. So the Israelites did everything the LORD commanded Moses; that is the way they encamped under their standards, and that is the way they set out, each of them with their clan and family (Num. 2.32–34).

The affirmation of Moses' compliance in doing what was 'ordered or commanded' (צוה) underlines his leadership ability in accomplishing the census work as directed. This recurring refrain throughout the book of Numbers defines his organizational skill and prophetic leadership competencies in applying the instructions of Yahweh.

Much ink has been used to explain what is deemed as incredulously high numbers for the tribes, clans and population of Israel which left Egypt and migrated to Mount Sinai to ratify a covenant with Yahweh. However, the opening chapters in Numbers are in agreement on the registration numbers of the men fit for battle and display a remarkable accuracy in textual transmission and in mathematical calculation. Some rounding of figures may be evident, but the biblical record is consistent and emphatic that the census totals amount to 603,550 in both chapters (Numbers 1 and 2; cf. also in Exod. 38.26). Furthermore, the tabulated record agrees with the account in Exodus 12.37–38. 'The Israelites journeyed from Rameses to Sukkoth. There were about six hundred thousand men on foot, besides women and children. Many other people went up with them, and also large droves of livestock, both flocks and herds' (cf. Num. 11.21). With these citations the total numbers of the men are recorded five times![22] The importance of the census indicates the biblical notion that each individual was considered a blessing and an important part of Israel. It also affirms the need for order in the camp and the necessity of counting the mili-

---

22 An interesting observation is made by Rashi regarding the need for the census.
    Because they were dear to Him, He counted them often. When they left Egypt, He counted them (Exod. 12.37); when [many] fell because [of the sin] of the golden calf, He counted them to know the number of the survivors (Exod. 32.28); when He came to cause His Divine Presence to rest among them, He counted them. On the first of Nissan, the Mishkan was erected, and on the first of Iyar, He counted them (Cf. Rashi on Num. 1.1; Exod. 30.11–13).

tary men for planning. With various attempts made to alter the literal meaning of 'thousand' (אלף), Levine is adamant that it must surely mean a numeric thousand—the other numbers used in the section are also literal.[23] Additionally, the context is using military formulas in the census record to establish the total numbers, so the 'eleph is a 'literal thousand' and does not refer to a social unit or 'clan' in this context. Other commentators who explain the numbers as symbolic gematria, metaphoric or formulaic to mean something less, have not been able to produce definitive conclusions for the theories.[24] Some suggest that if there was a formula used to present numbers that were not to be taken literally, then the formula was lost.[25]

Yes, the numbers are staggering when women and children are added to the census numbers. Moreover, the exodus account indicates that there were 'many other people' who left Egypt with the Israelites. Therefore, speculation that there were just over two million people is a lean suggestion. The main rejection over the large numbers has to do with the reproductive ability of a small group of seventy who enter Egypt (Exod. 1.5) to the 603,550 men (Exod. 38.26) in the census. However, it must be remembered that this census accounting is tabulated four hundred years later. The theme of reproductive blessing is noted early in Exodus in that 'the Israelites were fruitful and multiplied greatly and became exceedingly numerous so that the land was filled with them' (Exod. 1.7). It was this rapid growth that becomes an issue for the Egyptians who feel insecure and threatened by the Hebrews, which leads to their enslavement. Another remark declared by the midwives explains that 'Hebrew women are not like Egyptian women; they are vigorous and give birth before the midwives arrive' (Exod. 1.19-20). Under these circumstances the people increase and become unusually more numerous, compared to other people groups, due to the providential care of God.

The second primary issue with the high numbers has to do with the ability of procuring sufficient water, food, and shelter resources for such a large pop-

---

23   Levine, *Numbers 1-20*, pp. 139-140.
24   Allen provides a thorough overview of various theories set forth by commentators regarding the large numbers. These include corruption in transmission, different or dual meanings in terminology, symbolic meanings, and finally his own suggestion: 'I suggest the possibility that the large numbers in the census lists in the Book of Numbers are deliberately and purposefully exaggerated as a rhetorical device to bring glory to God, derision to enemies, and point forward to the fulfillment of God's promise to the fathers that their descendants will be innumerable, as the stars' (Allen, *Numbers*, p. 688; cf. pp. 680-691).
25   Since the theories have not been proven, Milgrom concludes that 'there is no choice but to assume that the number 600,000 was meant to be understood literally' (Milgrom, *Numbers*, p. 339).

ulation that is dwelling in a wilderness context. Feeding and hydrating a few million people takes miraculous provision! Ultimately, some theological assertions need to be taken into consideration. Notwithstanding the need to analyze the difficulties rationally, in the end the formulas which may have been used are no longer available—the textual confirmations must be taken at faith value. Theologically, the covenantal promises for numerous descendants are realized according to the Exodus record. Israel develops into a numerically large and great nation. The Abrahamic promises of uncountable progeny were finally coming to fruition. "He took him outside and said, 'Look up at the sky and count the stars—if indeed you can count them'. Then he said to him, 'So shall your offspring be. Abram believed the LORD, and he credited it to him as righteousness'" (Gen. 15.5–6).

It is Abraham's faith in this promise that establishes his righteousness (cf. Gen. 17.4–6, 22.17–18). It is the multiplication of descendants that verifies the progressive fulfilment of the divine promise. It is the Pentateuchal record that records the faithful and miraculous provisions of Yahweh for Israel during their epic journey from Egypt to the promised land. The God who leads them through the Reed Sea also provides for them in consistent, regular, and spectacular ways (Exod. 16.11–35; Deut. 7.18–23; 8.2–5). Finally, a probable refrain of Moses when the Israelites broke camp for their journeys is recorded in Num. 10.35–36. 'Rise up, LORD! May your enemies be scattered; may your foes flee before you. Whenever it came to rest, he said, Return, LORD, to the countless thousands of Israel'. Indeed, there is an emphasis on the countless, myriads, and multitudes of people!

Reflection and Response
Numbers 2: Countless People Camping with Yahweh
Reflection

Chapter two is another demonstration of incredible order as God's people are positioned around the Tabernacle in their encampment. All residents are in proximity to the Tent of Meeting and in community with family and clan. Their binding unity comes from their covenant with Yahweh, institutional commitments, and unified preparations for a journey. And the people are many.

Commentators have been exorcised about the perceived largess of the populations recorded in Numbers. Many have tried to reject their literal reality. However, the numbers have stood the test of time and the total of over 600,000 men is affirmed five times (Num. 1.46; 2.32; cf. Exod. 38.26; 12.37; Num. 11.21). Typical of patriarchal practice, no details are given on how many women and children are part of the community, nor birth rates. However, the texts in Exodus and Numbers are in agreement on the headcount for the military divisions.

The mathematics in Numbers is meticulous and accurate. The writer loves to record metrological information, headcounts, and materials! It is apparent that numerals are meaningful and important.

There are many factors which have been analyzed in order to make sense of how such a large group of migrants could leave Egypt and then survive in the wilderness for forty years. But questions remain, like how could the Israelites be so fertile and productive? Did the writers hyperbolize the headcounts? Was there a certain formula that the recorders used to arrive at the larger numbers? Is there a misunderstanding in the numerical terminology used? Are the numbers symbolic or metaphorical? How many firstborns can there be among the twelve tribes? Are the numbers inflated to give the impression of covenantal fulfilment? All these factors and more indicate difficulties in explaining the numbers. Details seem to be missing to provide a more realistic population. Or are they?

When it is all said and done, the texts record specific numbers and claim that a large population of migrants moved from Egypt to Canaan. They also affirm that a whole generation of people passed away during a forty-year period in the wilderness. This is the word of the Lord reflected in the Pentateuch. And this is very important information for us today. We live in a world of unprecedented populations, countries and nations that have challenges of epic proportions. There are principles in Numbers that help leaders to figure out solutions to real life problems.

What is essential for our understanding is the affirmation that Yahweh fulfils the words of promise given to the patriarchs. A nation would develop. The population would multiply along with the needs of the people. These are important reminders for our present situation where the population on earth is higher than ever—already well over 8 billion. So many countries and cities have incredibly high numbers of citizens to care for and provide resources for daily life. The challenges are staggering. Employment, purpose, and meaning for life is essential in our contemporary contexts. Leadership is required at every level of society. Organization structures, together with trained leadership teams, clear role descriptions, the provision of adequate materials to meet the needs of the populace—are all factors that must be set in place.

Response

Numbers records some of the challenges that Israel had to address—provision of resources, threats of war, migration, plagues, and segregation. Compared to current world population, these may seem like micro-problems. However, there are principles, wisdom, and insights for contemporary situations which will help in the organization and management of people. There is also the clear affirmation that many problems in life will require divine intervention, provision, and miraculous assistance for human progress to take place. Moreover, spiritual insights are provided in the scriptures regarding the need for faith and obedience to the mandates of divine law. These insights indicate skillful ways of life, approaches to development, guidelines for moving people forward in faith, and principles that can guide all citizens of earth—not just Israel.

How can our communities respond to the current challenges in the world which call for believers to provide assistance? Leadership, resources, and relief programs are essential elements in meeting the needs in the world. People are wandering in many diverse wilderness experiences and require tangible resources for life. The need to bring the nations of the world around the 'Tabernacle' of God's presence and his word has never been greater. This is not a time to ignore what is happening globally but an opportunity to partner with God in bringing hope, provision, and meaning to the nations of the world. How can we address the manifold needs? What can individuals and our church communities do to alleviate pain and suffering? Giving, going, sending, interceding and mediation are all necessary elements in kingdom work, requiring faith and obedience to move forward with action.

3.1–51—The Levites and the Aaronides

The Levites have an elevated role and prominence in the book of Numbers. Their rise to positions of service begins in Exodus with a further detailing of roles presented in Numbers. The introductory verses in Numbers 1.47–53 summarizes their prominent position near the Tabernacle and affirms the enormous responsibilities the Levites have over the sacred sanctuary. Their exclusion from the common census is explained because of their duties with the Tabernacle, its furnishings and overall security of the sanctuary. They will be counted separately by Moses and Aaron.

Levites are made responsible for the cultic ministry in the Tabernacle as replacements for the firstborn sons in Israel (Num. 3.12; 8.10, 16). Their roles include the dismantling, carrying, and erecting of the Tabernacle according to Yahweh's direction (Num. 1.47–54). They camp around the sanctuary (Num. 1.51–53) and serve the priesthood (Num. 3.5–10). The Levites are considered substitutes and representatives of the 'firstborn' (בכור) of other tribes so that the firstborn sons could serve their family needs (Exod. 4.22; 13.12–13; 29.9, 44; 40.15). It was the Levite's devotion to uphold the covenant by being instruments of judgment that elevates them to the sanctuary services (Exod. 32.25–29; Deut. 10.6–9). They react against the sacrilege and idolatry of the people, thereby showing their devotion to the holy things of God. For this act, Moses announces their consecration to Yahweh and pronounces the divine blessing upon them (Exod. 32.29).

3.1–4—Levitical Families

Chapter 3 begins with a reflection and 'genealogy' (תולדת, 'toledot'), of the priestly family, descendants of Levi.[26] The genealogical connection with the patriarchs highlights the importance of Aaron and Moses in the salvation history that is taking shape for Israel. The setting is at Mount Sinai where Yahweh speaks to Moses in the months which followed the covenantal events. There Moses receives numerous instructions concerning the Tabernacle and sacred practices. The family account begins with the firstborn son Aaron, followed by his brother, Moses. Of the 78 times the two brothers are mentioned together, Aaron is presented first in only five of the genealogical references.[27]

After Moses is called to Egypt, Aaron serves as the initial spokesman for Moses in the disputes with the pharaoh (Exod. 4.15–16; 7.1–2). In that sense he is called a 'prophet' and included in some of the covenantal events. Aaron is implicated in Israel's idolatrous failure in the golden calf debacle. His impropriety on this occasion was monumental but he is partly redeemed through the Levite's actions in bringing judgment upon the revellers (cf. Exod. 32.25–29). Aaron continues to serve in aspects of priestly service until he is installed as the chief priest in Israel (Lev. 8.31–36; 9.8–24; cf. Exodus 28–29). In the completion and dedication of the Tabernacle, the Aaronides are consecrated for sacred duties in sacrifice and ritual.

In Numbers 3 the Levitical and priestly duties are distinguished and the role of Aaron and his four sons, who are ordained to serve as priests, is affirmed.[28] Terms used for priests and the priesthood in the OT are referred to over 900

---

26   The Hebrew 'תולדות' is usually translated 'generations' to designate descendants and family lineage (occurs 28 times in the Pentateuch). In the Torah it is used in reference to several distinguished individuals including Adam (Gen. 5.1), Noah (Gen. 6.9; 10.1), Shem (Gen. 11.10), Terah (Gen. 11.27), Ishmael (Gen. 25.12), Isaac (Gen. 25.19), Esau (Gen. 36.1, 9), Jacob (Gen. 37.2), Levi (Exod. 6.16, 19), and Aaron (Num. 3.1). It is also used in reference to each one of the twelve tribes (12 times in Num. 1.20–42) and translated 'descendants' or 'account' in the NIV.

27   Milgrom, *Numbers*, p. 15.

28   The consecration of the priests transfers them from the profane to the sacred realm. 'The priests thus stand in a special relationship with Yahweh and as such belong to the divine sphere itself, a situation imposing on them the obligation to maintain cultic purity and enjoining the congregation to accord them special respect'. Cf. H. Ringgren, 'קדש', *TDOT*, XII, p. 533.

times, indicating their essential work in Israel. Aaron's priestly role becomes primary, and he is personally referred to over 350 times in the OT. The importance of the priesthood is developed early in Israel's history with the appointment of the Levites and ordination of the Aaronides. 'The priests represent Israel's relationship with God; in a sense, they are mediators of the covenant. The high priest, bearing the names of the twelve tribes on his breastplate, represent as it were the entire nation. The priests actualize Yahweh's presence in the words of their many liturgical functions. The holiness that worship demands is symbolized in the priesthood, which makes a visible statement that Yahweh is the Lord and master of the nation'.[29]

The priesthood comes from the tribe of Levi while the High Priest comes from the family of Aaron (also a Levite). Aaron and his sons are chosen to minister as priests at the altar and Holy Place (Exod. 28.1, 40–43; Leviticus 8). They carry out the daily round of sacrifices and oversee the sanctuary. They are anointed for this purpose (Leviticus 8; cf. Num. 3.2–4; 20.22–29). As the priesthood develops in Israel, their duties and obligations are substantial. Responsibilities include the guarding of the sanctuary, giving oracles through the 'Urim and Thummim', teaching the law, diagnosing diseases, and administering all aspects of the cultus (cf. Num. 27.21). They are obliged to intimately know and understand the cult requirements and conditions for people to participate in worship and community life (cf. Lev. 7.12 ff.; Num. 6.10).[30]

The legacy of Aaron is not completely free of critical contentions. It was Aaron who succumbed to the demands of the people to 'make gods' for Israel in the prolonged absence of Moses (Exod. 32.1–6, 21–24). Surprisingly, his pitiful response does not end with severe consequences. However, his sons Nadab and Abihu perish in the wilderness for failing to observe sacred instructions. After many privileges including audience with Yahweh (Exodus 24), they fail to implement some expected instructions of Yahweh by offering 'unauthorized fire with incense' and are consumed by fire (Lev. 10.2). The exact nature of the offence is not clear, but the divine displeasure in their sacrilege brings about an immediate act of judgment. On that occasion, Moses reminds Aaron concerning the holiness of Yahweh who said. 'Among those who approach me I will be proved holy; in the sight of all the people I will be honoured' (Lev. 10.3). This stern example of judgment and warning becomes a formidable reminder to the Levites of their sacred obligations.

---

29   Cf. W. Dommershausen, 'כהן', *TDOT*, VII, p. 74.
30   Cf. Dommershausen, 'כהן', pp. 66–70.

Eleazar and Ithamar, the remaining two sons are also anointed and ordained to serve as priests during Aaron's lifetime (since Nadab and Abihu have no sons). The procedures of 'anointing' (משח) and ordaining (a seven-day process) were carefully regulated.[31] Specific instructions are given in Exodus and Leviticus concerning the anointing of priests (Exod. 28.41; 29.7; Leviticus 8). 'Then Moses took some of the anointing oil and some of the blood from the altar and sprinkled them on Aaron and his garments and on his sons and their garments. So he consecrated Aaron and his garments and his sons and their garments' (Lev. 8.30). Additionally, the tabernacle furnishings are to be anointed, indicating their transfer from ordinary profane use to that of sacred cultic use (Exod. 40.9–15; Lev. 8.10–13). The anointing oil is for sacred use and must be made by a specific person, initially Bezalel, who is filled with the Spirit for his tabernacle-related duties (Exod. 37.29). Later, Eleazar son of Aaron takes on this task (Num. 4.16). The oil requires special ingredients such as liquid myrrh, fragrant cinnamon, fragrant cane, cassia, and olive oil (Exod. 30.22–33). The anointing oil symbolizes the divine presence that empowers the priests to fulfil their sacred duties. The extensive ceremony of 'ordination' (מלא; literally 'to fill the hand') provides the enablement and the authorization to function as priests (Num. 3.3).

3.5-10—*The Aaronides*

In the introductory verses to Numbers 3 the role of Aaron and sons is affirmed for the continuation of priestly duties. Although the Aaronides are also Levites, their roles are elevated over the tribe of Levi. In the Pentateuch the distinction between priests and Levites is maintained by certain limitations on roles. The Levites are set apart and consecrated for specific functions that could be considered their 'job description' which has two main elements. The first aspect concerns the Tabernacle and furnishings. Moses is instructed to present the Levites before Aaron—they would be subordinates to the sanctified priests, but essential dedicated servants who are responsible for specific physical work (עבדה). This includes the transporting and setting up of the Tabernacle (משכן), its furnishings, and other related work in the sanctuary. For this segment of responsibilities, Levites who turned fifty years of age are exempt from heavy lifting and only available for basic supports (cf. Num. 8.24–26).

---

31   The verb for 'anoint' (משח) occurs more than 68 times and mainly denotes 'the act and process of wetting, rubbing, smearing, or anointing something, exclusively and usually implicitly with oil'. Cf. K. Seybold, 'משח', *TDOT*, IX, pp. 44–45. Usually, the anointing oil is applied to a variety of things including cultic paraphernalia, kings (mostly), priests and prophets. For the consecration of the high priest (Exodus 29; Leviticus 8; cf. Num. 7.1) the anointing oil functions to sanctify the priest for sacral duties.

The second aspect of Levitical obligation has to do with security roles in keeping the sanctuary safe from encroachers. This pertains to 'guard duty' (משמרת) in protecting the Tabernacle which is a lifelong duty (cf. Num. 1.53). These two elements of the Levite's work are important to distinguish in the many references made in Numbers considering the Levitical guard.[32] Even though it appears that the Levites have a subordinate role to the Aaronides, they have the sacral duty of defending the sacred place and furnishings with the authorization to inflict a death sentence when warranted. It appears that the military role of defending holy things, as occurs in Exodus 32, is an essential part of their service. They are to be both strong porters as well as sacral warriors who surround the Tabernacle for the protection and benefit of the whole community.

Finally, the Levites are assigned to Aaron and his sons to serve according to the institutional needs. This apparent subordination of the Levites to the Aaronide priests becomes a point of contention for some Levites in recurring instances throughout the book of Numbers. Aaron and sons are the appointed priests with their own specified role and duties, but they also supervise the Levites. As representatives and mediators between God and man, the priests are called to a life of holiness, consecration, and devotion. Before ministering on behalf of others, they also needed purification (Exod. 28.36; Lev. 9.8–12; 21.6).

3.11–13—The Firstborn

Several affirmations are emphasized in these verses with a note concerning the 'firstborn' (בכור) male offspring in Israel. Firstborn sons are consecrated to the Lord (Exod. 13.1–2) as a reminder of how Israel's sons were protected from the death sentence on the firstborns in Egypt (Exod. 11.4–7).[33] Yahweh protected them and instituted the great Passover celebration to commemorate his salvation and act of deliverance. Before this development regarding the firstborn, Yahweh refers to Israel as his firstborn son (Exod. 4.22), thereby showing the elective element in Israel's nationhood (Exod. 19.5–6). The chosen nation

---

32 Cf. J. Milgrom, L. Harper, 'משמרת', *TDOT*, IX, pp. 73–74.
33 On the redemption of the firstborn, Kellermann comments,
> According to Exod. 13.11–16, all firstlings have belonged to Yahweh since the day on which Yahweh slew all the first-born of Egypt (Exod. 12.12–29). Exod. 13.2 contains a commandment of Yahweh transmitted to all Israel through Moses, stated in imperative form. 'Consecrate to me all the first-born'; Num. 3.12, by contrast states the requirement in personal terms. 'Behold, I have taken the Levites from among the people of Israel instead of every first-born ... they shall be mine'. Here we have a clear expression of the 'elective initiative of God'. (Kellermann, 'לוי', VII, p. 501).

becomes the firstborn in the sense of Yahweh selecting Israel to be his special treasure and kingdom of priests with a great responsibility in the world.

The firstborn males are favoured with a double portion of inheritance but before they can ever receive that, there are many onerous family obligations to look after (cf. Deut. 21.15–17). Additionally, as in many cultures of the world, the firstborn has additional responsibilities, often including the burial rites of parents. Emphatic in these verses is the Lord's affirmation that the Levites belong to him just as the firstborns do and are set apart to the Lord. The Levites serve in the cultic sphere as substitutes and are dedicated for sacred purposes just as the firstborn animals, and firstfruits in produce are given sacrificially to the Lord (Lev. 19.23–25). Although the Levites serve as substitutes for the firstborns, they are still considered exclusive possessions of the Lord (cf. Num. 3.40–51).

3.14-39—*Counting the Levites*

Once again Moses is instructed by the Lord and in this instance must count all the males that are over a month old in the Levitical families and clans. The names of the sons of Levi that Moses records include three main groups—the Gershonites, the Kohathites and the Merarites. Moses obediently takes the census of the Levite clans and records the information in an orderly systematic way. Each of these clans are counted, their placement around the Tabernacle allotted, their leadership roles distinguished, with specific responsibilities presented.

Beginning with the Gershonite clans, the Libnites and Shimeites, the total number of all the males a month old or more is 7,500. Their placement camp is on the west, behind the Tabernacle. The leader of the Gershonite families is Eliasaph (meaning 'my God has added'), son of Lael (meaning 'belonging to God').[34] Their specific duties at the Tent of Meeting include the care of the Tabernacle and tent, its coverings, the curtain at the entrance to the tent of meeting, the curtains of the courtyard, the curtain at the entrance to the courtyard surrounding the tabernacle and altar, the ropes—and everything related to their use. Very detailed instructions are given in Exodus 26 regarding the fabrics and making of these materials. Here the emphasis is on the maintenance and care of the furnishing for their transport from place to place as directed by Yahweh.

The second group consists of the Kohathite clans which include the Amramites, Izharites, Hebronites and Uzzielites. The number of all the males a

---

34   The theophoric name meanings cited in this section are from Allen, *Numbers*, p. 725.

month old or more is 8,600.³⁵ Their placement is on the south side of the tabernacle. The leader of the families of the Kohathite clans is Elizaphan (meaning 'my God has protected'), son of Uzziel (meaning 'my Strength is God').

The Kohathites are responsible for the overall care of the 'sanctuary' (הקדש), including care of the ark, the table, the lampstand, the altars, the articles of the sanctuary used in ministering, the curtain, and everything related to their use. This is the first occurrence of 'הקדש' in Numbers signifying the holy place and contents of the sanctuary. Typically, the *mishkan* refers to the 'Tabernacle' (משכן) but here the 'sanctuary' (הקדש) is the referent for the holy place. Also, in Numbers 4 and 18, the 'holy things' are featured.³⁶ Due to the extra precaution required for the most sacred objects listed here, the Kohathites need additional supervision. For this role, the chief leader of the Levites, Eleazar son of Aaron is appointed over those who are responsible for the sanctuary furnishings. Whereas the Gershonites and Merarites can use the ox carts for transporting materials, the Kohathites carry the furnishings on poles across their shoulders for additional protection of the items.

The third group consists of the Merarite clans which include the Mahlites and the Mushites. The number of all the males a month old or more who are counted is 6,200. The leader of the families of the Merarite clans is Zuriel (meaning 'my rock is God'), son of Abihail (meaning 'my Father [God] is Might'). Their placement for encampment is on the north side of the tabernacle. The Merarite's responsibilities include the care of the frames of the tabernacle, its crossbars, posts, bases, all its equipment, and everything related to their use, as well as the posts of the surrounding courtyard with their bases, tent pegs and ropes.

The last group placement is for Moses with Aaron and his sons who are to camp to the east of the tabernacle, toward the sunrise, in front of the tent of meeting. Due to their overall role of caring for the sanctuary on behalf of the Israelites, they have a prominent placement. Facing east, the rising sun shines upon the sacred Tabernacle where Moses meets with Yahweh. Anyone else who

---

35   The number here has a textual variant in the LXX reading which reduces the count to 8300.
36   In the OT there are 842 occurrences of the Hebrew root 'קדש' signifying holy and separated things for cultic purposes. Leviticus uses the term the most at 152 references and Numbers employs the term 80 times. Cf. W. Kornfeld, 'קדש', *TDOT*, XII, p. 527. The consecration of utensils and furnishings used in the cultus transfers things from the profane to sacred realms. According to Ringgren, the Priestly use of the term 'primarily in the cultic sense and especially in connection with the sanctuary, cultic utensils, priests, and sacrifices, developing in the process an impressive theology of the sanctuary regulating virtually everything associated with it'. Cf. Ringgren, 'קדש', p. 533.

approaches the sanctuary without permission or appropriate respect is to be put to death. The severity of a death sentence to be enacted by the Levites is for the benefit of the whole community. Any encroachment on the Tabernacle by those not authorized could jeopardize the nation. An example of a type of encroachment is presented in Numbers 16–18 with several incidents that involve Korah and other leaders. The violation of sacred space and objects is considered a serious act of irreverence which could bring divine wrath upon intruders (this stern warning appears four times in Num. 1.51; 3.10, 38, 18.7).

When the total number of Levites is counted, the number including every male a month old or more, is 22,000. This indicates a relatively small number in comparison with the other tribes recorded in Numbers 1. Furthermore, the number of able-bodied men to do the work is also limited but still sufficient for the main tasks. The two main specific tasks are guarding the Tabernacle when camped, and dismantling the Tabernacle, its furnishings and materials for transport, re-location and setup. This is their sacred work, duty and worship on behalf of the whole community. For the physically demanding work, men between thirty and fifty years of age are responsible.

A recurring refrain in Numbers 3–4 is the repetitive phrase 'at the command of the LORD'. The seven utilisations of this phrase in this section alone, emphasizes the obedient work of Moses and Aaron in counting the Levites as commanded (Num. 3.16, 39, 51; 4.37, 41, 45, 46). This exercise shows the personal interest of the Lord in each of the individuals who are to serve the nation in close proximity to the sacred Tabernacle. It also affirms the intimate knowledge of Moses and Aaron regarding the servants that are responsible for the most sacred service in Israel.

3.40–51—Redemption Fees

This last section of chapter 3 provides further specifications for the meaning behind the redemption of the 'firstborn' (בכור) Israelite males who are a month old or more.[37] Their names are to be recorded and the Levites become substitutions for the firstborn of the Israelites. The Levites take the place of the first-

---

[37] The importance of the firstborn is often noted in Torah narratives and reflected in the number of times the firstborns are singled out for attention. The term occurs about 132 times in reference to firstborn sons as well as animals in the OT (out of 26 in Numbers the firstborn sons are noted 20 times). Regarding the firstborn, 'Israel adhered to the laws of primogeniture through the father' Cf. M. Tsevat, 'בכור', TDOT, II, p. 125. 'The religio-phenomenological basis for God's claim on the firstborn is his mighty acts in Israel's history (Num. 3.13; 8.17; Ex 13.15), when God slew 'all the firstborn in the land of Egypt' (!), all the firstborn fell to him (cf. Ex 12.12f., 23)', Cf. p. 127.

borns for the Tabernacle services. As noted above, this selection by Yahweh provides a special status to the Levites who belong to him (Num. 3.44). However, the counting of the firstborns reveals an excess number compared to the Levites, so a redemption fee or 'ransom' (פדוי; noted 5 times in Num. 3.46–51) is instituted. Through this process the status of the Levites as belonging to the Lord in a special sense, is affirmed once again—'they shall be Mine' (Num. 3.12–13, 45).

The redemption of the firstborn is a fundamental principle in Israel. It is based on the recognition of the value and importance of the first child to evidence the procreative strength of the father which symbolizes the blessings of God on the family. The son is a highly valued individual in whom the family takes much pleasure. The firstborn is given much respect but is also depended upon for managing family responsibilities. In order for the son to be free from external incumbrances so that they can perform domestic and secular tasks, they have to be redeemed or 'ransomed' (Num. 18.15–17; Deut. 14.23–26). The principle of the firstborn is also applied to the livestock belonging to the Levites. Substitution for the firstborn of the livestock of the Israelites is an important lesson for the nation. Other legislation applies to the sacrifice of appropriate animals, but this procedure of redeeming the firstborn is an essential practice and is emphatically required by Yahweh's affirmation. 'I am the LORD'.

The redemption process and purpose are further illustrated here. When Moses completes the headcount of all the firstborn of the Israelites, the total number of firstborn males a month old or older, listed by name, amounts to 22,273. With the additional number of 273 firstborn, Yahweh instructs Moses to collect five 'shekels' (silver) for each one, according to the sanctuary shekel, which weighs twenty 'gerahs' (ca. two ounces). This collection is designated for the use of Aaron and his sons. The total amount comes to 1,365 shekels of silver and is presented to the priests (ca. just over fifteen kilograms). This becomes one of the important support systems set in place to look after the needs of the priesthood and Levitical guard (Num. 18.8–32).

4.1–49—Census of the Levites

After the general overview of the Levite's roles and placements, Chapter Four provides further specifications and details. In this second census the focus is on all the men between the ages of thirty and fifty who can do physically demanding work in addition to looking after their own family matters. The census begins with the Kohathites and is taken by Moses and Aaron.

4.1–20—*The Levitical Census and the Kohathites*

There is a change in the order of the Levite clans from Chapter Three as the record starts with Kohath who is the second born. Often in Genesis the choice of the younger over the elder is based on character or a significant life event. At times a surprising choice is made by divine selection where different criteria are applied (instances include Isaac, Esau, Reuben and David). This practice of 'choice' is an understandable requirement in life—someone must be selected for specific duties. The theological import of this is that Yahweh ultimately applies his benchmarks for the roles and tasks he has in mind. In the case of the Kohathites it is apparently due to the higher risks involved in the process of transporting the most sacred materials. Indeed, the Kohathites are responsible to 'care for the most holy things' (קדש).[38] This required a very careful implementation of specific procedures in managing the revered utensils.

The materials included in the Tabernacle are a remarkable, colourful and valuable catalogue of furnishings. The following details indicate that there are six key parcels each carried by porters with poles on shoulders. The cloth and quality of covers placed on the articles conveys the escalating order of sanctification. These articles are part of the offerings given by the Israelites (cf. 'These are the offerings you are to receive from them. gold, silver and bronze; blue, purple and scarlet yarn and fine linen; goat hair; ram skins dyed red and another type of durable leather' Exod. 25.4). Pride of place are the blue (violet), purple, and crimson (scarlet) coverings. A yellowish orange colour is also produced when skins are dyed and used for very effective protective coverings. These colours reflect the different levels of holiness and are made to display an impressive visual spectacle.

The Kohathites had to coordinate their work together with the preparations of the priests. Their tasks are carefully supervised by Aaron and his sons. The following details are meant to prepare the holy materials in a reverential manner as well as with protective packaging (referred to here as 'parcels').

The First Parcel. The priests had to enter the Tabernacle before the Kohathites to take down the shielding curtain which is placed over the ark of the covenant law (cf. Num. 1.50–53). This screening curtain separates the holy of holies from the rest of the sanctuary and is used to protect the priests who

---

[38] The sacred utensils are sanctified and rendered 'holy' (קדש) signifying their special designation for cultic purposes. Cf. Kornfeld, 'קדש', p. 527. The consecration of utensils and furnishings used in the cultus transfers them from profane to sacred realms, requiring very careful guardianship by the Kohathites.

are not permitted to see the ark. The ark is covered with colourful and protective materials, including the shielding curtain. Over these materials is placed a durable leather cover (probably the hide of an aquatic animal) with the additional solid blue cloths and carrying poles in place.

The Second Parcel. Over the table of the 'Presence' they are to spread a blue cloth. On it are placed the plates, dishes and bowls, and the jars for drink offerings. The bread is to remain on the table with a scarlet cloth over the twelve loaves (cf. Lev. 24.5–9) and covered with durable leather for transport with poles.

The Third Parcel. They are to take a blue cloth and cover the lampstand that provides light, together with its lamps, its wick trimmers and trays, and all its jars of olive oil which are used to supply the lamps. They are to wrap it with all the accessories in a covering of the durable leather for placement on a carrying frame.

The Fourth Parcel. Over the gold altar they are to spread a blue cloth which is covered with the durable leather and carried with the poles in place.

The Fifth Parcel. This includes all the articles used for ministering in the sanctuary, wrapped up in a blue cloth, covered with the durable leather and placed on a carrying frame.

The Sixth Parcel. They are to remove the ashes from the bronze altar and cover it with a purple cloth. Then all the utensils used for ministering at the altar, including the firepans, meat forks, shovels and sprinkling bowls are gathered together, and covered with durable leather. The package is then carried with poles in place.

Only the Aaronides are permitted to see and package the holy furnishings and the sacred articles. They are responsible to instruct each Kohathite porter on the work they are responsible for. Eleazar gives oversight to all the detailed procedures having to do with the Tabernacle materials and their transport. Eleazar also 'supervised' (פקדה) the holy materials used in the Tabernacle's service. He is responsible for the stewardship of the oil for the 'light' (מאור), the fragrant 'incense' (קטרת), the regular grain 'offering' (מנחה), and the 'anointing' (משחה) oil. He is put in charge of the entire sanctuary with its holy furnishings and articles. The materials used for the required offerings are a substantial amount and are carefully itemized in Numbers 7, 15, 28–29.

Offerings are an essential part of the daily routines of worship and attendance to elements of the cultus which require careful implementation. The main purpose is to bring gifts that bring 'satisfaction' in its offering to Yahweh. Details will be discussed in chapters where the regulations for cultic observance are presented. It is notable that the 'offerings' (מנחה) listed in Numbers are mentioned more than in any other OT book with 58 occurrences—more than the 37 referents in Leviticus. In the Pentateuch the term is used 113 times out of the 211 in the Hebrew OT.[39]

The Kohathite porters are not involved until everything is ready for transport according to the strict guidelines—infractions or disregard for the careful instructions could result in death. This threat reinforces the concept of holiness that is an essential revelation for the nation in their covenantal relationship with Yahweh.

4.21-28—*The Gershonites*

The census process continues with the enumeration of the Gershonite men between thirty to fifty years of age who are selected for their specific duties. They prepare the transport of Tabernacle curtains, its covering, and its outer shell of durable leather (probably dolphin skin; cf. Exod. 26.14), the curtains for the entrance to the tent of meeting, the curtains of the courtyard surrounding the tabernacle and altar, the curtain for the entrance to the courtyard, the ropes and all the equipment used in the service of the tent. The 'work' (עבדה) of transporting these materials refers to the general tasks pertaining to the sacred furnishings (cf. Num. 4.23, 24, 30, 47). This term is employed to signify the general 'burden' of caring for the sacred materials, but in some contexts is used to signify cultic 'service' (עבד).[40] With these materials the Gershonites are not under the same restrictions as the Kohathites who carried the main inner sancta—they prepare for transport but do so under the direction of the Aaronides—and more specifically, Ithamar.

4.29-33—*The Merarites*

For the Merarites, the instruction regarding the count are the same but their responsibilities are focused on the frames of the tabernacle, its crossbars, posts and bases, the posts for the courtyard with their bases, tent pegs, ropes, all their equipment and everything related to their use. Each man has specific things to carry and must work under the direction of Ithamar.

---

39. Cf. H.J. Fabry, 'מנחה', *TDOT*, VIII, p. 412.

40. The verb 'service' (עבד) occurs 271 times in *qal* form, designating work in the general sense but also difficult or heavy work as in Num. 4.47 for carrying the Tent of Meeting. The majority of references pertain to cultic service at the Tent of Meeting as determined by the context (Num. 4.33, 35, 39, 43; 8.24; 18.4, 44). Cf. H. Ringgren, 'עבד', *TDOT*, X, pp. 381, 403.

4.34–49—*Counting the Servants of the Cultus*

This section is a reiteration of the census results and the procedures of the count taken by Moses, Aaron and the leaders of the community. Each statement is a stylized report that repeats the basic details and tallies the headcount. For the Kohathites, all the men from thirty to fifty years of age amount to 2,750. For the Gershonites, all the men from thirty to fifty years of age are 2,630. For the Merarites, all the men from thirty to fifty years of age are 3,200. The total comes to 8,580, fulfilling the instruction of Yahweh to Moses and provides a significant work force of men who are trained and prepared for the Tabernacle duties.

The repeated affirmations of Moses' compliance with the Lord's instructions and the concluding verification that each individual Levite is given their basic job description, presents a positive picture of the Levitical guard who are poised and prepared for their sacred duties. Without their care and attention to the tedious tasks of the maintenance and transport of the sanctuary, the priests would not be able to perform the cultic services in the nation's 'worship' of the Lord. That is the divine purpose for leading Israel out of Egypt to serve God on the 'mountain' (Exod. 3.12; cf. 4.23; 7.16; 10.3–26; 12.31). The ministry of the Levites prepares the venue and the materials that are used for worship.

5.1–31—Physical and Spiritual Conditions

Whereas the first few chapters in Numbers focus on the personnel and tasks of the military, priests and the Levites, the book then turns to several conditions and behaviours that could affect community life. The content pertains to the nature of the sacred place and the presence of Yahweh in the camp. As a sacred habitation requiring a sanctified community, it must not be profaned through defilement or certain conditions of social disharmony. The context has to do with daily life in the camp where a whole range of circumstances and social interactions could cause contamination. The stresses of daily life in the wilderness setting, in addition to neighbour's tents pitched in close proximity to each other, is a challenging setting for a large population. Additionally, the daily preparation of food necessities, issues of hygiene and domestic matters are demanding. The threat of profaning the sacred space and offending Yahweh must be regulated with reverence and much care. Due to the spiritual and sacral issues involved, the priests are integrally involved in the counselling and officiating of the ordeal outlined in this case.

5.1–4—*Maintaining Purity in the Camp*

Three contagious conditions or experiences are presented which require isolation for people with certain afflictions. Quarantine is expected to keep the sacred space pure of defilement and to keep people free from contagion. Specifically, persons with visible skin conditions or bodily discharges of any kind, and those who come into contact with a corpse, are considered ceremonially 'unclean' or in a state of 'defilement' (טמא).

Skin Disorders

The first disorders that are discussed have to do with skin conditions. An extensive list of the types of skin conditions which could defile those who come into contact with afflicted people are presented in Leviticus 13.1–46. Visible skin disorders could be rashes, boils, swelling, and open sores. Such symptoms require specific procedures for diagnosis by the priest with follow-up checks. It is assumed that family members or friends are to be involved and concerned for members with issues and would bring them to the priest. Basic requirements include these steps.

> The LORD said to Moses and Aaron, 'When anyone has a swelling or a rash or a shiny spot on their skin that may be a defiling skin disease, they must be brought to Aaron the priest or to one of his sons who is a priest. The priest is to examine the sore on the skin, and if the hair in the sore has turned white and the sore appears to be more than skin deep, it is a defiling skin disease. When the priest examines that person, he shall pronounce them ceremonially unclean. If the shiny spot on the skin is white but does not appear to be more than skin deep and the hair in it has not turned white, the priest is to isolate the affected person for seven days. On the seventh day the priest is to examine them, and if he sees that the sore is unchanged and has not spread in the skin, he is to isolate them for another seven days. On the seventh day the priest is to examine them again, and if the sore has faded and has not spread in the skin, the priest shall pronounce them clean; it is only a rash. They must wash their clothes, and they will be clean. But if the rash does spread in their skin after they have shown themselves to the priest to be pronounced clean, they must appear before the priest again. The priest is to examine that person, and if the rash has spread in the skin, he shall pronounce them unclean; it is a defiling skin disease'. (Lev. 13.1–8)

Those who are 'defiled' (טמא) in one of these ways, whether male or female, are to be sent outside of the camp where they would not defile others or be in the camp where Yahweh's presence dwells. Special places for the period of segregation are set up outside of the sacred camp. Ultimately, the seriousness of these conditions and the fear of segregation is meant to motivate the community to be very health and hygiene conscious. The safety and health of the wider community appears to be the main consideration here. Isolation or quarantine is designed to keep others from contagion. Israel also had a real concern for how other people groups would view them and therefore, dealt strictly with sickness for the benefit of the whole community and their neighbours.

Bodily Discharges

The second condition of concern has to do with bodily discharges that could indicate a health problem or simply cause contamination. Leviticus 15 details a variety of bodily functions that would defile both male and female. Fluid discharges could stem from a disease or even from normal bodily functions like sexual intercourse or monthly menstruation. Semen, blood, and other secretions could contaminate individuals and even others who might have contact with contaminated articles. The risk of contact with things that cause impurity is exacerbated by the close living conditions in the camp. Such incidents must be dealt with through several procedures to bring about cleansing and to contain contagion from community spread. Considerable water resources are required for bathing and washing clothes or any other articles that are contaminated. In addition, offerings and sacrifices are required for some things, and include the action of a priest. Stern warnings underline the importance of cleanliness in the camp and compliance with the regulations. 'You must keep the Israelites separate from things that make them unclean, so they will not die in their uncleanness for defiling my dwelling place, which is among them' (Lev. 15.31).

Death and Corpses

The third defiling condition is brought about by proximity to a 'corpse' (נפש)—the body without the animating principle of life. Although the book of Numbers could be referred to as an obituary for a whole generation of people, there is a dearth of detail regarding the dead, the interment, place of burial, and actual procedures regarding burial rites. Nevertheless, affirmations of a whole generation of people passing in the wilderness are clear (cf. Num. 26.64–65). Death in the camp with consequent burials are probably a daily regimen in Israel. Although death is an inevitable fact of life, Yahweh's declaration of judgment over the exodus generation is certain. A whole generation lives under a death sentence. However, the way that most people died and what procedures were followed for body preparation, committal and periods of grief are not explained. There is almost an avoidance of the subject of death. Only a few specific examples are noted, including a group at Kibroth Hattaavah (Num. 11.31–34); Miriam (Num. 20.1); Aaron (Num. 20.23–29); Korah and 250 leaders consumed by fire and another group of 14,700 by plague (Num. 16.35–49); plus, another 24,000 die of a plague (Num. 25.8–10). Yet a whole generation passes after the first census. 'For the Lord had told those Israelites they would surely die in the desert, and not one of them was left except Caleb son of Jephunneh and Joshua son of Nun' (Num. 26.65). Typically, due to the warm climate, a burial takes place as soon as possible within a twenty-four-hour period. With the threat of segregation for being defiled by a corpse, people have to be quick to deal with the dead body in an appropriate manner. However, even the Book of Leviticus is rather quiet on the subject and details surrounding death.

The subject matter of death gives rise to biblical notions concerning holiness and purity. The ideal has something to do with concepts of wholeness and what is considered 'unblemished'. The ideals of being undefiled, untainted by human sin, devoid of depravity and the damages caused by these conditions, are important concepts for Israel. However, the consequences of the 'fall' (Genesis 3) which bring death, sickness, disease, and all manner of unfortunate suffering on earth are ever-present realities to deal with. Perhaps due to this the legislation and instructions in the Torah are more focused on the living and their needs to keep the community 'clean', than on details regarding the dead. Typically, the rights and procedures regarding the dead and the procedures for preparing the body for interment are elements left to the dictates of each culture.

Conditions of impurity are brought about by anything that causes decay and is associated with death—close contact with death brings about a state of contamination and defilement. Associated elements have to do with blood, semen, and skin conditions. Blood and semen are symbols of life forces. Furthermore, visible problems with the protective skin covering of an individual which exhibits decay are viewed as potential indicators of disease, infection and decay, which could lead to death. Therefore, in these matters, the community needs standards with procedures for dealing with cases to control impurity and hygienic problems. Failure in observing such standards could affect their relationship in the community as well as with God. The following insights of Milgrom are pertinent here. 'Thus, biblical impurity and holiness are semantic opposites. And since the quintessence and source of holiness resides with God, it is imperative that Israel control the occurrence of impurity lest it impinge upon the realm of the holy God. The forces pitted against each other in the cosmic struggle are no longer the benevolent and demonic deities who populate the mythologies of Israel's neighbours, but the forces of life and death set loose by man himself through his disobedience to or defiance of God's commandments'.[41] In this regard the Leviticus injunction is clear. 'You must obey my laws and be careful to follow my decrees. I am the LORD your God. Keep my decrees and laws, for the person who obeys them will live by them. I am the LORD' (Lev. 18.4–5).

5.5-10—Relational Restitution

The next example is ambiguous but indicates that personal conflict between individuals also affects their relationship with Yahweh. The actual social offence or wrong action is not specified here but the consequences of behavioural conduct that brings injury to others is considered sinful. However, in Leviticus 6.2–5 the potential offences are very detailed, including:

> If anyone sins and is unfaithful to the LORD by deceiving a neighbor about something entrusted to them or left in their care or about something stolen, or if they cheat their neighbor, or if they find lost property and lie about it, or if they swear falsely about any such sin that people may commit—when they sin in any of these ways and realize their guilt, they must return what they have stolen or taken by extortion, or what was entrusted to them, or the lost property they found, or whatever it was they swore falsely about.

Such behavioural actions bring disharmony in domestic and community contexts, but these wicked actions also show unfaithfulness to the Lord. Incidents of sin against one's neighbor make the perpetrator guilty and in need of forgiveness. The process begins with the acknowledgement of wrong-doing and a consequent confession of sin. Secondly, full restitution is required (in cases which involved tangible materials) with an additional value of one fifth given to the offended person. In a case where the restitution cannot be given to the person involved or to a relative, the sum is given to the priest. Additionally, the offering of a ram is expected. All this could amount to substantial expenditure but is required to indicate the level of harm brought to another person. It also communicates the penalties which serve to restrain individuals from anti-social behaviours and from offending the Lord. With true repentance, restitution and sacrifice, atonement could be realized. The intention of these actions is designed to restore harmony in the community.

---

41   Milgrom, *Numbers*, p. 346.

5.11–31—A Marital Conflict

Another case is presented from the intimate marital context, describing potential conditions that could bring serious threat to family harmony in the home. In the patriarchal narratives there are ample stories which illustrate the types of domestic challenges that arise from favouritism, immorality, idolatry, envy, ambition, and jealousy. In Numbers five the issue deals with matters of adultery and covetousness. More significantly, it deals with a potential breakdown in marital fidelity (cf. Gen. 20.6; 26.10; 39.9). Leviticus 18 is a whole chapter dedicated to the exposition and warning of sexual practices and behaviours that could lead to social destruction and breach of relationship with God. This text in Numbers 5 'speculates' a case where a wife may have strayed and become 'unfaithful' (מעל) to her husband (Num. 5.6, 11, 12, 27; 14.33; 31.16). The term signifying 'broken faith' is also used in regard to God's covenantal love for Israel which is often depicted with a marriage metaphor.

The text refers to a case where the truth is hidden, there is no human witness and where the woman is not caught in the act of adultery. There is no proof of infidelity—just the breakdown of trust and confidence which leads to insecurity and jealousy for the man. Verse 14 indicates that a 'spirit' of jealousy comes over him—it is a psychosomatic term indicating the growing disposition or nagging sense that something is not right. There is a perception or condition that brings mistrust into the relationship. When not dealt with, such situations may lead to domestic violence or abuse and must be resolved. Due to the circumstances of the situation, it must be solved with divine assistance and priestly mediation.

In this passage (Num. 5.11–31), the main characters are Yahweh (mentioned seven times), the priest, a husband, and his wife. The process of resolving the conflict calls for the husband to take his wife and appear before the priest with an appropriate offering (barley flour; no olive oil or incense). The fact that both must appear before the priest, forces an intentional meeting, and indicates that both parties are prepared to work out the situation in a mutual way. In cases like this, compliance by the couple to be present before the priest is essential, and by doing so, they are also considered present 'before the LORD' (Num. 5.16).

5.11–17—An Unusual Test

There is a complex ritual to undergo which in the end has a cause-and-effect result. The priest mixes 'holy water' in a clay jar with some dust from the tabernacle floor. The fact that the dust is taken from the sacred space may indicate its powerful effectiveness. The priest loosens the woman's hair, and places in her hands the grain offering for jealousy. The priest holds the bitter water that 'brings a curse' and places the woman under an oath. If innocent, the water would have no consequences but if guilty the woman would be accursed among the people. Furthermore, her womb would miscarry and her abdomen swell. To express her innocence, the woman is to say 'Amen' in agreement, declaring that the curse should come upon her in case she is guilty.

The ritual continues with the priest writing the associated curses on a scroll and then washing them into some bitter water which the woman must drink. Sacrifices are offered and the following consequences are to be observed. if guilty, the woman will suffer physical problems and miscarriage. She will come under a curse and consequently be sterile. However, if innocent, she will be cleared of guilt and able to have children. Presumably, the husband would be satisfied with the verdict and recommitted to his wife. Several commentators provide analogies in the Ancient Near East where examples like this are common and resolved in some way but often ending in death for the woman. Similar practices continue to be used in cultures of the world where functionaries apply rituals for guidance. In the biblical example, the resolution to a tragic situation requires divine assistance, vulnerability, and trust. The husband and wife must submit their predicament to the priest and follow through with the ordeal, so that the marital relationship can be restored. If guilty, the consequences are still severe in that the woman would become barren. However, the overall harmony of the community is in view through the resolution of the matter.

For those who are appraised of the situation, the incident is a powerful example to the community on the importance of marital fidelity and moral purity. Although the example has patriarchal elements of cultural practice which may seem unfair from contemporary perspectives, in the context of ancient near eastern practice it is considered an appropriate process with a positive result in view. The role of the priest is integral to provide for the conflict resolution and to bring the woman back into relationship with her husband ('to bring her near').

5.18–31—The Curse

There is considerable repetition in this text which makes it a very detailed and extended example. In these verses the procedures take on greater significance as the rituals and inclusion of curse terminology are employed. The ramifications of this seem to emphasize the importance of marital fidelity. The pronouncement of the curse is an indicator of the need for harmony in families and in the extended community in order for divine blessings to be realized. The opposite of blessing is the concept of cursing which is a major theme in Scripture (cf. Introduction). In Numbers 5 the case of the marital issue may result in the realization of a curse for the woman who is proven guilty. In verses 5.18–

27, two terms are employed ten times for the curse. The first one is the primary term (ארר) that may be translated 'curse or spell' (used 6 times in Num. 5.18–19, 22, 24, 27). The second term also refers to the 'curse' (אלה; cf. 4 times in Num. 5.21, 23, 27). The effect of the curse is to bring the guilty person who is placed under the curse into an unfortunate position, affecting marital status and physical well-being. This occurs when a person swears under 'oath' (שבע) to their innocence but may be found guilty.[42] The negative effects of the curse may cause alienation, bitterness, defilement, illness, or reproach.[43] The curse or 'execration' is perceived to have inherent power to affect a reversal of the state of 'blessing' (ברד) or to set into effect misfortune.[44]

The ordeal or test is described in much detail and illustrates fairly common procedures in ancient cultures to determine the truth that may be hidden from view. The ordeal involves certain risk for the guilty but pardon and restoration for the innocent. The test is facilitated by the priest who serves as Yahweh's representative to mediate the rituals involved. The rituals include the offering of barley grain and the taking of an oath in submission to the words of a curse spoken by the priest. It is understood that the spoken curse would go into effect and have a spell like power over the guilty party. Another significant act in the ritual is the recording of the words of the curse onto a scroll which is then transmitted into the bitter water for ingestion by the woman. The whole humiliating ordeal includes the public appearance before Yahweh and the priest who 'loosens' her hair in an act which diminishes her identity and pride. Based on the consequences of taking the bitter water with the unique ingredients, the woman's future is determined—the guilty one could lose a fetus, become barren, or become a social outcast in the community. However, the innocent one would be affirmed, restored and established in the home and society as a godly person.

Although the rituals and implications of this instance may appear foreign to people in some contemporary contexts of the world, there are elements in the text and in the test that continue to be employed in numerous cultures of the world. In such contexts the worldview of the physical and spiritual worlds are interwoven and work together to provide insights for life on earth. However, there may also be a macro-element in the case which illustrates Yahweh's relationship with Israel. The marriage metaphor is used extensively by OT prophets

---

42   Taking the oath by swearing to innocence places the person at the discretion of the deity who may intervene accordingly. Cf. W. Kaiser, 'נדר'. *TDOT*, IX, p. 244.

43   J. Scharbert, 'ארר', *TDOT*, I, pp. 412–425.

44   The term bless (ברד) occurs in a variety of forms approximately 370 times in the OT with about 14 references in Numbers. Cf. J. Scharbert, 'ברד', p. 296.

to explain the covenantal relationship between Yahweh and Israel. Jealousy, love, and covenantal commitment are emotional elements in marital relationships which also illustrate Israel's covenantal relationship with Yahweh. Weinfeld avers that, "Although the idea of marital love between God and Israel is not explicitly mentioned in the Pentateuch, it seems to exist there in a latent form. Following other gods is warned against with the statement, 'For I the LORD your God am a jealous God' (Exod. 20.5; Deut. 5.9; cf. Exod. 34.14; Josh. 24.19)".[45] This becomes an issue in the second part of Numbers where Israel's behaviour is referred to as 'unfaithfulness' and the nation is warned to 'not prostitute yourselves by going after the lusts of your own hearts and eyes' (cf. Num. 14.33; 15.39). A very serious incident of this figurative connotation is described in Numbers 25 when the Israelites align themselves with the Baal of Peor. Particularly the prophets apply this figurative meaning for Israel's covenantal failure and apostasy (cf. Ezek. 16.8; 23; Hos. 4.13–15; Mal. 2.10–16).

6.1–27—The Nazirite Vow

Legislation concerning the ministries which the Levites and priests are responsible for are detailed requirements that ensure the personnel are sanctified and protected in sacred spaces where they serve. Their roles are essential in the cultic observances which Israel had to implement and for this reason they are addressed so often in the book of Numbers.

Regulations for Levites are quite demanding as they must handle their sacred duties before Yahweh with precision. It is not a surprise therefore, that individual Israelites were also required to observe certain regulations for their personal sacred commitments. For some Israelites, there was an intense desire to be spiritually attentive and in a position of consecration to the Lord. Motivation for this form of dedication is no doubt diverse—it could be for a specific provision in life or simply for a spiritual experience. Whatever the reason, the Lord instructs Moses regarding such desires, in order to ensure that the person understood the conditions and expectations for the taking of a 'vow' (נדר). Numbers 6.5 and 13 make it clear that the vow is not for a career or lifetime

---

45 Cf. M. Weinfeld, 'ברית', *TDOT*, II, p. 278. Furthermore, the terms to be jealous and to play the harlot are used for both human and the covenantal relationship between God and Israel. The covenantal formula for legal marriage is expressed in the phrase 'I will be your God, and you shall be my people' (Lev. 26.12; Deut. 29.12). The covenant is a commitment confirmed by an oath which has binding validity for the partner (cf. Gen. 26.28; Exod. 19.8; Deut. 29.9 ff.).

status as a 'Nazirite' (נזיר), but for a temporary period of separation from things or experiences that could bring pleasure or even improve health. The connotation of the root word for the vow and *'nazir'* in Semitic languages has to do with withdrawal from ordinary life or certain practices so that the individual could be set apart for a specific purpose.[46] In Numbers the subject matter of vows is noted more than thirty times—primarily for the Nazirite vow, an individual's vow (Numbers 30), but also as a community vow (Num. 21.2).

6.1–12—*The Nazirite and the Vow*

In Numbers 6 the Nazirite vow is an expression of desire by a man or a woman to move from the profane physical realm to a more sacred spiritual sphere, with the core purpose of being in closer relationship with Yahweh. Regarding the religious use of making a vow or promise, there often are personal circumstances that motivate the individual to take the oath and make the personal sacrifices. 'An oath is a solemn promise to a deity to perform a certain act if the deity acts in a certain way. It is thus a prayer demanding emphatically that God act. A special form is the unconditional self-imposed obligation that binds the person making the vow to a particular way of life for a period of time or perpetually'.[47] To be in that sacred place in a spiritual sense, there are specific procedures to implement, beginning with the vow of dedication.

Additionally, there are three requirements of abstinence followed by several sacrificial rituals. Firstly, the person must abstain from anything associated with the grape—neither seed or skin, nor fermented wine, juice, sour wine vinegar or even raisins could be consumed during the vow's undertaking. Other fermented drink includes beer from grains. Therefore, anything that could cause intoxication which limits clear thought or causes a diversion from sacred contemplation. The actual period for the vow is established by the individual so careful thought has to be given to determine the extent of time they want to remain under their Nazirite vow.[48]

Secondly, the vow includes the external symbol of a Nazirite, namely the unshorn head of hair. No razor is to be used on the head. This contrasts with other cultures where people, like the Egyptian priests, shave their heads. In Israel, the priests are expected to trim the hair so in this act of dedication by the Nazirite their long locks are a visible sign of dedication and holiness. Thirdly,

---

46 Cf. G. Mayer, 'נזר', *TDOT*, I, pp. 306–311.
47 Kaiser, 'נדר', p. 244.
48 The primary form of a vow of abstinence in the OT concerns the Nazirite vow of dedication (Kaiser, 'נדר', p. 254).

the Nazirite vow restricts the individual from having any contact with a corpse. This restriction includes the normal family duties of preparing the dead for burial. The reason has to do with becoming ceremonially unclean—in other words to be 'defiled' (טמא). This restriction is even stronger for the Nazirite than it is for the role of a priest who is expected to assist with the immediate family member's burials (Lev. 21.1–3).

In this case it appears that the attitude towards death shows another dramatic display of anguish for the individual. The sentence or the curse of death (Gen. 3.19) is something to be symbolically portrayed as negative or evil and not in God's original plan. Avoidance of the dead is a dramatic portrayal of separation even from things and people that are dearest to the Nazirite. In this sense, sacrifice and suffering is part of the ordeal. Moreover, due to the wilderness context and issues of hygiene, there are perceptions that contact with the dead might even cause contamination in the long hair which could be defiled by contact with decay. Even the accidental death of a person in the immediate presence of the Nazirite under the vow necessitates extreme consequences including shaving of the head.

After an event where the period of consecration is interrupted, the Nazirite has several actions and rituals to perform. A period of cleansing is initiated and after seven days the head is shaved. The second ritual occurs on the eighth day where a sacrifice is delivered to the priest at the Tent of Meeting. Either two doves or two pigeons are sacrificed—one is a sin offering and the other is a burnt offering. Whether accidental or deliberate, being in proximity to the dead is viewed as a transgression that requires cleansing and forgiveness. This condition must be dealt with by 'atonement' (כפר) to cover any kind of transgression. Once completed, the vow is initiated again, with a fresh consecration to the Lord that begins with the initial time period of the vow. Thirdly, another costly sacrifice is brought to the Lord involving a year-old male lamb as a guilt offering.

6.13–21—*Finalizing the Vow*

At the end of the undertaking made by the individual, the Nazirite has to appear at the Tent of Meeting with three specific animal 'offerings' (מנחה). A year-old male lamb without defect for a burnt offering, a year-old ewe lamb without defect for a sin offering, and a ram without defect for a fellowship offering. The three-fold process of making the burnt offering, receiving the forgiveness of sin, and the consequent fellowship experience, brings about a satisfactory end to the vow. Additionally, a presentation is made by the priest of other products that had been carefully prepared by the Nazirite, including grain and drink offerings. Bread is made with the finest flour and olive oil without yeast. Then the Nazirite concludes their time of dedication by shaving their head and burning the hair along with the sacrifice of the fellowship offering. With this act the de-consecration of the person from the vow is completed.

The priest concludes the vow's duration with the appropriate rituals and formalities. The offerings and process take considerable time but eventually they are finalized with these actions. the priest places a boiled shoulder of the ram, and two loaves of bread in the hands of the Nazirite. The priest then takes them back for a wave offering before the Lord and retains them for a meal. At the conclusion of everything, the Nazirite is released to a mundane, pre-vow lifestyle including the right to drink wine.

It is obvious from these regulations that the Nazirite vow is a demanding, and costly act, taken for spiritual, physical, and sacred purposes, known primarily between the Nazirite and the Lord. The summation of the vow indicates the essential element of the vow's intention—it is not the Lord who initiates the period of dedication—it is the person. But once made, the Lord holds the individual accountable to fulfil all the requirements of the Law of the Nazirite. However, the Nazirite could also exceed the normal expectations of the requirements of the vow by making an additional offering. 'This is the law of the Nazirite who vows offerings to the LORD in accordance with their dedication, in addition to whatever else they can afford. They must fulfil the vows they have made, according to the law of the Nazirite' (Num. 6.21). The offerings and acts of abstinence are to show the intensity of the practitioner's consecration. When it is all over, the Nazirite anticipates the spiritual results and answers to prayer that motivated the vow in the first place.

6.22–27—*The Divine Blessing*

After the regulations concerning the Nazirite vow, Moses is instructed to deliver to Aaron and sons a remarkable benediction. The 'blessing' is to be administered by the priests in Israel and reflects the agenda of the Lord to bring the promised blessings of the covenant upon the people of Israel.

The positioning of the benedictory blessing appears to be in an unusual place in Numbers. However, the words of blessing follow an important theme from the preceding instructions concerning vows. The Nazirite desires to be consecrated to the Lord for a sacred spiritual exercise of devotion. To show the seriousness of taking such a vow there are strict guidelines and practices required by the devotee involving abstinence as well as sacrifice. This is where the priest's involvement is compulsory. The Nazirite must present sacrificial gifts at the Tent of Meeting for the priest's actions. Additionally, the opening chapters of Numbers emphasize the role and duties of the Levites along with the priest's responsibilities. All of their work and ministry is focused on bringing the Israelites into the presence of Yahweh for worship. Their benedictory blessing would become the concluding element of officiating the sacrifices and offerings of the people.

The Nazirite vow necessitates devotion, sacrifice, self-control, and consecration. In a sense, the placement of the vow may be an indicator of what is intended by Yahweh for the whole nation. The journey to the land of promise is not to be a vacation but a very demanding pilgrimage that takes courage and commitment. For the pilgrimage to be successful, Israel requires the continual blessings of Yahweh. The people's oath and vow to accept the covenantal obligations are implicit requirements for the blessing to be effective. 'All that the LORD has spoken we will do' (Exod. 19.8). The Nazirite vow and sacrifices were only effective when the Nazirite took the commitment seriously. The application of the extreme measures reflects the necessary devotion to the Lord and the commitment to restrict activities which could defile. In a similar sense, the priest's blessing over the Israelite community would be voided if the people were not in compliance with the covenantal standards of the nation. Only the Lord could affect the blessing and bring about the special circumstances declared by the priest.

Once again Moses is instructed to communicate one of the priest's crucial roles. Aaron and his sons have the responsibility and privilege to speak a benediction of blessing over the community. Pronouncement of the blessing recorded in Numbers is an additional feature in the work of the priests who officiated and consecrated the sacrificial system. In Leviticus, this act of benediction is illustrated.

> Then Aaron lifted his hands toward the people and blessed them. And having sacrificed the sin offering, the burnt offering and the fellowship offering, he stepped down. Moses and Aaron then went into the tent of meeting. When they came out, they blessed the people; and the glory of the Lord appeared to all the people. Fire came out from the presence of the Lord and consumed the burnt offering and the fat portions on the altar. And when all the people saw it, they shouted for joy and fell facedown. (Lev. 9.22–24)

This record of events is a powerful indicator of the priest's function with consequent blessing in Yahweh's presence.

The 'blessing' (ברך) is presented in three stanzas of connected and climactic affirmations that begin with three Hebrew words, and end with seven words.

> The LORD said to Moses, 'Tell Aaron and his sons,
> "This is how you are to bless the Israelites. Say to them,
> 'The LORD bless you and keep you;
> the LORD make his face shine on you and be gracious to you;
> the LORD turn his face toward you and give you peace.'"
> So they will put my name on the Israelites, and I will bless them.' (Num. 6.23–27).

Each line invokes Yahweh to look upon the community with a favourable disposition and then act in accordance with the needs of the people. The context for the blessing appears to be communal gatherings near the Tent of Meeting. There the people would gather for a variety of occasions with the desire to witness the 'divine countenance' shining upon them.

The invocation calls upon the Lord to 'bless' (ברך) and to 'keep guard' (שמר) over the community. The theme of blessing is one of the predominate interests in the Pentateuch with about eighty references in Genesis and almost fifty in Deuteronomy. Biblical concepts of blessing feature elements of fertility, progeny, strength, and vitality for work—in essence, the 'blessing' promotes the essentials of life. Blessing generates the fulfilment of the divine purposes.

In the context of Israel embarking on their pilgrimage to the promised land, the priest invokes Yahweh's protection—security from enemies behind as well as before. Fresh in their minds was the terrifying flight from the armies of Egypt and the continuing need for a safe journey ahead.

This scenario sheds light on the benediction. The name of the Lord is invoked over the community who are challenged to step out on a faith journey that would cause them to invade the property belonging to others. This formidable task would only be possible if the same Lord who brought them up out of Egypt would be present with them towards the conquest and habitation of Canaan. For the Lord to bless, his presence must be evident. His protection and communication are essential for Israel to realize the gracious 'shalom' of God. In this sense the benediction takes on a whole new dimension of meaning for the community. The regular pronouncement of blessing over the people would be a source of strength and encouragement in their gatherings and journeys. The invocation functions to remind Israel of their daily need for blessing and protection on their way forward towards their inheritance.

The entreaty continues for the Lord to 'shine' (אור) his 'face' (פנים) towards his people—to look upon them with pleasure and concern so that his grace and mercy would be made known. His shining countenance would be a light on their path, guiding them forward. The alternative is something to be feared by

Israel where God's wrath and displeasure would be made known. In fact, such times of wrath did come on the nation during events of defiance and rebellion (Num. 11.33; 14.11–12). Another fear would be for God to turn away from his people and ultimately be silent. Thus, the desirable provision from the Lord is for his 'gracious' (חנן) care and favour to be bestowed on the nation.

The culmination of the benediction reiterates the importance of the divine face to shine forth in order to implement the wholistic blessing of Yahweh on them—his 'shalom'. This blessing would be evident when the Lord keeps his focus on the community to bring about a state of 'rest' and well-being in the promised land. Peace is a major element in the overarching sense of well-being (שלום), and the opposite of fear, danger, and insecurity. However, the attainment of peace is not something that mankind can manufacture—it is only realized through the blessing of Yahweh. In fact, in the only reference to 'shalom' in Leviticus, Yahweh makes significant promises. 'I will grant peace in the land, and you will lie down, and no one will make you afraid. I will remove wild beasts from the land, and the sword will not pass through your country. You will pursue your enemies, and they will fall by the sword before you' (Lev. 26.6–7). Peace is promised but it will come according to the providential acts of the Lord. In this context, shalom in the land refers to the 'all-embracing state of well-being' which all people covet.[49]

Peace is an ultimate blessing for Israel to desire but the interesting reality is that the term (שלום) is moderately rare in the Pentateuch, with most of the 24 references referring to peace between individuals.[50] The reality is that there is not much peace between people and nations. Instead, there is conflict, aggression, conquest, and plunder (Genesis 14; Exod. 17.8–16; Numbers 21–23). Peace in the true sense of 'shalom' is a concept and condition that is hoped for in Israel's history, but rarely achieved! It is something that is primarily apprehended through the messianic work of kings and wise leaders.[51] Peace is therefore a key goal of the blessing that is brought about by the Lord who works through the efficient and obedient leaders of his people.

---

49 Cf. F.J. Stendebach, 'שלום', *TDOT*, XIV, p. 28.
50 The only other reference to shalom occurs when Phinehas the priest intervenes in the debacle reported in Numbers 25. Due to Phinehas' zealous intervention, he assuaged Yahweh's anger. For this action, the Lord makes a 'covenant of peace' with him and endorses a covenant of a lasting priesthood for the Aaronides (cf. Num. 25.10–13 and commentary section).
51 The noun '*shalom*' (שלום) appears 237 times in the OT but mainly in the prophetic books with the concept of wholeness or well-being brought about by Yahweh. Depending on the context, the term has a variety of dimensions in meaning.

There is a definite context to the divine blessing which reveals the consistent character and nature of God. A rich example of the blessing appears in the extent of the gracious blessings of God experienced by Moses in the divine—human element of friendship (Exod. 33.11). This provides the main component in the meaning of the term. It is the relational condition of well-being in the presence of Yahweh who welcomes and blesses his people with his manifestation. When Yahweh instructs Moses to proceed on the journey towards the land of promise he indicates that there would be formidable situations to work through. However, Yahweh would provide an angel to deal with the inhabitants of the land and drive them out. That is the good news! But Yahweh also threatens to not be present during this leg of the journey. The stubborn behaviour of the pilgrims who left Egypt irritates the Lord to the extent that judgment is immanent. Moses speaks freely with Yahweh, appealing for reconsideration with these words:

> You have been telling me, 'Lead these people', but you have not let me know whom you will send with me. You have said, 'I know you by name and you have found favor with me'. If you are pleased with me, teach me your ways so I may know you and continue to find favor with you. Remember that this nation is your people. (Exod. 33.12–13)

Moses' bold intercession brings forth a positive response from Yahweh who not only promised his presence to continue with his chosen leader but affirms the divine pleasure in his servant. Emboldened once again, Moses requests to witness the divine glory to which Yahweh responds.

> I will cause all my goodness to pass in front of you, and I will proclaim my name, the Lord, in your presence. I will have mercy on whom I will have mercy, and I will have compassion on whom I will have compassion. But, he said, 'you cannot see my face, for no one may see me and live'. (Exod. 33.19–20)

There are some definite paradoxes here because verse 33.11 states 'The LORD would speak to Moses face to face, as one speaks to a friend'. The anthropomorphic language used in this chapter affirms several things which have a bearing on Numbers 6. The presence of Yahweh and his glory are palpable, powerful realities which Moses has the pleasure of witnessing during the last forty-year segment of his life. Not only does Moses experience this divine presence but his apprentice Joshua is known to bask in the Lord's presence as well. 'Then Moses would return to the camp, but his young aide Joshua son of Nun did not leave the tent' (Exod. 33.11). Moreover, the text affirms that the communication between Yahweh and Moses is an intimate, friend to friend relationship. In part, this is the intent of conferring the blessing on the people of Yahweh.[52]

In Numbers 6, 'shalom' is the substance and result of Yahweh's favour with the idea of comprehensive well-being.[53] The protection and blessing of the Lord is like a protective shield over the community which produces peace, contentment, and relationship. The benediction ends with the affirmation that as the divine name is spoken over the community, Yahweh would indeed bless them.

Another ramification of the divine blessing needs to be observed here. As stated elsewhere, the covenantal blessings recorded in several passages are being fulfilled in the wilderness journey—the Lord is moving the nation forward, even though the pace seems slow. This unprecedented instruction to put the name of Yahweh on the Israelites so that they would be blessed, reveals the divine intention to see the promises come into reality. However, blessing as a theme in Numbers is an implicit, hidden, yet pervasive motif. There are glimmers of the Lord's care, provision, protection, and presence, but the full realization of rest in the land is only a hope that keeps the people moving forward.

Threats to the blessing are illustrated in the Balaam section where a diviner, turned prophet of sorts, is hired to thwart the blessings of Yahweh on the Israelites in order to curse them. The divine blessing functions to protect Israel from false prophets who seek to curse Israel and reverse the protective hand of Yahweh over the nation. The Balaam narratives depict the very essence of why Israel needs to pray for divine blessing, protection, and well-being. Numbers 22–24 are crucial chapters in Numbers which feature the threats to the nation which only the blessings of Yahweh can reverse. The episodes highlight the blessing and curse controversies between Balak and Balaam concerning Israel (cf. Numbers 22–24). However, the divine blessing in Numbers 6 and the Balaam section indicate that the blessings of the Lord are brought to bear on Israel through both the ministry of priests and implicitly through the prophetic leadership of Moses. The narratives are an effective depiction of prophetic conflict which serve to contrast the effective leadership of Moses and the unsuccessful attempts of the false prophet Balaam to curse Israel.

---

52   A further dimension of the presence of the LORD with Moses and leaders is developed in Numbers 11 through the sharing of the Spirit that is on Moses with the seventy elders. The ultimate desire is for all of God's people to experience the presence of God in daily communion.

53   Cf. Stendebach, 'שלום', p. 28.

Reflection and Response
Numbers 3–6: Levites and Priests Serving as Clergy

Reflection

The prominent roles of priests and Levites appear to give preferential position to the Levitical tribe. Leaders such as Moses, Aaron, priests and Levites, certainly had prestige and power. However, the roles they were called to fill came with incredible accountability, responsibility, and risk. While it is true that the vestiges of the priests are impressive and colourful, the ceremonial elements of their work are occasional. The daily work is more tedious as the sacrificial system demands rigorous activity, butchery, and burning. Furthermore, the daily work of guarding and occasional work of transporting the Tabernacle calls for strenuous labour for the Levites. The reality is that sacred ministry is a call to service. It requires daily and constant devotion. The clear job requirements given to the Levites come with reminders of the sacred nature of their work on behalf of the nation.

The Levitical role to guard the sanctuary also comes with considerable risk. Failure to comply with strict regulations and reverence could cause judgment and death. Allowing encroachers on sacred ground could also cost them their lives. Protecting the wider community from threats requires constant vigilance.

The substitutionary role of the Levites is also a reminder of their salvation history. While the firstborns in Egypt are taken in an act of judgment, Yahweh spares the firstborns in Israel. In a special way, they 'belonged to Yahweh' and he cares for them. To reciprocate his care, the firstborns have important roles to fulfil in their own family and community. Their responsibilities give them purpose and meaningful work in life. The selection of the Levites allows for the facilitation of family and community services to continue and benefit the nation. With the Tabernacle centrally located with the Levites and priests around it, the visibility of the clergy in Israel is a powerful reminder to the nation of Yahweh's presence and care. Consequently, one of the great privileges of serving the nation is in their access to the Lord through ministry, devotion, and support of Israel—the Levites are allowed to 'draw near'.

Response

The role of clergy and laity has often brought a level of tension to communities of faith, with the apparent implication that clergy are more holy or closer to God. However, the importance of the Torah's teaching affirms that the Lord desires to select and authorize servants for certain sacred functions. This is evident from the selection of tribes for certain duties as well as for individuals. Although Moses and Aaron are the most prominent leaders throughout the book of Numbers, the 'burden' of their leadership tasks is immense. They are often overwhelmed with the challenges they are forced to deal with.

Of course, clergy must earn respect—too often in Israel, individuals like Nadab, Abihu, and sons of Eli did not match their calling with their character and behaviour. They brought reproach and disdain on their office. This is evident in church history to this day—in fact in all religions we see that functionaries often feel entitled to respect, honour, and privilege. Too often they end up failing their communities. But the fact is, God still calls, he sets apart, he delegates sacred duty and requires devotion from leaders. There is burden and toil, but the service of the Levites was meant to instil reverence in the people by teaching them how to approach holy sacred things, and to reject the profane. Their effective service would be observed through the blessings conferred in the nation in their experience of order and productive life.

What is the role of the laity in all this? What are the best forms of support that laity can offer to leaders? How should clergy balance their sacred offices and maintain a passionate pastoral concern for the people in their care? In fact, an interesting example follows these chapters in Numbers on clergy services with a domestic situation. The priest is an integral part of family issues that arise in the community. Through careful processing of marital troubles, the priest administers and mediates to re-establish harmony in the home. The role of the priest includes the diagnosis of health issues as well as services to eliminate matters that bring about a 'curse'.

In Numbers Six, the priest also helps to facilitate the Nazirite's vow. Moreover, instructions are given for one of the priest's greatest liturgical ministries, which is to pronounce the divine 'blessing'. But this chapter highlights another very important reality which brings the clergy and laity divide into perspective in a comparative way. The Nazirite makes a sacred vow to accomplish spiritual goals by foregoing many personal privileges. Their example in pursuing the Lord's blessing and consecrating themselves for a designated period, is a profound lesson for the clergy. Those who are set apart for divine service, must take their calling seriously and honourably, fulfilling their sacred duties.

7.1–89—The Tabernacle and Altar Dedication

The Tabernacle is crafted and built according to the specifications of the Lord as revealed to Moses on Mount Sinai. The instructions given to Moses disclose several important elements regarding the 'sanctuary' (מקדש), and the 'Tabernacle' (משכן) according to the Book of Exodus. 'Then have them make a sanctuary for me, and I will dwell among them. Make this tabernacle and all its furnishings exactly like the pattern I will show you' (Exod. 25.8–9). The sanctuary terminology usually refers to the whole sacred complex where the Tabernacle is located. This is the place where Yahweh is considered to dwell among the people who would worship and offer sacrifices as instructed. The specific details regarding the Tabernacle are revealed to Moses according to a 'pattern' (תבנית), suggesting an architectural design. Furthermore, the revelation includes the furnishings, size specifications, and some of the material quantities (Exodus 25–27; 30). The anointed workmen who are chosen for the construction, Bezalel and Oholiab, are filled with the Spirit of God and given the necessary skills, abilities and knowledge to build the Tabernacle according to the specified design (Exod. 31.1–11; 35.30–39).

The Tabernacle is the special sanctuary of Yahweh (Exod. 25.8–9), and along with the Tent of Meeting it becomes the central focal point for Yahweh's presence in Israel and the vital place of connection for sacred matters. It represents the sacred place where the presence of Yahweh is revealed to the community in a tangible way—particularly when the nation gathers for sacrifices and communal services. Specifically, it is the place where Yahweh communicates with Moses, as he previously did on the Mount of Sinai. When the Tabernacle is finally completed, the Tent of Meeting becomes a part of the sanctuary and references to it in Numbers reflect the merging of Tent and Tabernacle.[54]

The procurement of materials, process of construction, and manufacture of all the pieces of the Tabernacle takes the better part of one year to build. Exod. 39.32–43 registers the completion of the project and after inspecting the materials, Moses affirms the work and blesses the craftsmen. When the 'Tent of Meeting' (אהל מועד) is erected, the furnishings are placed, consecration by anointing done, and everything is finalized (Exod. 40.1–33). All that remains is the Lord's confirmation and blessing with his presence. 'Then the cloud covered the tent of meeting, and the glory of the LORD filled the tabernacle. Moses could not enter the tent of meeting because the cloud had settled on it, and the glory of the LORD filled the tabernacle' (Exod. 40.34–35). This remarkable event sets the tone for Israel's experience in worship and confirms that the constructed Tabernacle is built according to the pattern. The nation is prepared for the next part of the journey (cf. Numbers 1).

---

54   For a detailed overview of the intricate elements, Cf. R.E. Averbeck, 'Tabernacle', *DOTP*, pp. 807–827.

7.1—Consecrating the Tabernacle

In Numbers 7, preparations continue to be implemented for the Tabernacle worship requirements as well as the transportation needs for the Levites. Numbers 1–4 focusses on the personnel resources required for the leadership of the people and the worship system. Now the attention turns to the physical resources needed for the Levites and the priests to do their work and offer the required sacrifices. The Tabernacle is crafted and erected but for it to be used, Moses must prepare for its functions by 'anointing' (משח) and 'consecrating' (קדש) all its furnishings, the 'altar' (מזבח) and its utensils. This process facilitates the transfer of the materials from the profane sphere to the sacred for use in Israel's cultus. The focal point in the chapter is the altar (mentioned 6 times in Numbers 7) which is dedicated or more specifically initiated for the sacrificial system.[55] The consecration of holy things relegates them for exclusive use in the holy cultic sphere of use. The pouring of the anointing oil is an important visible ritual that symbolizes the actual transferring of the altar to the sacred realm for cultic use. From the consecration of the altar in verse 1 to its official dedication offerings in verse 88, the chapter presents a processional of 'offerings' (מנחה) given by tribal leaders for the altar.

7.2-11—Bringing the Offerings

Preparations for the use of the altar follows its careful crafting out of acacia wood (the frame) and overlay of bronze metal (the main surface area). It is a significant size at five cubits square (ca. 2.3 metres each side) and three cubits high (ca. 1.4 meters high). Each of the four corners have a horn that is also overlaid with bronze. The altar has bronze rings installed for transportation by acacia wood poles that fit through the rings. The grating, ledge and utensils that are required for ash and coal removal are also important tools for managing the requirements of the sacrificial system. The placement of the altar is near the entrance where the sacrifices are offered in an open-air space for the smoke, blood, and ash management systems.

Once the altar is ready for use, the sacrifices and offerings needed to be secured. These are provisions from the tribes and are recorded as a lasting witness for all to observe. The materials and resources for the cultus system are documented as given by each tribe. These gifts are significant 'offerings' (קרבן) and are brought to the Lord by the tribal leaders according to the name listings in Numbers One and in the order of tribal representation in

---

55 With about 360 references for the 'altar' (מזבח) in the OT, most of the citations occur in Exodus 58 times; Leviticus, 73 times and in Numbers, 26 times.

Numbers Two. Twelve tribal leaders present generous offerings which provide what is needed for daily sacrifice.

Other gifts are presented for the transport of the Tabernacle during the anticipated journey. The six carts which are needed by the Gershonites and Merarites are supplied by two tribes who share in donating a cart together. Each tribe also gives an ox so that the expectations for work in transporting the sanctuary could be accomplished by the Levites. The Gershonites receive two carts and four oxen, while the Merarites receive the remainder. The Kohathites do not need a cart or oxen since they carry the sacred furnishings on their shoulders. All of these arrangements occur under the oversight of Aaron's son, Ithamar.

7.12–83—Leader's Contributions

The presentation of 'offerings' (מנחה) are presented in an orderly and dramatic fashion, providing each tribal leader with a distinct day to bring gifts in appreciation for the altar dedication. Each leader is presented by name along with the same list of offerings. The leader's names are identical to the census listing in Numbers One and Two, and each one comes on successive days over a period of twelve days as follows.

> Nahshon son of Amminadab of the tribe of Judah;
> Nethanel son of Zuar, the leader of Issachar;
> Eliab son of Helon, the leader of the people of Zebulun;
> Elizur son of Shedeur, the leader of the people of Reuben;
> Eliasaph son of Deuel, the leader of the people of Gad;
> Shelumiel son of Zurishaddai, the leader of the Simeonites;
> Elishama son of Ammihud, the leader of the Ephraimites;
> Gamaliel son of Pedahzur, the leader of the people of Manasseh;
> Abidan son of Gideoni, the leader of the people of Benjamin;
> Ahiezer son of Ammishaddai, the leader of the people of Dan;
> Pagiel son of Okran, the leader of the people of Asher;
> Ahira son of Enan, the leader of the people of Naphtali.
> Each leader presents the following gifts on behalf of their tribe.

One silver plate (or bowl) weighing a hundred and thirty shekels (ca. 3 pounds). One silver sprinkling bowl (or basin) weighing seventy shekels (ca. 1 ¾ pounds), and each filled with the finest flour mixed with olive oil as a grain offering. One gold dish (or ladle) weighing ten shekels (ca. 4 ounces), filled with incense. Animals for sacrifice include one young bull, one ram and one male lamb a year old for a burnt offering; one male goat for a sin (or purification) offering; and two oxen, five rams, five male goats and five male lambs a year old for sacrifices as fellowship offerings.[56] These offerings are collected by the priests and used in the cultus worship system as needed. The priests offer the required sacrifices according to the scheduled burnt, grain, fellowship and purification needs. The generous donations are equal in amounts from each tribe showing the unified dedication of the people in supporting the Tabernacle requirements.

7.84–88—The Altar

The summation provides a total inventory of the offerings, their weight, and the numbers of animals presented over the twelve-day period.

> These were the offerings of the Israelite leaders for the dedication of the altar when it was anointed. twelve silver plates, twelve silver sprinkling bowls and twelve gold dishes. Each silver plate weighed a hundred and thirty shekels, and each sprinkling bowl seventy shekels. Altogether, the silver dishes weighed two thousand four hundred shekels, according to the sanctuary shekel. The twelve gold dishes filled with incense weighed ten shekels each, according to the sanctuary shekel (ca. 28 kilograms). Altogether, the gold dishes weighed a hundred and twenty shekels (ca. 1.4 kilograms). The total number of animals for the burnt offering came to twelve young bulls, twelve rams and twelve male lambs a year old, together with their grain offering. Twelve male goats were used for the sin offering. The total number of animals for the sacrifice of the fellowship offering came to twenty-four oxen, sixty rams, sixty male goats and sixty male lambs a year old. These were the offerings for the dedication of the altar after it was anointed (Num. 7.84–88).

The overall effect of the report indicates the leader's ability to persuade the people to make the lavish donations for the altar. It may also indicate the level of comprehension the people are gleaning regarding the importance and cost of the sacrificial system, how it functions, and overtime, what the meaning behind each ritual is.

---

56   The gifts and offerings which are presented to Yahweh in the cultus amount to a profound quantity of materials which are regularly brought as offerings. These are not just rituals that consumed the ingredients in fire but are meaningful presentations of sacrifices that give a pleasing odour to the LORD. It becomes a satisfying fragrance (cf. Lev. 2.14f.), and together with the spices in the incense which cause the pleasing smell actually 'constituted the high point of the sacrificial ritual' (cf. M. Weinfeld, 'מנחה', *TDOT*, VIII, pp. 417–420).

7.89—Moses before the Lord

At the conclusion of the twelve days of presentation, Moses enters the Tent of Meeting to speak with the Lord. Notably, in Exodus 40.35 Moses could not enter the 'Tent of Meeting' (אהל מועד) because the glory cloud fills the Tabernacle. It appears that there are some significant changes in the communication between God and Moses after the Sinai and Exodus revelations. Once the Tabernacle is complete and consecrated, there are limitations and conditions in approaching Yahweh. The anthropomorphic statements where God speaks face to face with Yahweh (Exod. 33.11; Numbers 12) are meant to convey that of all people, Moses had incredible access to the presence of God. However, the priests and Levites must follow strict procedures in the Tabernacle and are not permitted to look upon the ark of the covenant. A protective veil hangs between the two cherubim above the atonement cover on the ark of the covenant law and the place where Moses stood to hear the voice of Yahweh.

This is the most sacred area and place of communication between Moses and Yahweh. According to Numbers, they meet there often. The 'ark' (ארון) of the covenant contains portions of the Torah and above it is the gold 'cover plate' (כפרת), referred to as the 'mercy-seat' or place of atonement. On the gold cover are two gold cherubim with wings spread upward at each end. In Exod. 25.22 Yahweh promises, 'There, above the cover between the two cherubim that are over the ark of the covenant law, I will meet with you and give you all my commands for the Israelites'. Now as promised, when Moses enters the tent, the Lord speaks with Moses who hears the 'voice' (קול). This is a fitting conclusion to a remarkable achievement by the Israelites in fulfilling the explicit detailed instructions for the Tabernacle materials and furnishings—Yahweh speaks to him.

8.1–26—Consecration of the Levites

The focus on the Tabernacle functions continues with specific instructions for the lighting of the seven-branched lampstand, the *'menorah'* (מנורה). This introduction is followed by the segregation of the Levites to their sacred work.

8.1–4—The Seven-Branched Lampstand

One of the main furnishings for the Tabernacle is the lampstand or *menorah*. In addition to the regular daily functions of the priests in making sacrifices on the altar (Exod. 29.38-43), they also attend to the *menorah* each morning and evening (Exod. 27.20-21; 30.7-8). The process includes the lighting of the lamps each evening with oil and replenishing wicks after cleaning each morning. Specially prepared refined olive oil is used for the lampstand and Yahweh makes it imperative that the lamps should burn continually (Lev. 24.1–4). Moses stipulates that Aaron must position the *menorah* so that all seven lamps cast their light forward to illumine the altar of incense and the table with the bread of the presence.

The description of the *menorah* indicates that it is a very ornate and valuable lampstand. The summary in Num. 8.4 is very brief compared to the details given in Exod. 25.31–41. The pattern for the lampstand is presented to Moses by revelation during a Mount Sinai excursion. Whereas other furnishings include gold plating, the lampstand is made from a solid piece of pure gold. The base represents a tree ornamented with flowerlike cups, buds, and blossoms. It includes four cups like almond flowers with buds and blossoms. The lamps are on top of arm like branches on each side of the base. They too are ornamented cups shaped like almond flowers, buds, and blossoms. Together with the lamp on top of the base there are seven lights signifying the perfect and complete set of lamps for the Tabernacle. The almond blossom is one of the first to bloom in the spring and probably symbolizes the renewal of life. But most importantly, the light is to shine continually, symbolizing the ever present life-giving force of Yahweh who dwells among the people of Israel.

The light emanating from the lamps and Tabernacle expresses an important truth about the nature of God who is light and in him there is no darkness. In fact, the first step in God's creative work is to declare 'Let there be light', and he separates the light from the darkness (Gen. 1.3–4). The lamps are fuelled with clear oil of pressed olives which radiate light from the lamps. Aaron and his sons are given a considerable responsibility to ensure that the lamps keep burning before the Lord from evening till morning.

8.5–7—*Consecration of the Levites*

Much of the preliminary content of Numbers is focused on the Levitical responsibilities. Their choice and status as firstborn replacements is established. The importance of their role in guarding the sanctuary from improper intrusion is emphasized (Numbers 3). The details of their responsibilities in transporting the sacred articles and furnishings are made clear (Numbers 4). Now the attention is turned to the physical and spiritual rituals which are to prepare and qualify the Levites to do the Tabernacle services.

Purification rites for all Levites with sacred responsibilities are arranged for them to become ceremonially 'clean' (טהר) and 'cleansed from sin' (כפר). The purification rites authorize them for their service and protects them from the potential judgment of God in situations where the wrath of God could be meted out. The procedures for the Levitical cleansing are different from those of the priestly sanctification rituals in Exodus because the functions and roles are distinctive. The Levites have more of the regular chores that handled the take-down, transport and set-up work of the sanctuary. To prepare for their sacred yet menial duties, they are sprinkled with the water of cleansing, and they must shave their whole bodies—a significant chore for Semitic men! Their clothes are washed for the purification rites which concludes with ritual bathing for the physical cleansing process.

8.8–13—Sacrifices

After the cleansing rites, procedures for the sacrifices are made clear. This includes a young bull, and grain offerings made with the finest flour mixed with olive oil. An additional young bull had to be offered for a sin offering to achieve the ethical purification requirements. The official sacrifice and ceremony take place with the Levites at the entrance of the Tent of Meeting before the whole Israelite community. The ritual participation of the 'community' (עדה) is evident where the congregation witnesses the cleansing of the Levites for their role of service in the nation. They show their support by laying hands on the Levites which 'transfers authority' over to them (cf. Num. 27.23). Although the 'Israelites' are to lay their hands on the Levites, it is probably the representative elders who gather behind them that do so. The entire community is involved because of the importance of the Levitical role in the Tabernacle. The community witnesses the rites associated with the priestly duties and ordination, thereby lending legitimacy to the installation of those who serve on behalf of the community (cf. Lev. 8.3–5; 9.5). With this ceremonial service they declare their acceptance of the Levitical ministry.

The action of presenting the Levites before the Lord as a 'wave offering' is called the *'tenufah'* (תנופה; Num. 8.11, 13, 15) which implies that the Levites are presented like sacrifices brought before the Lord for the sacred work (cf. Lev. 1.4; 3.2; 4.15).[57] This is a special ceremony or elevation service which signifies their complete dedication to the Lord's service in a symbolic way. The word *tenufah* implies physical movements of some kind to display their passion in readiness for service. Wave offerings typically present the grain or meat before Yahweh and then the persons offering it receive it back for their own use. Similarly, the Levites are offered to the Lord but in a sense are now promoted and commissioned to assist the priests for the Tabernacle services. In this instance, the Levites are presented as literal sacrifices for the Lord's purposes.

---

57   Cf. Milgrom, *Numbers*, p. 369–371 for an extensive excursus on the Levitical status and duties.

Another element in the proceedings of the ritual involve animal sacrifices brought by the Levites. Two bulls are brought by the Levites who must lay their hands on the heads of the bulls. The first bull is for a sin offering to the Lord, and the second bull is for a burnt offering. This symbolism is both substitutionary as well as an atonement for any moral issues the Levites are guilty of. The atonement is not only for the purging of sin but also for protection 'so that no plague will strike the Israelites when they go near the sanctuary' (Num. 8.19). The term for 'atonement' (כפר) is important and frequent in the Pentateuch because of the essential need for reconciliation between Israel and Yahweh (cf. Num. 8.12, 19, 21). Usually, atonement is made for individuals but there are a whole range of contexts where objects are also atoned for (both cultic and home or land). In such contexts the meaning is to be distinguished between the ritual purification rite, or in the sense of redeeming something that is defiled or evil, in the sense of a ransom. Therefore, the context and grammatical tense of the word may indicate a diversity in meaning.[58] In chapter 8 it mainly refers to the removal of that which would defile the Levite rendering them unable to perform their services in the cultus.

8.14-19—Set Apart for Yahweh

Now that the Levites are set apart, purified, and presented, they are ready for work. The substitutionary element in their selection in taking the place of the firstborns in Israelite families is reiterated. The affirmation that the Levites are substitutes for the firstborn and that they belong exclusively to the Lord, is a recurring refrain in several texts (Num. 3.12, 45; 8.14) with an emphatic, 'they shall be mine'. Numbers 8.16–18 is a wholistic summation of the core elements for the Levites selection and service.

> They are the Israelites who are to be given wholly to me. I have taken them as my own in place of the firstborn, the first male offspring from every Israelite woman. Every firstborn male in Israel, whether human or animal, is mine. When I struck down all the firstborn in Egypt, I set them apart for myself. And I have taken the Levites in place of all the firstborn sons in Israel. From among all the Israelites, I have given the Levites as gifts to Aaron and his sons to do the work at the tent of meeting on behalf of the Israelites and to make atonement for them so that no plague will strike the Israelites when they go near the sanctuary. (cf. Num. 3.11–13)

---

58 The term for 'atonement' (כפר) occurs 15 times in Exodus, but most frequently in Leviticus, 52 times, and 18 times in Numbers, in a variety of tenses. Cf. B. Lang, 'כפר', *TDOT*, VII, pp. 292–301.

Several affirmations are repeated here from Numbers 3 with a further explanation regarding the 'firstborn' (בוכר) male offspring in Israel. Firstborn sons are consecrated to the Lord (Exod. 13.1–2) as a reminder of how Yahweh protected Israel's sons from the death sentence on the firstborns in Egypt (Exod. 11.4–7). The valuation of the firstborn should not be underestimated. As the firstborn in a family, the child receives the full attention and love of the parents during their early childhood years. Consequently, as other children come along and the family grows, the firstborns have more responsibilities to attend to. This domestic reality also has applications for the firstborn concept in Israel as a nation.

Once again, the Lord confirms his consecration of the Levites and affirms that they are His—through special election they are chosen. In this way they become 'gifts' for Aaron and sons in support of the Tabernacle services. This substitution is meant to inspire appreciation among the Israelites for the ability of retaining firstborn sons for family responsibilities. The apparent subordination of the Levites to the Aaronide priests becomes a point of contention for some Levites in recurring instances throughout the book of Numbers. Kellermann claims, 'The complex nature of the P materials reveals a power struggle still underway between the Aaronite (and Zadokite) priests and the Levites on the one hand and among the individual groups of Levites on the other. Num. 3.5–10, for example, emphasizes that the Levites are subordinate to the priests, while underlining their significance for the community, for whom they minister vicariously as they carry out their duties at the sanctuary. There was obviously recurring rivalry among the individual Levite families as we can see in Numbers 4, where the genealogical sequence of Gershon, Kohath and Merari (Num. 3.17; etc) is changed to give precedence to Kohath. Probably the Kohath group is based on the same clan that lies behind the name Korah. Thus Numbers 16–18 with its various strata reveals conflicts, shifts of emphasis, and attempts to voice or realize the special hopes of individual groups'.[59]

Finally, a unique situation is presented in this passage with the two rites of laying hands on the bulls and the elevation offering. These actions are typically reserved for animal sacrifices which are then burnt or waved before the Lord. Here it is the Levites who become 'human sacrifices on behalf of' the Israelites—in essence they are the ransom for the people—an offering for the well-being of the nation in a vivid, symbolic way (cf. Num. 18.21–23).

---

59   Cf. Kellermann, 'לוי', p. 498.

8.20–22—*Applying Instructions*

The summation affirms that Moses, Aaron and the whole community dedicated the Levites according to Yahweh's instructions. The Levites are cleansed, consecrated, and atoned before the Lord. The whole ceremonial event is a remarkable presentation and community celebration of the Lord's provision for the nation. Now the Levites are prepared for action to begin their work at the Tent of Meeting.

8.23–26—*Retirement Option*

Lastly in this section, Yahweh provides for the retirement of Levites from the heavier duties of Tabernacle transportation work. There seems to be a discrepancy, however, from the age limits presented in Num. 4.3, 23, 30 where the men who are thirty to fifty years of age are assigned to this type of work. Here the age is lowered to those who are twenty-five years of age for work at the Tent of Meeting. While there is no resolution to this difference it seems plausible that the twenty-five-year-old men could be apprenticing for regular duties from age 30 to 50. The men who turn fifty are no longer tasked with the heavier work of transporting materials, but they are allowed to assist the younger Levites with the guarding of the Tabernacle (cf. Num. 3.5–38).

Reflection and Response
Numbers 7–8: The Lord Communicates
Reflection

One of the greatest claims in scripture is that the God of the universe speaks with humankind. From the opening verses of the Torah, God declares words and issues creation commands. In the book of Numbers, it is the narrator who affirms over and over the seemingly regular and constant communication between Yahweh and Moses. From the prolonged sessions on Mount Sinai, the Lord continues to instruct Moses for the benefit of the nation. From the vociferous theophanic displays on Sinai, the Lord accepts the people's request to speak through Moses and the prophetic nature of their communication is confirmed. In Numbers 7 the very special place of communion is revealed. In the Exodus account, Moses often meets with the Lord at the Tent of Meeting which eventually transitions to the holy place in the Tabernacle. There Moses hears the voice of God and applies what he learns to the national interests of Israel. Legislation, interpretation, and general communication is a continual experience for the prophet who shares his encounters with the community.

It is also evident from Numbers that the Lord does not censor Moses' words and responses. Several times the humanity of Moses springs forth as he utters strong words, careless desires, and harsh thoughts in his dialogues with the

Lord (Numbers 11). However, although the people are usually the cause of Moses' burden, he still intercedes on their behalf. Although the Lord tells Moses he would not go with the people to the promised land due to their stubborn rebellion (Exod. 33.3), he allows the intercession of Moses to change his decree. "And the LORD said to Moses, 'I will do the very thing you have asked, because I am pleased with you and I know you by name'" (Exod. 33.17). This is exhibited in the staggering example where Moses' intercession is not only heard by Yahweh but, persuades him to change his intent to punish a rebellious people (Num. 14.10–20). Moreover, the volume of times the Lord is recorded to speak with Moses, Aaron, leaders, and the community is astonishing and mentioned in every chapter (approximately one hundred and fifty times in Numbers). The characteristic phrase, 'the LORD spoke to Moses' highlights the fact that God desires to communicate with his creation. Just as he spoke with Adam and Eve in the garden of Eden, and with Abraham in Canaan, so he continues to speak to the covenant people.

Yahweh's speech may be evident in explicit instruction (Numbers 1; 4), warning (Num. 1.51–53; 4.17–20), explanation (Num. 3.11ff.), testing (Numbers 5), and in blessing (Num. 6.22–27). In Exodus the favoured place of communication is on Mount Sinai but also in the Tent of Meeting. In Numbers, Yahweh usually meets Moses and leaders at the Tabernacle but also in the Tent of Meeting. 'When Moses entered the Tent of Meeting to speak with the LORD, he heard the voice speaking to him from between the two cherubim above the atonement cover on the ark of the covenant law. In this way the LORD the spoke to him' (Num. 7.89).

Response

God is a communicator. Are we ready to listen? Does the Lord continue to speak to people in similar ways as he did in the book of Numbers? Does he prefer to speak to selected leaders who are then to mediate instructions to others? Is there a specific place that the Lord prefers to communicate with people? As we read through the scriptures and reflect on both Old and New Testament revelation, the answers to these questions change. However, several lessons may be gleaned. It does appear that the Lord continues to call and speak through leaders who have an enormous responsibility to communicate accurate, biblical knowledge in community contexts. God uses people who have a heart to hear and obey his instructions so that they may be effective instruments in his hands.

At the same time believers should recognize the voice of God for themselves and should dig into the written record of his word to discern what the Lord is saying. Do we have a special place where we open our ears to hear what the

Spirit is saying? Scripture is the foundational word of the Lord which the Spirit loves to apply to our hearts, minds and lives. Blessed is the person who takes time to meditate on the word and the law for edification, direction and specific application.

Both personal and congregational listening is required. Leaders and pastors are used by God to shepherd and guide the flock. However, daily personal reading, listening, reflecting with anticipation is an essential part of life. The diligent will definitely hear the Lord's instructions for the journey, whether in personal, family life, or work contexts—he is faithful to speak to those who will hear and obey.

9.1–23—The Passover and the Cloud

After the intensive work on the Tabernacle, the census undertaking, and the organization of the camp, Israel is finally positioned to resume their journey. The Tabernacle is erected, the Levites and priests are informed of their responsibilities, and a year has passed since Israel's exodus from Egypt. The historical occasion to be commemorated is the second 'Passover' (פסח) celebration by the nation. However, this one is different in that the people are no longer in Egypt but are free from their oppressors and are camped at Mount Sinai.

A number of itinerary notices are presented in several texts that provide a chronological timeline for the events which take place in the second year after the exodus. Num. 9.1–3 opens with a notice that marks an important event in the timeline. "The LORD spoke to Moses in the Desert of Sinai in the first month of the second year after they came out of Egypt. He said, 'Have the Israelites celebrate the Passover at the appointed time. Celebrate it at the appointed time, at twilight on the fourteenth day of this month, in accordance with all its rules and regulations'".

With other chronological indicators, a synopsis of the calendar events which occur to this point are as follows. One year after Israel's departure from Egypt, on the first day of the first month, the Tabernacle is completed. The offerings for the altar are presented and the ordination process for the priests is initiated (cf. Exod. 40.2; Lev. 1.1; 8.1; Num. 7.1–3). On the eighth day of that month the ordination service for the priests is completed (Lev. 9.1). On day twelve of that month the offerings for the altar are given and the Levites go through a purification rite (Num. 7.78; 8.5 ff.). The second official Passover celebration by the Israelites occurs on the fourteenth day (Num. 9.2).[60] The actual census recorded in Num-

---

60   Due to the number of texts with chronological markers and events that are transmitted

bers 1 does not begin until the second month, first day. On the fourteenth day of the second month, another Passover is celebrated by those who are ritually unclean during the first month (cf. Num. 9.11, 22). Finally, Num. 10.11 reports the moving of the cloud, indicating that the camp is to begin its wilderness trek on day twenty of the second month.

9.1-5—*The Passover*

The occasion is marked by specific instructions from Yahweh who communicates directives to Moses in the first month of the second year after the departure from Egypt. Israel is to observe the Passover event according to the precise time and instructions which are given in Exodus 12 when Israel is still under the bondage of the Egyptians. The Passover event would be celebrated in the first month of Israel's year—the month of Nisan. Due to the explicit and repetitive instructions to 'celebrate at the appointed time', the text affirms that the Israelites accomplish everything as commanded (Num. 9.5; cf. Lev. 23.1-5).

The importance of the Passover celebration for Israel is monumental and is mentioned seven times in Num. 9.2-14 (also cf. Num. 28.16; 33.3).[61] It is forever rooted in one of the greatest stories of deliverance from oppression in the OT and perhaps even in all human history. It is rooted in Israel's psyche for antiquity and is foundational to the nation's existence, hope and constitution. For Israel, the Passover story and exodus provided hope, purpose, mission, and direction as a people. Whereas other nations disappear in the annals of time, Israel survives incredible challenges through the foundational covenantal agreement and interventions of Yahweh. According to the Pentateuch, Israel as a community was instructed to observe three annual feasts or 'festivals' (חג)

---

over extensive periods of time, there are a number of variations in the Torah references. These are discussed by J. Van Goudoever, *Biblical Calendars* (Leiden: Brill, 2nd rev. edn, 1961), pp. 54-61, based on the main references in Exodus, Numbers and Joshua (cf. Ezek. 40.1-2). He concludes that 'in the Book of Exodus the three annual feasts are all described as being celebrated by Moses himself. The Passover and the Feast of Unleavened Bread in connection with the Deliverance from Egypt, and the Feast of Tabernacles in connection with the erection and dedication of the Tabernacle in the wilderness' (p. 60).

61 Scholars have offered many interpretations of the Passover rite and the actual meaning of the term (cf. E. Otto, 'פסח', *TDOT*, XII, pp. 7-8), but the historical connection between the events surrounding the event and its cultic observances rooted in Exod. 12.13-27 as described here continue to be understood as primary concepts for the Passover celebration. There are three records of Passover celebrations from Exodus to Joshua. The first one is after the exodus event (Exodus 12); the second is in the wilderness as noted in Numbers 9, and the third is in Joshua after the people enter into the promised land (Josh. 5.10-12).

at specific times of the year. These are the Feast of Unleavened Bread which began with the Passover in the spring. The Feast of Harvest or Weeks come at the end of the wheat harvest. Lastly, the Feast of Ingathering or Booths comes at the end of the fruit and grape harvest (Exod. 23.14–17; 34.23; cf. Deut. 16.16). These periods of celebration are connected to seasons and the agricultural cycle, beginning with the full moon in spring and ending with the autumn harvests. The annual commemoration provides the historical context for what God has done thereby instilling hope for the nation in what God would do—his provision, guidance, and protection.

The background of the tenth plague brought upon the Egyptians highlights the incredible role the Passover plays for all affected Israelite families and particularly the firstborn. Whereas the Egyptians experience the death of their firstborns (Exod. 12.29–30), Israel is kept safe. Death passes over all homes with blood over the door frames. This is the judgment of God on Egypt and the redemption event for the Hebrews. The first 'Passover' (*pesach*; פסח) is observed in Egypt but now Israel is to observe the Passover on the eve of their journey to the land of promise.

On the fourteenth day of the month the whole community of Israel is to celebrate the Passover with families in their homes. The male representative in each family is responsible for the preparation of a lamb, which could be shared with neighbours if the household is small and provides carefully selected portions for all. The choice lambs are to be one-year-old males without defect (use of sheep or goat is permitted). For four days the lambs would be cared for and then slaughtered on the fourteenth day of the month at twilight. Some of the lamb blood is to be smeared on the sides and tops of the doorframes of the houses where the meal is to be taken. The lamb must be prepared over a fire and served with bitter herbs and bread made without yeast. It is to be eaten after roasting along with the head, legs and internal organs. Any leftovers must be burned. To indicate their preparation and anticipation for action, they are to eat the meal quickly, with cloaks tucked into belts, sandals on with a staff in hand (cf. Exod. 12.1–11). The actions dramatically remind the participants of the deliverance acts of Yahweh.

These instructions are very clear, precise, and demanding, but still etched in the people's memory from the first Passover in Egypt. They require careful preparations and procedures that are significant but more importantly, symbolically meaningful. The basis for Passover and the ritual meanings could easily become lost when rituals become rote action without reflection. To ensure that this would not occur, the family takes time to reflect and retell the Exodus story. There is a process and specific 'order' (*seder*) to the service which is scheduled for the spring season and set apart as a holy commemoration. This service (as sketched out below) developed over time as people made adjustments for cultic restrictions which refocused attention to liturgy and symbolic representation.

The order of service begins with a blessing spoken over wine to sanctify the Passover meal. A cup of wine is consumed, and a second cup is poured. Hands are washed in preparation for the consumption of a vegetable (usually parsley). The parsley stem is dipped in salt water, symbolizing the tears shed in the land of oppression where the nation suffered slavery. Three pieces of unleavened matzah bread are on the table—one is broken and set aside for partaking later in the service. A highlight in the ritual meal is the reciting of the Exodus story where several questions are answered to instill the memory of Yahweh's actions on behalf of Israel. The story affirms what happened and applies its importance for the present. At the conclusion of the narration, the second cup of wine is consumed.

Another ritual hand washing is conducted in preparation for the eating of some matzah bread but first a blessing is pronounced over the cherished grain for bread. This is followed with another blessing spoken over a bitter vegetable (like horseradish), symbolizing the cruel bitterness of slavery. However, the bitterness is taken with a mixed paste of apples, nuts, cinnamon and wine, to remind Israel of the building cement they had to use in Egypt in building Pharaoh's kingdom. More bread is consumed with the paste mixture and then the meal is respectfully eaten. Prayers of thanksgiving are offered, and further blessings are made with the singing of psalms. The benediction is made with hope for future blessings in the land of promise.[62]

It is important to note that the commemoration of the Passover event has developed significantly since the first Passover detailed in Exodus 12–13. The commentary here reflects the pre-Deuteronomic emphasis where the sacrifices were attended to in a domestic context. With the centralization of the sacrificial system reflected in Deuteronomy 16.2–3, 5–7, the Passover becomes a pilgrimage with community observances. Rituals become more symbolic, and the lamb sacrifice must be done at the temple.

> You must not sacrifice the Passover in any town the LORD your God gives you except in the place he will choose as a dwelling for his Name. There you must sacrifice the Passover in the evening, when the sun goes down, on the anniversary of your departure from Egypt. Roast it and eat it at the

---

62 Cf. C.E. Armerding, 'Festivals and Feasts', *DOTP*, pp. 300–313 for further details. Cf. B. Bokser, *The Origins of the Seder* (Berkeley: University of California Press, 1984).

place the LORD your God will choose. Then in the morning return to your tents. For six days eat unleavened bread and on the seventh day hold an assembly to the LORD your God and do no work. (Deut. 16.5–7)[63]

Although the Passover feast is focused on the exodus deliverance events, the timing of the celebration in spring also combines the festivities to the Lord's blessing on the land. The rains bring the required resources to fructify the land and initiate the agricultural season. Israel finds ample reason to celebrate not only the Passover events but also the Lord's provision and sustaining grace. The Passover celebrated by the community with Joshua in the promised land was a significant milestone marking the end of their forty-year wilderness trial.

On the evening of the fourteenth day of the month, while camped at Gilgal on the plains of Jericho, the Israelites celebrated the Passover. The day after the Passover, that very day, they ate some of the produce of the land: unleavened bread and roasted grain. The manna stopped the day after they ate this food from the land; there was no longer any manna for the Israelites, but that year they ate the produce of Canaan. (Josh. 5.10–12)

9.6–13—Passover for the Unclean

A question concerning the Passover arises regarding a case of defilement. This text provides an example of how Moses communicates with Yahweh on behalf of the people. Moses receives the law and legislative instruction on Mount Sinai, but as life in the community develops, there are always situations which require consideration, interpretation, and guidance. Here the question is posed concerning individuals who encounter or contact a corpse. This situation is probably quite common, and results in 'defilement' (טמא), a state of contamination which restricts participation in the Passover.

The weight of the law which calls for segregation proved to be heavy for those who desire to observe the day along with the community. They are not allowed to bring offerings and must remain at a respectable distance, observing the rules of defilement. Moses takes the dilemma to Yahweh and is instructed that for situations of contamination or travel which keep men from their community at the Passover time, they are permitted to observe the same arrangements as instructed. Allowances are made for those who desired to observe and celebrate, but at a different time—one month later. Additionally, a strict rule is

---

63   Cf. B.A. Levine, 'Leviticus in the Ongoing Jewish Tradition', in *Leviticus. The JPS Torah Commentary* (Philadelphia: The Jewish Publication Society, 1989), pp. 215–238.

imposed for those who fail to observe the Passover. By rejecting the important covenantal provision, they face the serious penalty of being 'cut off' (כרת) from the people and are made responsible for their own sin. The law of the *'karet'* is a very serious consequence relegating a person to life outside of the community. This is a notable form of 'excommunication' which is referenced several times in Numbers (cf. Num. 15.30–31; 19.13, 20).

9.14—*Passover for Foreigners*

In Exodus 12 where the Passover instructions are recorded there are also restrictions presented for some people who left Egypt with the Israelites (Exod. 12.38). Details regarding who these people are, is not clear, but they may have included other Semitic people groups and slaves who were also oppressed by the Egyptians. For those who are considered foreigners to Israel or slaves, they are not permitted to eat the Passover meal unless all the males in the respective household are circumcised. The meal had to be eaten inside the house and no bones could be broken in the lamb. Otherwise, they are included in the festivities and are only to abide by the same regulations as are the Israelites.

9.15-23—*The Guidance and Presence of the Lord*

With the Passover celebration falling on the same day as the completion of the Tabernacle, the text turns to the presence of the Lord. The divine presence is indicated by the 'cloud' (ענן) which is focalized by eleven references in eight verses.[64] Moreover, this passage affirms that it is Yahweh who guides Israel through the wilderness by his seven-fold commands (Num. 9.18, 20, 23). The other emphases in these few verses are in regard the divine presence over the Tabernacle (referred to 7 times) and the Tent of Testimony or Meeting (אהל העדת). The text verifies that no one moves until Yahweh signals the timing for departure. No person, priest, or prophet determines the timing for travel—it is Yahweh. Departures, rests, and camp sites are determined by the movement of cloud and fire. Periods of rest and camp could last for days, weeks, months or even years! Whatever the length of time, the people are to be in total obedience to rest or journey following the movement of cloud or fire. This text reiterates the basic content of Exodus 40 but features the presence of Yahweh in the cloud (ענן) and fire (אש) over the Tabernacle. Several texts from the period of Israel's wilderness wanderings merge the cloud and the pillar motifs. How-

---

64 The cloud is referenced 20 times in Numbers with 51 occurrences in the Pentateuch. Numbers 9–10 provides the 'densest cloud concentration' indicators in the whole OT with 14 mentions. Cf. D.N. Freedman, 'עָנָן', *TDOT*, XII, pp. 253–254.

ever, the main concern of these texts is to feature the cloud and the pillar of cloud as the location of Yahweh's presence to lead, speak, or act. The pillar or the cloud plays a role in each special revelation of Yahweh.[65] In addition to the guidance motif, the cloud is also evident in a variety of contexts which may include divine action and even judgment (cf. Numbers 11; 12).

The main role of the cloud and the pillar (עמוד) is for guidance and protection.[66] This is the dominant theme in Exod. 13.17–14.31 when Israel embarks on their journey from Egypt. 'By day the LORD went ahead of them in a pillar of cloud to guide them on their way and by night in a pillar of fire to give them light, so that they could travel by day or night. Neither the pillar of cloud by day nor the pillar of fire by night left its place in front of the people'. It is not surprising, considering the threatening conditions, that God gives a visible beacon for the people to see while on their journey (cf. Exod. 40.38). In Exod. 14.20, the same pillar of cloud moves behind the camp of Israel, before the crossing of the Reed Sea, in order to protect and conceal them from the Egyptian army. From the cloud, Yahweh 'looked down' on the enemy and threw them into a panic and confusion (Exod. 14.24).

Through the cloud, the glory and presence of Yahweh are revealed. When the Tabernacle is completed 'the cloud covered the Tent of Meeting, and the glory of the LORD filled the Tabernacle' (Exod. 40.34ff.). Yahweh showed his acceptance by covering the Tent of Meeting with a 'glory cloud' indicating his presence filling the tabernacle. The presence of Yahweh is so intense that Moses could not enter the Tent of Meeting. The 'glory cloud' (כבוד) is referred to 24 times in the Pentateuch. In reference to Yahweh's glory it is usually in connection with his appearance in the Tabernacle and by his all-consuming fire surrounded by a cloud (Exod. 24.17; Lev. 9.6, 23).[67]

The cloud and fire in Num. 9.15–23 appears to be the same referent as the 'pillar of cloud and pillar of fire' in the Exodus accounts.[68] However, in Num.

---

65 In addition to these symbols, the angel of the LORD is also at work in connection with the pillar of cloud. In Exod. 14.19, the angel of the LORD moves with the pillar to protect Israel. 'Then the angel of God, who had been traveling in front of Israel's army, withdrew and went behind them. The pillar of cloud also moved from in front and stood behind them, coming between the armies of Egypt and Israel'.

66 The pillar of cloud and pillar of fire must have been a spectacular sight for Israel and this phrase is perhaps the best way to communicate the 'theophanic concept' which described Yahweh's glorious presence. Cf. D.N. Freedman, 'עמוד', *TDOT*, XI, p. 187.

67 M. Weinfeld, 'כבוד', *TDOT*, VII, p. 27; cf. pp. 22–38.

68 In Num. 11.25 the Spirit of God and the cloud function together when Yahweh shared the Spirit that was on Moses with the seventy elders. 'Then the LORD came down in the cloud and spoke with him, and he took of the Spirit that was on him and put the Spirit on the

14.14, Moses describes how the Lord reveals himself to Israel, similar to how he appears at the Tabernacle incident with Moses, Miriam and Aaron (cf. Num. 12.5; Num. 14.14—pillar, cloud, fire). The JPS makes this clear: 'You, O LORD, appear in plain sight when Your cloud rests over them and when You go before them in a pillar of cloud by day and in a pillar of fire by night' (Num. 14.14). The theme of guidance is emphasized in Numbers as Israel prepares for their pilgrimage to the promised land. In Numbers 10 they are ready for battle, unified, disciplined, and obedient with Yahweh in their midst, symbolized by the cloud. The cloud not only leads the people during the day and night, but it also regulates their times of travel and times of rest (Num. 9.15–23). In addition to the guidance theme, the movement of the cloud and its presence over the Tabernacle is to replicate Israel's experience at Mount Sinai where the presence of the Lord in theophany is visible. The cloud over the Tabernacle affirms his presence but also conveys a similar degree of segregated access. The summit represents the inner sanctum and Holy of Holies where only Moses and the high priest are permitted entry. The mid-point of the mountain is like the outer court which is sanctified for the priest's ministry and the base of the mountain represents the outer court that is the boundary for the people (cf. Exod. 19.12–25).[69]

At the Tabernacle the goal and symbol of God's redemptive work, the worship of God, is achieved. The presence of God now rests on his earthly dwelling. The symbols of Yahweh's presence are transferred to the Tabernacle (cf. Num. 9.22), and the people are prepared for their journey.

10.1–36—Moving Forward to a Promised Land

After a year of preparation and work in the shadow of Mount Sinai, the Israelites are deemed ready for their wilderness trek to the land Yahweh prepared for them to inhabit. Finally, the journey is set to begin, and the remaining arrangements are set in place.

10.1–7—Trumpet Signals and Departure
Specific instructions are given to Moses for the crafting of two trumpets made out of silver. These are to be differentiated from the *shofar* which is made from a ram's horn. Typically, the signal from the horn rallies the military forces and

---

seventy elders. When the Spirit rested on them, they prophesied, but they did not do so again'. In this text, God visibly manifested the divine presence to the people and moved upon the elders, who manifested their reception of the Spirit by prophesying.

69   Cf. Sarna, *Exodus*, p. 105.

at times is deployed in battle to strike fear into the hearts of enemy armies (a type of psychological warfare). Later in Israel's monarchy the horn is also used in coronation ceremonies. Here in Numbers 10 the purpose of the trumpet sounds is to signal a number of actions required by Yahweh. Instructions for the crafting of the trumpets appears at the beginning of the chapter, signaling those events leading to Israel's departure are ramping up.

The trumpets are to be fashioned with hammered silver work (similar to the fabricating of the golden *menorahs*). In the book of Exodus, the sound of trumpets is heard at Mount Sinai as part of the theophanic appearance of God. The incredible trumpet sounds are amplified as the first sound of the trumpet is heard along with thunder. The trumpet blast in the morning strikes fear into the hearts of the whole community (Exod. 19.16–19).

Several purposes are given for the use of the two trumpets. The first signal is to summon the whole congregation to the Tent of Meeting when both trumpets are blown together. The amplified sound is required to reach all parts of the camp to alert the vast group of people for the gathering. When only the heads of clans are summoned, one trumpet is used for the signal. Another audible blast signified an alarm that is meant for those people who are camped on the east side of the Tabernacle. A second audible blast indicates the alarm for those people who are camped on the south side. These signals, short or long blasts, stress that immediate action must be taken to muster people for action.

10.8–10—*Priestly Privilege*

Further instructions indicate that only the sons of Aaron are qualified to blow the trumpets. This is a special legislated duty for the priests, and they must use the trumpet functions for two key purposes. The first has to do with sounding the battle alarm. Israel is going to war against adversaries and the use of the alarm signals their need for help from the Lord. The sound is also meant to strike fear into the hearts of the enemy. Yahweh would then 'remember' his people and act on their behalf. The secondary use of the trumpets is for use in the cultic context. The trumpet sound announces community gatherings for appointed festivals, feast days and the beginning of each calendar month. The priests use the trumpets when sacrifices are performed on behalf of the congregation—for burnt and peace offerings. The sacrifices and trumpet sounds are meant to remind Israel that Yahweh is their sovereign God—a covenantal reminder and affirmation that, 'I am the LORD your God'.

10.11–28—*Preparing for Departure from Mount Sinai*

All of the preparations for the trek to the land of promise are now set in place and it is time for Israel to move. The section from Numbers 10.11–12.16 is the record of the initial trek from Mount Sinai into the wilderness of Paran. The wilderness is a vast area and Israel must make a number of stops before reaching 'Paran' (cf. Num. 12.16).

The main signal for the departure is the cloud ascending from over the Tabernacle of the Testimony (cf. Num. 1.50–53; 17.4–10; 18.2). The visible symbol of the Tabernacle with the ark containing the covenantal documents serves to provide confidence in the forward movement of the people at Yahweh's leading. The term for 'testimony' (עדות) is used 12 times in Numbers (1.50–53; 4.5; 7.89; 9.15; 17.4–10; 18.2). The root word signifies 'witness or attestation' (עוד) in the sense of a symbolic record of an agreement or covenantal commitment. The 'Tabernacle of the Testimony' points to the ark where the written document of the covenant was kept as a visible reminder of Israel's covenant with Yahweh (Num. 4.5; 7.89).[70] Additionally, Moses gives the signal for the camp removal when he discerns the Lord's motion. Then the vast group of people rose to follow the cloud and the Tabernacle to new destinations and places of rest. It may be assumed that the trumpets sounded the appropriate signal for departure (Num. 10.1–7).

The order of deployment occurs as revealed in preceding chapters. Here another detailed listing of tribal leaders is repeated (cf. Num. 1.4–16; 2.1–32; 7.10–83). Their period of training, learning, and building is now over and the new phase for the orderly planned pilgrimage has begun. Once the journey is initiated the tribes move forward in what would have been a formidable procession of divisions in a single, massive column of humanity. Leading the contingent of people are the sons of Judah, with Nahshon the son of Amminadab, over its army. Also, Nethanel the son of Zuar, over the tribal army of the sons of Issachar, and Eliab the son of Helon over the tribal army of the sons of Zebulun.

As instructed, the Tabernacle is taken down and the prescribed materials are moved by the sons of Gershon and the sons of Merari. Along with the Levites are those in the camp of Reuben led by Elizur the son of Shedeur, over its army. Also, Shelumiel the son of Zurishaddai over the tribal army of the sons of Simeon, and lastly in this formation, Eliasaph the son of Deuel with the tribal army of the sons of Gad. Behind this group come the Kohathites, carrying the most sacred, holy cultic articles. They follow the group so that the Tabernacle could be set up at the next camp location and be ready for the direct installation of the sacred furnishings upon their arrival.

---

70 Cf. Simian-Yofre, 'עדות', x, pp. 497, 512.

Following this group are the sons of Ephraim, with Elishama the son of Ammihud over its army, Gamaliel the son of Pedahzur over the tribal army of the sons of Manasseh, and lastly in this group, Abidan the son of Gideoni over the tribal army of the sons of Benjamin. Finally in the rear guard come the sons of Dan, with Ahiezer the son of Ammishaddai over its army, Pagiel the son of Ochran over the tribal army of the sons of Asher, and Ahira the son of Enan over the tribal army of the sons of Naphtali.

In accordance with all the instructions given to Moses by Yahweh, the orderly, disciplined preparations for the journeys ahead are implemented. The people of Yahweh are obedient and ready for their trek!

10.29–32—Guidance on the Journey

One of the core themes which runs through Numbers 9–10 is the motif of guidance. Up to this point in the documentation the people are generally positive and cooperative after their escape from Egypt. However, the future trip to an undisclosed 'promised land' is no doubt a venture that brings a variety of perspectives to the Israelites. Of fundamental importance for a successful pilgrimage is confidence in the travel itinerary and perhaps more importantly, confidence in the guide for the expedition. They need a shepherd to lead the community—as Moses eloquently implores in Num. 27.15–16. "Moses said to the Lord, 'May the Lord, the God who gives breath to all living things, appoint someone over this community to go out and come in before them, one who will lead them out and bring them in, so the Lord's people will not be like sheep without a shepherd'". Israel needs a shepherd to lead them through the valleys, wilderness, and mountainous regions to their destination.

Several guidance measures are put in place to provide a stable, consistent system of direction for Israel. Trumpets are used to signal alarms, instructions and celebratory sounds with notes that have meaning (Num. 10.1–10). The glory cloud of the Lord is a stable presence for all the Israelites to see and follow when in motion. The presence and glory of the Lord symbolizes his divine kingship in the nation—he rules from the centralized Tabernacle in their midst (Num. 9.15–23). The prophet Moses provides prophetic leadership that mediates Yahweh's instruction and indicates when the migration is to begin. Moses would literally lead them out and bring them in, until they reach each destination. Furthermore, Moses requests an additional helper to be on the migration team in the person of Hobab who is stated to be the son of Reuel the Midianite, Moses' father-in-law.[71]

---

71 The specific identity of Hobab is disputed due to the claim that Moses' father-in-law is

Finally, in the chapter, the ark of the covenant is involved in the leading of the nation, again symbolic for the presence of the divine king (Num. 10.33–36). The 'ark of the covenant of the LORD' leads the way for three days to escort the people to their place of rest. This is the first reference to the term 'covenant' (ברית) in Numbers although the 'ark of the testimony' (עדות) is mentioned twelve times in Numbers (1.50–53; 4.5; 7.89; 9.15; 17.4–10; 18.2). In these references, the testimony is a parallel term for the covenant which serves as a visible reminder to Israel of their commitments made by oath to serve, obey and follow the Lord. The covenant is a commitment confirmed by an oath which has binding validity for the partner (cf. Gen. 26.28; Exod. 19.8; Deut. 29.9 ff.) The term 'covenant' (ברית) appears 79 times in the Pentateuch, predominately in Genesis (26 times) and Deuteronomy (26 times). In Numbers 10.33; 14.44; 18.19; 25.12–13, the covenant is referenced in unique ways. The term for 'testimony' (עדות) in its root form signifies 'witness or attestation' (עוד) in the sense of a symbolic record of an agreement or covenantal commitment.[72] As the ark moves forward, the nation confidently follows Yahweh to the place that is promised on oath to be their habitation.

In the Exodus accounts, Reuel is the father of seven daughters and is called a priest of Midian. He seems to be an individual of stature within the community, an owner of animal flocks and someone with religious duties. In fact, the name Reuel means a 'friend of God' (Exod. 2.18). He becomes Moses' father-in-law upon his marriage to Zipporah. The naming of his firstborn son Gershom (meaning 'I have become an alien in a foreign land') signifies Moses' status as a foreigner from his people back in Egypt (Exod. 2.22). The next episode with Moses' father-in-law refers to him as Jethro, who gives Moses leave for his mission to Egypt (Exod. 4.18–20). At some point, Jethro journeys to Mount Sinai where Israel is camped in order to return Zipporah and sons to Moses. Apparently, Zipporah had returned to her father's home after the incident of circumcision described in Exod. 4.24–26.

During their reunion described in Exodus 18, Moses apprises Jethro of all the good things that Yahweh has done for Israel in rescuing them from their oppressors in Egypt. Jethro, priest of Midian makes a tremendous statement of faith, saying 'Praise be to the LORD, who rescued you from the hand of the Egyptians and of Pharaoh, and who rescued the people from the hand of the Egyptians' (Exod. 18.10). Not only does Jethro acknowledge that Yahweh is greater than all

---

named Reuel (Exod. 2.18) and Jethro (Exodus 18). Cf. Milgrom, *Numbers*, p. 78 for various considerations. It appears probable that Hobab was the brother to Moses' wife and someone that Moses knew well from his time spent in Midian.

72 Cf. Weinfeld, 'ברית', pp. 256–257.

other gods, but he then administers a burnt offering and other sacrifices to Elohim. It is a sacrificial communion meal with Moses, Aaron, and all the elders of Israel in the presence of God. The second important element in the narrative presents Jethro as a wise advisor. He witnesses the tremendous judicial role of Moses in providing legislative instruction for the people and makes this recommendation.

> You must be the people's representative before God and bring their disputes to him. Teach them his decrees and instructions and show them the way they are to live and how they are to behave. But select capable men from all the people—men who fear God, trustworthy men who hate dishonest gain—and appoint them as officials over thousands, hundreds, fifties and tens. Have them serve as judges for the people at all times but have them bring every difficult case to you; the simple cases they can decide themselves. That will make your load lighter because they will share it with you. If you do this and God so commands, you will be able to stand the strain, and all these people will go home satisfied. (Exod. 18.20–23)

The priest of Midian is a man of great wisdom, character, and leadership whom Moses respects. Jethro's advice is followed and implemented. However, after this incident, Jethro is sent home by Moses (Exod. 18.27). It appears that Hobab remains with the Israelites after Jethro's departure. At this interval when Israel is ready to begin their journey, Moses appeals to Hobab to trek with the nation and serve as an additional guide to the promised land. Moses entreats Hobab with a two-fold promise to treat him well with the blessings the Lord pledged to Israel.[73] The main reason for the entreaty is Hobab's knowledge of the wilderness. 'Please do not leave us. You know where we should camp in the wilderness, and you can be our eyes'. Although Moses indicates full confidence that Yahweh is now prepared to take the nation to the land of promise and that the Lord's purposes for them are good, it appears that he also relies on the human helper. It seems strange that with all the faith Moses has in Yahweh's leading, and with his own wilderness experiences of forty years, that he still appeals to Hobab to serve as a tour guide in the wilderness!

Here is another instance where the human element in Moses' leadership is recorded and appears to be an incident where he lacks faith. Several exam-

---

73   It appears from Judg. 1.16 that the descendants of Moses' father-in-law did travel with the Israelites and were given a place to live as promised.

ples could be cited in Genesis of Abraham and the patriarch's similar failings in managing challenges with cultural remedies. Alternatively, Moses indicates his prowess in adding an advisor to help with the wilderness trek. It also illustrates family and cultural respect for his father-in-law's family. There appears to be many cultural affinities behind Moses' request and promise to sharing God's blessings with relatives. Even with Moses' forty years of experience in the wilderness, he wants to ensure that all the assistance that may be needed is available to the nation. Moses shows that he cherishes Hobab's abilities and solicits his help in a gracious and dignified manner. This is another example of how some in Israel receive foreigners into their midst and treat them as equals—even to the extent of providing land inheritance in the promised land (also in the case of Caleb, Numbers 14), and blessings for Hobab.

10.33–36—The Ark of the Covenant

In the inner sanctum of the Tabernacle is the ark of the covenant law which is the most sacred area and place of communication between Moses and Yahweh. Instructions for the construction of the 'chest' are given in Exodus 25 stipulating an ark made from acacia wood. The ark is almost four feet long and two and half feet wide. The wood is overlain with gold on the inside and outside with additional gold moulding around the edges. For transportation the directives are clear. 'Cast four gold rings for it and fasten them to its four feet, with two rings on one side and two rings on the other. Then make poles of acacia wood and overlay them with gold. Insert the poles into the rings on the sides of the ark to carry it. The poles are to remain in the rings of this ark; they are not to be removed' (Exod. 25.12–15). Inside the 'ark' (ארון) is the sacred Torah 'covenant' (ברית) with the cover of the gold plate (כפרת)—the 'mercy-seat' or place of atonement. On the gold cover are two gold cherubim with wings spread upward at each end. It is between the two cherubim that are over the ark of the covenant law, where Moses receives Yahweh's commands for Israel (he hears the divine voice).

The 'ark of the covenant of the LORD' contained the tablets of the commandments and perhaps some of the laws of the covenant as they were added (cf. Num. 1.50–53; 4.5; 7.89). The book of the covenant (Exod. 20.22–23.19) was part of the developing corpus of legislation attributed to Moses and may have also been deposited in the ark for protection.

Upon receiving the signals for moving the Israelite camp, the processional sets forth with the ark of the covenant leading the way, and the cloud overhead. The initial trek is a three-day journey from Mount Sinai on their way to places of rest. The ark of the covenant, the cloud of the presence, and the command of Moses converge to signal the departure from the camp and forward march of the people (and presumably the trumpet sound).

Moses' rallying cry calls upon Yahweh to lead into battle. 'Rise up, LORD! May your enemies be scattered; may your foes flee before you'. Whenever it came to rest, he said, 'Return, LORD, to the countless thousands of Israel'.[74] This poem is probably used when Israel is involved in a holy war and calls upon the Lord to fight on behalf of the nation (cf. Num. 14.44; Josh. 3.4–6; 6.6–7). In Israel's exodus tradition the people discover the power of Yahweh as a warrior through the religious conflict with Egypt and composes this song. 'I will sing to the LORD, for he is highly exalted. Both horse and driver he has hurled into the sea. The LORD is my strength and my defense; he has become my salvation. He is my God, and I will praise him, my father's God, and I will exalt him. The LORD is a warrior; the LORD is his name' (Exod. 15.1–3). The battle cry in the context of the ark leading out and coming to rest, affirms the symbolic presence of the Lord as king on his throne. It serves to not only muster the community but to exhort and encourage the people to confidently move forward with Yahweh leading the way.

Reflection and Response
Numbers 9–10: Shepherds for the Wilderness Itinerary
Reflection

Life on earth has always been fraught with challenges, danger, and limited knowledge about creation, environment, weather and how things in the world function. Adam and Eve discovered this in Eden as they were set in a garden and learned to 'cultivate' the soil for produce as well as 'cultivating' their spiritual lives. They were filled with curiosity and were able to learn from God in the cool of the garden about the world and their commission to procreate and exercise dominion over the animal world and their 'paradise'.

In a similar way, Israel is set to embark into an unknown world. They completed a year of life with purpose at Mount Sinai but are now poised for something totally new—a trek to a promised land that they know nothing about. Their preparations are concluded, and Moses has them ready to follow the Lord's cloud as they did when they left Egypt. Life is exciting and adventure is in the air.

These chapters present spectacular modes of guidance and direction for Israel as the nation embarks on their epic journey to the promised land. Of course, the main guide for the sojourn is the divine shepherd who superintends

---

74 The poetic battle cry at the end of the chapter signals the forward movement of Israel. In the MT this poem is book-ended by two inverted nuns which may signify the ancient nature of the invocation (cf. Levine, *Numbers 1–20*, p. 318; for rabbinic views cf. Milgrom, *Numbers*, p. 375–376).

the nation's itinerary for the expedition from Egypt into the wilderness regions of the Sinai Desert. The clear and visible forms of leading the nation are supernatural because the nature of their journey is dangerous and demanding. With so many people in the caravan, the tangible presence of the Lord is there to encourage the people's confidence and compliance. It may be surmised from the narratives depicting Israel's exodus journey, that the Lord provides the guidance that is required for the expedition at hand. For Israel, the promised land is a destination that the nation dreamed about for a long time. However, for the dream to be realized with the acquisition of land, the trek required immense effort and divine assistance. The Lord who initiated their journey had to be trusted to bring them to their final destination.

In the early days of Israel's encounters with Yahweh the nation is dependent on God's revelation. This occurs in unique ways due to the limitation of stories and developing prophetic record, and limited Torah records. They had the angel of the Lord and the cloud of fire. The verification of God's presence in the camp is so evident in the passage with numerous cloud references and compliance to divine direction. This is not a mirage. The Lord is among his people in a visible cloud. Moreover, the presence of Yahweh over the Tabernacle and in the journey provides the nation with a strong sense of security and protection. The implication of this strong sense of God's presence in the midst of the people causes amazing unity and response from the people. No person, priest or prophet determines the timing for travel—it is Yahweh. Departures, rests, and camp sites are determined by the movement of cloud and fire.

In short, the book of Numbers asserts that the nation has all the resources they require to know they are headed in the right direction. This is emphasized in the positive tone of chapters 1–10 where the prophet and the priest work in tandem to prepare for departure with an organized contingent of leaders. Moses gives strong prophetic leadership that effectively mediates and implements Yahweh's instructions. The divine shepherd and the prophetic shepherd work together to lead the people forward to their destination. Prophetic direction, trumpet sounds, the glory cloud, the tribal leaders, the ark of the covenant and a human guide with knowledge of the wilderness topography—all melded together to instill confidence in the journey's forward direction.

Response

Although Moses has several support systems in place for the journey to the promised land, it is evident that he is very concerned about the details for the trek. He does not have a map. He needs divine guidance for the journey, and he makes it clear to the Lord that he would not depart on an expedition without the divine presence. 'If your Presence does not go with us, do not send us up from here. How will anyone know that you are pleased with me and with your people unless you go with us? What else will distinguish me and your people from all the other people on the face of the earth? (Exod. 33.15–16)'. Israel's journey to their inheritance offers many lessons for communities of faith who are led forward to accomplish spiritual and ministry ventures with the Lord.

There are also personal ventures in faith to realize God's purposes. How does a believer navigate the daily challenges of life? How do we accomplish and realize the goals that we believe the Lord has set before us—in the short and the long term? Does God still provide visible guidance and confirmations along the way? Will God shine a light to indicate the path we are to take? How do we prepare for difficult transitions in life? Although we should not expect a visible cloud or a pillar of fire to lead us around, the Lord prefers to be present with his people in genuine relational ways. With the prophetic word available to believers, there is no excuse for not understanding what the will of God for our lives is. He provides direction through the principles, instructions and examples as noted by the apostle Paul in his exhortation.

> For I do not want you to be ignorant of the fact, brothers and sisters, that our ancestors were all under the cloud and that they all passed through the sea. They were all baptized into Moses in the cloud and in the sea. They all ate the same spiritual food and drank the same spiritual drink; for they drank from the spiritual rock that accompanied them, and that rock was Christ. Nevertheless, God was not pleased with most of them; their bodies were scattered in the wilderness. Now these things occurred as examples to keep us from setting our hearts on evil things as they did. (1 Cor. 10.1–6)

Furthermore, we have leaders, community, the Spirit of God who inspires, calls, guides, and provides as is evident in the Acts of the Early Church narratives. Signs and wonders continue to be experienced by those who fervently desire to follow the Lord according to his plan and purpose, along with authentic confirmations. When the internal nudging of the Spirit is clear and the discernment sensed is confirmed, we must count the cost, prepare effectively with the leaders and community, trust the direction, and then embark.

11.1–25.18—Hardships, Conflicts, Rebellion and Judgment

11.1–35—Prophetic Leadership

The first ten chapters of Numbers focus on the preparations that are necessary for Israel's next phase in their journey. These introductory chapters with records of leaders, responsibilities, offerings, and legislative materials are largely positive, providing a solid foundation for the nation's future aspirations. They provide insight into the administrative structure and leadership preparations in the nation for the epic transition to the land of promise. The people are prepared for their trek from Mount Sinai in an orderly and impressive formation.

At the end of Numbers Ten, a formidable force of people with their hearts set on a journey to the place pledged by Yahweh are assembled. The patriarchal promises are foundational to their dream and the Sinaitic covenant verifies their trust that Yahweh would lead them there. With the Tabernacle and ark in their midst, trained leaders in the ranks, the cloud of presence and Moses leading the way, the journey seems to be on a very positive course. However, the chapter begins and ends with concerns about food resources for the massive group of migrants. Furthermore, several conflicts develop that have implications for Moses' leadership. The people not only call into question his ability to manage the daily burden of the people's essential needs, but they question whether they want to move forward with Moses.

For this challenge of relocating a nation from one country to another, Moses requires the miraculous intervention of Yahweh as well as human leadership assistance. For so many people to reach the covenant land promised by Yahweh, an immense quantity of resources and stamina must be realized. The challenges involved for leaders will be the subject matter of several chapters in Numbers beginning with chapter 11, which features the task of leadership, a primary theme in the book. Leadership of the nation is a focal part in the book beginning with organizational matters (Numbers 1–10). Leadership continues to be the essential motif during the whole course of the journey. At the end of Moses' life as a prophetic leader, his primary concern is for the right successor to take his place.[1]

---

[1] Moses' concern is justified and reflects his desire for the nation's well-being: 'May the LORD,

11.1–25.18—HARDSHIPS, CONFLICTS, REBELLION AND JUDGMENT

After a largely positive experience for Israel leading up to chapter 11, these events vividly present the immense challenges faced in the wilderness. Chapter 11 records the first of several serious complaints that are voiced by various people, mainly against the leadership abilities of Moses (cf. Num. 12.1–2; 14.1–4; 17.6–7; 20.2–3; 21.5).[2] The text fluctuates between food issues (Num. 11.4–13, 18–20, 31–34) and leadership matters (Num. 11.16–17, 24–30, 12.1–15) which feature crucial principles for the community in the wilderness and for Israel's future development.[3] Furthermore, there are blended resolutions to the issues through the provisions of God and the work of Moses. This includes several dramatic acts of judgment and correction meted out by Yahweh. The departure from Egypt and pilgrimage to the promised land calls for a disposition of faith, trust, and cooperation. Yet, Israel characteristically is dismayed by the unanticipated hardships and reacts negatively. In Numbers eleven there are two basic but recurring challenges of life in the wilderness, namely, how will the nation's physical needs be cared for and who will adjudicate the domestic issues that arise?[4]

11.1–3—The Complaint

The positive tone of Numbers 1–10 suddenly changes in chapter 11 with the distinctive complaining of the people which begins soon after the exodus events (cf. Exod. 14.10–12; 16.1–3). No doubt the wilderness deprivations are demanding but Yahweh's deliverance and covenant provisions with promises of care are being realized. Now the pent-up aggravations of the 'hardships' in the wilderness begin to spill over and are vocalized by the people. The occasion brings about the wrath of the Lord who hears their grumbling and becomes 'incensed with anger' (חרה).[5] Immediate judgment is delivered by Yahweh who causes

---

the God who gives breath to all living things, appoint someone over this community to go out and come in before them, one who will lead them out and bring them in, so the LORD's people will not be like sheep without a shepherd' (Num. 27.16–17).

2 Milgrom, *Numbers*, p. 82.
3 Ashley, *Numbers*, pp. 206–207.
4 This chapter is also addressed in the *Festschrift* for R.J. Stronstad. Cf. W. Hildebrandt, 'Man Shall Not Live on Bread Alone: The Burden of Prophetic Leadership in Numbers 11', in R.P. Tuppurainen (ed). *Reading St. Luke's Text and Theology: Pentecostal Voices Essays in Honor of Professor Roger Stronstad* (Pickwick Publications: Eugene, OR: 2019), pp. 197–208.
5 The expression of the LORD's anger is very intense with several words to emphasize his 'burning wrath'. The verb used to express the LORD's 'anger' (חרה) occurs 33 times in the Pentateuch, mainly in narratives. In Numbers the anger of the LORD is 'kindled' 8 times, with 3 occurrences in ch. 11 (Num. 11.1, 10, 33). Divine anger is caused by Israel's wrong behaviour and rebellion as well as with some of Moses' actions (cf. Exod. 4.14). But his main source

fire to strike the outskirts of Israel's 'camp' (מחנה). The location of the judgment and fiery outbreak becomes a reminder of the incident and is named a place of 'burning' (*Taberah*; תבערה). The swift divine reaction comes as a response to the people's complaints early in their journey as an important lesson.

Just as the people cry out for deliverance from Egypt and are heard by God (Exod. 2.23–25), so here, they cry out to Moses for help and protection (Num. 11.2). This is a vivid and dramatic episode which depicts some of the typical flaws in human nature. The initial complaints and judgment will soon be forgotten, but another episode of grumbling will begin. However, Moses responds to the people's cries and appeals to the Lord on their behalf. His prophetic response of intercession results in the quenching of the fire by the Lord.

11.4–9—*The Provisions*

In a second instance of discontent, a group of instigators are referred to as the 'rabble' (אספסף)—a term used only once in the OT. The apparent derogatory term refers to a mixed multitude of foreigners who determine to exit Egypt and attach themselves to the Israelites for the exodus from Ramses to Sukkoth (Exod. 12.38).[6] Ostensibly, these foreigners prefer to align themselves with the Israelites rather than remain in Egypt under precarious circumstances. Moreover, the Israelites do not seem to have an issue with the people and in due course the nation's legislation would formulate laws for their well-being and protection.

In this episode the issue involves cravings for food variation, but the people's complaints are vocalized in wailing. The clamour intensifies as the people lament the loss of their Egyptian menu and coveted fish, cucumbers, melons, leeks, onions, and garlic (Num. 11.4–6). They quickly tire of the daily 'manna' (מן) provisions even though manna appeared to be tasty, nutritious, and easy to prepare for a nomadic situation (Num. 11.7–9). It is like coriander seed but when

---

of anger pertains to the people who commit idolatry (Exod. 32.10–19) and fail to move forward in faith (Numbers 13–14; cf. Num. 32.10–13). In the golden calf episode and in the nation's refusal to enter Canaan, the Lord threatens to consume or destroy the people, but Moses' intercession brings about a resolution. In fact, Moses reminds Yahweh that: 'The LORD is slow to anger, abounding in love and forgiving sin and rebellion' (Num. 14.18a). Cf. D.N. Freedman, J.R. Lundbom, 'חרה', *TDOT*, V, pp. 173–175.

6 This theme of foreigners attaching themselves to Israel is frequently attested in the OT. Even though unusual terms are often used like the 'rabble' or a mixed multitude, aliens and foreigners, they often make positive contributions. They are the 'foreigner or stranger' (גר) among the Israelites but are often named and valued in the nation (i.e., Hobab, Jethro, Zipporah, a Cushite wife, Caleb, etc.).

prepared is like bread which 'tastes like wafers made with honey' (cf. Exod. 16.31–32). The consistent faithfulness of Yahweh provides the manna which is to be gathered daily, crushed, cooked, and made into loaves for consumption. Understandably, the same diet each day becomes tedious, but this episode so early in their journey indicates a profound rejection of Yahweh's sustaining provisions. The people desire 'meat' (בשר) to 'eat' (אכל).[7] Similar to a funeral dirge the people voice their anguish by wailing at their tents.

11.10–15—Moses Protests

Upon hearing the wailing of 'every family at the entrance of their tents', Yahweh becomes intensely 'angry' (חרה), and Moses becomes troubled. On most occasions of conflict, Moses is usually quick to intercede on behalf of the people (Num. 11.2; cf. Exod. 17; 32.11–14), but the compounding of daily issues to deal with, takes its toll. Moses launches into a blunt and aggressive lament: 'Why have you brought this trouble on your servant? What have I done to displease you that you put the burden of all these people on me? Did I conceive all these people? Did I give them birth? Why do you tell me to carry them in my arms, as a nurse carries an infant, to the land you promised on oath to their ancestors? Where can I get meat for all these people? They keep wailing to me, 'Give us meat to eat!' I cannot carry all these people by myself; the burden is too heavy for me. If this is how you are going to treat me, please go ahead and kill me— if I have found favor in your eyes—and do not let me face my own ruin' (Num. 11.11–15).

Moses' queries include several legitimate observations. As the servant of Yahweh with a calling, the task includes 'trouble' as well as the 'burden' (משא). In Num. 4.15–49 the burden terminology (9 times) is used specifically for the Levitical duties connected with the Tabernacle. Now, Israel is the 'burden', and caring for a large population of people that he 'did not conceive', is not Moses' idea. He confesses that he still does not understand why Yahweh calls him to safely shepherd the people to the land of promise. He admits that he cannot carry the burden of the people by himself. In despair Moses declares he would rather die due to his fear of personal ruin. Moses cannot perceive where sufficient meat would be found for the multitudes. However, he also makes a perceptive and crucial observation. Yahweh's promise to bring Israel into the promised land is not in doubt, because he swore on 'oath' (שבע) to the forefa-

---

7. The emphasis on 'eating' (אכל) appears seven times (Num. 11.4, 5, 12, 18 twice, 19, 21). The desire for 'meat' (בשר) is referenced eight times (Num. 11.4, 13 twice, 18 thrice, 21, 33). Apparently, they are more concerned about their menu than their mandate.

thers that he would take them there (Num. 11.12; cf. 14.16, 23; 31.11). Moses' problem concerns the toll that his leadership demands require of him for resources and for the care of people who did not fully understand the purposes of their journey.

11.16–23—Yahweh's Response and Moses' Negotiation

Yahweh responds to this situation with two instructions.[8] The first directive is similar to how the Lord deals with Moses when he tries to evade his prophetic calling. He encourages him to trust and obey but also provides a helper and supportive 'signs'. When Moses claims he cannot speak properly as a prophet to Pharaoh, Yahweh provides Aaron to assist in the communication and persuasion process. Now to help with the daily burdens of the people, Yahweh calls for seventy 'elders' (זקן) who function as leaders and officials among the people, to be selected and presented for a commission. The explanatory report in Deuteronomy elucidates what this selection of leaders is meant to accomplish:

> So I took the leading men of your tribes, wise and respected men, and appointed them to have authority over you—as commanders of thousands, of hundreds, of fifties and of tens and as tribal officials. And I charged your judges at that time, 'Hear the disputes between your people and judge fairly, whether the case is between two Israelites or between an Israelite and a foreigner residing among you. Do not show partiality in judging; hear both small and great alike. Do not be afraid of anyone, for judgment belongs to God. Bring me any case too hard for you, and I will hear it'. And at that time I told you everything you were to do. (Deut. 1.15–18)

In this way the burden would be shared.

These elders are to be selected from leaders whom Moses has experience with. Elders have the closest connection to the people as tribal representatives and are integral for the management of the nation. The seventy elders as a group are also active as leaders in Exodus where they witness some of the awesome revelations of Yahweh (cf. Exod. 3.16–18; 12.21; 24), but it is not clear if

---

8 Numbers 11 exhibits several counterparts to details and events that occur in Exodus 16–24. This includes the complaints about food, the daily provision of manna and the arrival of quail. Furthermore, the heavy burden of Moses is addressed with the solution of elders to be additional helpers. Cf. J.R. Levison, 'Prophecy in Ancient Israel: The Case of the Ecstatic Elders', *Catholic Biblical Quarterly* 65 (2003), p. 514.

these are the same elders referred to in Numbers 11.[9] One of the main distinctions concerning the choice of helpers for Moses between Exodus 18, 24 and Numbers 11 is in the selection process. In Exodus 18 it is the human advice of Jethro that establishes judicial aides-de-camp for Moses' 'burden'. In Numbers it is by divine command that Moses brings seventy known leaders and officials (elders) for the specific role of assisting the encumbered leader.

In this way Yahweh addresses Moses' primary problem of 'the burden' (משא) which is the heavy load of leadership to carry Israel forward. This burden includes many elements which are common challenges for leaders. It encompasses the primary need of determining clear communication between the Lord and the people. It encompasses the daily pressure of providing huge quantities of water and food resources. It demands clear guidance through the wilderness and enemy territory. It necessitates judicial rulings for domestic situations that arise among people who live in close proximity to each other. The burden of concern includes community standards, health matters, birth and death—literally, the weight of a nation needing special care is upon Moses. The burden was real, demanding, and unrelenting. Typically, leaders in the OT try to avoid the prophetic call and evade the 'mantle' (cf. Moses; Jeremiah; Jonah; Ezekiel)! However, Yahweh's answer in this case is to provide helpers who are recognized leaders, empowered and fortified to keep the team and mission on the right path towards the 'promised land'.

How would these elders be equipped and enabled to assist in the task? Apparently, through the sharing of some of the power of the 'Spirit' (רוח) that is on Moses, these elders would be able to help with the 'burden' and care of the people (Num. 11.16–17; 24–25). This is the first time in Numbers where the 'רוח' is referred to as present with Moses.[10] Knowledge of the 'Spirit of God' and how the divine presence will animate leaders is a developing concept for Israel, and one that is not clearly explained here. However, this reference and thematic development proves to be a powerful and desirable part of Israel's

---

9   The 'elders' (זקן) were respected leaders within specific social groups and gave tribal representation at meetings. They voice the concerns of their communities and exercise local jurisdiction for key decisions (cf. Deut. 21.1–9, 18–21; 25.5–10; Exod. 24.1–9). Cf. J. Conrad, 'זקן', *TDOT*, IV, p. 123. Cf. Hildebrandt. *An Old Testament Theology*, p. 110–111.

10 S. Tengström, 'רוח', *TDOT*, XIII, pp. 372. רוח occurs 378 times in the OT plus 11 times in Aramaic. In the Pentateuch it appears 38 times but only a few of these references are to be translated as the 'Spirit' of God. Typically, רוח refers to wind, breath, or spirit in humankind. Numbers 11 mentions רוח 6 times for 'thematic dominance' (p. 391). However, Tengström claims that the 'universal dissemination of the prophetic spirit (Num. 11.29) is a notion of the postexilic period, bringing the text close to Joel 3.1–2 (2.28–29)', p. 391.

understanding of how Yahweh empowers leaders for service.[11] In compliance with Yahweh's directive, a gathering of leaders is organized for a ceremony at the Tent of Meeting where Yahweh promised to show up, speak, and transfer some of the Spirit's power from Moses to the elders.

The second directive announces the word of the Lord for the situation at hand—the grumbling and wailing. This directive relates to one of the primary roles in prophetic leadership, namely, to hear Yahweh's word and to announce the events that will come to pass. This process reinforces Moses' prophetic role and verifies that Yahweh is addressing the problems in the camp. The people are directed to prepare for a day of feasting by consecrating themselves. Yahweh promises to attend to the food issue at hand so that their craving for meat would be satisfied, but preparation for the feast is required before they could receive the miraculous provision. However, the provision of meat will be mixed with a dose of judgment because of their 'rejection' of Yahweh's care and presence, as well as their persistent longing for Egypt. They would be fed with an abundance of meat for a month until sickened of the diet they demand. Their craving would turn to loathing. The feast is to be another dramatic lesson concerning the prerequisite trust in the Lord. The Lord who delivers and directs, is also able to sustain, provide and guide like a good shepherd.

Even Moses is incredulous that such a large population, including 'six hundred thousand men on foot' would actually have enough meat, whether flocks, herds or fish, for a month! His usual comportment is reduced to that of 'complainer' and 'mistruster' in Yahweh's ability. The Lord's reply addresses both issues of leadership burden and food: 'Is the LORD's arm too short? Now you will see whether or not what I say will come true for you' (Num. 11.21–23). The Lord's response makes it clear that a lack of provision is not the issue, nor the lack of power—he is able to bring into reality the words that are declared. Moses' role is to declare the message of Yahweh and prepare the people for the divine interventions.

11.24–30—*Sharing of the Spirit*

As instructed, Moses communicates the words of the Lord and gathers the elders around the Tent of Meeting. Yahweh appears in a cloud, speaks with Moses, and then 'withdraws' (אצל) a portion of the 'Spirit' (רוח) that is on Moses. With the Spirit 'deposited' on the elders and 'resting' (נוח) on them, the elders

---

11 As Levison clearly argues, this passage is not to be compared or explained with the ecstatic or analogous texts in the former prophets where Saul exhibits 'frenzy' and other experiences under the possession of the Spirit. Cf. Levison, *Prophecy in Ancient Israel*, pp. 506–512.

spontaneously begin 'prophesying' (ויתנבאו). Concerning the interpretation of 'prophesying' (ויתנבאו) in Numbers 11, many scholars have concluded that the incident portrays ecstatic behaviour similar to narratives which present Saul and a few other prophets behaving ecstatically. This appears logical since the *hithpael* form for prophecy usually indicates some form of ecstatic behaviour with verbal expression. However, this episode appears to present some development in a form of prophetic speech, with some similarities to other cultures, but with theological momentum in Numbers.[12]

It is not clear what the act of prophesying entails but the fact that it is audible, and observable by others indicates the externally visible and auditory nature of the encounter. The withdrawal of some of the Spirit that is on Moses and shared with the elders signifies that a level of leadership authority and practical skill is transferred to the elders. This transfer gives credibility and authority to the elders for their daily work among the people and the encouragement required for ministry. With the sharing of the Spirit, the burden of leadership is delegated and distributed to presumably reduce Moses' burden. The experience of prophesying is limited to this one occasion and the elders do not 'continue' with prophetic activity once they leave the Tent of Meeting. The implication is that the elders do not become prophets in the same way that Moses functions as leader and spokesman for Yahweh. The encounter empowers the elders and publicly authorizes them to assist as leaders. Moses continues to be the prophetic leader of the nation with the full authority of his Spirit-endowed position.[13]

The encounter with the Spirit has several implications and functions. This event verifies that Moses, the chosen leader, is positioned and authorized for his role as primary leader of the nation by the Spirit upon him.[14] The occa-

---

12   In his perceptive article, Levison makes a legitimate case for verbal and thematic links to Exodus and dismisses that prophesying here describes an ecstatic state. Rather, '... prophesying entailed a more ordered experience that served to assist Moses as he led Israel'. Levison, *Prophecy in Ancient Israel*, p. 514.

13   Cf. L.R. Martin, 'The Charismatic Spirit in the Torah and Former Prophets', in R.P. Tuppurainen (ed). *Reading St. Luke's Text and Theology: Pentecostal Voices Essays in Honor of Professor Roger Stronstad* (Pickwick Publications: Eugene, OR: 2019), pp. 185–197.

14   Levison, *Prophecy in Ancient Israel*, p. 513, makes important observations regarding the connection with the Exodus 24 account and the orderly tenor of the Spirit encounter. However, this was more than a visionary experience. He claims,

> By the same token, Exodus 24 supplies what is implicit in the narrative of Numbers 11: prophesying consisted principally of a visionary experience within a controlled central setting, with an established social hierarchy and an appointed locus of revelation. The elders had been appointed earlier to bear Moses' burden with him, had gathered at a locus of revelation, on Mt. Sinai, and had participated in a communal visionary experience alongside Moses.

sion provides a tangible, audible, prophetic experience that the community witnesses to solidify the elder's roles publicly. It provides an internal confirmation for the seventy elders that they are authorized but also qualifies them to serve in greater ways due to the Spirit's impartation. The encounter signifies to the community that the Lord is present and working on the nation's behalf through the expanded leadership cohort who are touched by the Spirit. The event is described in similar theophanic terms as Exod. 19.9–11 where the Lord descends in a dense cloud and speaks to Moses in an audible way to evoke the trust of the people. 'Then the LORD came down in the cloud and spoke with him, and he took some of the power of the Spirit that was on him and put it on the seventy elders'. The divine presence in the cloud makes the event a vivid and memorable occasion for the people. The Spirit on leaders provides the 'prophetic element' and gives an example of Moses' experience in speaking God's instructions. The elders will not prophesy after this event, but they will provide counsel, resource management, and assistance for the community as needed.

The narrative also reports another act of prophesying in the location of the camp. Two other elders named Eldad and Medad who remained behind, also experience the Spirit's 'deposit' on them and are 'prophesying' (מתנבאים) back in the camp location (מחנה). The JPS translation adds an important insight here which underlines the observable external nature of Spirit-induced prophecy: 'Eldad and Medad are acting the prophet in the camp!' This incident usually gives rise to several views ranging from that of illegitimate prophecy to a threat of ambitious leadership. However, the two do not manufacture this encounter—the Spirit 'rests' (נוח) on them, verifying the divine inclusion of Eldad and Medad in the prophetic activity. Also, the location of their act of prophesying is accentuated as being in the camp (4 times in 11.27–30; מחנה), the same locale of judgment described in Numbers 11.1 and in 11.31–32 (3 times). This emphasis appears to infer that Eldad and Medad intentionally remain in the camp with the people, presumably to attend to the people's needs or serve in some capacity. The unusual occurrences of Yahweh's judgment on the camp as well as the withdrawal of leaders to the Tent of Meeting, would have caused significant trepidation among the people.

Furthermore, it should be observed that Eldad and Medad are listed among the elders and, therefore, are legitimate 'registered' leaders. They too are positioned to assist Moses with his leadership burden and Yahweh allows the Spirit to rest on them, causing them to prophesy where the people could witness an authentication of their inclusion with the elders. When Joshua hears about this situation from a young informant, he apparently views it as a potential threat to Moses' leadership, an impingement on his authority, and wants their charis-

11.1–25.18—HARDSHIPS, CONFLICTS, REBELLION AND JUDGMENT

matic activity stopped. However, Moses perceives a desirable development in this episode as noted in his response: 'Are you jealous for my sake? I wish that all the LORD's people were prophets and that the LORD would put his Spirit on them!' (Num. 11.29). Moses assures Joshua that this blessing of Yahweh's presence signified by prophesying is desirable for all his people. His aspiration for the people is rooted in his own experience of what a 'prophet' (נביא) is to be and should encounter. Namely, Spirit-reception, prophetic insight, an intimate relationship with Yahweh and leadership authorization (similar to the democratization of Israel as a 'Kingdom of priests' in Exodus 19).

The sharing of the 'Spirit' (רוח) that is on Moses with the elders, does not diminish his leadership responsibilities, but actually enhances his ability to focus on the essential matters of directing the nation towards the goal of the promised land. This is affirmed when Joshua is appointed as Moses' successor. Num. 27.16–20 presents the thematic thesis for a paradigmatic leadership transfer in answer to Moses' prayer for God to provide authorized leadership. Joshua has the 'spirit' of leadership and as commissioned, will take Israel into the land of promise. However, this is not a sudden matter as it took extensive time for Moses to mentor his protégé who was known to linger at the tent of meeting (Exod. 33.11) and was among the elders who prophesied. Moses is instructed by Yahweh for the divine appointment: 'Take Joshua son of Nun, a man in whom is the spirit of leadership, and lay your hand on him. Have him stand before Eleazar the priest and the entire assembly and commission him in their presence. Give him some of your authority so the whole Israelite community will obey him'. In this provision, Israel would have leaders to guide, instruct and provide for their daily needs. The overall import of this unique experience introduces the concept that Spirit authorized leadership may be limited in OT documents, but at some future time, experiencing the Spirit's presence will be shared with all of God's people.[15]

Moses welcomes the 'prophetic' activity because he views it as a partial answer to the 'burden' (משא). People hear the prophesying elders and could now have confidence in authorized elders who may help them with their social and domestic issues. The act of prophesying here accentuates verbal expression. Levison considers it a visionary experience for the elders in a communal context, but it is impracticable to see how a communal vision would have any impact on the people. Unless a vision is communicated by a prophet in verbal terms, the vision is a personal experience—rarely a communal one. Prophecy is mainly a verbal function to communicate and affirm the divine will, includ-

---

15   This theme is developed in the prophet Joel's message (Joel 2.28–30) indicating that Moses' desire will be realized in a future event as the Spirit is poured out upon all flesh.

ing the ability to speak judicial wisdom and comfort into situations that arise. After the momentous experience at the Tent of Meeting, Moses and the elders return to the camp.

11.31–35—An Abundance of Quail

The narrative returns to the opening theme concerning the people's desire for meat. As promised by Yahweh (Num. 11.18–23; also cf. Exodus 16), an extraordinary provision of quail is brought to the people by a 'wind' (רוח) of the Lord (cf. Gen. 8.1; Exod. 14.21), which drives the quail from the sea to pile up around the camp. The description of the amounts and the people's greed in gathering the quail are extraordinary: 'It scattered them up to two cubits deep all around the camp, as far as a day's walk in any direction. All that day and night and all the next day the people went out and gathered quail. No one gathered less than ten homers. Then they spread them out all around the camp'. A homer may refer to 'heaps' but also more than a ton! The amount of meat gathered and then spread out for drying was staggering but so was the gorging of quail by the people. The feasting initiated another severe act of judgment as the Lord's anger 'burned' once again (cf. Num. 11.1–3). Another place name is given as a reminder of this episode, *Kibroth Hattavah*—a grave for those who crave. Many of the people are struck with a severe 'plague' (מכה), and some of them are buried in the wilderness.[16] The numbers and the identity of those who are stricken are not indicated here, although some commentators believe it mainly affects the 'riffraff'.[17] It is also supposed that others who are not stricken with plague, continue to eat the quail for a month (Num. 11.19). This incident becomes an historic reminder for the nation (Pss. 78.26–31; 105.40).

12.1–16—Family and Leadership Conflict

The incidents at *Taberah* and *Kibroth Hattaavah* feature the stressful elements of the wilderness trek which require enormous resources and wise leadership. The events also reveal the theological implications of the divine anger on those who complain about the 'limited' provisions that are made in the forward march to a better place. The episodes highlight another element in the developing challenges which include the expansion of the leadership base and the role of the elders. Moreover, these elders now have an experiential encounter

---

16 This term is only used once in Numbers in the sense of a 'plague' indicating a sudden sickness caused by the ingestion of meat.
17 Cf. Milgrom, *Numbers*, p. 92.

with the same Spirit that animates Moses and are elevated to new leadership responsibilities. This context of the elders prophesying appears to inform the episode in Numbers Twelve concerning Miriam, Aaron, and Moses.

A continuation of the conflict motif is apparent in a narrative which begins with a family issue that indicates developing domestic tensions between siblings. This is inevitable taking into consideration the stresses of life that are taking shape in the wilderness. Moreover, sibling rivalry and family drama is a typical human experience and quite prominent in the patriarchal narratives. Themes of envy, jealousy, intrigue, birthright, and cultural diversity exhibit a variety of conflicts which cause serious consequences for families. In chapter 12, Moses continues to face criticism from an unanticipated source—his sister and brother.

12.1–2—*Family Tensions*

Two matters are presented here which require resolution. It appears that Miriam and Aaron take issue with Moses' wife and whatever problems they feel she is causing. Secondly and more prominently, they challenge Moses' prophetic leadership status and his apparent right to be the sole spokesman on behalf of Yahweh. Both of these issues are connected to the preceding events where the 'rabble' or non-Israelite people begin the confrontational complaining about food and are singled out. Now 'the Cushite wife' of Moses becomes a problem for Miriam and Aaron. Added to this annoyance for the sister and brother-in-law, is the prophetic encounter they miss. It appears that they are excluded from the encounter at the Tent of Meeting where the Spirit on Moses is shared with the elders who experienced a taste of 'prophesying'. The incident brings to the fore Moses' status and primary leadership role by virtue of the Spirit upon him. Although the Spirit is shared with other leaders, Miriam is not included, perhaps intensifying the aggravation that leads to her question, 'Has the LORD only spoken through Moses?'

According to Num. 26.59, Miriam is the elder sister of Aaron and Moses.[18] Although not named in Exodus 2, her first appearance in scripture is tradi-

---

18 The second census in Numbers 26 includes the Levitical lineage with the mention of Miriam:

> These were the Levites who were counted by their clans: through Gershon, the Gershonite clan; through Kohath, the Kohathite clan; through Merari, the Merarite clan. These also were Levite clans: the Libnite clan, the Hebronite clan, the Mahlite clan, the Mushite clan, the Korahite clan. Kohath was the forefather of Amram; the name of Amram's wife was Jochebed, a descendant of Levi, who was born to the Levites in Egypt. To Amram she bore Aaron, Moses and their sister Miriam. Aaron was the father of Nadab and Abihu, Eleazar and Ithamar. But Nadab and Abihu died when they made an offering before the LORD with unauthorized fire (Num. 26.57–61).

tionally held to be in Exod. 2.4–10 where she helps in the providential rescue of her brother Moses who is under threat of the Pharaoh's design to kill the Hebrew boys. If this is Miriam, she is a wise and shrewd woman who providentially finds favour with the Pharaoh's daughter and through it all, her baby brother is saved and raised in the royal palace. After the great exodus event, Miriam is referred to as a prophetess and leads the women in a song of victory (Exod. 15.20). The song of exaltation is an extensive theological presentation of Yahweh's deliverance and military victory as Israel's warrior. Miriam leads the women in dancing and encouragement through the refrain of exaltation: "Then Miriam the prophet, Aaron's sister, took a timbrel in her hand, and all the women followed her, with timbrels and dancing. Miriam sang to them: 'Sing to the LORD, for he is highly exalted. Both horse and driver he has hurled into the sea'" (Exod. 15.20–21). This seems to be the important element in Miriam's prophetic expression—inspiration with the ability to sing prophetic truth resulting in the encouragement of the people. With this positive familial background, and her influence in the nation with Moses and the Israelites who are unified in their celebration of deliverance, it is a surprising turn that Miriam takes issue with Moses' marriage as well as his prophetic status.

The implication in the passage is that Moses' first wife Zipporah who was a Midianite (Exod. 2.21), is no longer alive and that Moses may have remarried a Cushite woman. Alternatively, some commentators surmise that the term Cushite may mean 'beautiful' and still refers to Zipporah who does not rejoin with Moses until after Jethro travels to meet his son-in-law (cf. Exodus 18). Moreover, the incident where Zipporah refers to Moses as a 'bridegroom of blood' due to the circumcision rite (Exod. 4.24–26) may have caused her to return to her father in Midian at that time. Whether the issue is with Zipporah or another marriage to an actual Cushite woman from Ethiopia, there are serious rifts which develop and cause Miriam to be critical of her brother.

It is not clear if Miriam's offense is racial, with implications on cultural differences and practices, or whether it is on religious grounds and the cultus requirements. Perhaps it is simply domestic tensions that are common in all households as amply described in the patriarchal narratives. Surely the Israelites would question why Moses would marry a foreigner rather than a Hebrew. Intermarriage is permitted when religious compatibility is evident, but there are several narratives that indicate negative connotations on cultural mixing (Gen. 24.3; 27.46; 28.1–9; Exod. 34.16; Lev. 21.14). Surely Moses the great lawgiver is aware of this! Whatever the case, Miriam and Aaron take up their offenses with their brother.

12.3–5—Moses' Humility

Once again, the incredible level of communication between Yahweh and Moses is evident through the repetition of the phrase, 'The LORD spoke to Moses' (approximately 150 times in various forms in Numbers). Therefore, the questions voiced by Miriam, 'Has the LORD spoken only through Moses?' 'Hasn't he also spoken through us?' seem incredulous and confrontational. The role of Aaron in Exodus is quite clear—he is a prophet in the sense that he presents the words of Moses given by Yahweh to the Pharaoh and people (Exodus 7). However, his role as a spokesman for Moses diminishes overtime as Moses finds the confidence and ability to lead and speak for himself. Aaron transitions into his appointed priestly functions. In the case of Miriam, however, other than her prophetic singing, there is no record of what prophetic words she received from Yahweh (cf. Exod. 15.20).

Moses' attitude in this provocative situation inspires the probable editorial comment concerning his superlative quality of humility! Moses is the most 'humble' (ענו) man on earth! Although this assertion has brought about much speculation as to its origin, it undeniably reflects the core character quality of Moses. Commentators have used this verse to verify their conclusion against Mosaic authorship. However, editorial comments can also verify the truth of this assertion—especially when one takes into consideration the characteristics of Moses' leadership record. With reference to Moses, the term 'humble' (ענו) indicates that he is unpretentious at the core. It is not just characteristic of his humility on certain occasions, but it is a foundational quality that is shaped through the joys and hardships of life. Moses falls from the heights of status in the Egyptian palace with all of its luxury and educational opportunities, to the valleys of the Midian wilderness where he is excluded from the ranks of his Hebrew family and culture. Although he may have been content in Midian, it certainly is a formidable challenge to envision a return to the Pharaoh's court to confront a regent and demand that the Hebrew slaves be released from their labour. However, this is the reality that he is presented with and eventually Moses accepts the task to lead Israel out of Egypt towards an undisclosed land of promise.

Humility is reflected in his initial call to leadership where his reluctance leads to several concessions by Yahweh. His arguments concerning the call and role that Yahweh has for him are rooted in his own valuation of himself. 'Who am I that I should go to Pharaoh and bring the Israelites out of Egypt?' (Exod. 3.11). More than a lack of confidence, Moses has reasons for his reluctance—historically, he flees Egypt due to the fear of reprisal for his murderous action. Now he argues extensively with the Lord and tries to shirk his leadership calling (Exod. 3.11–4.17). His final reluctance is based on his perceived lack of eloquence with 'slow speech' and tongue. If this concern is based on speaking Egyptian to Pharaoh after so many years in the wilderness of Midian, then perhaps he does have an issue with confidence in the language. Finally, his request for the Lord to send someone else, is still not an acceptable option for Yahweh—Moses is his choice. Moses has the background and training for the role and there is no one else. However, a concession is made for him in that Aaron would be his spokesman. This facility is acceptable to Moses, and he works in tandem with his brother in confronting the Pharaoh. But Aaron's eventual loss of his speaking role may have also exacerbated his relationship with Moses who soon gained the confidence to be the primary spokesman.

Moses is indeed a humble man. Many examples could be listed to show Moses' humility. It is evident in his pronouncement concerning Eldad and Medad, and the desire that all of God's people would have prophetic insight. Humility characterizes Moses' persistent intercession on behalf of the Israelites, even when their behaviour exasperates him. He exhibits humility in most of the instances where Israel criticizes his role in taking them out of Egypt into the wilderness. It is evident when there are attempts to take over his leadership position and status, whether it is Miriam, Aaron, or the sons of Korah. His humility is evident when one analyses the whole record of his life and observes the levels of service he performs for the nation. He remains a faithful, humble 'servant' (עבד).

Alternatively, Miriam and Aaron appear to be envious of Moses' standing with Yahweh and are summoned before the Lord. This must have been a terrifying situation reminiscent of a court hearing. The Lord comes down to the entrance of the Tent in a pillar of cloud and calls them out, 'Aaron and Miriam!' (Num. 12.5).

12.6–8—*The Prophetic Blessing*

Numbers Six ends with the familiar divine or 'Priestly Blessing' that has become a refrain for believers in benedictions. To a degree Numbers Twelve may illustrate what could be considered 'a Prophetic Blessing' in that God provides the nation with a leader who has the best interests of the people in mind. In these verses, the function and magnitude of the prophetic role in Israel is presented. Even though the terminology of prophecy is just developing in the Pentateuch, the declaration by Yahweh sets the precedent of what is involved and how prophecy in Israel should operate going forward.

This narrative exposes a potentially serious situation that initiates immediate action by Yahweh who hears the allegations of Miriam. The text implies that Miriam and Aaron are talking about Moses' marriage in public and spreading discontent. While the murmuring may be behind Moses' back, it is not hidden from Yahweh who hears it and takes action. The Lord summons Moses, Aaron, and Miriam to the Tent of Meeting where the cloud descends over the tent entrance. Yahweh speaks directly to Aaron and Miriam with judicial force, calling them to hear these words concerning Moses and particular modes of revelation.

> When there is a prophet among you, I, the LORD, reveal myself to them in visions, I speak to them in dreams. But this is not true of my servant Moses; he is faithful in all my house. With him I speak face to face, clearly and not in riddles; he sees the form of the LORD. Why then were you not afraid to speak against my servant Moses?

Firstly, Yahweh speaks about individuals who arise as a 'prophet' (נביא) and experience the typical format of revelation through 'visions' (מראה) and 'dreams' (חלום). The term 'prophet' occurs fourteen times in the Pentateuch, referring to Abraham (Gen. 20.7), Aaron (Exod. 7.1), and predominately Moses (Deut. 34.10). In connection with this title, Abraham is told to make intercession for Abimelech as he does earlier for Sodom (Gen. 18.17). Like the latter prophets, he receives divine instructions and speaks with God personally (Gen. 15.1ff.). Aaron is Moses' prophet in the sense of being his spokesman. The request of Israel for a prophet in the capacity of a mediator arises in connection with the theophany at Mount Sinai. Expressing fear and awe for Yahweh's presence, Israel responds to Moses, 'Speak to us yourself and we will listen. But do not have God speak to us or we will die' (Exod. 20.19; cf. Deut. 5.23–27).

From the Pentateuchal understanding of what it means to be a prophet for Moses, the experience begins with a call (Exod. 3.1–4) that singles him out from all other people and includes intimate 'face-to-face' (פנים אל פנים) communication with Yahweh (cf. Exod. 33.11; Deut. 34.10). These experiences with Yahweh are what make Moses the paradigmatic prototype of a prophet (cf. Deut. 18.15–18). His relationship with Yahweh and his power in leadership are unequaled. 'For no one has ever shown the mighty power or performed the awesome deeds that Moses did in the sight of Israel' (Deut. 34.12). It is this dimension of communication that is prophetic—the prophet becomes Yahweh's spokesman as the divinely revealed messages are declared. To be clear, the title 'prophet' (נביא) is used very sparingly in the Pentateuch. It is a developing role in Israel which takes decades of advancement before becoming one of the most powerful leadership roles in Israel. In Numbers it is only used twice (as discussed in Numbers 11.29 and in this passage), although the activity of prophesying in conjunction with the Spirits' work is also evident. Additionally, there is an implicit assumption that all of Moses' leadership activities, including the dramatic mode of reception of the divine word, was prophetic. Elements of prophecy and prophesying are also illustrated in the Balaam narratives (cf. Numbers 22–24).

The mode of revelation to prophets mainly consists of a 'vision' (מראה) and in this instance, the root word signifies something that others cannot see. Prophetic words are revealed in visionary form. For example, the pattern of the lampstand and the sanctuary are 'shown' to Moses (Num. 8.4; cf. Exod. 25.9; 27.8). As prophecy develops in Israel, the main term for visionary experiences from which the prophet receives divine messages is 'to see' (ראה). Another term for 'visions' (מחזה) occurs in the Balaam section where he receives revelation (Num. 24.4, 16). This word is associated with pre-prophetic seers but later becomes synonymous with 'seeing' (ראה). However, the main term used for visionary experiences in reference to the prophets is 'see' (ראה). The context must be carefully analysed since (ראה) occurs 1303 times in the OT, with 39 references in Numbers that have a variety of meanings.[19] In the ancient near east there were many diviners and clairvoyants who served in king's courts to reveal messages purportedly from gods. For the true prophet in Israel the vision would be something orchestrated by Yahweh for the prophet to know and understand and communicate. Dreams are another method that Yahweh uses. The 'dream' (חלום) is illustrated in several examples in scripture where a variety of people have dreams inspired by Yahweh. This may even include individuals who are not prophets like Jacob and Solomon, or even the Pharaoh in Egypt. But dreams also require interpretation and could take considerable time for fruition and realization (cf. Joseph and Daniel narratives). As prophecy develops in Israel, the vision and dream motifs for revelation become the typical mode of message reception.

With Moses, revelation is unique. Yahweh speaks with him directly, 'face to face', or more literally in this verse 'mouth to mouth' (פה אל פה). Both of these phrases for divine communication are anthropomorphic terms describing the most intimate type of interaction, and with clear messages, not with riddles. The mode of revelation is not a one-way communication because God allows Moses to intercede on behalf of the people (just as Abraham is permitted to negotiate for Sodom and Gemorrah). Furthermore, Moses is allowed to perceive the 'form' (תמונה) of the Lord (various terms that provide insight into the 'form' could be image, likeness, representation, semblance).

The reason given for this level of access is that Moses is the most trusted 'servant' (עבד), and the one whom Yahweh trusts with the 'household'. Namely,

---

19   Cf. H.F. Fuhs, 'ראה', *TDOT*, VIII, pp. 212–239.

the precious, treasured people of God (Num. 12.7–8; cf. Deut. 3.24; 34.5; Josh. 1.1–15; 22.2–5). Moses is the relentless servant who approaches Yahweh when summoned but also intercedes for the nation many times—thereby showing his care and service for the people of God. Milgrom carefully describes the introverted structure of these phrases where each line has a specific number of syllables. The pivot in the declaration comes in the middle phrases: 'Not so with My servant Moses; He (alone) is trusted in all My household'.[20] Yahweh affirms that Moses is his special servant and has earned the unique and direct form of communication that other prophets could only hope for. For Moses, the blessing of prophecy allows him to speak with the Lord 'mouth to mouth' and meet with God 'face to face' where he receives the divine revelation for Israel.

In this context the two references to Moses as the servant of Yahweh are used as 'an honorific title of the mediator of revelation rather than an official title, and as referring to the special status of his relationship with God'.[21] This distinctive process includes mountain climbing, remaining in the presence of Yahweh for extensive periods, hearing, recording and proclaiming the divine word. However, Moses is more than a prophet, he is the Lord's trusted servant. Miller features the main portraits of Moses according to Deuteronomy, but they equally apply to the Mosaic' roles in Exodus through Numbers. As the central character in Deuteronomy, Moses is the amazing teacher of the law who receives it and interprets it (Deut. 4.5, 14; 5.31; 6.1). Moses is the model prophet (Deut. 18.15, 18; 34.10–12), exemplified in his intercessory activity for the people (Deut. 9.7–29; 10.10–11; Exod. 32–34). The Lord listens to Moses's prayer and heeds it (Exod. 32.14)! But he is also the 'suffering servant' of God. 'The dominant view of Deuteronomy is that Moses is the Lord's faithful servant whose death outside of the promised land is due to the Lord's anger on account of the people. Moses is clearly identified with the people in the punishment that is placed upon them, but the judgment on Moses is for their sin (Deut. 1.34–37)'. Therefore, according to Deuteronomy, Moses is not allowed into the land on account of the people's sin.[22]

12.9–16—Divine Judgment

The implication in this episode is that Miriam and Aaron have the audacity to challenge Moses' marital relationship and leadership status when all their brother cares about is the well-being of the nation. This situation brings about

---

20   Milgrom, *Numbers*, p. 95.
21   H. Ringgren, 'עבד', pp. 394–395. Hebrews 3.5 affirms Moses' faithfulness as a steward and servant.
22   Miller, '"Moses My Servant": The Deuteronomic Portrait of Moses', p. 309.

the burning anger of Yahweh upon them, similar to the incidents that occur at *Taberah* and *Kibbroth Hattaavah*. As Yahweh departs from the Tent, Miriam is left with a visible skin condition and flaky white covering. Although this condition is not leprosy and more like psoriasis, it still is a frightening and instant punishment which renders her unclean (cf. Exod. 4.6–7). This shocking sight causes an immediate reaction from Aaron who petitions Moses with the title 'Adonai' (אדון). In repentance of their sinful behaviour, he begs for Miriam's restoration. Moses' response is also immediate, and he pleads for Miriam to be healed. True to his prophetic role and humble spirit, Moses intercedes for his sister. However, the punishment is permitted to finish its course.

The serious miscalculation of Miriam's conduct exacts a harsh lesson for the community to comprehend—it is not beneficial to accuse the Lord's servant before people or the Lord. A crude cultural practice is referred to which indicates that defilement must lead to exclusion. When a father spits in the face of his daughter, she would be rendered unclean, humiliated and segregated for a period of seven days. There is no indication that Miriam is healed immediately. However, the implication is that she is allowed to return after her period of exclusion based on a clear diagnosis, usually from the priest. After seven days outside of the camp, Miriam is re-admitted, and the Israelites continue their march from Hazeroth into the wilderness of Paran where they camp. As is customary in inclusive or high-context culture communities, the punishment of one person affects the whole, and Israel's trek is delayed.

Reflection and Response
Numbers 11–12: Prophetic Leadership in the Wilderness
Reflection

Numbers Eleven is a classic narrative describing some of Israel's wilderness adversities and the divine response through human leadership to meet the people's needs. For Israel's epic migration to the land of promise, the difficulties are intense and require physical and spiritual stamina. In this section of Numbers, a transition occurs in the way God provides for Israel's needs from patriarchal to prophetic leadership positions. Yahweh provides leadership as required and delivers the daily resources needed to sustain the nation in the wilderness with physical sustenance, guidance, and instruction—through the prophet Moses. The Lord supplies the support system that Moses needed to be more effective in looking after the people's physical, mental and spiritual well-being. Although many leaders are selected for roles in the community, Numbers 11 adds a new element in the development of leadership structure to the Pentateuch. The chapter corroborates the necessity of the Spirit resting on leaders to animate them for service.

The narrative reveals that Moses functions in his role with an endowment of Spirit upon him. In fact, the presence of Spirit with Moses is so powerful that 'sharing' the Spirit with seventy elders for authorized leadership duties in the nation to lessen the 'burden', is made possible. This revelation gives insight for leadership qualifications and partly describes what prophetic leadership entails. This is the first clear passage that indicates how Yahweh empowers his chosen leaders with the Spirit. It marks the beginning of the developing revelation of how Yahweh moves the nation forward through leaders to accomplish the divine will. Moses' power and endurance in ministry comes from the Spirit that is on him (Num. 11.17). The episode further illustrates another dimension of the characteristic presence of the Lord experiences at the Tent of meeting.[23] Furthermore, the Lord shows his amazing care, provision and miraculous interventions for the nation in numerous ways, through Moses' charismatic administration.

Moses' call to leadership occurs after two major segments of his life provide him with educational development (in Egypt) and experiential reflective growth (in Midian). His 'call' comes in fulfilment of Yahweh's prophetic statements to Abraham regarding the exile of his people in Egypt and the 400 years of their time there (cf. Gen. 15.13; Exodus 3). The timing of Moses' leadership call comes in answer to the Israelites' cry for relief from the Pharaoh's oppression. In fulfilment of the Lord's words to the patriarch, God hears the people's lament, is concerned about their sufferings, and responds by calling, instructing, and commissioning Moses. It becomes apparent from this example, that when the outcry from humanity for deliverance is heard, God prefers to work in partnership with select individuals to address the need.

The call upon Moses is not a secular form of leadership involving power and military force but a special divine summons where he is constrained to obey the will of Yahweh. His life experiences prepared him for this specific assignment. Moses is convinced through his epic burning bush experience that God called and commissioned him for a leadership task. Moses is not referred to as a 'prophet' directly (cf. Num. 12.6–8), but he occupies this role for the last

---

23   This is made explicit by the prophet Isaiah:
   Then his people recalled the days of old, the days of Moses and his people—where is he who brought them through the sea, with the shepherd of his flock? Where is he who set his Holy Spirit among them, who sent his glorious arm of power to be at Moses' right hand, who divided the waters before them, to gain for himself everlasting renown, who led them through the depths? Like a horse in open country, they did not stumble; like cattle that go down to the plain, they were given rest by the Spirit of the LORD. This is how you guided your people to make for yourself a glorious name. (Isa. 63.11–14)

forty years of his life. Not only is he lauded the greatest prophet at the end of his life, but he is the one to be emulated by all other prophets (Deut. 18.18–19; 34.10). He is also referred to as the servant of Yahweh, indicating his faithful stewardship of the Lord's people. Moses obediently tells Israel the words which Yahweh inspires him to speak, and he leads them through the tumultuous days of the wilderness era. Prophecy is the chosen method of communication with the nation and Yahweh primarily speaks to his servant Moses through whom he leads Israel (cf. Num. 11.25; 12.6–8).

Although there are several occasions in the wilderness where Moses wants to give up his role, he serves faithfully until his death is immanent. Up until this time, he carries the prophetic 'burden' of moving the nation forward in accordance with Yahweh's covenantal promises. He does so through many hardships and leadership conflicts when his abilities and vision are questioned. He understands what it means to be appointed to the task of leading the Lord's people by example, by protecting them, and by providing for them (cf. Psalm 23). At the end of his life his main concern is the people's well-being as his entreaty for his successor indicates (cf. Num. 27.16–17). The prayer of Moses reveals several dynamic truths. Firstly, it is in the providence of God to make the selection and appointment of leaders. Secondly, good leaders are influential in discipling, training and mentoring other leaders (Moses and Joshua). Thirdly, leaders actively look for their successor to take over responsibilities for the care of people. Fourthly, leaders are integral to the way God chooses to look after people who are 'like sheep', needing the care and guidance of the shepherd.

Several times in Numbers there are chaotic situations that occur, and in those episodes, leaders jump into action to bring order out of chaos. Some of the challenges in Numbers are demanding, including the preparation of young men for military assignments, training the Levites for risky work around the most sacred duties of the cultus, confronting conflicts in leadership challenges concerning competency, and moving the nation forward to realize the divine vision. One of Moses' positive characteristics is his inclination to accept help. He is magnanimous in working with Aaron, other leaders, and elders to accomplish the divine will for the benefit of the nation (Exod. 3.16, 18; 12.21). Even with the immense talents and roles that Moses exhibits, along with the privileges accorded to him on Mount Sinai in the presence of God, he is just a man with all the limitations that entails. He gets angry, tired, distraught, and frustrated.

When Moses requires assistance, he is ready to receive and endorse leaders for service. Thus, the authorized elders would function to provide resource management, instruction, and application of the law to people's domestic or community disputes, thereby lessening Moses' burden. At the Tent they have a remarkable spiritual experience but then take this new authority into the camp where the daily needs of people are managed. Although the seventy elders also experience prophetic inspiration and leadership opportunities, Moses remains their leader.

The conflict that arises with Miriam and Aaron is another disappointing situation for Moses to navigate. There is something to be said about God's choice of families for leadership roles, but this does bring certain dynamics into play. Power struggles can often get in the way of the core issues and main mission. However, it is up to individuals to find their role with humility and understanding rather than selfish ambition and conflict. Miriam and Aaron learn this lesson in a powerful way. Each person must find their place in a supportive team context because there are higher stakes in play than personal goals. The whole leadership enterprise is to move the nation forward in the fulfilment of the Lord's purposes. For this process, the Spirit empowers the leader with vision and the abilities to press onward.

Response

Numbers 11 and 12 calls for leaders to make some careful adjustments and commitments. Are we going to be the cause of certain conflicts and problems, or the solution to them? Do we really want to complain and grumble about menus if we have enough food, shelter, and nutrition (unless we are in situations of poverty, homelessness, refugees in migrant camps, etc.)? Are we so keen to turn back to life in 'Egypt' just because the trek to the 'promised land' is too difficult to manage? Are we ready to support the leaders and burden carriers who are in positions of authority over us? Could it be that our actions reveal subversive tendencies with an unauthorized vision? These narratives and several which follow, encourage God's people to promote unity and compliance with leaders. May the words of Moses and his desire that all of God's people would experience the benefits of 'prophets', resonate in our spirit's and empower our leadership responsibilities.

13.1–14.45—The Reconnaissance Mission

These two chapters are very carefully structured with an introverted arrangement in parallel sections.[24] The content may have divergent traditions or

---

24 Milgrom carefully presents the structure of the narrative according to 5 sections with a pattern that has 3 thematic components featuring destruction, intercession and the resulting judgment or calamity (cf. *Numbers*, pp. 387–390).

sources behind them which are now intricately woven together. This assumption is common in critical commentaries due to several factors observed in the texts. Complications arise concerning the place names, extent of the itinerary, specific characters and their roles (Caleb and Joshua), as well as some duplication of content.[25] Gray points out the 'numerous incongruities' in the details of the narrative and concludes that a few sources lie behind the present text. In his commentary he propositions that three sources are woven together to show that the whole land of Canaan is explored (not just the southern region as some verses imply) and that both Caleb and Joshua are involved in promoting positive perspectives (Num. 14.24; cf. 14.6–7, 38).[26]

Perhaps the best way to understand these narratives is to acknowledge two different, yet complimentary perspectives, namely the prophetic and the priestly view. Both of these traditions with their thematic emphases are interwoven, and although they seem to be stitched together into a congruent narrative, the final editors keep certain variations in the final document. An important observation concerns the exhortations given by Caleb in Numbers 13 which are further elaborated on by both Caleb and Joshua in chapter 14. The same is true for Yahweh's proclamation or divine judgment in Num. 14.11–12 which is then revised and mitigated after Moses' intercession in Num. 14.26–35. If these details represent two different traditions, in the final documentation, they feature the development of what actually takes place in this intense watershed event for Israel. In its current textual form, the narrative elevates the pivotal nature of the historic land exploration for the exodus generation. The episode provides a solemn warning for Israel's future generations that Yahweh values reliance and faith in matters concerning the covenantal promises. Yahweh also requires trust in divine leadership administered through servants who are willing to risk potential danger in realizing the divine provisions afforded to the nation in the promised land. The covenantal promises are secure but must be apprehended through confidence and action.

---

25 Cf. Hymes, 'A Pluriform Analysis of Numbers 10.11–14.45'. His analysis of the textual and thematic variations in different traditions (Masoretic, Samaritan, Septuagint, and Josephus) from a Pentecostal position is very insightful and rich in content. His analysis of the pluriform traditions provides an example of the complexity in these chapters which gave rise to the many historical-critical methods applied to the texts. Hymes adds to the discussion through a 'synchronous approach using narratology, intertextuality and rhetorical criticism, are combined with a diachronic and comparative analysis' (p. iii).

26 Gray proposes that the Jahwist and Elohist traditions were combined and then supplemented with a Priestly version of the events. Cf. G.B. Gray, *A Critical and Exegetical Commentary on Numbers* (Edinburgh: T & T Clark, 1903), pp. 129–133.

The main topics in Numbers 13–14 include the selection of leaders that are commissioned to explore the land (13.1–24) and the exploration reports (13.25–33). These are followed by the people's responses (14.1–10a). Yahweh is infuriated by the negative reactions and lack of faith, but Moses intercedes for the nation (14.10b–38) and Yahweh relents. Realizing their failure and severe judgment, the people propose to enter the land on their own initiative (14.39–45). These incidents prove to be so critical that Moses features them in his covenantal sermon in Deuteronomy.

According to Moses' extended discourse, there are two monumental failures in Israel which bring about the nation's epic wilderness judgment. The first instance is recorded in Exodus 32 and comes right after the nation is established at Mount Sinai. There, Israel grows impatient at Moses' lengthy absence and falls into the idolatrous worship of the golden calves. The nature of that critical failure is historic as it shatters the covenantal agreement to worship Yahweh as the sole deity. This event becomes a trend setting practice whereby the nation often reverts to the worship of local gods according to the depraved religions of the ancient Near East (cf. Numbers 25). The judgment is quick and harsh due to incremental 'rebellion' of the people:

> Remember this and never forget how you aroused the anger of the LORD your God in the wilderness. From the day you left Egypt until you arrived here, you have been rebellious against the LORD. At Horeb you aroused the LORD's wrath so that he was angry enough to destroy you. (Deut. 9.7-8; cf. 9.12–25)

The second instance which seals Israel's fate in the wilderness is the exploration mission of the promised land. This turns out to be another instance of rebellion when ten representatives instigate the majority of Israelites to reject Moses' leadership (Numbers 13–14; cf. Deut. 1.22–45). By doing so they also reject the leadership of Yahweh. In this failure, the response of the nation distains the covenantal promise of land by refusing to move forward.

> But you were unwilling to go up; you rebelled against the command of the LORD your God. You grumbled in your tents and said, 'The LORD hates us; so he brought us out of Egypt to deliver us into the hands of the Amorites to destroy us. Where can we go? Our brothers have made our hearts melt in fear. They say, "The people are stronger and taller than we are; the cities are large, with walls up to the sky. We even saw the Anakites there."' Then I said to you, 'Do not be terrified; do not be afraid of them. The LORD your God, who is going before you, will fight for you, as he did for you in Egypt,

before your very eyes, and in the wilderness. There you saw how the LORD your God carried you, as a father carries his son, all the way you went until you reached this place'. In spite of this, you did not trust in the LORD your God. (Deut. 1.26–32)

The allegations of Israel stated here are momentous, including the conjecture that the Lord hated them!

The fear of the Amorites is another matter but the assumption that the Lord's motivations are evil went too far, illustrating their lack of trust. In these narratives the wrath and anger of the Lord is described to highlight the culmination of rebellious behaviour which finally is eclipsed with his judgment. The resulting failure indicates two main problems. The first has to do with the original mandate of God for his people, in taking dominion of the earth or land, and ruling in the sacred space according to the laws of the Lord (Gen. 1.26). The second has to do with the apprehension of the land of promise according to the covenant made at Mount Sinai.[27]

Rather than pressing forward to take dominion and expand the kingdom of God, they reflect on a few pleasant memories of Egypt—preferring the 'easier life of slavery' in the building of the Egyptian kingdom, than the forward movement in freedom to establish Israel's kingdom. In this event, the nation shows evidence of not understanding their covenantal role as a nation. Yahweh chooses Israel as a treasured possession; he makes them a kingdom of priests—a holy nation that would receive the gift of land and take dominion for Yahweh to rule. Instead of pressing onward, the majority desire to return to the land of subjugation.

In both of these pivotal events, the wrath of the Lord initiates a potentially devastating judgment which jeopardizes the covenant. Yahweh proposes to punish Israel and begin afresh with Moses who launches into an extensive intercession and arbitration with the Lord. In a metaphoric way, these chapters reflect the descent of Israel from a covenantal high on Mount Sinai to a very low valley in the shadow of death where they experience judgment, wasted opportunity and a lost generation in the wilderness.

---

27 According to Deuteronomy, the culmination of these events brings about the divine resolution:

> When the LORD heard what you said, he was angry and solemnly swore: 'No one from this evil generation shall see the good land I swore to give your ancestors, except Caleb son of Jephunneh. He will see it, and I will give him and his descendants the land he set his feet on, because he followed the LORD wholeheartedly'. "Because of you the LORD became angry with me also and said, 'You shall not enter it, either'". (Deut. 1.35–37)

11.1–25.18—HARDSHIPS, CONFLICTS, REBELLION AND JUDGMENT

13.1–3—Selecting Leaders for the Exploration

While Israel is camped in the wilderness of Paran, Yahweh instructs Moses to send a 'leader' (נשיא; or chief) from each of the twelve tribes into the 'land of Canaan' (ארץ כנען) for 'exploration' (תור 'to scout or spy'). Their reconnaissance mission is to determine the strength of the inhabitants in the land to ascertain what resources are needed for the incursion. This is the land of promise that the Lord presents to Abraham who dwelt there by faith.[28] Finally, after many years of exile and oppression in Egypt, the Israelites are poised for entry into their own real estate. Regardless of what these leaders would find in Canaan—this is the gift of property that Yahweh intended to grant his people.[29]

13.4–16—Selected Explorers

Once again, the twelve tribal names are recorded with the specific name of a selected leader as well as the father's name. The order of the tribal names is slightly different from Numbers One, but each selected person is notably a leader in the tribe and selected as the representative who will bring back a report to their own people. A variety of epithets are used for the leaders such as spies or scouts, but the parameters of their assignment implies that they are explorers. The fact that these are different leaders from the earlier listing indicates a significant leadership structure for each tribal group to ensure representation for the needs of so many people. The leaders are:

> from the tribe of Reuben, Shammua ('renowned') son of Zakkur ('mindful');
> from the tribe of Simeon, Shaphat ('has judged') son of Hori ('white bread');
> from the tribe of Judah, Caleb ('dog') son of Jephunneh ('he will be facing');
> from the tribe of Issachar, Igal ('he redeems') son of Joseph ('Yahweh has added');
> from the tribe of Ephraim, Hoshea ('salvation') son of Nun ('continue or increase');

---

28 The reaffirmations of land ownership promised to Abraham are numerous (Gen. 12.7; 13.15, 17; 15.18; 17.8; 24.7; 26.3 f.; 28.13 f.; 35.12; 48.4; 50.24).

29 The main term for 'land' (ארץ) occurs 1472 times in the OT alone! However, the context determines whether it refers to the earth in a cosmic sense, land, or ground (cf. M. Ottosson, 'ארץ', *TDOT*, I, pp. 393–401). In Numbers it primarily refers to the gifted inheritance of land in its 87 references. The predominate chapters where land is featured are in Numbers 13–14 (36 times) and 45 times in Numbers 32–35.

from the tribe of Benjamin, Palti ('my deliverance') son of Raphu ('healed');

from the tribe of Zebulun, Gaddiel ('God is my fortune') son of Sodi ('acquaintance');

from the tribe of Manasseh (a tribe of Joseph), Gaddi ('My fortune') son of Susi ('my horse');

from the tribe of Dan, Ammiel ('my kinsman is God') son of Gemalli ('camel driver');

from the tribe of Asher, Sethur ('hidden') son of Michael ('who is like God');

from the tribe of Naphtali, Nahbi (also means 'hidden') son of Vophsi ('rich');

from the tribe of Gad, Geuel ('majesty of God') son of Maki ('decrease').

The selected and registered representatives from the twelve tribes are probably younger men than those listed in previous records. These are men who are strong and capable for the exploration task as well as potential skirmishes. Some of the names have impressive meanings but two of the names will be singled out due to the nature of the positive reports they bring, namely Caleb from the tribe of Judah, and Hoshea from the tribe of Ephraim. Moses renames Hoshea with the theophoric 'Yehoshua' (יהושע; 'Yahweh is salvation'), which becomes very significant based on the considerable interaction and experiences he has with Moses (cf. Exod. 17.9, 13; 24.18; 32.17; 33.11; Num. 11.28). Joshua is an eager student, intern, and devoted servant who exhibits positive traits as he moves forward in his leadership development.

13.17–24—*The Commission*

Instructions for the dozen explorers are specific and include some military type of assessments. They are to observe and analyze the productivity of the land, as well as the type of inhabitants. They are to examine the land's quality, presumably for agriculture, as well as the types of trees and produce. They are to take stock of the people's population numbers as well as the strength of their fortifications and types of housing. Finally, they are tasked to return with some of the fruit in the land.

The pattern of this passage appears to fall into a type of 'testing' narrative. The covenantal partner is given promises which are then tested according to an obedience and fulfilment grid. Several examples are evident in the Pentateuch beginning with Adam and Eve who are instructed to enjoy all the products of Eden except for the produce from the tree of the knowledge of good and evil. Noah is instructed to build the ark for reasons unknown to him. Abraham is told to leave Ur for an unknown land and after realizing the promise of a son, he is tested on Moriah to sacrifice his firstborn son Isaac. Similarly, Moses faces the formidable test of returning to Egypt to remove God's people from their oppressors. Likewise, the exploration of the land assignment, appears to be a significant test for the selected leaders and for Israel. Will the scouts take an inventory of the situation in order to determine the resources required for a military incursion into the land?

The itinerary is extensive and ranges from the Negev, the dry southern area, up to the northern hill country. The range is from the southern Desert of Zin as far as northern Rehob, toward Lebo Hamath, which eventually forms the boundary for Israel (cf. Num. 34.7–9). The city of Hebron is in the south and the explorers have to go through it on their return. The text notes that Hebron—a city seven years older than Zoan in Egypt, is inhabited by Ahiman, Sheshai and Talmai, the descendants of Anak. This reference implies that Hebron is a significant city in comparison to Zoan which becomes a main administrative centre in Egypt. Reference to the Anakites suggests that the inhabitants are either very powerful rulers, or very large people.[30] Whatever the case, they are depicted as formidable obstructions for Israel.

The exploration of the territory corresponds to the similar sojourn made by Abraham who also traversed Canaan to see the land gifted by Yahweh. According to Gen. 12.6–9,

> Abram traveled through the land as far as the site of the great tree of Moreh at Shechem. At that time the Canaanites were in the land. The LORD appeared to Abram and said, 'To your offspring I will give this land'. So he built an altar there to the LORD, who had appeared to him. From there he went on toward the hills east of Bethel and pitched his tent, with Bethel on the west and Ai on the east. There he built an altar to the LORD and called on the name of the LORD. Then Abram set out and continued toward the Negev. (Gen. 15.6)

Abraham traverses the whole region to discover the promised property and he begins to believe in the eventual ownership of the land. In fact, the covenantal renewal reiterates the promise of the son and the ownership of the land based upon Abraham's belief in the Lord. "On that day the LORD made a covenant with Abram and said, 'To your descendants I give this land, from the Wadi of

---

30 Milgrom, *Numbers*, p. 103, suggests, based on the Genesis 23 background, that they were perhaps Hittite noblemen.

Egypt to the great river, the Euphrates—the land of the Kenites, Kenizzites, Kadmonites, Hittites, Perizzites, Rephaites, Amorites, Canaanites, Girgashites and Jebusites'" (Gen. 15.18–21). Hebron is a special place for Abraham who receives Yahweh's promises there. Hebron is also a burial place for some of the patriarchs. The nations listed here will figure into the historical events that take place during the wilderness and conquest period for Israel.

After following the instructions of Moses, the explorers return with a selection of produce to provide evidence of a fertile and productive agricultural land. It is harvested from the Valley of Eschol, presumably in the southern region near Hebron, on their return trip. Pomegranates, figs, and an enormous cluster of grapes are carried for the community to observe and taste. The quality of grapes are important to inspect since not all varieties are good. The metaphor of grapes and wine is used in scripture to determine or test the quality of relationship with Yahweh. Nations are judged according to what they 'produced', and Yahweh is the divine vintner who inspects his crop to determine its quality (cf. Isa. 5.1–7).

13.25–29—Forty Days in the Promised Land!

The whole trek takes the explorers forty days—a significant trip that amounts to approximately 800 kilometers (Num. 13.25). They return to the Israelites who are camped at Kadesh which marked the southern boundary to the land of promise. Kadesh is on the outskirts of two large wilderness regions of Zin and Paran. Upon returning to the encampment, the surveyors present their findings to the leaders and gathered community. Indeed, the land they saw was good! The presentation of fruit is impressive and their account of a land flowing with milk and honey is an appropriate metaphor for a special place of fruitfulness and abundance. In reference to Canaan there is special theological significance for the promised land, but the area is not always clearly defined. Its greatest extent is referred to in the expression 'from the river of Egypt to the Euphrates' but most often in the general sense of 'the land of the Canaanites' (Num. 34.2). The land belongs to Yahweh and is his 'heritage' to give. He owns it and rules over it.[31] It has paradisiacal characteristics as the abundantly blessed, glorious land, flowing with milk and honey (Num. 13.27; 14.7–9; 16.13–14; Deut. 6.3; 11.9). However, the reports of positive blessings are offset by the fortifications that the

---

31 'As Yahweh's inheritance, the land has exuberant epithets. It is the good land (Exod. 3.8; Num. 14.7; Deut. 1.25) an expression that combines fruitfulness, wealth, beauty—in short, the fullness of blessing'; (cf. Ottosson, 'ארץ', p. 403). Tigay states that "'A land oozing milk and honey' came to be a proverbial description of the fertility of the land of Israel, representing the products of animals and the earth, of herders and farmers". *Deuteronomy*, p. 438.

'powerful' people inhabit. Typical fortifications of walled cities could reach ten metres in height with stones up to four metres wide! To emphasize the danger of going back to this place, the explorers noted the presence of the descendants of Anak. Not only are these people portrayed as formidable foes, but many other people groups inhabit the promised land: 'The Amalekites live in the Negev; the Hittites, Jebusites and Amorites live in the hill country; and the Canaanites live near the sea and along the Jordan'.

Some of these people are nomadic with cattle and require considerable pastureland and water resources. The Hittites, located in the northern region are considered an intimidating force. The Jebusites are inhabitants around the area of Jerusalem while the Amorites are located in the Transjordan regions. While the term 'Canaanites' could refer in general to the population of people living in Canaan land, they are also a distinctive group with their own culture and religious practices. The report is factual and concise, yet comprehensive in summarizing the key inhabitants as well as the four main regions encompassing the promised land of Canaan.

13.30–33—*The Exhortation*

Sensing the effect of the negative conclusions with biased opinions of the majority, Caleb (כלב, which means 'dog') interjects a more positive perspective and courageous estimation: 'We should go up and take possession of the land, for we can certainly do it'. Caleb represents the tribe of Judah and becomes an eloquent spokesperson. His heritage appears to be Kenizzite, the son of Jephunneh (Num. 32.12) and according to the lineage in Genesis 36 is a descendant of the Edomite clan fathered by Esau (Gen. 36.11). Kenaz is a son of Eliphaz and one of the chiefs in the Edomite clan (Gen. 36.15, 42) but somewhere along their interactions they attach themselves to the tribe of Judah where Caleb rises to leadership. He is another example of how a variety of foreigners affiliate themselves to Israel and are often exemplary persons of faith like Jethro (Exodus 18). For his faith and inspirational outlook, Caleb is rewarded with assurance of an inheritance in the land (Num. 14.24; cf. Josh. 14.7 ff.).

With two very diverse standpoints, the confrontation begins to heighten as the majority of explorers enlist the people's support. Their claim that the inhabitants are powerful is declared and they promote the idea that Israel is not able to take the land. Not only do they exaggerate the negative elements of the report, but they depict a dangerous land that 'devours' those who live there. This could be a metaphoric way of depicting land that would not support agricultural production and may even indicate a famine or drought situation. However, this is not a reference to the good agricultural soil but to the threat of defeat by people who are stronger and perhaps better prepared for battle. 'All the people we saw there are of great size'. The strength and size of the people are hyperbolized with a reference to the Nephilim. To this day the identity of the Nephilim remains a controversial and misunderstood reference, first mentioned in Gen. 6.4. The technical meaning is the 'fallen ones' giving rise to interpretations of fallen angels. In the Septuagint the rendering 'giants' has promoted speculative interpretations. The most likely explanation for these 'descendants of Anak who come from the Nephilim' is that they are powerful, aggressive rulers who are capable of securing their fortified cities and resisting invaders. The grasshopper metaphor implies how small or impotent they feel in the presence of such dominant people with garrisoned cities. With the rejection of Caleb's call to action, the scene quickly deteriorates.

14.1–10a The People Protest

On this occasion the whole 'community' (עדה) 'assembles' (קהל) together to confront and object to the leadership of Moses (Num. 14.1-4). This gathering implicates the entire community for their involvement in the rebellion against the leaders (cf. Num. 13.26; 14.1, 2 twice, 5, 10, 27, 35, 36). The community is swayed by the negative presentation of the spies who fail in their military function of motivating the community to accept their role in the conquest of the land promised by Yahweh. The community vocalizes their dissent with emphatic loud cries that are not easily consoled. In fact, the people weep throughout the night.

The emphasis on the whole assembled community serves to expose a unified consensus against the leadership of Moses, Aaron and Yahweh. The nation even alleges malicious intent on the part of Yahweh to see them die in the land by the sword. The people's evaluation of Yahweh's purposes are not accurate considering his deliverance acts through the exodus events. Their response illustrates the fickleness of people who are easily swayed to believe the false report. Even though they witnessed a staggering emancipation, they fear that Yahweh would allow their children and wives to be carried off into exile. The fear of war is justifiable, but the fear of becoming 'plunder' is paradoxical. Yahweh delivers them from the Egyptian military and when they depart from the land of oppression, they actually 'plundered' the Egyptians, taking gifts of gold, silver and clothing (Exod. 12.35–36). He is more than capable of doing this again.

Yet their confrontational stance before the leaders is clearly stated with two preferences: they preferred to have died in Egypt or in the wilderness. Death is favoured over putting trust in Yahweh to lead them in his good plans towards their designated inheritance. Finally, their indignation formulates into a plan to select a leader who would take them back to Egypt. With this strong motivating opinion against the positive exhortation of Caleb and Joshua, their judgment would be severe and their desire to die in the wilderness, granted. Numbers 14 ends with a military defeat after many people carelessly move ahead against their leaders' warnings.

Knowing how perverse and treacherous this proposition is, Moses and Aaron fall prostrate before the community to symbolically indicate their horror, but also to be in a posture of intercession (cf. Num. 14.5; 16.4, 22, 45; 20.6). The calibre of Joshua and Caleb becomes evident as they rise to the challenge of responding favourably to the divine plan. There is so much human drama in this episode which heightens the tremendous implications of how Israel responds. Joshua and Caleb tear their clothes to indicate their grief and indignation with the crowd. With their leaders on the ground, they exhort the nation, appealing for a rational response:

> The land we passed through and explored is exceedingly good. If the LORD is pleased with us, he will lead us into that land, a land flowing with milk and honey, and will give it to us. Only do not rebel against the LORD. And do not be afraid of the people of the land, because we will devour them. Their protection is gone, but the LORD is with us. Do not be afraid of them. (Num. 14.7–9)

These two reputable witnesses verify the excellence of Yahweh's gift of land, as well as his ability to protect the nation due to his presence with them. They call for trust and courage and warn against fear and rebellion.

Whereas the first appeal for compliance is made by Caleb alone, now both Joshua and Caleb promote their appeal for trust in tandem.[32] Both individuals have impressive backgrounds with Caleb representing the tribe of Judah. The stamina and calibre of Caleb is summarized in Josh. 14.6–11 when he approaches Joshua on behalf of Judah to claim Hebron as their inheritance. Caleb is forty years old when Moses sends him out with the explorers. It is because of his wholehearted trust in the Lord's provision of land that he exhorts the people and for this act of faith, Moses promises Caleb an inheritance: 'The land on which your feet have walked will be your inheritance and that of your children forever, because you have followed the LORD my God wholeheartedly' (Josh. 14.9). Forty-five years later Caleb stakes his claim and vows to drive out the Anakites from their fortified cities according to the promise and assistance of the Lord.

---

32 Although Caleb (9 times) and Joshua (11 times) are usually named in tandem, Joshua is mentioned slightly more often due to his mounting leadership profile (cf. Numbers 27). In the book named after him, 'Joshua' is referred to more than 150 times.

Exodus 17 presents Joshua as a victorious military leader who defeats the Amalekites, thereby advancing his leadership prowess. He becomes Moses' assistant and devoted attendant who patiently waits for Moses at Mount Sinai. Joshua is an eager intern of Moses but also displays his intense desire to know Yahweh by lingering at the Tent of Meeting and serving as needed (Exod. 33.11). His selection to represent the tribe of Ephraim among the group of twelve leaders who travel to Canaan indicates his developing reputation. His leadership and courage is publicly displayed with Caleb, providing another stage for Joshua to become the selected leader for the conquest. In recognition of Joshua's aspiring leadership role, Moses changes his name from Hosea to Joshua.

14.10–12—Yahweh Responds with a Devastating Change in Itinerary

In Numbers 13–14 Yahweh speaks several times, beginning with the initial instruction to explore the land (13.1–2). In 14.11–12 Yahweh questions Moses about the people's behaviour and then pronounces the divine intent to punish. The details regarding the divine perspective and intention is further elaborated on in two extensive declarations which clearly explain the impending consequences and reasons for the judgments that follow (Num. 14.20–25, 26–35; cf. Genesis 3).

Further drama takes place as the people resolve to stone the witnesses (Num. 14.10). Intervention comes from Yahweh who not only restrains the people's actions with his presence in the glory cloud, but he speaks to Moses in exasperation. 'How long will these people treat me with contempt? How long will they refuse to believe in me, in spite of all the signs I have performed among them? I will strike them down with a plague and destroy them, but I will make you into a nation greater and stronger than they'. The response of Yahweh is warranted in the light of the recurrent 'rebellious' (מרד) 'contempt' (נאץ; spurn or despise) exhibited by the community. This word for 'contempt' (נאץ) is a strong term used in contexts of a divine and human encounter where the people expressly scorn Yahweh's beneficence.[33] The characteristic fickleness of human nature is exposed as they soon forget Yahweh's provisions and 'signs' (אות) among them. Yahweh threatens to judge them with a destructive plague and proposes to begin again, solely with Moses (as he did previously with Noah and Abraham). The allegations against the people include the omission of faith, and the commission of distain for Yahweh's leading.

Yahweh's response is similar to what happens after the Mount Sinai revelation and the golden calf episode: 'I have seen these people', the LORD said

---

33   Levine, *Numbers 1–20*, p. 364.

to Moses, 'and they are a stiff-necked people. Now leave me alone so that my anger may burn against them and that I may destroy them. Then I will make you into a great nation' (Exod. 32.9–10). The core problem in this episode is the rapid digression from covenantal expression to that of rebellion and idolatry. In Exod. 19.8 the people proclaim, 'We will do everything the LORD has said'. However, the pattern of sin which occurs in incidents after creation with Adam and Eve, during the Exodus events, and with the Mosaic covenant are intensifying actions which amount to serious relational breaches that affect the whole community. Although the covenantal promises are still attainable, the repercussions for a whole generation of people are staggering.

14.13–19—Moses Intercedes

No doubt Moses is reminded of the golden calf events and discerns the ominous portents of judgment on the horizon. He responds with passionate intercession to dissuade Yahweh from his intent to strike the people with a plague. Moses approaches the Lord with a diplomatic, courageous, and pastoral mediation. His appeal is similar to the prophetic intercession of Exod. 32.11–13 where he negotiates, "why should your anger burn against your people, whom you brought out of Egypt with great power and a mighty hand? Why should the Egyptians say, 'It was with evil intent that he brought them out, to kill them in the mountains and to wipe them off the face of the earth'? Turn from your fierce anger; relent and do not bring disaster on your people. Remember your servants Abraham, Isaac, and Israel, to whom you swore by your own self: 'I will make your descendants as numerous as the stars in the sky and I will give your descendants all this land I promised them, and it will be their inheritance forever'". The prayer of Moses appeals to the Lord's covenantal love and promises. His intercession is effectual and brings about a favourable response from Yahweh who relents. Disaster is averted. Moses then makes another passionate appeal, replete with an historical witness of Yahweh's miraculous interventions on behalf of Israel.

In Num. 14.13–16, Moses' appeal is a more concise arbitration focused on two core elements. The first concern is for Yahweh's reputation among the nations—particularly Egypt.

> Then the Egyptians will hear about it! By your power you brought these people up from among them. And they will tell the inhabitants of this land about it. They have already heard that you, LORD, are with these people and that you, LORD, have been seen face to face, that your cloud stays over them, and that you go before them in a pillar of cloud by day and a pillar of fire by night.

Moses may be presumptuous in his claim that the Egyptians know all these things, but the facts presented are clear: Yahweh does indeed deliver Israel from Egypt. The Egyptians do witness the incredible plagues of judgment. They have first-hand knowledge about the presence and power of Yahweh with his people. Apparently, many have also witnessed the revelation of Yahweh displayed in the theophanic-glory cloud and fire.

The second element Moses portrays has to do with the power of Yahweh to complete his purposes for Israel. Moses exposes the human tendency to allege that Yahweh is impotent to bring Israel into the promised land. Furthermore, the people's allegation that Yahweh is incapable to fulfil his promises to them could cause speculation that he acts as an executioner. In fact, their allegation is that Yahweh would rescind the patriarchal promise he swore 'on oath' that he would give them the gift of land (Exod. 13.11). 'If you put all these people to death, leaving none alive, the nations who have heard this report about you will say, "The LORD was not able to bring these people into the land he promised them on oath, so he slaughtered them in the wilderness."' Moses concludes with a request for the Lord's power to be displayed according to the revelation Yahweh provides after the giving of the law on Mount Sinai—there God reveals his nature and character to Moses in a dramatic vivid covenantal renewal: 'Then the LORD came down in the cloud and stood there with him and proclaimed his name, the LORD. And he passed in front of Moses, proclaiming',

> The LORD, the LORD, the compassionate and gracious God, slow to anger, abounding in love and faithfulness, maintaining love to thousands, and forgiving wickedness, rebellion and sin. Yet he does not leave the guilty unpunished; he punishes the children and their children for the sin of the parents to the third and fourth generation. (Exod. 34.5-7)

Exod. 34.6-7 is a concise but deep level synopsis of God's character and nature. In Jewish liturgy it is referred to as the 'Thirteen Attributes of God' and is often recited in religious gatherings.[34] The verses are based on the second commandment which states:

> You shall not make for yourself an image in the form of anything in heaven above or on the earth beneath or in the waters below. You shall not bow

---

34. Sarna, *Exodus*, p. 216. The Talmud expands on the meaning of the attributes, but the main elements are rooted in the LORD's compassion, grace, mercy, truth, and loving kindness. It features his desire to forgive all iniquity and bring cleansing to those who repent and intercede.

> down to them or worship them; for I, the LORD your God, am a jealous God, punishing the children for the sin of the parents to the third and fourth generation of those who hate me, but showing love to a thousand generations of those who love me and keep my commandments. (Exod. 20.4–6)

The second commandment makes clear that idolatry, which is often considered spiritual adultery, is a rejection of God and his loving intentions for humankind. The ramifications of idolatrous practices are that they may initiate a trajectory which affects families and communities for many generations, unless eradicated.[35]

The Numbers intercession follows a more concise rehearsal of Yahweh's character and covenantal promise with Moses' appeal for forgiveness on behalf of the nation. The petition appeals for Yahweh to implement his power which is foundational to his magnificent character. His declaration affirms Yahweh's patience without denying his wrath. He affirms Yahweh's incredible 'loving kindness' (חסד), which sustains the covenantal commitments made at Sinai (Num. 14.18–19). This covenantal term only occurs here in Numbers (2 times) to affirm the Lord's enduring affection even though the punishments for disobedience will be extensive. Furthermore, Moses affirms Yahweh's ability and propensity to forgive sin and rebellion. However, this does not mean that the guilty walk away without consequences.

> Now may the Lord's strength be displayed, just as you have declared: 'The LORD is slow to anger, abounding in love and forgiving sin and rebellion (פשע). Yet he does not leave the guilty unpunished; he punishes the children for the sin of the parents to the third and fourth generation.' In accordance with your great love, forgive the sin of these people, just as you have pardoned them from the time they left Egypt until now. (Num. 14.17–19)

These verses are theologically loaded with terminology that is descriptive and illustrative of deep, spiritual implications.

---

35 Kaiser, *Exodus*, p. 423, comments,
> Children who repeat the sins of their fathers, evidence it in personally hating God; hence they too are punished like their fathers. Moses made it plain in Deut. 24.16: 'Fathers shall not be put to death for their children, nor children put to death for their fathers; each is to die for his own sin'. The effects of disobedience last for some time, but the effects of loving God are far more extensive: to a thousand [generations] (v. 6).

The mediation is embedded in covenantal theology and rooted in the nature of God. Even though the Sinai covenant is established in God's election of Israel, the 'firstborn'—there are covenantal obligations. The wayward son would be punished. Pardon (סלח) or 'taking away' the transgression (נשא) is available, but consequences do follow sinful actions. Reconciliation is possible but there are repercussions for the pattern of rebellion that is forming in Israel. How would this take place? The 'sin' (עון; depravity) of the fathers will have lasting effects on the children and generations to follow. In part, this concept is common in high context cultures or collectives where the group dynamics are more important than individual liberties. The actions of the father and mother have significant corollaries on the whole family and extended group. The contemporary conduct of family members would have impacts on future generations unless there is an intervention. Furthermore, recurrent rebellion will be punished by Yahweh as it is displayed from one generation to another. Rather than a devastating punishment as seen with the generation of Noah and Babel, the punishment is moderated. However, Yahweh would continue to actively 'punish' (פקד) in accordance with the requirements of divine justice. The children would witness the effects and have to make their own covenantal choices. If they learn from their errors and amend their religious affections, a transformation is possible (cf. Deut. 5.9–10; 7.9). Therefore, the importance of fidelity to the covenant is crucial for Israel so that faithfulness could be rewarded.

The importance of Exodus 34 is vital background in order to comprehend the gravity of what happens from Yahweh's perspective. There Moses appeals for Yahweh to not only forgive 'sin' (חטאה) and 'wickedness' (עון), but to remain with the 'stiff-necked' people and to take them to the Lord's inheritance. Yahweh responds affirmatively and renews his 'covenant' (ברית) with Israel in clear terms:

> I am making a covenant with you. Before all your people I will do wonders never before done in any nation in all the world. The people you live among will see how awesome is the work that I, the LORD, will do for you. Obey what I command you today. I will drive out before you the Amorites, Canaanites, Hittites, Perizzites, Hivites and Jebusites. (Exod. 34.10–11)

This affirmation is followed by an extensive list of warnings and commands which reinforce the devotion Yahweh demands in order to take Israel into the land of promise. These warnings are no doubt foremost in Moses' mind as he witnesses the incident of the exploration reports with the people's response and fears for divine retribution.

14.20-25—*Yahweh Relents*

Moses' intercession is met with Yahweh's concession: Israel is 'pardoned' (סלח) and Yahweh's anger subsides, but the consequences of the people's actions are staggering and extensive. The gravity of the situation is embedded in the fact that Israel witnesses the incredible revelation of Yahweh's glory as well as the tremendous signs performed in Egypt—including the ten plagues of the religious conflict. Moreover, the Lord gives provisions and performs many signs in the wilderness. Rather than allowing these experiences to increase their faith and trust, they characteristically disobey and actively test Yahweh 'ten times'. This reference brings to mind the Egyptian conflict and ten times that the Pharaoh refuses to comply with Yahweh's demands to let the people go (Exodus 7–11). At the end of the cycles of ten plagues, the Pharaoh's resistance finally come to an end and Israel is released. In a similar cycle of resistance, Israel does not comply with Yahweh's plans for them, and their rebellion finally results in judgment. Based on this ten-fold summary, a rabbinic tradition was formed concluding that there are ten (עשר; actually, ten times and not 'many' as some translations) trials in the wilderness where Israel 'tests' (נסה) Yahweh and does not heed his voice. These are prime examples of treating Yahweh with 'contempt'.

Allen provides a reasonable summary of the main instances of Israel's reactions in the wilderness journey:

> The ten times of the rebellions of the people against the grace of the Lord perhaps may be enumerated as follows: 1. At the Red Sea where it seemed that Pharaoh's army would destroy them (Exod. 14.10–12). 2. At Marah where they found bitter water (Exod. 15.22–24). 3. In the Desert of Sin as they hungered (Exod. 16.1–3). 4. In the Desert of Sin as they paid no attention to Moses concerning the storing of the manna until the morning (Exod. 16.19–20). 5. In the Desert of Sin as they disregarded Moses concerning the gathering of the manna on the seventh day (Exod. 16.27–30). 6. At Rephidim as they complained for water (Exod. 17.1–4). 7. At Mount Sinai as Aaron led the people in making the golden calf (Exod. 32.1–35). 8. At *Taberah* where the people raged against the Lord (Num. 11.1–3). 9. At *Kibroth Hattaavah* in the grumbling provoked by the rabble for quail (Num. 11.4–34). 10. At *Kadesh* in the Desert of Paran when the people refused to receive the good report of Joshua and Caleb but rather wished themselves dead. (Num. 14.1–3)[36]

---

36   Allen, *Numbers*, p. 822.

For this continuous pattern of disobedience, sin and failure, Yahweh is adamant to affirm the guilty would not see the land (and just as he promises on oath to bring them into the promised land, so now he affirms the guilty will not see the land). However, the leadership of Caleb is commended. Caleb has a different 'spirit' emulated by whole-hearted devotion combined with a positive vision. The difference is notable in comparison to the explorers who do not trust in Yahweh's provision, power and beneficence. Caleb believes in the divine plan, encouraging the nation to move forward in faith to the fertile gift of Yahweh who is present with them and able to overcome the inhabitants. For this Caleb and his descendants would be fairly rewarded with an inheritance of land.

However, the disobedience of the majority engenders a change of plans. The implication is that Yahweh would no longer fight on behalf of Israel. Without divine assistance the people are vulnerable to the Amalekites and the Canaanites who dwelt in the region. The itinerary is changed to divert the nation through the desert along the route to the Red Sea. Their journey no longer has a clear destination in sight, nor do they need to prepare for battle with the people of Canaan.

14.26–35—*Yahweh Pronounces the Judgment*

Yahweh has more to say, and the proclamation of judgment is announced to both Moses and Aaron. The Lord's patience finally wore out and the recurrent grumbling of the people needed to be addressed. He hears Israel's murmuring about food, leadership, water, enemies, and other inevitable hardships that arise in the adverse wilderness context. Whereas some of the grievances may be warranted due to the need for water and nutrition, many of the complaints are based on peripheral preferences. Yahweh's pronouncement of judgment is devastating and far-reaching: 'In this wilderness your bodies will fall—every one of you twenty years old or more who was counted in the census and who has grumbled against me' (Num. 14.29).

What the people ask for would in fact be realized (cf. Num. 14.2; 26.63–65). A generation would meet their demise in the wilderness. Whereas Adam and Eve are excommunicated from the garden of Eden, a generation of Israelites would not even be allowed to enter the promised land. This 'curse' would not be retracted and is declared with two paradoxical assertions. None of the individuals who are counted in the census of those who are over twenty would be permitted to enter the land that Yahweh swore to provide as a home, with the exception of Caleb and Joshua. Moreover, the people's fear that their children would be captured as plunder would not be realized because Yahweh ensures their entry into the land.

Although the children would enter the promised land, they too would face a wearisome period of wandering until the forty years of judgment are concluded—one year of punishment per day of exploration which results in the 'unfaithful' (זנות) response and rebellion, rather than covenantal faithfulness.[37] Yahweh's forbearance would be turned against them just as they turned away from him. This is the consequence for the 'wicked community' that first turned against Yahweh in recurrent measure after Israel's election, protection, and deliverance from Egypt. They would wander aimlessly under a generational death sentence for the same period of time that Moses was in Midian—40 years as a shepherd! The children of a faithless generation would suffer a type of curse, on behalf of their parents in the wilderness. During this period, they also witness the demise of their folks who perish and are buried outside of the land of promise. The suffering they endure for their 'sins' (עון) is intensified by the knowledge that Yahweh is 'against' them for rejecting his guidance. The punishment is reiterated with a solemn decree: 'I, the LORD, have spoken, and I will surely do these things to this whole wicked community, which has banded together against me. They will meet their end in this wilderness; here they will die' (Num. 14.35).

14.36-45—A Death Sentence and Further Repudiation

Ten of the explorers meet their fate for the rebellion instigated by their inflammatory report. Their judgment is immediate death by plague (מגפה)—only Joshua and Caleb are spared.[38] When Moses reports this consequence, the people mourn bitterly for the dead. However, their period of grieving is very limited, and they make two resolutions. Recognizing the gravity of what had occurred along with the devastating pronouncements of judgment, the people confess their sin. Secondly, rather than seek guidance they determine to force their way into the land of promise on their own initiative. Despite Moses' stern warnings that their intentions are disobedient, that their defeat is guaranteed for turning against the Lord, the people press onward. His prophetic word that the Lord would not be with them is ignored. Therefore, their defeat by the sword would be realized.

---

37   The term 'זנות' is a strong word that may mean harlotry in certain contexts (cf. Num. 25.1-3).

38   Several terms are used to indicate death by plague in Numbers but most often 'מגפה' indicates a sudden outbreak (cf. Num. 14.37; 16.48, 49, 50; 25.8, 9, 18; 26.1; 31.16). This form of the verb 'נגף' which appears 46 times in the OT usually refers to a 'striking down' by plague. In Num. 14.37 the punishment by plague is 'a sudden punitive blow or sudden death, sent by Yahweh to punish people for turning from him to Baal-peor or for rebelling against their leaders'. Cf. H.D. Preuss, 'נגף', *TDOT*, IX, p. 212.

Notwithstanding this dire prediction, the people move forward without Moses or the ark of the 'covenant' (ברית) in their midst.[39] The ark of the covenant not only symbolizes the Lord's presence but must be transferred by the Levites according to strict procedures. By not following them, the people show their rejection of both prophetic and priestly leadership in their quest. Without the symbol of the Lord's presence in their quest, the people repudiate the words of Moses and the requirements of Yahweh for direction in battle. Against Moses' double warning and clear command not to proceed with their planned attack they press onward to take the land by their own means. From a highpoint near Arad in the Negev, the Amalekites and Canaanites overpower the Israelite invaders, pushing them back to Hormah and eventually forcing a remnant back into the wilderness (cf. Num. 21.1–3). While there is no report concerning the quantity of dead from this incursion, the people suffer a resounding defeat.

All this occurs in accordance with Moses' warning that Yahweh would not fight for them—they are to heed the divine warnings, judgment, and head in a different direction. Their abandonment of Moses and Yahweh ends in failure and the beginning of the demise of a whole generation. Although the incidents of death seem limited in several passages (cf. Num. 11.33–34; 14.37; 16.49; 21.6; 25.9; 26.10; 27.3), the assertion of Num. 26.63–65 regarding the second census is clear: 'These are the ones counted by Moses and Eleazar the priest when they counted the Israelites on the plains of Moab by the Jordan across from Jericho. Not one of them was among those counted by Moses and Aaron the priest when they counted the Israelites in the Desert of Sinai. For the Lord had told those Israelites they would surely die in the wilderness, and not one of them was left except Caleb son of Jephunneh and Joshua son of Nun'.

Reflection and Response
Numbers 13–14: Shepherds and Spies for the Wilderness Itinerary
Reflection

The events that are recorded in these two chapters begin with an adventuresome reconnaissance mission but end with several devastating developments for the community. The detailed instructions for the mission are carried out by selected leaders who fulfil their purposes in observing what the land has to offer and surveying what the hurdles in taking the land might be.

---

39   The term 'covenant' appears five times in Numbers with important ramifications (cf. Num. 10.33; 14.44; 18.19; 25.12–13). cf. M. Weinfeld, 'ברית', pp. 269–279.

Yahweh's plans for Israel are always good and the blessing of land with abundant resources is to be an unconditional gift. This truth is verified in the covenantal statements and the Lord's 'oath' in several texts leading up to the land inspection. However, the timing and extent of land ownership is regulated by the covenantal curses and blessings (Deuteronomy 28–29). There are standards to be met, there is a relationship with Yahweh that must be honoured, and there is respect for leaders that must be exhibited.

The intentions of Yahweh include the forward movement of the nation in faith and development to take dominion over the land and to exercise service and care for people. The gift of land is never in question. All the land belongs to the Lord who has the right to allocate it according to his purposes. However, the behaviour of the inhabitants did have implications because realizing the purposes of God required faith, obedience, and action. The question for Israel: Will they move forward in obedience with Yahweh?

A few crucial observations from the exploration episode should be noted. It is Yahweh who commissions the explorers to survey the land of Canaan that he intended for Israel. The instructions for the mission are very clear. After forty days of surveying the land, the twelve explorers verify that the quality of land and produce is good. Their responsibility in reporting accurately and without personal bias is anticipated. However, the narration illustrates several realities of the human condition. It is much easier for people to contemplate life in a familiar setting than it is to imagine life in the unknown. The ten spies cannot visualize how Israel would be able to defeat the inhabitants of Canaan. They find it easier to persuade people to abort the divine mission through fear mongering, than to persuade people in the advancement towards a better, albeit an unknown, risky future. Only some leaders are able to envision a future where the risks are worth taking. The final verdict of the Lord is severe due to the extent of rebellion that had affected the response of the whole community. Unfortunately for Israel, the people choose to trust the negative reports in opposition to Yahweh's affirmation of a bright future in a special land.

Moses, Aaron, Caleb, and Joshua provide resilient and consistent direction for the community. However, their exhortations and intercession could not overcome the persistent negativity of the ten spies who convince the majority of people that taking the land is too difficult. Positive views are rejected in the light of hyperbolized danger. However, with Yahweh's leading and promised protection, the nation is expected to hear, learn, and move forward in trust. The crux of the positive words from Caleb and Joshua from a military perspective is what the Lord anticipates: 'We should go up and take possession of the land, for we can certainly do it'. This proactive exhortation is reinforced with a prophetic vision:

> The land we passed through and explored is exceedingly good. If the LORD is pleased with us, he will lead us into that land, a land flowing with milk and honey, and will give it to us. Only do not rebel against the LORD. And do not be afraid of the people of the land, because we will devour them. Their protection is gone, but the LORD is with us. Do not be afraid of them.

However, human nature and trepidation takes over and the community prefers a different direction with new leaders.

The forty-year wilderness judgment is a devastating lesson for the nation to learn but eventually the second generation are given another opportunity to move forward under the leadership of Joshua. Yahweh's exhortation provides all that is needed for the community to forge forward in faith:

> Now then, you and all these people, get ready to cross the Jordan River into the land I am about to give to them—to the Israelites. I will give you every place where you set your foot, as I promised Moses. Your territory will extend from the desert to Lebanon, and from the great river, the Euphrates—all the Hittite country—to the Mediterranean Sea in the west. No one will be able to stand against you all the days of your life. As I was with Moses, so I will be with you; I will never leave you nor forsake you. Be strong and courageous, because you will lead these people to inherit the land I swore to their ancestors to give them. Be strong and very courageous. Be careful to obey all the law my servant Moses gave you; do not turn from it to the right or to the left, that you may be successful wherever you go. (Josh. 1.2–7)

If Israel had heeded the Lord's direction earlier in their migration, a whole generation of people could have experienced life differently!

Response

Israel is on the brink of realizing new life with an inheritance gift of land. The conquest of the land has significant implications for the nation in fulfilling the kingdom expansion designed by Yahweh. The narrative provides several lessons for believers, calling for discernment and trust in the Lord's leading for institutional and personal guidance. Leaders who are responsible for communities of faith must be very clear in hearing, seeing, and envisioning the Lord's direction. They are responsible for persuading the community to move forward in taking dominion and developing the kingdom of God in whatever dimensions that may mean—micro or macro levels. This requires inspirational words, intercession and prophetic vision as exemplified by the primary leaders in this episode.

Moving forward by faith into unknown territory is never easy. Where there is no vision, the people lack clarity in purpose and may even perish. However, the Lord's direction is available. The divine interests are made known to prophetic leaders and Moses communicated the vision faithfully. Unfortunately, the lessons for those who refuse to follow Yahweh's instructions were staggering. They face a monotonous existence in the wilderness, some perish, and others are defeated in the unauthorized incursion into Canaanite territory. This latter incident illustrates the fluctuating decisions made by people without vision. By rejecting the direction of Moses and leaders, people proceed into a precarious situation and end up in a chaotic situation. The intercessory work of Moses is a constant reminder to leaders of the essential work to be done for people who are often frail, fearful, resistant to change and maybe even fickle when it comes to making hard decisions. Forward motion is always anticipated and valued. Failure to move results in stagnation, living in the former memories of life in Egypt.

Every community of faith in every generation is faced with situations that require reflection and response to the Lord's leading for the expansion of the kingdom. The way forward may seem formidable, but when God is in it, all things are possible. My wife and I faced a life-changing decision many years ago when tasked with a mission assignment in East Africa. The task before us was daunting and we realised how dependent we were in the Lord's provisions. Yet, moving forward into the unknown for ministry was the best choice we ever made. Likewise, many of our family and friends faced their life-changing decision to move forward in God's providence to leave persecution in Europe for distant lands of promise. Each generation faces their divine venture. God waits for the positive response.

15.1–41—Cultus Offerings and Sacrifices

The completion and dedication of the Tabernacle is described in Numbers 7–8. In honour of the Lord and his exalted place in the community, the people express their appreciation by presenting generous gifts for the place of worship. In Numbers 15, Yahweh provides further instructions to Moses regarding the cultus requirements for both private and public sacrificial rituals. These are additional clarifications which assume knowledge of the details in Lev. 6.1–11 and 7.11–34. Although the sacrifices are carefully described here, the desire to give sacrifices and offerings to God seems to be rooted in the human heart.

People in the ancient Near East commonly presented sacrifices to their deities, primarily for thanksgiving but also for provision and protection. In the Pentateuch, Moses mediates the regulations for giving that are requirements for both public and private sacrifices.

The content and placement of this chapter, with sacrificial and legislative themes, may seem out of place after the land exploration debacle. However, the beauty of the introduction is in its communication of hope renewed. Yahweh does not give up on a faithful remnant nor on his role in leading Israel. 'After you enter the land—where I am taking you' provides a positive vision of a future habitation in the promised land and affirms the Lord's commitment to bring them home (Num. 15.1–2). One day the covenant people will be settled in their own place and will enjoy the produce of the land. This crucial affirmation is reiterated by Moses to provide confidence and vision for their future. Yahweh's intentions for blessing are still possible for those who will enter the land and follow the required protocols. 'When you enter the land to which I am taking you and you eat the food of the land, present a portion as an offering to the LORD' (Num. 15.18–19).

The position and arrangement of Numbers 15 serves several functions. It clarifies some of the expectations regarding sacrifices and offerings. But it also addresses sins that may be inadvertent and others that are premeditated, or 'done with a high hand'. It could be speculated that the ordeal with the ten negative spies reveals that sins of commission are committed and the chapters to follow provide clear examples of sin. In other cases, however, where crowds of people are involved, the probability of many innocent people carried along with the mob are also affected. One example of flagrant behaviours is also recorded here to remind people of the sabbath requirements and commands that must be taken seriously. The thread of upholding the Mosaic laws runs through the chapter and culminates in the final instruction to affix tassels to their clothing for reminders: 'Then you will remember to obey all my commands and will be consecrated to your God' (Num. 15.40).

15.1–16—Cultic Requirements

Here the specific procedures and requirements are given for the offerings to be carefully prepared and presented. It may seem self-evident but the details of the cultus institutions for sacrifice and offering within the cultic calendar, were developed over time. The Pentateuchal sources reveal the process and direction through Moses of what Yahweh has in mind for the nation's worship system. While there may have been similar forms and comparable systems in the Near East, the meanings are different for Israel. The Egyptian cultus and mythology proves to be very different from what develops in Israel. Numbers 15 depends on foundational material in Exodus and Leviticus which provide more details on the ingredients, meaning and process of sacrifice.

There is a refining and specification that now fills in some of the ritual functions. The two main sacrifices fall under the category of 'burnt offerings' (עלה) and public sacred 'festivities' (זבח) where animals, grains and libations are ritually prepared and offered. Typical sacrifices involve animals, but in Numbers 15 additional food items are incorporated. For most animal sacrifices the entire corpse is consumed by fire.[40] The sacrifices that are ignited by fire include animals, grains and wine. They are presented along with vows made by individuals who are included in the sacrificial rituals which also involve killing the animal. Freewill and voluntary offerings are also given as an act of spiritual worship. Annual festival offerings are presented in public. In addition to the sacrificial prescriptions recorded in Leviticus, Numbers 15 offerings include grain, oil, and wine.

The quality and portions ware clearly specified for the offerings of a lamb, a ram, a young bull, with increasing quantities of the main elements: grain with the best flour, oil, and wine. These products are offered with gratitude to Yahweh by appreciative individuals and become a pleasing aroma to the Lord (Num. 15.4–12). All of the foregoing expectations are now affirmed for worshippers who are native born Israelites as well as those who are aliens and foreigners. Anyone who attaches themselves to the nation is given equal standing with commensurate responsibilities to make offerings according to these specifications. This is also a lasting ordinance in Israel which affirms the acceptance and equality of all: 'You and the alien shall be the same before the LORD' (Num. 15.15).

Regulations regarding aliens in Israel and 'foreigners' (גר) who desire to attach themselves to the nation for whatever reason (such as security, refuge for the landless, love of Israel's culture or religion) are generally generous and inclusive. These are rooted in the reality that even Abraham was a foreigner to the promised land and needed acceptance from the inhabitants (Gen. 14.13; 23.4) just as Israel was in Egypt (Exod. 2.22; Lev. 19.34). Just as Israel is dependent on God's allocation of land for them, so too are foreigners dependent on Israel's care and beneficence in providing shelter (Lev. 19.10; 23.22; 25.6). Such sojourners are often vulnerable and poor, requiring protection from an accepting community. Although they are required to live under community

---

40 D. Kellermann, 'עלה', *TDOT*, 11, p. 99 (referred to 286 times in the OT).

expectations and laws, they do not have equal rights or status in Israel. As a balancing provision to this reality, foreigners are not obligated to fulfil all the expectations of Israel's cultus and could be selective in volunteering to bring some offerings.

Required food offerings from the herd or flocks, are to be given as burnt offerings or as special sacrifices pleasing to the Lord. There are a few notable differences for the burnt offering requirements in Num. 15.22–31 when compared to Lev. 4.3–21, indicating more specification with slightly different emphases.[41] Both of these passages provide instruction on the purification offering which deals with inadvertent omissions in meeting community standards. In Numbers 15 the emphasis is on commands that are not implemented and therefore, require the burnt offering of a bull and goat which serves to cover the oversights effectively.

TABLE 1   Offerings and sacrifices

Name	Main references	Required product	Offerings blended	Purpose
Burnt Offering עלה	Num. 15.1–16; Lev. 1; 6.8–13; 22.18–20	Male Animal; Ram; Dove or Pigeon	Grain & Libation	Voluntary Sin & Fellowship; Devotion
Sacrifice זבח	Num. 15.3	Animals; Herd or Flock		Festival מועד Freewill נדבה
Grain offering מנחה	Lev. 2; 6.14–23; Num. 15.24	Fine Flour מנחה סלת	Oil & Wine	Thanksgiving; Gratitude to God
Libation נסך	Num. 15.5, 10, 24	Wine; Oil	Grain & Drink Offering	Appreciation for Provision; Forgiveness

Sacrifices also have a variety of purposes, including special vows, freewill contributions or festival offerings. As these are prepared, there are specific elements to be included with measured portions and procedures followed. This includes grain, oil and wine offerings with qualitative requirements and measurements. Sacrifices which are properly prepared and given with the right attitude of gratitude result in a 'pleasing aroma' before the Lord. In other words, Yahweh accepts such an offering (cf. Num. 15.3, 7, 10, 13).

---

41 Milgrom, *Numbers*, pp. 402–405, offers extensive discussion in Excursus 35.

15.17–21—*Aspiration*

The future hope of entry to the promised land is once again reinforced—it is not 'if you enter the land' but 'when'. There they will eat the abundant food of the land. Specifically, the first of the grain harvest is to be prepared and baked into a loaf. In other words, the first products of the land are to be offered to the Lord in acknowledgement of the fulfilment of the promise to bring them to their land. The offerings are to be given from the threshing floor in response to Yahweh's provision and gifts. The threshing floor note is another indicator of hope for the people to be established in the land with fields to harvest and places to process the produce.

Although the loaves are presented to Yahweh, the priests will be beneficiaries of the bread (Num. 18.12). Once again, this offering will be expected throughout the generations to follow.

15.22–31—*Personal Responsibility*

Further details are provided here for the probable situation where individuals, or the community in general, fail to adhere to expected community standards—particularly due to ignorance, forgetfulness or other. Instructions here are rooted in the Leviticus 4 passage that also addresses required sacrifices. These verses seem to be connected to the foregoing details of chapter 15 but clearly address the importance of adherence to 'any of the LORD's commands' that have been relayed by Moses. This assumes that the commands revealed to Moses and presented to Israel, will continue to be made known, taught, and explained to the community. In situations where inadvertent sins of omission occurred, reconciliation through appropriate sacrifices has to be sought. This process requires the services of the priest, who oversees the burnt offering of a young bull along with the prescribed grain and drink offering. Additionally, the male goat is an obligatory sacrifice to cover the unintended sin. Through this ritual, the priest makes 'atonement' (כפר) for the whole community, forgiveness and reconciliation is granted and the community is restored to harmony (Num. 15.25, 28).[42]

Resolution is also provided for individuals who intentionally commit sin. In this circumstance, the perpetrator has to give a year-old female goat as a sin offering. A priest must officiate for atonement and forgiveness to be granted. The same procedure is required for a native-born Israelite or a foreigner. Very

---

42   Atonement is achieved for the community through the priest's ministry and sin offering. In verse 28 atonement is made for the errant individual. The term for 'atonement' (כפר) occurs 18 times in Numbers, in a variety of tenses. Cf. B. Lang, 'כפר', *TDOT*, VII, pp. 292–301.

serious repercussions are in store for the defiant sinner whose actions result in blaspheming the Lord. They are to be cut off (כרת), literally 'severed' from the community (this term is used 3 times in v. 30–31). The punishment is appropriate, since the offender despises Yahweh's word and breaks the commands which are meant to bring order in the community. Failure to abide by community standards brings its own consequences as the following example of the 'sabbath breaker' illustrates.

Rabbinic views concerning the law of community 'severance', maintain that the punishment comes directly from Yahweh who causes some kind of additional consequence. This could include barrenness, premature death, alienation from family or similar dispositions. It is considered a divine penalty because it relates to a spiritual or religious command that is ultimately perpetrated against Yahweh. The concept of 'cutting off' (כרת) in the Pentateuch, functions as a stern warning to the community for breaking communal standards. This threat of exclusion for individuals and descendants was alarming and meant to restrain wrong behaviour. This refers to community disruptions in Num. 9.13; 15.30–31; 19.13, 20 (also 5 references in Exodus and 17 in Leviticus with similar meaning: cf. Exod. 12.15, 19; 30.33, 38; Lev. 7.20–21, 25, 27; 20.3, 5–6, 18).

Milgrom claims that there are nineteen cases of the 'cutting off' (כרת) in the Torah and the following examples are specifically drawn from Numbers.[43] Neglecting the offering of the paschal sacrifice (Num. 9.13), encroaching on the sanctuary in an unauthorized manner by the Levites (Num. 18.3; cf. 4.15, 19–20), blaspheming or desecrating the Lord's name by actions (Num. 15.30–31), and finally, disregarding purification rituals after being in contact with the dead (Num. 19.13–20). The timing and the extent of the punishment may also vary as determined by Yahweh. Views regarding this 'severance' and divine punishment seem to develop and change in OT periods, but initially the individual and their descendants, suffer considerable reproach from the community. In a similar case of judgment for rebellion, a severe illustration of public punishment is presented in the Korah, Dathan and Abiram verdict, which brings about the loss of their lives as well as their families (Num. 16.33).

15.32–36—*Sabbath Observance*
An example of flagrant disregard for the sabbath command is recorded, illustrating the seriousness of breaking the regulation for the day of rest. Members of the community apprehend a man gathering wood on the sabbath. He is

---

[43] Cf. Milgrom, *Numbers*, p. 406.

brought before Moses and Aaron for a ruling on the consequences. This example illustrates a concept which runs throughout the chapter and will culminate with an emphasis on keeping the commandments of the Lord as an expression of holiness (Num. 15.37–41). The motif of 'justice' (משפט) is connected to keeping ordinances and community rules for the well-being of all members (cf. Num. 15.16, 24). Although some consequences for disobedience are harsh, there is also a way to achieve atonement.

The sabbath day commandment receives the most extensive elaboration of the ten commandments revealed to Moses on Mount Sinai. In Exod. 20.8–11 the basic injunction is to 'Remember the Sabbath day by keeping it holy', by resting and abstaining from any work. It is rooted in the six creation days of the Lord who also rests on the seventh day which is blessed and sanctified. Exod. 31.12–17 expounds the command which includes the death penalty for infractions: "Then the LORD said to Moses, 'Say to the Israelites', 'You must observe my Sabbaths. This will be a sign between me and you for the generations to come, so you may know that I am the LORD, who makes you holy. Observe the Sabbath because it is holy to you. Anyone who desecrates it is to be put to death; those who do any work on that day must be cut off from their people'". The passage goes on to stress a six-day work week followed by the strict observance of the seventh day as a day of sabbath rest, sanctified for the Lord. This lasting ordinance must be observed and celebrated by all subsequent generations as a lasting covenant. Sabbath observance is a 'sign' of Israel's covenant allegiance and is rooted in Yahweh's creative work ending on the seventh day when 'he rested and was refreshed'.

In this instance it appears that the man is guilty of desecrating the sabbath by intentionally disregarding the day of rest. In Exodus 31 there is a double consequence for such an infraction—death or being cut off from the community. Since this is a serious and probably a new offence, it requires an official judgment, so the man is brought to Moses for a determination. The man is kept in custody during the deliberation which ends with the declaration that the man must die.[44] A similar case is noted in Lev. 24.10–23 where an individual blasphemes the name of God with a curse. In both cases there is a period of custody, deliberation, and the resulting verdict by Yahweh that death by stoning should be carried out, outside of the camp. The severe judgment is a stern warning to keep the sabbath day sacred as commanded by the Lord. The capital

---

44 Moses takes the case to the LORD for insight and a verdict which is considered an 'oracular' procedure to receive guidance from Yahweh regarding the case. A similar procedure is taken for the case of blasphemy in Lev. 24.10–23.

death sentence is carried out by the community as instructed and customary in high context inclusive societies. 'So the assembly took him outside the camp and stoned him to death, as the LORD commanded Moses'.

15.37–41—*Remembering Commandments*

The theme of instruction and adherence to the commandments of the Lord culminates in the directive to add tassels to the corner of garments. The tassels or 'fringes' (ציצת) include a blue cord on each tassel having eight strands with five knots. The main purpose of the tassels, which are used for the prayer shawl (tallit), is for a memory device. When the tassels are observed with the 'royal' blue thread, the individual is reminded of the commandments of Yahweh which should restrain sin and promote obedience to act on the 'commands' (מצוה; *mitzvah*). The '*tzitzit*' (ציצת) letter values were tabulated to 600 plus 8 threads and 5 knots—a symbolic memorable device to recall instructions that were to be obeyed. Rabbinic views also use the pomegranate as a symbol of all the commandments in the Torah by claiming it has 613 seeds. The tassels function as a 'sign' with a theological motivation attached, to instill obedience and reflection on the commands of Yahweh.

This chapter's legislative content functions as another affirmation of the importance of the instructions and commands which must be observed to maintain community order and holiness to the Lord. The instructions are detailed and transmitted from Yahweh to Moses. Their overall placement in various chapters of Numbers indicates that they should be read within the context to elaborate content and observance. The rules or 'ordinances' (חקה) are for all community members (twice in Num. 15.15 for emphasis). The characteristic refrain 'to be a lasting ordinance for all generations' affirms the importance of the rules which are meant to bring harmony in society (Num. 10.8; 18.23; 19.10, 21; cf. Lev. 23.14–41). The 'laws' (מצוה) must be observed for societal stability (6 times in Num. 15.18, 22–23, 31, 39–40).[45] Warnings on observing the com-

---

45 Since the third century AD, the commands were counted by some rabbis who maintained there are 613 in the Torah. In the *Bavli Makkot* 23b–24a Rabbi Simlai expounded: '613 commandments were said to Moses, 365 negative commandments, like the days of the year, and 248 positive commandments, corresponding to a person's limbs'. The tendency to count and organize the laws was common in order to codify them in readable categories. This occurs in *talmudic* and *midrashic* manuscripts to claim that God gave Israel exactly 613 commandments. Referencing 16th century Rabbis Joseph Karo and Moses Isserles in the *Shulhan Arukh*, Watts observes that 'Scholars arrange the provisions of Torah to produce, for example, the traditional enumeration of 613 laws, codes of *halakhah* and comparisons of the regulations with their biblical and extra-biblical parallels'. Cf. Watts, 'Reader Identification and Alienation in the Legal Rhetoric of the Pentateuch', p. 102.

mands are designed to restrain the individual from chasing after the lusts of the heart and the eyes. The tassels are intended to reinforce the memorable 'sign' function—symbols with sacred meaning for the worshipper.

Several terms are used to feature the Lord's commands and instructions which convey the divine will and authority. The directives of Yahweh given through Moses are to be implemented and followed for the well-being of the nation. In the OT the term '*mitzvah*' is used 466 times (in the present or past tense). In the repetitive phrase 'as the LORD commanded Moses', the divine authority is affirmed in the transfer of instructions.[46] The book of Numbers employs the term (מצוה) seventy-one times and concludes the book with the refrain 'at the LORD's command', emphasizing that the work of Moses in communicating Yahweh's instructions was fulfilled. Other terms in the OT are also employed to convey the legal notions of divine authority which required that the rules, ordinances, statutes, and commands given through Moses are to be made public and obeyed because they are authoritative.[47]

In verse 39b, 'the lustful urges' are an apparent reminder of the golden calf incident and the necessity of serving only Yahweh when they come to the promised land. Israel is sternly warned not to 'prostitute' their relationship by chasing after the illicit lusts of the human heart and eyes. This warning is made clear in the covenant renewal after the calf incident: 'Be careful not to make a treaty with those who live in the land; for when they prostitute themselves to their gods and sacrifice to them, they will invite you and you will eat their sacrifices. And when you choose some of their daughters as wives for your sons and those daughters prostitute themselves to their gods, they will lead your sons to do the same' (Exod. 34.15–16).

The metaphor of prostituting themselves to other gods and on lustful urges after the desires of the heart and flesh are based on the word 'fornicate' (זנה). Just like the covenantal agreement has a metaphoric marital element, so the term 'prostituting' refers to the human tendency of straying or following after foreign gods. The OT reveals that there was a strong appeal towards the rituals

---

[46] Several terms are employed to communicate the authority of the LORD in revealing his instructions for Israel. These are summarized in Psalms 19 and 119 which feature the incredible value of the commandments of Yahweh, for instruction, teaching, testimony, precepts, commandment, fear or reverence, and ordinances. The '*mishpat*' (משפט) indicates the legal judgments of the Lord which are true (Ps. 19.8–10) and are designed to bring order in society. Additionally, the concepts of blessing and cursing are portrayed as consequences of obedience or disobedience to the commands of God (cf. Lev. 26; Deut. 28).

[47] Cf. H. Ringgren, 'מצוה', *TDOT*, VIII, pp. 505–507.

and beliefs of other religions due to fear and superstition. Furthermore, some foreign worship practices were less stringent and offered promises of blessings in fertility and security (cf. Numbers 22–24). Thus, the illicit allure of strange gods leads to moral defection and idolatrous behaviour (Numbers 25).

Essentially the instructions and warnings in Numbers 15 serve to motivate spirituality. They are to instill hope and faith that life in the promised land will be blessed and not cursed. This was God's intent from the beginning—he chose Israel, redeemed them from the land of oppression and revealed himself to Israel as Lord and God. The Sinai covenant laid out the conditions of the arrangement which consolidated the relationship and to this Israel said: 'All that the LORD has spoken we will do' (Exod. 19.8). The ideal covenantal relationship is affirmed when the tassels cause the people to remember the Lord's redemptive work on their behalf. 'Then you will remember to obey all my commands and will be consecrated to your God. I am the LORD your God, who brought you out of Egypt to be your God. I am the LORD your God' (Num. 15.40–41).

16.1–17.13—Leadership Ambitions

The leadership confrontations for Moses begin with the people's complaints in Numbers 11. The leadership burden upon him is immeasurably demanding, but Yahweh's Spirit on Moses enables him to lead the nation. Moreover, the Spirit on Moses is shared with the seventy elders to empower them for ministry among the people. Additionally, the tribal leaders, priests and Levites provide significant support for Moses. In Numbers 12, the allegations of Miriam and Aaron pose another type of conflict regarding Yahweh's choice for prophetic revelation and the preeminent position of Moses over the Israelites. Numbers 13–14 records the escalating defiance of the ten explorers who instigate a wide-spread community opposition against Moses and Aaron. The reconnaissance mission becomes a watershed moment for Israel. This episode is the capstone event that verifies Israel's characteristic contempt for Yahweh's divine plan for the nation to begin the conquest and inhabit their inherited property. The community rebellion solidifies their punishment of life and death in the wilderness.

As if those disturbing incidents are not enough for Moses to resolve, he faces another major offensive in Numbers 16–17 from certain leaders and groups with vested interests. Some of the issues involved have long standing historical backgrounds but they come to a climax in the context of the wilderness frustrations and delayed entry into the promised land. These chapters form a compendium of internal threats to Moses' leadership in particular, but also include threats to Aaron's priestly role and family functions. The narratives of aggression are a culmination of internal threats to Moses and Israel's destiny. They will be followed by the Balaam episodes which feature the external threats to Israel's inheritance and legacy.

The section comprising Numbers 16–18 has several problematic matters that give rise to theories of divergent traditions and details in the narrative. Specifically, there are sudden scene changes, interesting dialogues, and several repetitive sections. Commentators take a variety of positions in dealing with these elements and arrive at diverse conclusions. The source critical analysis work of Gray is still influential for the careful dissection and attribution of material to P and JE (Priestly; Jahwist; Elohist traditions). His theory in the development of the narrative includes the initial single authorship of a P strand that is expanded by other P interests over time and then integrated with details from JE. The important elements of theme, conflict, leadership ambition and tension are pieced together from several sources before final edits, resulting in the present narration of events.[48] Therefore, while it is evident that there is a long history of compilation, development and preservation going on here, the literary approaches taken by Alter, Milgrom and others inform a number of key theological teachings. One is Alter's assertion that the 'editorial combination of different literary sources might usefully be conceived as the final stage in the process of artistic creation which produced biblical narrative'.[49] This is part of the process and appears to be an ancient form of literary artistry that employs the discontinuities, duplications, and contradictions without feeling obligated to smoothen the reading or delete the different details of the narrative. Alter's example refers to Numbers 16 where Korah appears to be a kind of archetype of the wilful rebel against legitimate rule. However, the chapter suggests that 'two different rebellions were superimposed with the resulting contradictions as to the identity of the rebels, the purpose of the rebellion, the place of confrontation with Moses, and the manner in which the rebels are destroyed'. These differences are left in the text for distinctive reasons which will be observed.

Another variation occurs in the verse allocations made between the Hebrew MT text and English versions. The commentary below will follow the NIV verse references.

---

[48] Cf. Milgrom, *Numbers*, pp. 414–423; Gray, *Numbers*, pp. 197–202; Levine, *Numbers 1–20*, pp. 405–432.

[49] Alter, *The Art of Biblical Narrative*, pp. 133–134.

NIV & English	Masoretic text
16.1–35	16.1–35
16.35–50	17.1–15
17.1–13	17.16–28

A careful literary focalization on narrative features in this episode provides a clear picture of the controversies which Moses and Aaron face. The braiding together of the conflict events involves four distinct segments which portray leadership ambitions by named individuals with 250 supporters and presents them amid intensifying markers. The overall effect is to show that the leadership conflicts are not warranted nor prudent. The insubordinate actions are focused on the leadership of Moses and Aaron, but they also impinge on the choice and appointment of these leaders by Yahweh. The disputes concern the validity and selection of Moses as primary leader who is confronted by Dathan and Abiram. Additionally, some Levites are against Aaron which instigates a larger insurrection against him by tribal leaders. These episodes then give way to a general uprising of the whole community and once again, disagreement threatens the well-being of the Israelites.[50]

The importance of the Levitical role and functions are highlighted in Numbers to a greater degree than any other OT book. The Levites are referred to about 73 times in various contexts and several chapters detail their status, role, and prominence, with the risks involved in ministry responsibilities in the nation (Numbers 1, 3–4, 8, 18). The importance of their selection, positioning, and function is affirmed: 'The Levites, however, are to set up their tents around the tabernacle of the covenant law so that my wrath will not fall on the Israelite community. The Levites are to be responsible for the care of the tabernacle of the covenant law' (Num. 1.53; cf. 1.47–53). The nation is adequately warned that the Levites are protectors of the sacred materials and judgment will fall on those who do not observe the sanctity of the Tabernacle. A fitting summation of this is recorded in chapter 18 to round out the tragic events in chapters 16 to 17 and provide a recapitulation of the Levitical ministry tasks. For their considerable risk and role in carrying the sacred tabernacle fixtures, they are rewarded with practical, material benefits.

---

[50] For a detailed analysis of the relevant elements in these chapters see D.J. Taylor, 'A Narrative Critical Analysis of Korah's Rebellion in Numbers 16 and 17' (PhD Thesis, University of South Africa, 2010), pp. 90–108; 206 ff.

Although Numbers 16 to 17 shows evidence of careful editing and blending of stories, the overall effect of the narrative reflects design and purpose. With its placement in the centre of Numbers, the episode accentuates how serious the developing rebellion of leaders is for Moses and Aaron. It is a culmination of conflicts which have major impacts on the political and religious structures in Israel's leadership formation. The overall dramatic presentation is reinforced by the devastating judgments on those who confront not only Moses and Aaron, but Yahweh.

16.1–2—Confrontation

The record of conflict begins with the identification of leaders who take issue with the leadership powers of Moses and Aaron. The main instigators are introduced to set the scenes which follow. These characters are aggressive antagonists who vilify the leadership of Moses and Aaron. The concise introduction provides minimal but sufficient detail to introduce the background to the confrontation. The verbal expressions used in verses 1–2 indicate an 'insolent' emboldened grasp for power in opposition to Moses. The primary adversaries are Korah, Dathan and Abiram who influence another 250 well known and respected leaders in the community. Together, this formidable group of men are emboldened to challenge Moses and Aaron.

Korah, a descendant of Levi, appears to feel that as the eldest son of the second son of Kohath, he should have a higher position and not be omitted from priestly leadership. In fact, his main assertion appears to be that he too should have a role in the priestly services of the Tabernacle. There is a genealogical element to his contention indicating some family rivalry. In the case of Dathan and Abiram, their lineage is traced back to Reuben whose family blessing is reduced to a curse due to his impropriety with his stepmother (Gen. 49.3–4). Typically, in ancient near eastern cultural practices, such an act of impropriety often signifies leadership ambitions in the clan with intent to usurp someone's position. In this instance, the actions would illustrate the concept of 'the sins of the father' having an ongoing influence. Longstanding effects of such setbacks seem to carry forward their impact on Dathan and Abiram who take up their dissatisfaction with Israel's leaders. Also, mentioned in this verse is On, son of Peleth, who is part of the group and probably a Reubenite, but not referred to again.[51]

---

[51] Levine's analysis of the internecine conflict stated by the 'priestly writers' is meant to 'lock in the exclusive sanction of the Amramite family, the family of Moses and Aaron, within the larger Kohathite clan of Levites, as the sole legitimate priests'. Cf. Levine, *Numbers 1–20*, p. 424.

Adding to the intensity of these confrontations is the high number of influential leaders who take sides with the antagonists to challenge Moses and Aaron regarding their governance and religious status in the nation. These are not just individuals who like to join a protest but are men of reputation, some of whom are appointed members of the council. Altogether, this is a considerable force of people who defy Moses and Aaron. In the verses which follow, these three groups of people will bring their complaints before the leaders. Alter's conjecture regarding the fusing of two similar conflict episodes has considerable appeal in that 'perhaps there were compelling political reasons for fusing the two rebellions. Perhaps all these considerations of narrative coherence seemed less important to the writer than the need to assert thematically that the two separate events—the attempt to seize political power and the usurpation of sacerdotal function—comprised one archetypal rebellion against divine authority and so must be told as one tale'. Alter goes on to draw a connection between the first act of murder (Abel) whose blood seeped into the earth as well as the fire judgment on Sodom and Gomorrah. These two stories may prefigure all similar attempts of individuals to take illicit power and entire societal perversity and corruption. Both are serious archetypal human issues with commensurate divine judgments.[52]

16.3–11—Leadership Conflicts

The initial allegation at its core questions why Moses and Aaron have taken it upon themselves to hold authority over the whole 'community' of people. The claim of the instigators is that: 'You have gone too far'. In other words, they allege that the two primary leaders have taken too much power over the destiny of the nation. In the estimation of the accusers, the whole nation is 'set apart and holy' (קדוש) with Yahweh present among them. Why should Moses and Aaron establish themselves over the whole community and their destiny? Underlying the main contention is the fundamental issue of choice, role, and position. Who gets to choose leaders and their status? Is it Yahweh, family lineage or cultural values that hold sway? The ironic element in the allegation is that Israel's behaviour in the days preceding this rebellious episode prove that their actions have been anything but 'holy' before the Lord. This emphasis on 'holiness' (קדוש) is a principal theme that runs through the narrative (cf. Num. 16.3, 5, 7, 37, 38).[53]

---

52 Cf. R. Alter, *The Art of Biblical Narrative* (New York: Basic, 1981), p. 137.

53 The importance of holiness in the OT is obvious from the 842 occurrences of the Hebrew root 'קדש' signifying holy things and things separated for cultic purposes. Although Leviti-

In humility and fear for the community, Moses once again falls prostrate before the aggressors indicating his concern for the judgment that will come upon the rebels. From his intercession, he arises to address Korah and adherents. Moses defers to Yahweh's verdict in the matter and prophetically declares that in the morning, the Lord will designate who is holy and has legitimate status to serve. Moses discerns that the issue involves the determination of 'holiness' and who is in right standing to officiate the sacred aspects of the Tabernacle service. The situation involves an encroachment on the cultus, and a specific challenge on the priesthood (Exod. 28.1–4; Leviticus 7–8). The issue would be resolved with a test to determine the Lord's 'choice' (בחר)—the one who is selected for certain responsibilities (cf. Numbers 5; 7; 17.5). Along with the primary motif of Yahweh's selection that runs through the narrative, he will also determine who has the privilege to 'draw near' (והקריב אליו) to the Lord for sacral duties (cf. Num. 3.16; 16.5, 9, 10, 40; 17.13; 18.2).

Moses outlines the criteria of testing which will reveal the one Yahweh selects for the priesthood. The test comes with an odious warning that the leaders have overstepped their standing—the sons of Levi have gone too far with their ambitions. The test involves the offering of incense or coals in 'fire pans' (מחתה) before the Lord at the entrance to the Tabernacle. This offering is considered a priestly duty and not part of the Levitical responsibilities. The test is to determine Yahweh's verification of role distinction between priests and Levites. Furthermore, Moses is incredulous at their dissatisfaction with the role that Yahweh allocated to the Levites. The God of Israel selected them and sanctified them for special services in the cultus near the Tabernacle, but apparently, they disparage that privilege. In fact, Yahweh brings them near to himself and gives them the privilege of serving the community. Therefore, their actions are actually against Yahweh, thus heightening the nature of the confrontation.

Finally, Moses indicates his support for Aaron by asking why they are against him when he is chosen by Yahweh. By attacking Aaron, they are challenging Yahweh's decision to appoint him to the sacred office.

16.12–17—*A Summons and a Repudiation*

In verses 12–14, Moses turns his attention to Dathan and Abiram, summoning them to a hearing. Their rebellious refusal to appear is based upon their

---

cus uses the term the most to describe the cultic requirements for holiness with 152 references, Numbers employs the term 80 times. Cf. D. Kornfeld, 'קדש', *TDOT*, XII, p. 527. The consecration of utensils and furnishings used in the cultus transfers things from the profane to sacred realms. Cf. Ringgren, 'קדש', p. 533. Consecration of functionaries is also essential to make them sanctified personnel for service (cf. Numbers 3 and 7).

perspective that Moses is unable to bring them into the promised land. Their apparent claim is that Moses usurped the power to rule over Israel but is unsuccessful in bringing them into the land flowing with milk and honey. Moreover, they allege that Moses is cheating them out of an 'inheritance' (נחלה) of fields and vineyards.[54] Paradoxically, Moses leads them out from Egypt which they characterize as a land of milk and honey! So quickly do they forget the years of oppression and slavery in Egypt and once again long for the few benefits they have there. Instead, they are doomed to 'death' (מות) in the wilderness and imply that it is Moses' fault (the death motif is prevalent in Num. 16.13, 29, 41, 48, 49; 17.10, 13).

Adding insult to injury, they ask, 'Will you gouge out the eyes of these men?'[55] This query insinuates that Moses may avenge their behaviour or be the cause of such literal consequences by leading them into the land of the Canaanites without adequate preparation or support from Yahweh. For whatever reasons, they reject Moses' invitation and refuse to hear him. This episode, along with the Korah conflict, brings Moses to anger and his petition to Yahweh is that they will fail the test about to take place. Just as they rejected Moses' authority, so too should the Lord reject their 'offering'. Usually, Moses does not defend himself but here he affirms that he has not wronged the transgressors, nor has he taken anything from them—not even a proverbial donkey! Once again, the humility of Moses' response and attitude is demonstrated, but not without indicators of the toll which leadership confrontations exact on the leader.

16.18–34—The Contest

The dialogue returns to Korah and Moses who outlines the contest preparations which will go forward the next day. All those who contested Aaronic leadership are to appear before the Lord at the entrance to the Tent of Meeting, the next day. Each of the 250 followers are to come with their fire pans with coals and incense to present before the Lord. Moses and Aaron will also present the same and await the response of Yahweh. The nature of the contest clearly brings to mind the incident in Leviticus where the legitimate sons of Aaron are

---

54 This is the first reference to 'inheritance' (נחלה) in the sense of a property allocation in the promised land. From Num. 16.14, this becomes a prominent theme, especially in chapters 26–36. The term is used 43 times in Numbers with a flurry of 17 occurrences in Num. 36.2–12.

55 This is a literal interpretation, but other translations may refer to poor treatment including slavery. Budd notes the idea of deception in the insinuation that Moses was 'beguiling the people with false promises'. Cf. Budd, *Numbers*, p. 187.

killed for their improper approach to the altar. The main thematic connections are the fire offerings, the approach before the Lord, and the required holiness or sanctification.

> Aaron's sons Nadab and Abihu took their censers, put fire in them and added incense; and they offered unauthorized fire before the LORD, contrary to his command. So fire came out from the presence of the LORD and consumed them, and they died before the LORD. Moses then said to Aaron, 'This is what the LORD spoke of when he said: "Among those who approach me I will be proved holy; in the sight of all the people I will be honoured."' Aaron remained silent. (Lev. 10.1–3)

In this formidable instance, the sacredness of the priestly office is clearly affirmed and should have given Korah and followers pause. However, the fact that they follow through with the test seems to indicate their confidence for a positive result.

As the large contingent of individuals gather according to instructions, the glory of Yahweh appears to the entire community (cf. Num. 12.5). The ominous appearance of Yahweh affirms the dread that Moses has for the rebellious actions of Korah. When Moses and Aaron hear the verdict and instructions of the Lord, they are horrified and fall prostrate—once again Yahweh is prepared to exact destruction upon the 'whole community' (כל העדה) but will spare Moses and Aaron. The prophet intercedes and petitions the creator of humankind and Israel, to reconsider his judgment: 'O God, the God who gives breath to all living things, will you be angry with the entire assembly when only one man sins?' (Num. 16.22). Of course, the sins are more than one, but the petition is clear—the one who gives breath and life can also take it away. The appeal is for deference, that Yahweh would only punish the guilty perpetrators.

The intercession is effective, and Yahweh instructs Moses once again, but this time in preparation for acts of judgment. The people are warned to stay clear of the tents of the main instigators—Korah, Dathan and Abiram, who come out of their tents with their families. People are warned to touch none of the belongings of the 'wicked ones' which are under a ban. Moses presents the foreboding sign that will confirm his leadership calling and authority and verify their contempt before Yahweh. It proves to be a prophetic portrayal of a dramatic act of God. Just as the rebellion of the leaders is in public, so now their punishment would be a public event. As the prophet envisions, the earth opens in a sinkhole which literally swallows the families and their belongings of those associated with the Korah, Dathan and Abiram insurgency. It is a horrifying scene:

> As soon as he finished saying all this, the ground under them split apart and the earth opened its mouth and swallowed them and their households, and all those associated with Korah, together with their possessions. They went down alive into the realm of the dead, with everything they owned; the earth closed over them, and they perished and were gone from the community. (Num. 16.32–33)

Although the community of Israelites who witness the event flee in fear, the judgment is precisely enacted on the guilty parties (although women and children are innocents, in Hebrew collective culture the leader's choices also affect the extended clan). The cataclysmic event transfers them to the realm of the dead, a 'grave' ('sheol'; שאול). The authority of Moses who warns the people of their sin with an accurate depiction of consequences, is reinforced (cf. Deut. 11.6; Num. 17.5). The prophetic presentation of events which come to pass, reinforce the powerful role of Moses in declaring the words of judgment which are fulfilled by Yahweh in an unprecedented way (cf. Deut. 18.14–20). 'You may say to yourselves, 'How can we know when a message has not been spoken by the LORD?' If what a prophet proclaims in the name of the LORD does not take place or come true, that is a message the LORD has not spoken. That prophet has spoken presumptuously, so do not be alarmed' (Deut. 18.21–22). In most cases the fulfilment of prophecy is difficult to ascertain due to the expanse of time it may take. In this instance, the prophetic words of judgment are speedily realized, bolstering the standing of Moses, and vindicating him in an impressive way.

16.35-40—Sacred Office

But the judgment is not over with the earth swallowing catastrophic event. As in the *Taberah* judgment (Numbers 11), fire comes out from Yahweh and consumes the 250 men who are offering the incense. This second cataclysmic event, which is combined with the initial judgment, brings a surprising resolution to the intense conflict that affects the whole community. The judgments highlight the sacredness of the priestly office. The censors symbolize the act of encroachment on the sacred office of Aaron as well as the on Tabernacle. The divine judgment vindicates the selection and authorization of Aaron's family. The Lord now instructs Moses regarding the cleansing operation. Responsibility is given to Eleazar, the son of Aaron.

Eleazar, the legitimate descendant of Aaron, is instructed to collect the censors and prepare the charred remains for the altar. The burnt remains and coals are removed due to defilement, but the censors are recreated to serve as visible reminders of the rebellion. They are hammered into coverings for the altar to become a sign of the episode and a stern reminder that Aaron and descendants are the legitimate priests to burn incense before the Lord. The altar, covered with the censors, will be a lasting memorial and warning for all encroachers to be wary, as the editorial summation affirms:

> So Eleazar the priest collected the bronze censors brought by those who had been burned to death, and he had them hammered out to overlay the altar, as the LORD directed him through Moses. This was to remind the Israelites that no one except a descendant of Aaron should come to burn incense before the LORD, or he would become like Korah and his followers. (Num. 16.39–40)

In this vivid and dramatic display, the sanctity of the priesthood and consecrated utensils is accentuated.

16.41–50—Sacred Offering

The scene now shifts to the next day as the dawning of the horrific events sink in. However, even after the frightening displays of judgment, the murmuring and anger of the people continue. They resume their confrontation against Moses and Aaron whom they allege to be responsible for the death of those who were killed—considered the Lord's people. Once again, the Lord intervenes to defend the leaders and reveal his awesome presence in the cloud over the Tent of Meeting (cf. Num. 12.5). The threat of judgment is renewed and for the third time Moses and Aaron fall prostrate.

To avert further destruction, it is Aaron's turn to offer a sacrifice to turn the wrath of God aside. At Moses' directive, Aaron responds to the communities' needs. His priestly role is featured as he stands between the Lord and the people to present an 'atoning' (כפר) offering of incense (Num. 16.46–47). The atoning action brings reconciliation for the community through Aaron's actions.[56] He stands between the living and the dead to intercede and stop the 'plague' (נגף) which breaks out among the people.[57] Before the sudden outbreak of plague could be averted, 14,700 had already perished. In this episode, Aaron is featured as the brave, caring high priest who serves the people in the midst of a

---

56 Cf. B. Lang, 'כפר', *TDOT*, VII, p. 293.
57 Levine points out the ironic situation here in that the Levite's role was to avert God's wrath by maintaining order in the Tabernacle service, but here they arouse his wrath with their behaviour and cause the plague. Cf. Levine, *Numbers 1–20*, p. 421. This episode highlights the appropriate actions of Aaron and reaffirms his standing in the community.

plague even though the risk of defilement is high. Yet again, the implication is underlined—the Aaronides are the chosen lineage for the priesthood. They are to minister on behalf of the people, even in the midst of dangerous outbreaks. When it is all done, Aaron returns to his rightful place at the entrance to the Tent of Meeting with Moses at his side. Together, the prophet and the priest rise to the challenges presented by interceding and acting for the wellbeing of the nation.

Aaron clearly displays the obedience and support of Moses that is expected of the whole community of Israelites. His action is symbolic of the mutual respect for the diverse roles of leadership. Aaron is a man of action but few words. Initially, he is the spokesman who relays Moses' message. However, after the devastating event of the golden calf idolatry (Exodus 32) and the death of his sons Nadab and Abihu, Aaron 'remained silent' (Lev. 10.3). Perhaps not completely and not for long, but the traumatic experiences seem to have transformed him into a different man.

17.1–13—*Aaron Is Upheld*

The focus on Aaron continues with another dramatic test scene. The two-fold purpose of the narrative is to further underscore the validation of Aaron and descendants as the rightful high priests for Israel (cf. Lev. 16.2). Secondly, the negative attitude of the community is still not ameliorated and in fact, the severe judgments left a sense of foreboding over the nation. The community fears extermination (Num. 17.10, 12, 13). To put an end to the constant grumbling of the Israelites, Yahweh determines to settle these issues. The test will affirm God's selection of priests with a dramatic reminder that the people must refrain from their grumbling lest another severe punishment comes upon the generation in the wilderness.

The test requires community participation from each ancestral tribe. The *Leitwort* 'staff or tribe' (מטה) is featured in its usage (sixteen times in ten verses) to highlight the symbolism of the 'staff' for the selection of the Levitical 'tribal' representation. The term occurs 252 times in the OT and 111 times in Numbers where it usually means 'tribe'. It also means staff or stick for use in shepherding. For Moses, the staff he uses becomes an instrument of power when God uses it as his sign of divine action on behalf of Israel in Egypt (14 times in this sense in Exodus). Usually, the term takes the literal meaning of 'tribe' with sociological connections to family—a transition from the meaning of 'branch or rod' (cf. Num. 1.20–46; 2.3–31; 10.14–27; 34.18–28).[58] As Milgrom notes, 'The double

---

58 Cf. H.J. Fabry, 'מטה', *TDOT*, VIII, p. 245; pp. 241–246.

meaning of '*matteh*' is significant: The dead '*matteh*' (staff) comes to life and represents the living '*matteh*' (tribe) that God blesses'.[59]

Moses is to collect from each tribe an official representative staff of the leader and is instructed to inscribe the name on the staff. Whereas the walking staff is a common but necessary tool for shepherds, it also is a personal identification marker. It could also symbolize authority in the sense of a 'scepter' as is common in many cultures (cf. Gen. 49.10; Num. 20.8; 24.17). For Moses, it is an instrument of power that is used for miraculous interventions in the religious confrontation in Egypt. It is Moses' tool for shepherding sheep, transformed into a powerful symbol of leadership and labelled the staff of God (Exod. 4.1–3, 20; 9.23; 17.5–9). Aaron also has a staff that proves superior to the Egyptian sorcerers and swallows their staffs which become snakes (Exod. 7.8–12).

It seems remarkable that the leadership of Aaron is still contested after the revolt of the 250 ended in death by fire. This affirms the intensity of the confrontation and determination of the leaders to usurp Aaron's role. Therefore, on the tribe of Levi's staff, Aaron's name is to be written, for it is his role as high priest that is under question. Although the names of the tribal leaders are not listed here, the number of staffs are twelve. Since Aaron's staff is 'among them' it appears that there are 13 staffs placed before the ark. Verses 6–7 summarize that the instructions of Moses are followed, to verify the leader's compliance with the test and submission of their staffs to the divine verdict.

Another element of symbolic connotation is the placement of the staffs in the Tent of Meeting before the of the ark of the covenant law. This builds on the reference in Num. 16.5 which indicates the process of selection for sacred duties. 'In the morning the LORD will show who belongs to him and who is holy, and he will have that person come near him. The man he chooses he will cause to come near him'. Thus, the 'chosen' (בהר) staff will designate the legitimate one who will be authorized and affirmed for priestly duties in the inner sanctuary. Moreover, the results of the contest should settle the matter once and for all, causing the continual murmuring of the Israelites to subside.

With anticipation, Moses enters the Tent the next day and sees the choice of Aaron's staff clearly selected through a most dramatic display. The staff comes alive, and the metamorphosis is emphatically presented with three imperfect verbs to highlight that not only are there buds, but also blossoms and the actual production of almonds. This miraculous display occurs over night to finally validate the role of Aaron and his descendants for their prominence in priestly service. The transformation of the staff symbolizes the fruitfulness and bless-

---

59   Milgrom, *Numbers*, p. 142.

ing that Yahweh desires to bring upon the nation through the ministry of the Aaronides. There may not be an explicit connection here to the high priestly prayer which Aaron and his sons are to speak over Israel, but the implicit connotations are significant. The priestly ministry offered from the sanctuary through sacrifice and prayer is to bestow life affirming blessing and peace on the nation. Through the ministry of the priests, symbolized by the 'leadership' staff of shepherds, the nation would be kept, blessed and in shalom (cf. Num. 6.23–27).

No doubt it is a solemn occasion when Moses brings the staffs out of the Tent and returns them to each hopeful leader. The realization of Yahweh's choice is affirmed and rather than be consoled with peace, the response is one of fear and dread. 'We will die! We are lost, we are all lost! Anyone who even comes near the tabernacle of the LORD will die. Are we all going to die?' While these fears are justified, in reference to the preceding judgments in chapter 16, the episode is meant to be instructive, not punitive. However, the rhetorical questions are left unanswered at the end of the chapter—a device that should cause those who consider rebellion in the future, to reconsider. Moreover, Aaron's budded staff is placed before the ark of the covenant as an abiding reminder and warning sign against rebellion. The symbolic staff is intended to motivate obedience and support for the Aaronides in conformity to the obedience of Moses, namely, 'Moses did just as the LORD commanded him' (Num. 17.11). The fear of death is real, but Yahweh affirms that the end to grumbling will avert punishment and death. This truth will be reinforced in Num. 18.5 where through the effective ministry of the Aaronides, the wrath of Yahweh will be averted.

Reflection and Response
Numbers 16–17: Yahweh Determines Leaders
Reflection

The narratives which are set in the middle of the book of Numbers feature the surprising tenacity of those who delight in power and assert their ambitions in public. It reveals a paradox in life where chosen leaders often seek ways to avoid their calling while others try to usurp power, status, and rank. To a degree, the opponents to Moses and Aaron feel that they could provide better leadership with superior outcomes. Their attempts to grasp greater authority are aggressive. Their influence in gathering support from other leaders and the community in general is considerable.

Once again, the humility and deference of Moses and Aaron in the narratives is revealed. Prostration and intercession show their dependence on the Lord to bring vindication and resolution to the confrontations. Nevertheless, the human toll on the leaders is evident as their concern for the larger community and God's judgment is unmistakable. And the judgments are severe. Many people lose their lives in another dramatic display as Yahweh's control over fire, earth and plague are witnessed. Both Moses and Aaron are vindicated through the dramatic tests which are employed to show the Lord's chosen leaders. Many perish but in the end the community learns to respect and reverence the Lord.

Response

It is apparent from several stories in the Pentateuch that Moses and Aaron have significant shortcomings and flaws. They make errors in judgment, they get angry, impatient and are far from perfect. However, they are chosen by Yahweh who works through them and instructs them accordingly. When they fail, the Lord deals with them and exercises damage control as warranted. He supports them, he disciplines them, but he also vindicates them publicly. He does not tolerate leaders who seek to usurp power and roles that are not meant for them. He does not tolerate encroachment on sacred precincts, authorized leaders, or sacred responsibilities.

Leadership assignments from the Lord are often a mystery, but according to some scriptures they are rooted in responsibility. Selection is often rooted in character (Noah; Job; David) and a desire to wisely care for people (Moses; Solomon; Barnabas). Those who attend to God given work, with productivity, faithfulness, and stewardship, are rewarded with more work! Leaders must carefully adhere to the scriptural guidelines for their roles and focus on the requisite services for ministry in meek yet proficient ways. The NT warning from a very humble apostle is an applicable response: 'But if you harbor bitter envy and selfish ambition in your hearts, do not boast about it or deny the truth. Such "wisdom" does not come down from heaven but is earthly, unspiritual, demonic. For where you have envy and selfish ambition, there you find disorder and every evil practice' (Jas 3.14–16). In other words, it is essential to stick to the work and position which the Lord has allocated to leaders. It is unadvisable to criticize other authorized leaders for their shortcomings when we may have similar blind spots needing our attention. Of course, accountability and confrontation may be inevitable when God exposes sin or character issues, but such matters must be handled with care and appropriate Christian processes (Mt. 18.15–20; 2 Tim. 2.24–26). It may be anathema for hostile leadership bids which bring destruction and judgment on people, rather than blessing and development.

18.1–32—Protecting Sanctuary, Clergy and People

After the intense events of rebellion, the severity of judgment, and loss of life, the resulting societal trauma and apprehension in the nation is to be expected. At this juncture the narrative transitions to a number of legal ramifications for Aaron and the Levites. The tenor of the narration appears to address the fear of divine punishment and the people's dread of trespassing on the Tabernacle precincts lest they be killed. The context of the fear is two-fold. The first is the immediate situation and events which result in fire and plague judgments. However, the initial principle of approaching sacred space goes back to the revelation at Mount Sinai where limits are set for the people around the mountain. They are clearly warned not to approach the mountain or even the base of it lest they be put to death (cf. Exod. 19.12). The rationale is based on the human desire to approach God. However, the holiness of Yahweh is such that there are strict protocols and principles which must be followed in order for people to approach the Lord. They must follow instructions and proceed through the guidance of established leaders and priests. Details are communicated to Moses who was called to meet with the Lord on the top of Mount Sinai. There Yahweh instructs Moses to warn the people to maintain their distance and not approach the divine presence. Even the priests must be careful and consecrated. 'Moses said to the LORD, "The people cannot come up Mount Sinai, because you yourself warned us, 'Put limits around the mountain and set it apart as holy'." The LORD replied, "Go down and bring Aaron up with you. But the priests and the people must not force their way through to come up to the LORD, or he will break out against them."' (Exod. 19.22–24). The restrictions and approach to God is carefully regulated.

In Numbers 18, further clarity is given by Yahweh to Aaron concerning the risks, responsibilities, and benefits of the sanctuary duties. While the status and affirmation of Aaron's authority along with the experience of miraculous interventions are rewarding, there are concomitant liabilities that come with it. Therefore, as the Lord provides some consolation to the people concerning the tabernacle to motivate their continued respect for the sacred precincts, he also elevates the accountability of priests and Levites for cultus activities and sancta. As Milgrom notes, 'Chapter 18 is both the remedy and the consolation for what occurred—now the sacral guards will be responsible for lay encroachment which mainly refers to unauthorized approaches to the sanctuary and furnishings'.[60] A number of details concerning this theme are also presented in

---

60   Milgrom, *Numbers*, p. 424. He also compares the meaning of encroachment with Hittite

Numbers 3–5 where the Levitical and priestly duties are distinguished from the role of Aaron and his four sons who are ordained to serve as priests. The consecration of the priests transfers them from the profane to the sacred realm where their priestly responsibilities require strict protocols and cultic purity. They may have benefits but serve under demanding obligations.[61]

18.1–7—Instructions for the Priests

Only in this passage and in Lev. 10.8–11 is Aaron instructed directly by the Lord. By addressing Aaron directly, Yahweh affirms his choice and reinforces the authority that the consecrated priesthood commands. The former instructions concerning the Tabernacle and cultus have been clearly imparted in Exodus and Leviticus. Here the burden of responsibilities are once again reiterated and elevated. To a certain extent they clarify directives stated in Num. 4.1–20 and 7.9. The Kohathites will bear responsibility for any offenses connected with the security of the sanctuary. The Aaronides will bear responsibility for any offenses connected with the functions of the priesthood. Their duties mainly pertain to the regulations that are in effect when 'the sanctuary' (הקדש; Num. 18.3, 5, 16) is in the camp or when it is being transported to another location. The 'holy place' must be secure and free of contamination, at all times (cf. Exod. 40.34–38; Leviticus 16; Numbers 1–4).

For the priests, the regulations are extensive as recorded in Exodus and Leviticus and require meticulous adherence to proper dress, health, hygiene, and preparation for service. Supervision for the Levitical services and performance is under the jurisdiction of the priests and severe penalty of death is exacted for both Levite and priest who approach their work without due respect. Careful training and attentiveness is required for all Levites to know what sacred furnishings and areas of the sanctuary are accessible and how they are to be handled. Both priests and Levites have security duties at the entrance to the Tent where Israelites would also come to bring sacrifices at appropriate times and according to prescribed spaces. The risks involved are palpable and include death (Num. 18.3, 5, 7). The vital work of priests and the priesthood in the OT is featured by the 900 references to their essential work in Israel. Aaron's role becomes primary, and he is personally referred to over 350 times in the OT. The importance of the priesthood developed early in Israel's history with the

---

texts that catalogue items and actions that are considered improper. For Israel, the issues are mainly focused on the proper handling of sanctified materials, furnishings, and placement of the Tabernacle.

61   Cf. Ringgren, 'קדש', p. 533.

TABLE 2   Sacred roles and responsibilities

Verse	Sacral class	Responsibility for	Encroachment of
18.1b, 7a	Priests	Most Sacred Objects	Disqualified Priests
18.3	Priests & Levites	Most Sacred Objects (at rest)	Levites
18.1a	Kohathites	Most Sacred Objects (in transit)	Israelites
18.22–23	Levites	The Tabernacle (as a whole)	Israelites

appointment of the Levites and ordination of the Aaronides. As mediators of the covenant and representatives of Yahweh before the people, their roles actually outlast the roles of prophets. 'The priests actualize Yahweh's presence in the words of their many liturgical functions'.[62]

It is the ultimate form of service to willingly take the place of fellow Israelites to avert the wrath of God in matters concerning the holy place. But it is also an honour to be chosen: 'I myself have selected your fellow Levites from among the Israelites as a gift to you, dedicated to the LORD to do the work at the tent of meeting'. It is also a gift to be allowed to serve as a priest, attending to both Yahweh and the needs of the people. The roles of the sanctuary servants are summarized in Table 2.

18.8–19—Benefits for Priests and Levites

According to the detailed requirements of the cultus, the Israelites are obliged to bring offerings and sacrifices in worship of Yahweh. The Aaronides become the custodians of the offerings which are recorded in order from the 'sacred' contributions to the 'most sacred' offerings. Some are designated for the altar and burnt but other portions are allocated for priestly usage. These items are designated as 'holy' (קדש) and are to be handled with the utmost reverence (Num. 18.8, 9, 10, 17, 19, 32). In presenting these offerings the attitude of the participant must reflect the sacred nature of the occasion, along with a reverential disposition.

A distinction is made concerning the elements that may be eaten—some are only for the men (Num. 18.10) and others are for all who reside in the household. The offerings are to be of the best quality and freshness, including oil, wine, and grain. Some products are expected to be processed (cf. Lev. 2.12;

---

[62] Cf. W. Dommershausen, 'כהן', TDOT, VII, p. 74. Their priestly benediction and blessing is the pinnacle of their liturgical function.

TABLE 3 Offerings and ingredients

Most holy offerings	Ingredients	References	For
Grain	Cereal / Bread	Num. 18.9; Lev. 2.3; 6.7–9	Priest; some burnt
Sin / Purification	Meat	Num. 5.5–8; Lev. 4.25–26; 6.19; 7.7	Priest; some fat, organs & blood burnt
Guilt	Meat; Organs; Blood	Lev. 7.1–6	Yahweh; Priest; burnt

Num. 15.20–21). Featured contributions were the first fruits of the crops as they ripen—typically grains, fruits, and oils. The implication is that the offerings are joyfully brought to the sanctuary and given to the priests with gratitude for Yahweh's provisions. These gifts are also to be used by the priests to meet their daily needs.

A specialised offering is also given, called the 'wave offering' (תנופה) which are brought to the Tabernacle and presented in a dramatic 'elevation offering'.[63] It is a ritual presentation that goes along with several offerings (Lev. 7.30; 9.21; Num. 6.20; 18.18) which include the right hind thigh, bread, grain, material for the Tabernacle and oil. Additionally, reference is made to the gift or 'heave' offering (תרומה; the 'terumah' noted in Num. 18.8, 11, 19). Exod. 29.27–28 makes special references to this offering in the context of the ceremony that consecrates the priests for service. The breast of the ram is waved before the Lord, acknowledging his provision, and the consecrated elements of the ram become the regular share given by the Israelites to Aaron and sons for their nourishment. This ritual occurs during a variety of meaningful occasions in dedications, well-being, and fellowship offerings. The main distinction made between the wave and the heave offerings (Num. 18.8–19) is that the latter are dedicated to Yahweh outside of the sanctuary while the former are imparted in a presentation before Yahweh near or in the sanctuary.

Furthermore, everything that is 'devoted' (הרם) or proscribed, is also provided (Num. 18.14; cf. Lev. 27.28; הרם; 'herem'). Everything that is consecrated to the Lord under a 'ban' refers to the ultimate dedication of something that usually is destroyed so no one gets to benefit from it. Although this may seem like a waste of valuable resources, the intention is to break the motivation of desire

---

[63] Cf. Milgrom, *Numbers*, p. 151; Also see pp. 425–426 for an extensive excursus on usage and details. For the *terumah* offering see pp. 426–427.

TABLE 4 Offerings and products

Holy offerings	Products	References	Recipients
First fruits of soil	Processed goods: grain, wine, oil	Num. 18.12–13; Lev. 19.24–25; 23.10–11	All who are ceremonially clean
Products under 'Herem'	Meat, etc.	Num. 18.14; Lev. 23.20	Priests
Firstborn	First issue of womb (human or animal)	Num. 18.15	Priests, but males must be redeemed
Firstborn of pure cattle, sheep, goats	Sacrificed; burnt; Blood splashed on altar	Num. 18.17–18; Lev. 3.9; 7.3, 11–16	Yahweh offering & pleasing smoke; meat for Priests

and greed for material things. However, here the priest and his family are also to profit from the devoted offerings, which indicates an unusual generosity.

Another category of sacrifices are those designated 'holy' and of special quality—the best of the fresh oil, wine and grain, but differentiated from the 'most' holy offerings. These deserve special appreciation because they represent the blessings of Yahweh as the giver of life. It is the Lord who opens wombs and initiates production, giving breath to mankind (cf. Num. 16.22). The offering of produce to the Lord through sacrifice, is performed in recognition of his beneficence and in prayer for his continued provisions as illustrated in Lev. 23.10–11: 'When you enter the land I am going to give you and you reap its harvest, bring to the priest a sheaf of the first grain you harvest. He is to wave the sheaf before the LORD so it will be accepted on your behalf; the priest is to wave it on the day after the Sabbath'. In addition to the sacrificial element involved, this category includes a dramatic ceremonial presentation to reinforce the importance of the sacrament.

The matter of the firstborn requires considerable explanation and specificity with additional requirements concerning the 'firstborn' (בכור; cf. Exod. 13.12–13; 24.19–20).[64] There are three distinctive elements: the pure animals that are sac-

---

[64] The importance of the firstborn is reflected in the 132 references to firstborn sons as well as animals in the OT (out of 26 in Numbers the firstborn sons are noted 20 times; cf. Num. 3.2–50). Firstborns had special status but more responsibilities (cf. Tsevat, 'בכור', II, pp. 125–127). Israel is God's 'firstborn' among the nations but is also responsible to be 'a kingdom of priests' (cf. Num. 3.13; 8.17; Exod. 12; 13.15; 19).

rificed and may be consumed; the impure animals which may be redeemed by their owners, and the male child that must be redeemed by the parents. The redemption price is noted as five shekels of silver (cf. Num. 3.47). While this may seem like a simple transaction the overwhelming reality for the parents is to emphasize that the son belongs to God for his purposes. The whole matter is superintended by Aaron and sons and occurs when the child is one month old with a symbolic ritual of dedication. The principle of the firstborn is rooted in the example of Israel, chosen by Yahweh out of all other nations. This is a special choice of privilege but comes with responsibilities.

Finally, the summary affirms the extent of the provisions: 'Whatever is set aside from the holy offerings the Israelites present to the LORD I give to you and your sons and daughters as your perpetual share. It is an 'everlasting covenant' of salt before the LORD for both you and your offspring' (Num. 18.19; cf. Lev. 2.13).[65] The covenant of the priestly emoluments elaborated here are perpetual and the symbolic reference to salt (ברית מלח עולם) reinforces the lasting efficacy and validity of Yahweh's commitments. Salt is included in the ceremonial meal that ratifies the covenantal arrangements (cf. Gen. 26.30; Exod. 24.11).

18.20-24—God Will Provide

Just as the benefits are to accrue continually, so the 'tithes' (מעשר) provided by the Israelites are set in place for a lasting ordinance. This provision is made to replace land 'inheritance' (נחל) and has several details to ensure the recompense of Levites and priests. The Lord addresses Aaron for the third time (Num. 18.1; 8; 20) before turning his instruction to Moses (Num. 18.25). The Lord makes it clear that Levites and priests are not to anticipate land allocations but are to focus their attention on Yahweh and their required service. They are to understand that their daily earthly needs will be provided by Yahweh through the explicit allocation of tithes exacted from the Israelites. One of the reasons for this determination is theological in that 'Yahweh is their inheritance'. However, the Levites will also be given 'Levitical cities' for special purposes noted in Num. 35.2-8.[66]

---

65 The covenantal ceremonies are accompanied by sacrifices which affirm the intimate nature of the rites which have concepts of friendship, peace and benevolence associated (cf. Weinfeld, 'ברית', p. 258). The covenant is a commitment confirmed by an oath which has binding validity for the partner (cf. Gen. 26.28; Exod. 19.8; Deut. 29.9ff.; cf. Num. 10.33; 14.44; 18.19; 25.12-13).

66 The importance of the land allocations as an 'inheritance' to families and tribes is featured by the numerous references to the terms and concepts associated with it (6 times in 18.20-53; cf. Num. 26.53-62 [5 times]; Num. 27.7-11 [6 times]). In its verbal forms it occurs

There are clear principles and implications behind the tithing arrangements presented here. On one hand the instructions address the tremendous fear of the people regarding the potential death for trespassing on sacred space (cf. Num. 18.3–4, 7, 22, 32). The incidents with Korah and others are the backdrop to expectations and Yahweh comes to ensure Israel that the Levites will take the responsibility of securing the Tent of Meeting. Moreover, the Levites will bear the burden of safeguarding the sacred area and thereby protecting the people. No doubt that the implications of severe judgment which struck Nadab, Abihu, Korah, Dathan, Abiram and so many others, are to motivate the Levites to be fierce defenders of the Tent of Meeting.

Levites are accountable for the duties presented in Numbers and the ordinance is perpetual for the Levites for generations—it is a career. The tithes that are presented are considered an offering to Yahweh which is then allocated to the Levites. As prescribed in Lev. 27.30–31, tithes are regular offerings with specifications:

> A tithe of everything from the land, whether grain from the soil or fruit from the trees, belongs to the LORD; it is holy to the LORD. Whoever would redeem any of their tithe must add a fifth of the value to it. Every tithe of the herd and flock—every tenth animal that passes under the shepherd's rod—will be holy to the LORD.

Although the tithe is not a 'tax' as is commonly collected by kings in the ancient near east, the tithe is a compulsory requirement that is regularly calculated based on income and products.[67]

18.25-32—*Tithe Instructions*

In order to preserve order and reduce conflicts of interest, Moses is to oversee the instruction for the Levites. Moses makes it clear that the tithe will be theirs for their inheritance but from it they must carve out ten percent of it for the Lord's offering. This is then to be given to Aaron the priest and includes grain, wine and oil—products that are processed and valuable for nourishment and

---

59 times, and as a noun 220 times in the OT, and in most contexts. it pertains to the conferring of property allocations. Some contexts focus on the legal aspects (cf. Deut. 21.15–17; Num. 27.1–11) but the practical distribution of the lands will be done by Moses, priests, and tribal leaders. Evidence of the importance of inheritance procedures may be observed in its 36 references in the book of Numbers between chapters 16–36. Cf. E. Lipiński, 'נחל', *TDOT*, IX, pp. 319–335.

67 Milgrom, *Numbers*, p. 433.

sustenance. Moreover, it is to be of the highest quality of what is given. In this way it will be clear to the Israelites what their obligations to the Levites and priest will be. It is also clear that the tithe is to be considered the fair wages for their work and risk at the Tent of Meeting. Once the tithes are properly exacted and disbursed, the Levites can enjoy the proceeds for their households. Once again, the chapter ends with a warning. The best of the tithes must be properly disbursed so that the offerings are not defiled or profaned because the penalty of death is a factor.

Chapter 18 therefore, reflects an important premise. Levites and leaders serve at considerable risk. Yahweh protects and provides based on detailed conditions. Sacrificial offerings and service begets sustaining grace and providence.

19.1–22—Ritual Purification Rites

This chapter is unique in its carefully presented structure which spotlights seven topics that are repeated 'seven' (שבע) times in two distinctive panels. Featured in the two-panel presentation is the 'ritual law' which is the main emphasis throughout the chapter. Very meticulous requirements are to be followed in order to maintain ritual purity in the camp. Disregarding sacred precincts and conditions which render an individual 'unclean' bring about negative consequences. The placement of Numbers 19, after the priestly duties are presented, is significant as it deals with the rising death count in Israel after the judgments and plague outbreak described in Numbers 16 to 17. Furthermore, the content elaborates on themes addressed in Num. 5.1–4 and 6.6–12 where cleansing requirements are featured.

In the first section, the focalization is on the preparation of ashes and ingredients for the cleansing rituals. In the second section, the focus is on the things which cause defilement and consequent punishment. To be ritually 'clean' (טהור) is an essential requirement for all members of the community to remain in close relationship with family and Yahweh. Several factors in life could cause a person to become 'impure' (נדה) and, therefore, require segregation. For reconciliation with the Lord and community to be affected, certain rites are outlined for strict implementation. The three semantic domains in the use of the term include impurities connected to menstruation, abomination of some kind and defilement requiring purification rites.[68]

---

[68] J. Milgrom and D.P. Wright, 'נדה', *TDOT*, IX, p. 233.

TABLE 5   Septenary repetitions

Red heifer; no defects; no yoke	19.2, 5, 6, 10, 17
Burnt objects (hide, flesh, blood, organs, cedar wood, hyssop, red wool)	19.5–6
Sprinkle (blood; cleansing water)	19.4, 13, 18 (2×), 19, 20, 21
Washing	19.4, 6, 7, 8, 10, 19, 21
Things that contaminate	19.14–16
Things that are cleansed	19.18
Priests	19.1, 3, 4, 6, 7

The septenary repetitions of 'seven' occur with references to the specific objects, actions, and personnel which are addressed. Beginning in verse 19.4, the blood is to be sprinkled seven times toward the Tent of Meeting. References to the seven-day ritual requirements for purification caused by defilement are made seven times (cf. Num. 19.11, 12 [twice], 14, 16, 19 [twice]). The effect of this literary device is to feature the importance of the procedures for the health and well-being of the community in worship. It also points to the effectiveness of the rituals to finalize the cleansing process.

19.1–10—*Ritual Instructions*

An important premise lies behind the extensive meticulous rites that are described here. As noted elsewhere, specific references to death and burial arrangements in Numbers are considerable but limited, when the large population is taken into consideration. The fact that a death sentence hovers over a whole generation of Israelites ensures that death and corpse contact are a regular and constant reality. Due to the finality of death and decomposition of the body, corpse contact brings contamination to the individuals in proximity with the dead. This condition of defilement also affects the sanctity of the sacred areas around the Tabernacle. For order in burial and purification rites to be effective, Moses and Aaron are instructed to implement compulsory laws. Aaron is to supervise the ritual of the red heifer described here, but Eleazar officiates the sacrificial procedures. This is another example of the transition of responsibilities of Aaron to his son, but it also implies that Aaron is contaminated by the huge plague death count that he is surrounded by. 'He stood between the living and the dead, and the plague stopped' (Num. 16.48).

The focus on the 'ritual law' (חקת התורה; Num. 19.2a, 14a; cf. 31.21) highlights the importance of cleanliness which allows the worshipper to remain in the camp and interact socially with community members. To be ritually 'clean'

(טהור) is a vital necessity (cf. Num. 19.9 [twice]; 12 [twice]; 18; 19 [twice]) for the community, and the regulations set in place by the leaders are meant to educate the people on hygiene and death. The opposite of purity is to be 'impure' (נדה) or in some 'filthy' state that causes a person's defilement (cf. Num. 19.9, 13, 20, 21; 31.23).

The procedures are clearly presented by Yahweh to Moses for implementation by Aaron and the priests. A unique requirement specifies that a red heifer without defect or blemish and that has never been used for work under a yoke, was to be slaughtered outside of the camp. After the incision, Eleazar who is the designated officiant, dips a finger into the blood and sprinkles it towards the tent of meeting seven times. Then the whole carcass of the animal is burnt while Eleazar supervises the process to ensure that all parts including hide, flesh, blood, and intestines are transformed into 'ash' (אפר). Similar detailed procedures are outlined for sin offerings in Leviticus (cf. Lev. 4.1–23; 16.3–28; Num. 15.27–29), but the details on the choice and process for burning the red heifer are distinctive (cf. Lev. 1.3–9 for comparisons).[69]

To enhance the process, aromatic cedar wood and hyssop are added to the burning heifer. Additionally, a symbolic crimson coloured wool is added into the fire (also used in priestly garments and Tent curtain). The cedar wood and hyssop herb are important elements for the cleansing rites. Not only are they symbolic for cleansing but they also have elements which kill bacteria and disinfect—especially when burnt into 'ash' (אפר), the integral ingredient mixed with water.

Once the animal has been reduced to ash, the priest, and those who assisted with the burning, must attend to personal rites of decontamination. To be considered 'unclean' (טמא) is a very serious condition, as highlighted by the frequent references in the chapter (14 times in Num. 19.7, 8, 10, 11, 14, 16, 20, 21, 22 [thrice]). Defilement mandates considerable restrictions in daily lifestyle

---

69   Several details in the purification rituals as given to Moses and described in Leviticus are similar. The diseased person must remain outside of the camp until the priest examines them. The person undergoes a ceremonial cleansing and then they are considered 'healed' of their defiling skin disease. The cleansing process involves several items including two live clean birds, cedar wood, scarlet yarn, and hyssop. A precise process must be followed:

> Then the priest shall order that one of the birds be killed over fresh water in a clay pot. He is then to take the live bird and dip it, together with the cedar wood, the scarlet yarn and the hyssop, into the blood of the bird that was killed over the fresh water. Seven times he shall sprinkle the one to be cleansed of the defiling disease, and then pronounce them clean. After that, he is to release the live bird in the open fields (Lev. 14.2–7).

freedoms. The verb for 'unclean' appears 155 times in the OT and the noun, 136 times. Contexts for its usage refer to abomination and various sins including sexual uncleanness. Several things may defile and are considered unclean including certain animals, some diseases, sexual discharges and sexual aberrations, death, and a variety of idolatrous cultic activities. André elaborates:

> Ritual uncleanness is often linked with the sphere of death. The distinction between clean and unclean animals applies only to those used for sacrifice, offering the firstborn, or food, for all of which only 'clean' animals are permitted. A leper was kept apart like a corpse. The sexual discharge of a male and the menstruation of a female are life that is never realized and therefore have an aspect of death about them. Sexual intercourse, ejaculation, and parturition all contribute to the emergence of life, but they are also felt to be unclean and require purification.[70]

Priests are trained to determine those things that cause defilement and relegates matters into a category of the profane. Those things that bring about ritual impurity cannot be reconciled with the holiness of Yahweh.

Decontamination rites include washing garments and cleansing the body with water. This provides the segregated person with re-entry to the camp, but they are considered unclean until evening. The vital process of collecting all of the ashes after the incineration of the red heifer and products is done by a ceremonially clean person and then stored in a place outside of the camp. However, after this task is completed, the same cleansing procedures as required by the priest are to be followed. The essential ingredients are protected by the community specifically for cleansing rites. These instructions are applicable permanently (עולם), for all who reside in the community—both Israelites and foreigners.

19.11–13—*Cleansing Rituals*

Finally, in this section, specifications concerning impurity and how to deal with it are laid out. Those who come into contact with any human corpse are considered to be in a state of defilement for seven days. The process of returning to a clean state requires the cleansing water solution applied on the third and seventh day—without this, they remain unclean and are responsible for bringing defilement to the Tabernacle precincts (cf. Num. 19.13, 20). The punishment is

---

70 G. André, 'טמה', *TDOT*, V, p. 331.

severe, for that person who must be 'cut off' (כרת) from the community. In other words, strict compliance with the regulations of this ordinance are expected from all who reside in Israel.

19.14–22—*Further Lessons on Defiling Circumstances*

In the second panel of instructions, the focus is on experiences and specific incidents that elaborate on the causes of contamination. The first example is probably a constant reality and daily occurrence—entering a tent with a corpse in it causes immediate defilement. The potential contagion, depending on circumstances of illness leading to death, decomposition, heat and air-borne disease, is a continual challenge. All those affected by entering or being in a tent with a corpse are immediately considered unclean for seven days. After one week the rite of cleansing is completed with the pouring of the ash water solution over the unclean person. Furthermore, a ceremonially clean individual would then apply the cleansing solution to the tent, its furnishings and all who reside within by sprinkling the solution with a hyssop branch. The other element of defilement which occurs in a tent with a corpse is the contamination of uncovered food products. Such produce is to be destroyed and cannot be redeemed.

The second example is for defilement that occurs elsewhere. The same procedure is applied to others who may have touched a human bone, or dirt near a grave, or been near a person who is killed or dies a natural death. In short, this is the remedy for those contaminated: considered unclean for one week, they are sprinkled on the 3rd and 7th day with the cleansing solution. They then wash their clothes, bathe in the purifying water, and in the evening are considered restored to a 'cleansed' state. The penalty for not following through with the process is reiterated from verse 13: 'But if those who are unclean do not purify themselves, they must be cut off from the community, because they have defiled the sanctuary of the LORD. The water of cleansing has not been sprinkled on them, and they are unclean. This is a lasting ordinance for them' (19.20–21).

The focus in this chapter is on contamination having to do with the dead. Interestingly, the instructions only deal with the situation and the remedy. Many practical issues are not addressed such as: where is the corpse taken? Are the occupants of the tent permitted to stay there for the week of defilement? Did family members prepare the body for burial or are there professionals who look after that? Is the unclean status of the individual mainly there for their own protection from physical contagion? How does this process relate to matters of spiritual defilement?

Reflection and Response
Numbers 15–18: Attending to Spiritual Matters
Reflection

As noted in the commentary section, the cultic details in Numbers are further instructions based on the directives presented in Exodus and Leviticus. So much of daily life in the wilderness is consumed with the acquisition of resources and food preparation. Work and business affairs easily take over the people's prime time and concentration to meet the needs of family life and work responsibilities. For Israel, however, Yahweh ensures that the people also attend to matters of daily sacrifice to turn their attention to spiritual, covenantal, and eternal matters. This requires the focalization of peoples' devotion on the Tabernacle and the offerings conducted there on behalf of the nation and individuals.

The rites of Israel in the sacrificial system may seem like foreign practices for most cultures. However, the core purpose in the system is for Israel to be kept in right standing with Yahweh. In the light of God's holiness, the people have to be ritually pure to remain in relationship with him. Due to the inevitable problems of sin, rebellion, and defilement, the damage caused in the divine human relationship needs to be resolved through the process of atonement. This requires the priest's involvement in conducting prescribed sacrificial rituals combined with the personal acts of contrition so that reconciliation with Yahweh can be affected. When the essential sacrifices are made by the priests, purification is attained (cf. Leviticus 5).

The sacrificial system is the appointed means of providing for the forgiveness of sin and the maintenance of the covenant bond. Although sacrifice does affect cleansing, atonement and forgiveness, the system and rites require constant attention (Lev. 4.35). To be forgiven, the worshipper has to draw near to the sanctuary, kill the sacrificial animal and lay hands upon its head (Lev. 4.27–35). With this action completed, the priest can make atonement for the trespasser. This action underscores the personal recognition of responsibility for sin and the breach of the covenantal bond. It emphasizes the cost of sin and its consequences. Both premeditated and unpremeditated sins can be forgiven (Lev. 5.15; 15.29; 6.1–2) but repentance, restitution, and confession are required (Lev. 4; 5.1–6; 16.21; 26.40; Num. 5.6–8). The order of sacrifice in Leviticus 9 indicates that sin offerings are given for the forgiveness of sin. The burnt offerings indicate personal consecration and commitment, and the peace offerings initiate a celebration of reconciliation. A pinnacle for the annual Day of Atonement is when the High Priest makes sacrifices on behalf of Israel for the sins of the nation and the purification of the sanctuary (Exod. 30.10; Lev 16.29–34; Deut. 33.10). They sprinkle blood on the altar on behalf of the participant (Lev. 1.14–15; 5.8). They are cleansed and permitted to touch the sacred things but must abstain from anything that defiles (Lev. 21.1–6).

However, the Israelites also desire to show their gratitude to Yahweh by offering sacrifices and gifts to the Lord (Num. 15.17–19), in recognition of the Lord's amazing care, beneficence and providence. Their sacrifices acknowledge that he is the sustainer and provider of all they have. Their daily offerings of a percentage of what they receive are a constant reminder that Yahweh is their provider. Their continual support of the Levites, priests and Tabernacle maintenance are a vital part of their worship. In giving generously they acclaim Yahweh as Lord of land and produce.

Response

When the sacrificial system is no longer in place, Israel turns their devotional sight to the Torah readings, prayer, and community life. In lieu of an expensive, elaborate, and demanding system, they turn to a more relational, reflective participation in spiritual matters. So it is for believers today. How do we please the Lord in our daily lives? What does the Lord require of us to fulfil the duties we have in order to remain in close relationship with him? How do we transform the sacrificial requirements into genuine, personal acts of devotion that bring glory to God? Although the rituals are no longer necessary, daily devotional time spent in the scriptures with implementation of divine instructions and prayer are vital for life, productivity, and eternal matters.

20.1–22.1—Conflicts Escalate and Infuriate

After the purification instructions and details for sanctification in the camp, the record turns to narrative with several episodic stories. Incidents of death, travail, sin, plagues and wilderness troubles continue with both internal and external confrontations.

The initial matter has to do with the need for a massive supply of water that is a constant daily need during the wilderness sojourn. In the people's estimation the leaders should be ensuring that a water supply is always provided for. Their thirst appears to be the final straw in growing frustrations which spill over in their list of grievances—their brothers die before the Lord, the wilderness is a terrible place of death for people and livestock, there is no produce to eat and no water to drink! The food products they enumerate are the very things that were available in the promised land—grain, figs, grapes, and pomegranates (Num. 13.23). While there are legitimate issues to address, it is the tone and pattern of contention that indicates trouble ahead. Once again, they voice their death wish: 'If only we had died when our brothers fell dead before the LORD' (Num. 20.3).

20.1–5—Death of Miriam

The chapter begins with the rather terse report of the death and burial of Miriam. It ends with the more detailed report of Aaron's death and the transition of the priesthood to Eleazar. Regarding Miriam, there are no details regarding her demise or whether there is a mourning period. Just that she is buried, presumably at Kadesh. Concerning Aaron, however, the community will mourn for thirty days after his death. Not only is Aaron's death noted here but it receives further attention and detail in Numbers 33. The Israelites arrive at Kadesh in the Desert of Zin during the first new moon (beginning of the month). Although the material is not specifically dated, the text refers to the fortieth year of pilgrimage which is logged in the itinerary summary of Num. 33.37–39: 'They left Kadesh and camped at Mount Hor, on the border of Edom. At the LORD's command Aaron the priest went up Mount Hor, where he died on the first day of the fifth month of the fortieth year after the Israelites came out of Egypt. Aaron was a hundred and twenty-three years old when he died on Mount Hor'.

There is considerable debate among commentators concerning the references to Kadesh since Israel is camped there already in year one after their departure from Mount Sinai.[71] They are on location in Kadesh once again in Num. 13.26. Source critics analyze the materials to determine different traditions that may be combined, but it is more probable that Israel comes to the same place at different times in their journey (cf. Deut. 1.46; 2.14). The main implication here is that a generation of Israelites, including Miriam and Aaron, are losing their lives during the forty-year wilderness excursion which at times leads them in cycles of aimless wandering.

The first episode arises due to the lack of water which is understandable, but the complaint quickly develops into graver allegations. Although a new generation is in the process of taking over, a comparable pattern of complaining and confrontation continues to be evident. The people despair of their lives and question the purpose for their trek to the promised land. Once again they long for the life they knew back in Egypt! A similar episode regarding water deprivation is recorded in Exodus 17 and forms an important comparison with this text.

---

71 Cf. Levine, *Numbers 1–20*, pp. 90–91.

In the Exodus episode the Israelites depart from the Desert of Sin and travel according to Yahweh's directions until they camp at Rephidim. Due to the lack of water, they complain and blame Moses for the desperate situation they are in. Moses takes a defensive position and warns them about testing the Lord's patience. However, the people persist and question Moses' motivations for leading them out of Egypt into a dry desert.

> Why did you bring us up out of Egypt to make us and our children and livestock die of thirst? Then Moses cried out to the LORD, 'What am I to do with these people? They are almost ready to stone me'. The LORD answered Moses, 'Go out in front of the people. Take with you some of the elders of Israel and take in your hand the staff with which you struck the Nile and go. I will stand there before you by the rock at Horeb. Strike the rock, and water will come out of it for the people to drink'. So Moses did this in the sight of the elders of Israel. And he called the place *Massah* and *Meribah* because the Israelites quarreled and because they tested the LORD saying, 'Is the LORD among us or not?' (Exod. 17.1–7)

This parallel occurrence is similar in many respects but there are also several differences from the episode in Numbers 20. The main variance is the time span of almost forty years. In the initial occurrence at the beginning of Israel's trek, Moses is to strike the rock with his staff while Yahweh 'would stand' with them and cause the water to flow. When Moses follows the instruction, the water is provided. The incident in Exodus is serious but no judgment is recorded. The naming of the place *Massah* and *Meribah* is to mark the incident as memorable since the people both 'test' and 'quarrel' with Yahweh there.

20.6-13—*Moses Will Not Enter the Promised Land*

In characteristic fashion Moses and Aaron fall prostrate before the Lord at the entrance to the Tent of Meeting. This is their common reaction whenever the gravity of a situation escalates to a high level of conflict (cf. Num. 14.5; 16.4, 22, 45).

Yahweh appears in his 'glory' (כבוד) to provide instructions for the leaders. The sudden appearance of the divine presence at a time of calamity signals Yahweh's intention to intervene. He directs the leaders to gather the community. They are to carry the 'staff' (מטה) and are to speak to a specific rock (Num. 20.8–11).[72] According to these instructions, water would be produced to cater

---

72   Fabry, 'מטה', pp. 241–246. The term occurs 252 times in the OT and 111 times in Numbers

to human and livestock needs. It is not clear whose staff is referred to here because both Aaron and Moses have one. Aaron does use his staff during the conflict with Pharaoh (Exod. 7.9, 20; 8.1, 13). It is also his staff that 'buds' to validate his chosen role and is kept in the Tent of Meeting as a symbol of warning (Num. 17.25). Moses uses his staff several times in the wilderness and in a parallel occurrence at Horeb (referred to as *Massah* and *Meribah* after the event) to bring forth water (Exod. 17.1–17; cf. 14.16; 17.9).

Since Moses takes the lead in this episode, it is possible that it is 'his' staff that is used. However, due to the drastic turn of events that takes place here and the judgment to fall on Moses, it is preferable to accept that Moses takes Aaron's staff from the Tent which is to symbolize Aaron's choice as priest before Yahweh. The 'budded' staff also serves as an emblem of warning against future acts of rebellion. The reason for this conclusion is that the staff is to be a symbol and not an instrument—Moses is instructed to speak to the rock and trust that Yahweh would provide the miraculous river of water. By using the staff as an instrument and rhetorically asking the 'rebels' if he and Aaron should get the water out of the rock, Moses disrespectfully uses the symbol that produces almonds miraculously as if it were a magical tool. His motivations are clearly wrong and out of anger, but the actions still bring about a positive result: 'Then Moses raised his arm and struck the rock twice with his staff. Water gushed out, and the community and their livestock drank'. However, the Lord views Moses' behaviour as disrespectful and cuts to the issue at hand with a resoundingly severe judgment: 'Because you did not trust in me enough to honor me as holy in the sight of the Israelites, you will not bring this community into the land I give them' (cf. Num. 20.11–12). Moses is spared immediate humiliation before the community but will suffer consequences.

Due to the gravity of Moses' actions in Yahweh's estimation, Moses loses the privilege of leading Israel into the land of promise. Consequently, Moses will not be allowed to enter the promised land and the new generation will be led by new leaders. Apparently, the frustration of persistent habitual complaining that occurs over forty years of wilderness existence take an exacting toll on the 'senior citizen' in leadership. It is true that Moses characteristically prostrates himself before the Lord and depends on Yahweh's directives. However, in this instance he takes things into his own hands by trusting in the staff symbol and

---

where it usually means 'tribe'. It also means staff or stick for use in shepherding. For Moses the staff he uses becomes an instrument of power when God shows his sign in divine action on behalf of Israel in Egypt (14 times in Exodus). Usually, the term takes the literal meaning of 'tribe' with sociological connections to family—a transition from the meaning of 'branch or rod' (cf. Num. 1.20–46; 2.3–31; 10.14–27; 34.18–28). Cf. Fabry, 'מטה', p. 245.

acts as if he has the power to bring forth water with it. Apparently, this is not how Yahweh intends for Moses to end his career. The judgment specifies that he does not trust Yahweh to affirm his holiness and ability to provide for the people. A similar judgment is made in verse 24 alleging that both Aaron and Moses rebel against the precise command of the Lord. Due to their infraction, they will not enter the land of promise.

This judgment appears very harsh to many commentators and the debate regarding Moses' actual failure, sin and action which constitutes such a heavy punishment is lengthy. Milgrom offers a nine-page excursus on the 'Magic, Monotheism, and the Sin of Moses', where he reviews ten arguments that fall into three main categories. With a variety of variations by commentators they include: 1) striking the rock twice rather than speaking to the rock; 2) Moses showed his true character with an angry temper and failure to provide water as required; 3) his query implicitly indicates doubt of God's provision, and additionally alleges that the people are rebels.[73] However, Milgrom's perceptive observation is warranted. 'In the face of the magnitude of this sin, all prior incidents of Moses' petulance and doubt pale. Here, in a direct address to his people, Moses ascribes miraculous powers to himself and Aaron. Indeed, by broadcasting one word—*notsi*', 'we shall bring forth'—Moses and Aaron might be interpreted as having put themselves forth as God'.[74] The nature of prophetic leadership requires the prophet to follow Yahweh's instructions meticulously and to speak the words of Yahweh accurately. It is the Lord who is able to perform the miracles with authenticating signs of his leadership and provisions in Israel. In this case, Moses' humanity and personal issues are exposed, and the days of his leadership are now numbered.

The passage ends with another symbolic geographical reference ('strife; contention') which connects it to Exod. 17.7 as '*Meribah*' (מריבה). In Num. 27.14 it is referred to as *Meribah-Kadesh* as a reminder of the contentious manner in which the people argue with Moses and the Lord. At these places of habitual grumbling, the Lord still proves himself to be faithful in meeting the needs of Israel and by providing for them as the good shepherd. In this way Yahweh is proved holy among them.

20.14–21—*External Threats*

After their extensive wilderness journey the Israelites move towards the promised land from a different position than the southern entry point taken by the

---

73 Milgrom, *Numbers*, pp. 448–456.
74 Milgrom, *Numbers*, p. 452.

twelve spies (Numbers 13). The route they desire to take on the east of the Jordan is through a territory occupied by the Edomites. In order to avoid problems, Moses sends messengers to the king of Edom to communicate a diplomatic request. The address acknowledges the historical relational background that can be traced back to Jacob and Esau (Gen. 32.4–5). Based on this familial connection, Moses kindly requests safe passage through Edom's territory. The appeal includes an historical summary to apprise the king of the arduous situation suffered in Egypt. Moses also testifies to the intervention of Yahweh who is responsible for answering their cries and sending a 'messenger' (מלאך) to deliver them from Egypt (cf. Exod. 14.19). This latter information is a brilliant part of Moses' appeal, indicating the divine assistance in Israel's journey.[75] The request appeals for a sympathetic response and promises to limit any damage or trouble: 'Please let us pass through your country. We will not go through any field or vineyard, or drink water from any well. We will travel along the King's Highway and not turn to the right or to the left until we have passed through your territory' (Num. 20.17). Although the request is fair and reasonable, the Edomites feel endangered and respond with the threat: 'You may not pass through here; if you try, we will march out and attack you with the sword'. A second appeal with further assurances to limit trespass and even offering to pay for water is rejected.

Technically, the King's Highway should be accessible for travel, but the Edomites appear to remember the legacy of Jacob and Esau's history of conflict and are prepared to secure the road from a formidable number of Israelites. Faced with an external threat from the Edomite army, Israel turns away. Although the passage is brief and simply reports what occurs, it must be a blow to Moses' leadership to have the nation turn around and proceed to another place for re-grouping. The whole situation smacks of an unauthorized trek to this location which becomes another 'wandering' episode. However, later in his covenantal sermon Moses provides background material which adds another level of insight to the events with the Edomites.

---

75 In Exod. 14.19, the angel of the Lord moves with the cloud pillar to protect Israel. Not only is the angel leading in front of Israel's army, but also withdraws to come between the armies of Egypt and Israel. In other texts, the angel of the presence is sent in response to Israel's cry for deliverance (cf. Exod. 23.20–23; Isa. 63.9). Although the angel of the Lord is active before the exodus (Gen. 16.7, 9–11; 22.11, 15; 31.11; Exod. 3.2), the angel is the distinct helper of Israel during the wilderness pilgrimage and acts as the emissary of Yahweh. Cf. W. Eichrodt, *Theology of the Old Testament* (2 Vols.; OTL; Philadelphia: Westminster, 1967), II, p. 24 ff.

Then the LORD said to me, 'You have made your way around this hill country long enough; now turn north. Give the people these orders: "You are about to pass through the territory of your relatives the descendants of Esau, who live in Seir. They will be afraid of you, but be very careful. Do not provoke them to war, for I will not give you any of their land, not even enough to put your foot on. I have given Esau the hill country of Seir as his own. You are to pay them in silver for the food you eat and the water you drink."' (Deut. 2.3–6)

With these variations in detail, it appears that there are two attempts to travel through this region. By turning away from the initial threat, Moses indicates his leadership prowess and sensitivity for the needs of the people. The timing for entry into the land is not yet right. In Numbers, the Edomite episode mainly functions to introduce the beginning of a few external threats to Israel's final push into the land with several dramatic events before the new generation will enter their land.

20.22–29—*Death of Aaron*

Aaron (אהרון) has an impressive forty-year leadership career together with his younger brother Moses. His leadership definitely has its difficult experiences with the golden calf incident and the confrontational episode with Miriam. In a dignified report the Lord announces the impending death of Aaron in the metaphoric phrase: 'he will be gathered to his people'. The fact that Aaron cannot enter the promised land for his act of rebellion is reiterated. The location is Mount Hor in the vicinity of the Edomites. The arrangements are made for a major turning point in Israel's history. The first High Priest will be laid to rest and the priesthood will transition to his son Eleazar who already is serving on several important occasions (Num. 3.32; 4.16; 19.3). The procedure of garment transfer from father to son at the direction of Yahweh reinforces that the priesthood is inherited through the lineage of Aaron. The ceremony is simple but very dramatic. In sight of the whole Israelite community, who probably anticipates the event to follow, the leaders journey up the mountain where Aaron's priestly garments are removed and given to Eleazar. There on Mount Hor, Aaron passes into the next life. Upon hearing of Aaron's demise, the community enters a thirty-day mourning period. Typically, seven days are given for grieving but in the case of dignitaries the period is longer. The event verifies the declaration of Yahweh concerning Aaron's demise and the divine judgment concerning the land. It also provides the reader with the realization that the days of Moses' leadership will also come to an end before the promised land will be entered by Israel.

21.1–3—External Threats of the Canaanites

In addition to the threats of losing key leaders like Aaron, the narrative continues to present growing challenges for the nation. The continuing need for resources of food and water are obvious. Furthermore, the sizeable community is an evolving menace to the inhabitants of the land who determine to take action against Israel.

There are several difficulties in placing the exact geographical location of events and details described in this account.[76] After turning away from the Edomite threat (Num. 20.21), Israel ends up in another region in the Negev that is home to Canaanite people under the protection of 'the king of Arad'. The Negev is a large region in the south and the specific area is probably not far from Mount Hor where Aaron is buried. It appears that Moses is determined to forge ahead towards the promised borders and make an attempt to break through. News of a large group of people reaches the king who sends his forces to attack, and some people are captured. The Israelites make a 'vow' (נדר) while requesting intervention from Yahweh: 'If you will deliver these people into our hands, we will totally destroy their cities'. The vow and the promise to destroy the cities is in accordance with the 'ban' (חרם) whereby everything is devoted to the Lord, and nothing is kept for plunder. In this way the motivation for the battle is kept in focus. Consequently, the Lord hears Israel's appeal and allows them to completely destroy the Canaanites and their towns. With this victory in hand, the place is named 'destruction' (*Hormah*). This brief episode is an indicator of changing realities for Israel as their wilderness wandering period nears its final destination.

21.4–9—Complaints and Judgment

While the period of wilderness testing is apparently drawing to a close, the challenges of provision for food and water are exacerbated with growing external security issues. The apparent detour along the Red Sea route to avoid Edom is taking a toll on the nation. In another characteristic display of vexation, as the road seems never to end, the people confront God and Moses with a repetitious refrain, 'Why have you brought us up out of Egypt to die in the wilderness? There is no bread! There is no water! And we detest this miserable food!' (Num. 21.5; cf. 11.5, 18, 20; 14.2, 4; 20.5).

In their characteristic lack of restraint, the people vocalize their growing discontent and blamed Yahweh for the extent of their suffering. The escalation of the complaining rose to another climax. This situation proves to be a seri-

---

76   Cf. Milgrom, *Numbers*, pp. 457–458.

ous watershed moment for the nation is on the brink of a new generational beginning. The punishment that follows is immediate and shocking as 'fiery' or 'venomous' (שרף; 'seraph' or burning implies the symptoms and pain inflicted by the bite) 'serpents' (נחש) are released to attack people, and many are afflicted with deadly bites. Although the threat of vipers is always there, this was an authorized punishment which reflects the intensification of Yahweh's wrath. Many die from the outbreak. With this unforeseen punishment upon them, the people return to Moses with contrition and the appeal for intercession, that the Lord would take the 'snakes' away. The answer to the prayer involves a significant process.

The remedy for the plague of snakes requires the forging of a symbol as well as an act of faith from the people. Moses is instructed to make a symbol attached to a pole. The actual alloy to be used is 'copper' (נחשת) or bronze which apparently is common in that area.[77] The alloy has a reddish tinge to it—a vivid colour to display the feared deadly creature. For Israel the symbol of the snake would have been a common sight in Egypt where snakes were important representations on hieroglyphs and often affixed to mitres or amulets to ward off danger. Symbolically in Egypt the cobra represented royalty and sovereignty. The reddish cobra was common in Egypt and throughout the wilderness region. This passage is very brief, and the text does not indicate how long it takes for the symbol to be made. However, the main indicator that the threat is alleviated is Moses' prayer for protection. The importance of the symbolic provision of the snake on the pole is to assuage the fear of death going forward. Anyone bitten by a serpent has the recourse to look upon the standard with the vexing serpent and believe that healing is available through faith in Yahweh.[78] It is a memorable and powerful reinforcement of the Lord's victory over another terrible challenge. It is another victory to add to the many other provisions which culminated in the fact that Yahweh is indeed leading, providing and healing those who trust in him.

The 'serpent' (נחש) threat is a literal reality which receives a powerful symbolic meaning in this passage. The nature of the incident does call for reflection

---

77 H. Fabry, 'נחש', *TDOT*, IX, pp. 378–379, surveys several proposed explanations of the bronze serpent and its symbolic representations in foreign cultures. However, in this passage it only 'symbolized the salvific intervention of Yahweh. Later when it threatened to take on independent value as an image conveying grace, it was destroyed in the cultic reform of Hezekiah (2 Kgs 18.4)' (Fabry, 'נחש', p. 380).

78 It must be emphasized that there is no magical connotation to the symbol. 'The healing effect is ascribed only to obedience to Yahweh (paradigmatically expressed by looking up [at the snake]).' Fabry, p. 367.

on the Genesis episode concerning the serpent in Eden and the consequences that arise due to the curse. The serpent was the craftiest animal in Eden and effectively led Eve astray with the temptation to eat the desirable fruit. The incident illustrates the human propensity to desire what may look pleasing to the eye, like the menu in Egypt, but may not bring the anticipated satisfaction. Moreover, God provides everything for humankind but makes one prohibition as a test. In this regard Adam and Eve fail and the consequences are extensive, including death. The source of the temptation being a serpent makes the symbol particularly provocative in Numbers 21. The serpent is the cause of death by snake bite and has always struck fear and enmity into the hearts of mankind. The symbol is a vivid reminder of the cause of suffering for Israel all the way back to mankind's fall. It is a warning not to be deceived by the fruits of the world which may be very appealing but often lead to death. Israel's complaints with this context in mind are another example of a failure in realizing the higher purposes of Yahweh. Therefore, the 'cursed snake' which ultimately will be crushed, becomes a symbolic representation of the curse. The symbol calls upon Israel to see, remember, and trust Yahweh to reverse the curse and bring healing to the afflicted.

> So the LORD God said to the serpent, 'Because you have done this, Cursed are you above all livestock and all wild animals! You will crawl on your belly and you will eat dust all the days of your life. And I will put enmity between you and the woman, and between your offspring and hers; he will crush your head, and you will strike his heel.' (Gen. 3.14–15)

There is another example concerning symbols, snakes and staff that may be instructive in this context. When Moses requires support from Yahweh for his prophetic leadership, he is given a miraculous sign with his staff. As instructed, he takes his staff and when he throws it down it turns into a snake. When he retrieves it by grabbing its tail the snake turns back into a staff. In this instance the purpose of the sign and staff is to verify his calling, commission, and authority. 'This', said the LORD, 'is so that they may believe that the LORD, the God of their fathers—the God of Abraham, the God of Isaac and the God of Jacob—has appeared to you' (Exod. 4.3–5). Moses uses the staff in his confrontation with Pharaoh who requires miraculous sign verification.

> So Moses and Aaron went to Pharaoh and did just as the LORD commanded. Aaron threw his staff down in front of Pharaoh and his officials, and it became a snake. Pharaoh then summoned wise men and sorcerers, and the Egyptian magicians also did the same things by their secret arts:

Each one threw down his staff and it became a snake. But Aaron's staff swallowed up their staffs. Yet Pharaoh's heart became hard and he would not listen to them, just as the LORD had said. (Exod. 7.10–13)

In this last example Aaron's staff becomes a *'tannin'* which refers to a sea monster (Gen. 1.21) that swallows the other snakes.[79]

21.10–20—*Yahweh Will Bless*

As Israel continues to lose patience leading up to their fortieth year of sojourning, the nation begins to take a few risky jabs at their enemies. God is patient and actually helps them with some of their attempts, potentially to prepare the younger generation for the conquests that will come.

This section reports several itinerary movements that may be out of order in comparison to the places noted in Numbers 33. Several of the locations that are mentioned here are difficult to find on a map due to ancient developments, textual difficulties, and historic name changes. However, these are important notices of incursions into the Amorite-held territories. They are presented to reinforce the partial, stumbling, forward movement to the promised land and to register a few victories in the process. In fact, seven places in the Amorite regions are noted which may be another symbolic note of encouragement. Furthermore, the poetic and hymnic abilities of Israel are illustrated in a format that reminds the readers of the great Exodus deliverance event which inspires the nation with the song of Moses and Miriam in Exodus 15. They are small indicators that there is a light after the difficult events in the wilderness. Num. 21.10–35 is also a precursor to the Balaam chapters which follow. A similar theme of external threat is featured with poetic prophetic indicators of theological value. In this way Chapter 21 prepares the reader for Israel's arrival on the plains of Moab in 22.1.

The encampments are listed as follows:

> The Israelites moved on and camped at Oboth. Then they set out from Oboth and camped in Iye Abarim, in the wilderness that faces Moab toward the sunrise. From there they moved on and camped in the Zered Valley. They set out from there and camped alongside the Arnon, which is in the wilderness extending into Amorite territory. The Arnon is the border of Moab, between Moab and the Amorites. That is why the Book of the Wars of the LORD says: '… Zahab in Suphah and the ravines, the

---

[79] Fabry, 'נחשׁ', pp. 366–377.

Arnon and the slopes of the ravines that lead to the settlement of Ar and lie along the border of Moab'. From there they continued to Beer, the well where the LORD said to Moses, 'Gather the people together and I will give them water'. (Num. 21.11–15)

The vicinity of the locations are on the Transjordan range near the southern point of the Dead Sea which positions Israel between the Amorites and Moabites. Mention of the Book of Wars reinforces the place names as they once were, and then concludes the notation with a quoted poem. Evidently at some point there were records of war and victory kept as historical reminders of events, but none are extant. However, the citation strengthens the historical notice showing that Yahweh brings them to *Beer* (a well), to gather the community together for the provision of water—without the characteristic complaining! While the site of *Beer* is no longer known, the importance of a watering well to provide for the people's needs is obvious. It has a celebratory dimension to it with a joyful tone: 'Then Israel sang this song: "Spring up, O well! Sing about it, about the well that the princes dug, that the nobles of the people sank—the nobles with scepters and staffs"' (Num. 21.17–18). The song gives credit to the rulers who are responsible for digging the well and preparing it for servicing the communities. It includes the hope that the spring will continue to deliver its life-providing resource. The emphasis is on the authorities (princes; nobles) and their symbols of power ('scepters and staffs') which signify the responsibility of leaders to provide, protect and to steward them for their people. The import of the inclusion here is that Israel appears to acknowledge that Yahweh is indeed able to bring about the blessings he has promised, as manifest in the supply of water. Furthermore, the song is an implicit recognition that the land ruled by others will also be theirs.

A few more itinerary names are recorded but their specific locations are unknown: 'Then they went from the wilderness to Mattanah, from Mattanah to Nahaliel, from Nahaliel to Bamoth, and from Bamoth to the valley in Moab where the top of Pisgah overlooks the wasteland'. They end up in a valley on the eastern side of the Dead Sea which brings them another step closer to the territories of the Moabites.

21.21–22.1—*Victories in Battle*

Similar to the courteous appeal made to the Edomites for safe passage through their land, messengers are sent to Sihon king of the Amorites (cf. 21.26; 32.33). His actual status is unclear, but he is the leader and protector of people in the region. Israel's request to pass through the region on the King's Highway—even with assurances to not trespass or take water—is rejected. Not only so, but his army is mustered to confront Israel in their wilderness encampment near Jahaz. Sihon's attack is met with amazing force from Israel who not only rout the Amorites but take over land from the Arnon to the Jabbok. The land and cities taken by Israel are extensive and include the city of Heshbon and its surrounding settlements. This is a city taken from the Moabites by Sihon—now lost to Israel. The impressive victory is an example of the theological truth 'the LORD giveth, and the LORD taketh away!' It will be a foundational reminder to Israel when challenged with the extensive conquest invasion to come. A limit on their incursion, however, is evident up to the fortified border of the Ammonites. The occupation of the cities taken by the Israelites provides an introduction to their eventual settlement in the promised land and concludes with a summation:

> That is why the poets say: 'Come to Heshbon and let it be rebuilt; let Sihon's city be restored. Fire went out from Heshbon, a blaze from the city of Sihon. It consumed Ar of Moab, the citizens of Arnon's heights. Woe to you, Moab! You are destroyed, people of Chemosh! He has given up his sons as fugitives and his daughters as captives to Sihon king of the Amorites.' (Num. 21.27–29)

Commentators are puzzled as to the actual meaning and initial context of the poem. Typically, the ancients like to formulate summaries of historical events with memorable phrases which could be sung and easily remembered. If this is the purpose here, the poem verifies Sihon's defeat and the need to rebuild Heshbon after the 'fire' destruction and battle. The implication is that the battle is fierce and extensive, not just in Heshbon but the surrounding areas of the Amorites. It goes further to warn enemies of Israel, and specifically the Moabites, that their territory is also under threat. The nation of Israel whose God is giving them gifts of land is more powerful than Chemosh the main divinity of the Moabites. The threat to the people of Moab is clear—Chemosh will be unable to defend the sons and daughters of the Moabites. The danger is real as illustrated by the verbs used to feature the extent of destruction. Although verse 30 has several textual difficulties, the emphasis is on the overthrowing of the Amorites from Heshbon to Dibon and as far as Nophah to Medeba. Israel claims that they have dethroned, destroyed and demolished the Amorites so that the nation can begin settling into the land.

With this victory in place, Israel is emboldened to enlarge their territory. Moses sent spies to explore another site called Jazer, and this mission leads to the capture of surrounding villages. The Amorites, who are there, flee and Israel continues their attack northward to Bashan (cf. Deut. 3.1–11).[80] King Og of that city takes the initiative to confront Moses and the Israelites who fight at Edrei—a location in a northerly area of the Transjordan. The force and fortifications of Og are more than impressive, and Moses needs the encouraging word from Yahweh to not fear—the Lord promises to deliver the whole army into Israel's hands. Israel went to battle and struck down the army of Og, keeping no survivors and taking possession of the land. This battle report is abbreviated here but it is given a more detailed account in Deuteronomy:

> So the LORD our God also gave into our hands Og king of Bashan and all his army. We struck them down, leaving no survivors. At that time we took all his cities. There was not one of the sixty cities that we did not take from them—the whole region of Argob, Og's kingdom in Bashan. All these cities were fortified with high walls and with gates and bars, and there were also a great many unwalled villages. We completely destroyed them, as we had done with Sihon king of Heshbon, destroying every city—men, women and children. But all the livestock and the plunder from their cities we carried off for ourselves (Deut. 3.3–7).

22.1—*Camp on the Jordan*

This verse serves to encapsulate the journey from Paran to the plains of Moab, on the other side of the Jordan across from Jericho. The function of this verse according to Milgrom is an editorial transition to the final section of numbers 'which deals with events that occurred and laws given at the banks of the Jordan prior to entry into the promised land'. It forms an inclusion with the last verse in Num. 36.13, 'These are the commands and regulations the LORD gave through Moses to the Israelites on the plains of Moab by the Jordan across from Jericho'.[81] Furthermore, the location notice is a fitting hinge to the Balaam narratives which are woven into the next section of Numbers. In the itinerary of Num. 33.48, the place of departure is the mountains of Abarim. The plains of

---

80 More detail concerning locations are recorded in Deut. 3.3–11.
    So at that time we took from these two kings of the Amorites the territory east of the Jordan, from the Arnon Gorge as far as Mount Hermon. (Hermon is called Sirion by the Sidonians; the Amorites call it Senir.) We took all the towns on the plateau, and all Gilead, and all Bashan as far as Salekah and Edrei, towns of Og's kingdom in Bashan. (Og king of Bashan was the last of the Rephaites. His bed was decorated with iron and was more than nine cubits long and four cubits wide. It is still in Rabbah of the Ammonites).

81 Milgrom, *Numbers*, p. 184.

Moab are a stretch of land alongside of the Dead Sea on the northeast side (Cf. Num. 26.3, 63; 31.12; 33.38–50; 35.1; 36.13).

The thematic link to the next few chapters is that of further external threat to the progress of Israel in their pilgrimage to the land of promise. Whereas the gift of land is a wonderful prospect for Israel, the nations who hear of a horde of people with military abilities coming their way must have been a foreboding experience.

Reflection and Response
Numbers 11–21: Wandering in a Wilderness
Reflection

Life on earth is a blend of awesome experiences which are often mixed with tragic incidents and hardships. So it is for the Hebrews who enjoyed good times in Egypt until the political circumstances changed and life for many became something to be endured—filled with suffering and oppression. Israel's 'adventures' reflect the experiences of many on this planet. There are mountain top encounters as well as deep valleys of affliction. For those who kept in tune with world events during the pandemic, countless of heart-rending stories of suffering were witnessed. These occurrences in life may often seem meaningless and futile. However, this is where the wilderness experiences of Israel become more than just bewildering stories of old. The narratives and legal materials provide principles and applications for spiritual life and understanding during the good times and the tough ones. The turmoil of economic poverty, lack of food and water, challenges of disease and illness, the prospect of death and judgment—these are all relevant topics of concern which the book of Numbers addresses in a variety of ways.

All of life is a pilgrimage of sorts, but some periods in life involve transitions, changes, and travel. After the Exodus experience and journey from Egypt, God leads Israel through another wilderness sojourn (Exod. 13.17–18), traversing very difficult terrain and diverse locations (Deut. 1.19). To a degree, this trek is a period of testing for Israel to see how they would respond to God's leading and instructions (Exod. 16.4). However, during this time Israel also 'tests' the Lord (Exod. 17.2; Num. 14.22–23) as well as Israel's leaders. Already in Exod. 5.19–23 and 14.10–12, the elders and Israelite community are not happy with Moses' leadership—an early indicator that Moses' work in the nation would be a difficult assignment. And yet, many assignments with purpose and reward in life are like that. Leadership carries significant burdens and accountability. No wonder most people are reluctant to accept difficult positions of authority. However, there are always those people who aspire to leadership and power for various motivations. Selfish ambition is certainly an issue in political, religious, and economic structures. Some people seem to believe they can always do a better job than others and believe there are better ways to plan, manage and lead. The leadership conflict narratives feature many elements of controversy with diverse approaches, perspectives, and resolutions.

In Exodus the testing theme takes shape right after the victory song in Exod. 15.1–21. *Marah* is a place where the water is bitter, and people grumble against Moses. However, God responds by showing Moses a tree that makes the waters drinkable (Exod. 15.22–27). The divine instructions combined with Moses' obedience bring about miraculous provisions for the nation. Then the Lord brings the people to an oasis called Elim. Sometimes life is like that! But other times, life is more like a rollercoaster with its mountain top experiences followed by deep valleys of lows. In the wilderness of Sin, the people cry out for food and lament the loss of a 'good menu' in Egypt (Exod. 16.1–3). God answers with provision of quail and manna (Exod. 16.13–15; 31, 35). Again, at Rephidim (renamed *Massah* 'testing' and *Meribah* 'quarrelling'), there is no water (Exod. 17.1). The people complain and Moses is instructed by God to strike the rock (Exod. 7.1–7). Life may also be repetitive due to the fickleness of human nature. Sometimes our journey takes us into new and difficult circumstances which naturally cause us to reflect on the best of our past realities. If not careful, our human nature tends to wallow in despair without pressing on to forge new and better seasons in life. Too often we forget about God's provisions and lament the temporary deprivations that are an inevitable part of life.

The wilderness theme in Exodus is integral to our comprehension of why the judgments of the Lord appear to be severe in Numbers. A pattern is evident in several narratives which indicate the people have a valid need. Needs are met with a human and divine response, as well as some provision. Due to the nature of the conflict, behaviour and grumbling, a significant form of judgment is delivered. This pattern usually follows an expressed need. However, at *Taberah* the people are just complaining about the 'hardships' of life. In this case the Lord reacts in judgment and no provision is given (Num. 11.1–3). It is the incessant habit of complaining against leaders and God that ultimately culminates with devastating scenes of judgment. God is patient but there comes a time when actions speak louder than words. Moreover, there is something in human nature that causes people to eventually forget about the severity of suffering and makes them reflect on the positive elements.

At *Kibroth-Hattavah* the people complain about the lack of variety in their diet (Num. 11.4–34) although they have food. The Lord's provision of meat and quail comes with 'dessert' when he brings judgment. His anger burns and some die in a plague. A watershed moment occurs in the narrative of the twelve spies who are sent to explore their inheritance. The land proves to be productive with milk and honey, but people live in fortified cities (Num. 13.27–28). People grumble against Moses and accuse God of wanting to slay them—they want to return to Egypt (Num. 14.3–4). Here provision is not given but judgment by pestilence comes upon many (Num. 14.12). God promises further judgment for those who see his glory and signs yet test God ten times—they will not see the promised land (Num. 14.21–23). But some pass the test—Joshua and Caleb showed their faith and courage to press forward. The ten spies with the negative report died by plague.

In addition to complaints about hardship, food and water, the people are often critical against the leadership of Moses and Aaron. At times there are family frictions (Numbers 12), but often prominent leaders came against Yahweh's chosen men which ended in contests and cataclysmic judgments (Numbers 16–17). Even strong, chosen, and empowered leaders like Moses and Aaron succumb to the pressures of leadership and over-step their authority, which ultimately keeps them out of the land of promise (Numbers 20–21). Dramatic narratives, but full of leadership lessons on human nature, human depravity, principles of governance and divine justice.

Response

The wilderness testing era will often be returned to in scripture as a theological lesson for Israel to learn from (cf. Num. 33.1–53; Deut. 1.6–3.29; Pss. 78.17 ff.; 95.7–11; 1 Cor. 10.1–11). These passages often characterize Israel as a stubborn people who are dissatisfied with the provisions and care of Yahweh. The exhortation for readers is to learn from the past record in order to turn a new page that is filled with faith, trust, thanksgiving, repentance, and abundant life. How do we respond when life's challenges arise? Do we succumb to patterns of complaining? Do we respond to difficulties with a critical spirit that blames others for conditions and problems? Are we content with the blessings of God and the leaders he has set in place over us? The following table is a helpful reminder for us to learn from the wilderness episodes so that we may move forward in faith regardless of the circumstances that may arise.

TABLE 6 A summary of the conflict episodes in Numbers 11 to 21

Reference & place	Contention	Divine response	Punishment	Results
Taberah (11.1–3)	Food issues	YHWH is angered	Fire falls consuming camp outskirts	People cry out; Moses prays; fire dies down

TABLE 6   A summary of the conflict episodes in Numbers 11 to 21 (cont.)

Reference & place	Contention	Divine response	Punishment	Results
Kibroth-Hattaavah (11.4–35)	Menu issues	YHWH is angry; Moses is distressed but intercedes	Plague breaks out	Meat is provided but becomes loathsome (11.18–20, 31–32)
Hazeroth (12.1–15)	Miriam & Aaron challenge YHWH's choice	YHWH is angry & confronts leaders	Miriam punished with skin issue and segregation	Moses is upheld as YHWH's chosen prophet
Land expedition (13.1–14.38)	Scouts instigate fear & rebellion; people wish for Egypt	YHWH judges the lack of faith; Moses intercedes	A generation will perish in the wilderness; ten die	Moses intercedes; God forgives
Canaan border (14.39–45); Hormah	Sin confessed but Israel decides to press forward	Moses warns them not to go	Defeat at hands of Amalekites & Canaanites	Death for many
Encampment (16.1–40)	Korah & others rebel; accuse Moses & Aaron of power grab	Moses warns & intercedes; YHWH is angry	Judgment & death for many by plague, fire & earthquake	Leaders challenged; people warned; Moses affirmed
Encampment (16.41–50)	Moses blamed for punishments & death; Question Aaron's authority	Censors ordeal is arranged	Judgment & sacrifices	14,700 die by plague; Aaron serves to stop it plague; Aaron affirmed
Encampment; Tent of Meeting (17.1–13)	Leaders question the choice of Aaron as High Priest	Contest with staff is arranged	Aaron's staff comes alive	Aaron's role affirmed;
Kadesh (20.2–13)	Water complaints; laments	Moses & Aaron are to speak to rock; Moses strikes the rock	Moses punished; will not lead into promised land	Water given; Aaron dies
(21.4–9)	Laments for suffering	Snakes kill	Serpent symbol on stand is made	People live when they look on serpent

22.2–24.25—External Conflicts: Israel and Moab

For several commentators, the so-called 'Balaam Section' appears to be a random inclusion into the book of Numbers for several reasons. Moses is not mentioned in these three chapters. The use of a variety of names for God implies that different sources are used to weave the poetic and narrative sections together. The story about the talking female donkey seems to be out of place and includes a number of difficult contradictions. Furthermore, the status and role of Balaam is debated: is he a diviner, a seer, a real prophet, or a false prophet? Clearly, Balaam is an enigmatic person but his influence in Numbers as well as in several passages of scripture are substantial.[82] Therefore, the importance of the Balaam narrative, together with several oracles, must not be under-estimated. They serve a vital function in the overall purposes of Numbers and in the OT record.[83] These three chapters provide essential theological teaching regarding the calling, purpose and priestly service that Israel as a 'kingdom of priests' must provide to the nations. Moreover, they address the rise and functions of prophecy in the cultural milieu, where divination, sorcery and other forms of manipulation are employed to discern 'divine' activities which affect political regimes and life on earth. Although Moses is not mentioned in chapters 22–24, there are several correspondences which show Balaam to be cast in parallel, and perhaps competitive, activities done by Moses.[84] However, Moses does reappear to take charge of the Moabite and religious threats in ch. 25, in a 'prophetic style' confrontation. Moreover, the whole tenor of Balaam's activities in serving Balak provide a negative view on leadership. These narratives provide important insights into how the improper motivations of kings and diviners can lead to disorder and chaos for many people.

The richness of the 'Balaam narratives' is informed by unique devices commonly used in Hebrew story development which highlight the effects of oral transmission to instill memorable theological material. This is evident in the motifs of blessing and cursing; the seeing but not really 'seeing', the angel of the Lord with a sword, the use of repetitive triplets (Balaam and ass, altars and sacrifices), and the unique images used for Israel (as dust; a crouched lion; a star).

The overall activities of the narrative illustrate the vital concept of blessing and cursing which is a powerful motif flowing through the Pentateuch. The theme develops the theological worldview which is rooted in the creation

---

[82] Balaam is referred to 64 times in the Bible—mainly in Numbers 22–24, but also in several Old and New Testament texts (cf. Num. 31.8, 16; Deut. 23.4, 5; Josh. 13.22; 24.9, 10; Neh. 13.2; Mic. 6.5; 2 Pet. 2.15; Jude 1.11; Rev. 2.14).

[83] In fact, Levine, *Numbers 21–36*, dedicates 138 pages to the three chapters of the 'Balaam Pericope'. Milgrom writes four detailed excursuses: Balaam and the Ass; Balaam: Saint or Sinner?; Balaam: Diviner or Sorcerer?; and Balaam and the Deir 'Alla Inscription, pages 468–476. In the Deir 'Alla Inscriptions that are dated to 900 BC, Balaam is referred to as a 'seer' (חזה; *hozeh*). Although difficult to translate, the inscriptions add interesting insights which verify the typical practices of divination in the ancient near east.

[84] For example, the Lord speaks to both individuals; the angel of the Lord is active in several scenes; both individuals lie prostrate at times and both of them supervise sacrifices. They are leaders who give direction and receive prophetic revelation.

story of blessing for progeny (Genesis 1), in the consequences of sin narrative and curses (Genesis 3) and solidified in the Abrahamic covenant (Genesis 12) which features an essential truth: God blesses foreign nations according to how they deal with the covenantal people. It is a relational blessing that flows from Israel's covenantal relationship with Yahweh. When the nation is obediently worshipping the Lord, who redeems them from oppression in Egypt, blessings of all kinds ensue. To a certain extent the whole cultus and priestly service is to ensure the 'blessing' of the people through sacrificial offerings and the 'laying on of Yahweh's name' to bless Israel, the covenant people (Num. 6.22–27). On the other hand, when Israel follows the idolatrous ways of the nations which pervert their social communal ways, then curses cause the loss of land and numerous negative consequences (cf. Deut. 28.15–68).

This is the contextual background of the Balaam episodes which provides keen insights into the way Yahweh handles external threats to Israel as well as individuals and community. Another key element in the section is the whole discussion of prophecy and divination in the ancient Near East. Who speaks for God? How can humans influence God to intervene in the life of a nation? How do people find provision, security, and community in a world of competing people groups in the quest for survival? Who is a true prophet and a false prophet? With these narratives Israel is given a heads up regarding political science merged with supernatural powerful forces that can provide guidance and direction for nations and people. The king of Moab conspires with Balaam to bring harm to Israel through the professional diviner's application of curses. In this way the comparison of the true prophet Moses with the false prophet Balaam becomes clear. The lesson is that there will always be forces in play against the progress and development of God's people and their service to the world. There will always be those who employ the forces of evil to help them deal with the battle against enemies who want land, cities, security, and control.

In the end the lesson is clear: If God is for Israel, then who can come against the nation? If God desires to use Israel to be a kingdom of priests to the nations of the world, then what curses can be placed upon them to restrain their service?

22.2–6—*Balak, Moabites, and Midianites*

This section begins by introducing Balak son of Zippor (Num. 22.2) who is identified as the king of Moab (Num. 22.4). The first word devoted to the Balaam section introduces important themes and motifs that are developed to focalize the elements in the narrative. A *Leitwort* (leading word) 'to see' (ראה) will flow through the passage to feature the difference between physical sight and spiritual sight.[85] It will lead to the understanding of the nature of 'prophecy' (נאם) and how divine utterance and revelation are received (cf. Num. 24.3, 4, 15).[86] Balak 'sees' and understands that a great threat is coming towards the Moabite people with an incursion of Israelites into their territory.

With Israel's movement into the Amorite territories and their encampment near the Moabites, the people rightly feared for their security. Israel's fearsome reputation based on the Amorite invasion as well as their exodus from Egypt is known to Balak. Moreover, the population of the Israelites is viewed as a staggering horde. In addition to the threat of invasion the reality that such a population would consume all the resources is a realistic fear: 'This horde is going to lick up everything around us, as an ox licks up the grass of the field'.

Apparently, the people of Midian coexisted with the Moabites and rally together to deal with the current threat. Although the Moabites and elders of Midian view Israel's encroachment as a serious problem, they are not prepared to try military action. Instead, Balak, king of Moab, determines to hire the services of Balaam, son of Beor, who is known to function in the craft of 'divination' (קסם) (cf. Num. 22.7; 23.23; 24.1; cf. Josh. 13.22).

---

85   The *Leitwort* 'to see, perceive, look' (ראה) occurs 15 times in Numbers 22–24. In the OT it occurs 1303 times and 39 in Numbers with a variety of meanings. Cf. H.F. Fuhs, 'ראה', pp. 212–239. Another term for 'visions' (מחזה) occurs in Num. 24.4, 16 where Balaam receives legitimate revelation oracles. This word is used as a technical term specifying a form of revelation associated with pre-prophetic seers but later becomes virtually synonymous with (ראה). When Balaam 'perceives' an oracle (ראה), it is used as a formulaic introduction (Num. 24.17). Whatever the seer perceives in a visionary experience is transformed into a speech event (Num. 23.9, 21). The formula of presenting the utterance 'oracle of Balaam' is used to describe the 'seer's self-awareness and responsibility for giving his vision verbal form'. Cf. Fuhs, 'ראה', p. 237. The parallel term for 'vision' (חזה), in a technical usage for prophets, occurs in Num. 24.4, 16. This term with its derivatives occurs 129 times in the OT plus 45 in Aramaic. Typically, reception of the vision comes nocturnally but includes the revelation of a word. Cf. A. Jepsen, 'חזה', *TDOT*, IV, pp. 283–284. Therefore, the vision and word element in prophetic contexts has important ramifications for prophecy inspired by the Lord.

86   Alter, *The Art of Biblical Narrative*, pp. 104–107. The use of a *Leitwort* in repetitive forms of the word is a device which intensifies the thematic movement towards a climactic insight. Although the characters are able to see the immense population that is Israel, and they see the materials used for sacrifice—they do not have clear vision regarding the spiritual world and how the supernatural world functions. However, as Balaam works through his human understanding of divination and begins to comprehend how Yahweh determines the course of history, his eyes are eventually 'opened' to see the divine will.

The message and invitation from Balak is clear:

> A people has come out of Egypt; they cover the face of the land and have settled next to me. Now come and put a curse on these people because they are too powerful for me. Perhaps then I will be able to defeat them and drive them out of the land. For I know that whoever you bless is blessed, and whoever you curse is cursed. (Num. 22.5b–6)

Whether Balak's estimation is hyperbolic or not, the incursion of the people from Egypt that covers an area 'as far as the eye can see' is threatening. Balak rightly fears an invasion from people who seem to be stronger than Moab. The goal of the curse invocation is to immobilize the threat by defeating and driving the migrants away.

Balaam's reputation must have been impressive for the emissaries to go to such an extent to hire him. The near eastern concept of the power of the spoken word is reflected in Balak's invitation. A formulaic word or curse given by the empowered functionary with the right force and clarity is considered a mighty and terrifying power that could prove effective in various spheres of life. Balak's purpose in hiring Balaam to set a curse in motion becomes a dominate theme and *Leitwort* in the narrative. Two words for 'curse' are used with basically the same meaning. The first appears seven times (ארר), and the second term, ten times (קבב).[87] The curse or 'execration' is perceived to have inherent power to affect a reversal of the state of 'blessing' (ברך) or to set into effect misfortune. A magical understanding of the spoken word that could bring about the destruction of Israel and safety for Moab is evident in Balak's request. Typically, the curse motif is used against enemies or covenant partners who fail in their duties of not paying tribute, but also used in preparation for battle.[88] On the complete opposite scale of the curse is the positive act to bless. To 'bless' (ברך) is another *Leitwort* in the passage which focalizes the key issues involved in the Balaam narratives. Yahweh's blessings and protection are upon Israel which is a potential threat for the other nations.[89]

---

87   Scharbert, 'ארר', I, pp. 412–425; cf. Num. 22.6 (3 times), 12; 23.7; 24.9 (2 times); Num. 22.11, 17; 23.8 (2 times), 11, 13, 25, 27; 24.10, for קבב.
88   Levine, *Numbers 21–36*, p. 150.
89   The term 'bless' (ברך) occurs in a variety of forms approximately 370 times in the OT with about 14 references in Numbers. In Num. 22.6 the text 'assumes the benediction of a mantic endowed with special powers to bless and to curse' will in fact come about. Cf. Scharbert, 'ברך', p. 296.

22.7–12—The First Invitation from the Elders of Moab and Midian
Messengers well versed in divination practices are sent to a distant land in Pethor near the Euphrates River with the divination fee to solicit Balaam's services.[90] In the ancient Near East, divination is a popular technique which includes communication with supernatural forces and the manipulation of materials in order to influence powerful consequences. The elders of Moab and Midian who travel to fetch Balaam understand how divination works. In other words, they function in the same worldview and system, believing that Balaam's craft will bring about their security. The elders of Moab and Midian present Balaam with the terms and Balak's request. Before engaging the invitation, Balaam requests time to consider whether he should accept the assignment. Deliberations typically include rituals to determine what should be done. Often this could include a dream quest to determine the divine will.[91] Whatever the process entails, Balaam indicates that his response depends on the direction he anticipates from Yahweh (יהוה).[92] During the night Elohim (אלהים) communicates with Balaam, asking who the visitors are. Balaam repeats the message and identifies Balak as the one who is eager to hire a diviner with cursing skills.

The first references to Yahweh and God in this section occur in verses 8–9. In Numbers 22–24 there are 51 references to the divine name using five different forms.[93] The intent appears to highlight the reality that whatever happens to the people of God will be determined by the divine will and not by the human designs which will prove to be impotent.

---

90 According to the locations, a trek of about 640 kilometers is indicated. With four trips in view, this could have taken more than three months of time.

91 Dreams are a mode of communication used by Yahweh to reveal direction or future realities (Gen. 40.5–8; 41.1–8; 44.4,15; Dan. 1.17; 2.1–11). When given to certain individuals or prophets, it is Yahweh who provides the interpretation and meaning through Spirit-filled servants (e.g., Joseph and Daniel).

92 Divination is prohibited in Israel (Lev. 19.26; 20.27; 2 Kgs 17.17), especially when connected with magic and sorcery. In Deuteronomy such practices are viewed as occultic and forbidden:

> When you enter the land the LORD your God is giving you, do not learn to imitate the detestable ways of the nations there. Let no one be found among you who sacrifices their son or daughter in the fire, who practices divination or sorcery, interprets omens, engages in witchcraft, or casts spells, or who is a medium or spiritist or who consults the dead. (Deut. 18.9–11)

Diviners are usually associated with the false prophets (Jer. 27.9; 29.8; Ezek. 13.6–9, 23; Mic. 3.6f.; Zech. 10.2). Lots and dreams are occasionally considered valid forms of direction, but Yahweh is recognized as sovereignly involved in providing direction through such means (cf. Prov. 16.33).

93 Ashley, *Numbers*, p. 433.

TABLE 7   Diversity in divine names

Text	Yahweh; יהוה	Elohim; אלהים	El; אל	Shaddai; שדי	Elyon; עליון
22.2–21, 36–41	4	6	0		
22.22–35	12	1	0		
23.1–30	8	3	4		
24.1–25	5	1	4	2	1

God clearly tells Balaam not to accept the invitation and prohibits the cursing because they (Israel) are 'blessed' (ברך). Balaam reports his decision to the officials in the morning by stating that 'Yahweh' restrained him from proceeding with them. Surprisingly, they accept the reply and return to Balak reporting Balaam's refusal.

22.13–20—The Second Invitation from Distinguished Messengers

This does not deter Balak who sends another contingent of more dignitaries than the first group, with promises of greater reward and more persuasive terms. Yet, Balaam remains adamant in his reply: 'Even if Balak gave me all the silver and gold in his palace, I could not do anything great or small to go beyond the command of the LORD my God'. He also affirms that it is not the amount of gold that is at issue, but that Yahweh commands him not to comply. It is this affirmation that 'Yahweh' is Balaam's God that often brings some confusion to readers. Is Balaam a diviner, a 'seer', a false prophet or legitimate prophet?[94] It is possible that his reputation as a powerful diviner also includes his affiliation to Yahweh. However, he determines to put it before the Lord once again, with a surprising change of tone: 'Since these men have come to summon you, go with them, but do only what I tell you'. Balaam is permitted to go but with firm restriction on his actions to do as instructed. Yet even with Balaam's confession of being a Yahwist, the narration posits a glimmer of doubt.

---

94 It is because of the words he speaks, and not his practice of divination, that Balaam is aligned with the prophets. Balaam as a 'seer' may be capable of receiving divine revelations from Elohim (Num. 22.18), but he responds to inquiries for a fee. The seer in the OT is allowed by Yahweh to perceive a divine communication for specific situations (for example Samuel; cf. 1 Samuel 9).

22.21–35—Balaam's Journey and the Divine Messenger

Most commentators consider the story of Balaam and his talking ass as an interpolation of folklore replete with content that is meant to humiliate his character. Whereas the initial story of Balaam of Peor begins with portraying a positive character with affiliation to Yahweh, the narrative to follow shows a conflicted, unstable individual going down a slippery path. Nevertheless, the narrative is an essential teaching with many implications for the whole wilderness epic and appears to include a sarcastic comparison to Israel's stubborn resistance to Yahweh's leading.

With the divine nod to leave for Moab, Balaam prepares for the trek with the Moabite dignitaries and two of his personal servants. In an unusual choice for such a long trek, Balaam rides on his female donkey. The introductory note in the narrative indicates that things will go wrong, since God was very wroth as Balaam departs with the guests (Elohim 'burned with anger'). The 'angel' (מלאך) of the Lord is sent to block Balaam's path but he is oblivious to the divine messenger. Only the ass 'sees' the angel with a drawn sword in his hands.[95] To avoid the angel, the ass turns into a field causing Balaam to respond in anger.

On three occasions the ass 'sees' the angel of the Lord and the formidable sight scares her off the road. Balaam is not able to see the angel and does not understand why the ass is stubbornly refusing to comply. Balaam beats his animal three times with his staff (Num. 22.23, 25, 27) and is humiliated by the beast's lack of compliance in moving forward to their destination. Finally, the Lord gives the donkey the ability to communicate with Balaam. In his wrath, Balaam states that if he had a sword, he would kill the animal! An interesting conversation ensues with the ass reasoning with the diviner regarding his faithfulness. At this point, Yahweh 'opens' Balaam's eyes to see behind the physical realm and realise the angel's presence. In this way the narrative focalizes the *Leitwort* 'to see' (ראה) which occurs several times in a variety of ways (saw, see, seen) to feature Balaam's lack of spiritual insight. As a functioning diviner, he has other motivational aspirations that begin to change when Yahweh opens his eyes to see reality.[96] Of course it is difficult for rational peo-

---

95 The angel of the LORD is mentioned 11 times in Numbers, but 10 occurrences are in this pericope (Num. 22.22–35).

96 See Alter's perceptive analysis of the Balaam pericopes in *The Art of Biblical Narrative*, p. 104 ff. Alter summarizes the force of the narrative: 'Paganism, with its notion that divine powers can be manipulated by a caste of professionals through a set of carefully prescribed procedures, is trapped in the reflexes of a mechanistic worldview while from the biblical perspective reality is in fact controlled by the will of an omnipotent God beyond all human manipulation'.

ple to believe that a donkey can speak. However, the claim that 'the LORD opens the donkey's mouth' is similar to the claim that 'the LORD opens Balaam's eyes'. Both require a supernatural element and the faith to receive it. Similar to the talking serpent (Genesis 3), the talking donkey has a message. However, here the message serves to restrain the diviner from his foolish actions of going against the Lord's instructions.[97]

Although the story refers to a variety of unusual places such as fields, a vineyard, walls and pathways, the focalization is on Balaam's failure to see the angel of the Lord. Implicitly he has also failed to hear the word of the Lord and it takes the speech from the donkey to rally his attention. As the reality of what happens dawns on Balaam, he falls prostrate to the ground. When he realizes the gravity of his actions and the intervention of the Lord's angel with drawn sword, he is struck with his own sin in forging ahead to serve Balak. Now Balaam communicates with the angel of the Lord. The Lord sees Balaam's heart and motive—he is on a reckless path of action and the angel is prepared to kill him. Paradoxically, Balaam is saved by the ass (Num. 22.33). He offers to return home and end the assignment, but for the second time is mandated to carry on with strict instruction to only speak as directed.

22.36–23.12—*Balak and Balaam*

With anticipation, Balak goes out from his place to meet Balaam in the northern locale of Moab on the Arnon border.[98] He scolds Balaam for not heeding his initial invitation which has only increased his anxiety and resolve to deal with the Israelites. Balaam repeats his mantra that he must only speak what Elohim inspires him with. There is an obvious tension between what Balak desires and what Balaam will be able to act upon. However, the men proceed to *Kiriath Huzoth* where Balak sacrifices oxen and sheep in preparation for the work of Balaam. By serving some of the meat to Balaam and the officials, the offerings are similar to a fellowship meal and an appropriate way to serve the travellers after a long arduous trek.

The next morning, they move to an elevated area named Bamoth Baal, where they could see a portion of the Israelite camp. Now Balaam begins his craft in earnest. In characteristic fashion for diviners, there are rituals to follow and

---

97 Some of the parallels that are evident from Genesis 3 are the talking animal which seeks to convince Eve to 'take and eat'. Also, the 'opening of eyes': 'Then the eyes of both of them were opened'. Other comparisons include the cursing of the serpent, Eve and Adam, the cherubim angel with a sword, and the blocking of the path to Eden.

98 Commentators who consider Num. 22.21–35 a fictional tale, view it as an interpolation that should be omitted up to the point of Balak's arrival.

interpretations to determine.⁹⁹ Balaam directs the preparations for his work requiring seven altars, seven bulls and seven rams. Not only does the number 'seven' (שבע) figure prominently in scripture, but it is theologically meaningful in Israel's cultus and the ordering of life, affirming completion and levels of perfection (the number is used 12 times in Num. 23.1–29).¹⁰⁰ Not only does the preparation of seven altars require significant work and effort but the sacrificial animals are costly. The offering rituals are meant to predispose the deity toward the petitioner in order to accomplish the curse that Balak is paying for. Both Balaam and Balak officiate the sacrifices simultaneously until Balaam seeks solitude to receive the divine message. Sure enough, Elohim manifests himself to Balaam and inspires him with the specific divine words for Balak. Dutifully, Balaam returns to Balak, the dignitaries and the place of sacrifice, to deliver an astounding 'oracle' (משל; literally a proverb or parable but also a prophetic proclamation):¹⁰¹

> Balak brought me from Aram, the king of Moab from the eastern mountains. 'Come', he said, 'curse Jacob for me; come, denounce Israel'. How can I curse those whom God has not cursed? How can I denounce those whom the LORD has not denounced? From the rocky peaks I see them, from the heights I view them. I see a people who live apart and do not consider themselves one of the nations. Who can count the dust of Jacob or number even a fourth of Israel? Let me die the death of the righteous, and may my final end be like theirs! (Num. 23.7–10)

The oracle relates the historical context of how Balaam and king Balak have come together through the summons to travel from Aram in order to curse Israel. Balaam announces his inability to curse Israel because Yahweh has not permitted the verbal execration. From his perch, Balaam witnesses first-hand

---

99   Diviners devised operational or magical means of communication. Various technical means were devised that were thought to have magical potency in manipulating the actions of the gods for the benefit of human beings. This included operational means such as the casting of lots or smoke from a censor to indicate a yes or no answer by the deity. Magical conceptions held that the deity produced changes in natural phenomena such as the weather, stars, or animal viscera based on a code acceptable to both the deity and the diviner.

100 Over 300 occurrences of seven, seventh, seventy are used in the OT, often with metaphoric import. In some form, 'seven' (שבע) occurs approximately 65 times in Numbers.

101 The word also has its place in prophetic proclamation, where it refers to an oracle spoken as the result of a vision or inspiration (cf. Balaam oracles in Num. 23.7, 18; 24.3, 15, 20 f., 23). Cf. K.M. Beyse, 'משל', TDOT, IX, p. 66.

the vast population of Israelites, whose numbers are compared to 'dust'. The metaphor is an indicator of the covenantal promises which compares Abraham's descendants to sand, stars and dust. 'I will make your offspring like the dust of the earth, so that if anyone could count the dust, then your offspring could be counted' (Gen. 13.16; cf. 22.17). Balaam also notes their special status. They are not as the other 'nations' (גוי), they live apart. They are not reckoned among the other nations. In part this may refer to their 'secure' position, but it also brings to mind their covenantal status: 'Now if you obey me fully and keep my covenant, then out of all nations you will be my treasured possession. Although the whole earth is mine, you will be for me a kingdom of priests and a holy nation' (Exod. 19.5–6). Israel is chosen by Yahweh and although the nation responds in many disappointing ways, the Lord is not casting them aside but is prepared to lead them and bless them. Balaam concludes the oracle with a personal wish to die a righteous and blessed man and thereby share in the nation's destiny (cf. Gen. 12.3; 22.18; 28.14). Balak is stunned by the oracle which states the opposite of what he hopes for. In fact, he discerns the underlying reality that Balaam supports the blessing of Israel. Balaam is adamant that his warning is true—he can only communicate what the Lord puts in his mouth.

23.13–26—Balaam's Second Oracle

Undeterred, Balak takes the diviner to another location where they have a different view of the Israelites, on the summit of Pisgah. There Balaam repeats the required assembling of seven altars with a bull and a ram offering on each one. Once again, he orders Balak to remain with the offerings while he seeks audience with the Lord.

This process brings about the reception of the second oracle which Balaam pronounces to the king and the officials: 'Arise, Balak, and listen; hear me, son of Zippor. God is not human, that he should lie, not a human being, that he should change his mind. Does he speak and then not act? Does he promise and not fulfil? I have received a command to bless; he has blessed, and I cannot change it'.

> No misfortune is seen in Jacob, no misery observed in Israel. The LORD their God is with them; the shout of the King is among them. God brought them out of Egypt; they have the strength of a wild ox. There is no divination against Jacob, no evil omens against Israel. It will now be said of Jacob and of Israel, 'See what God has done!' The people rise like a lioness; they rouse themselves like a lion that does not rest till it devours its prey and drinks the blood of its victims. (Num. 23.18–24)

After Balaam receives the second word from God, he summons Balak to attention and provides some keen theological instruction. It appears that both Balaam and Balak learn things about God as the episodes of sacrifice and oracle reception play out. God is not like a man in regard to changing his mind about important matters. He is not capricious—what God promises he also brings to fulfilment. Therefore, Balaam can only bless what God has blessed. In this regard, blessing is observed in the rich historical experiences of Jacob and Israel whose temporary misfortunes are turned to positive blessings (cf. Gen. 50.20). Yahweh is their God, and the people worship him as their king through song and praise (Exodus 15). Evidence for this is the exodus from Egypt which God directed and superintended. Israel's 'strength of a wild ox' is evident in the historical events that bring them from Egypt through the wilderness to Moab. Israel has the power of a lion which is keen on hunting its prey to drink blood, therefore, a real threat for the Moabites. The real crux of the oracle comes in verse 23. Divination nor augury with omens will work against Israel.[102] In other words, Balaam declares that his use of divination, rituals and offerings will not be able to change what God has purposed for Israel. That is, God guides Israel by prophecy and not through magical arts to determine his will. God's plan for the nation will be fulfilled through his blessing and no curses or magic can come against his promises. The divine plan to choose a people for himself to be a kingdom of priests through whom he would bless the nations will be realized.

On this occasion, Balak is incensed at another positive oracle for Israel. He blurts out that Balaam should neither curse nor bless! Balaam reminds Balak of his limitations and yet, they proceed together to another venue.

23.27–24.9—*Balaam's Third Oracle*

As they move to another location, Balak is more subdued in his hopes: 'Perhaps it will please God to let you curse them for me from there'. From Peor overlooking the wasteland, Balak is instructed to build yet another seven altars for another seven bulls and rams. Balaam's third oracle is an even stronger and more impressive affirmation of the nation, than the first two oracles. He is very bold to declare it due to the positive pronouncements for Israel that continue to pour from his mouth:

---

102 According to Milgrom, the main difference between a sorcerer and a diviner is that the former tries to alter the future through the use of curses or blessings, whereas the diviner mainly tries to ascertain the future and foretell events to come. Balaam is considered to be a diviner through his craft of reading signs or omens on hilltops—and by not complying with Balak's expectation to curse Israel through sorcery. Cf. Milgrom, *Numbers*, pp. 271–273.

The prophecy of Balaam son of Beor, the prophecy of one whose eye sees clearly, the prophecy of one who hears the words of God, who sees a vision from the Almighty, who falls prostrate, and whose eyes are opened: 'How beautiful are your tents, Jacob, your dwelling places, Israel! Like valleys they spread out, like gardens beside a river, like aloes planted by the LORD, like cedars beside the waters. Water will flow from their buckets; their seed will have abundant water. Their king will be greater than Agag; their kingdom will be exalted. God brought them out of Egypt; they have the strength of a wild ox. They devour hostile nations and break their bones in pieces; with their arrows they pierce them. Like a lion they crouch and lie down, like a lioness—who dares to rouse them? May those who bless you be blessed and those who curse you be cursed!' (Num. 24.3–8)

As Balaam seeks the divine message for the third oracle, he changes his approach due to the realization that it pleases Yahweh to bless Israel. In fact, he does not use his divination skills, nor does he seek out a private spot to hear the message of God but turns his face toward the wilderness. Apparently, Balaam is learning about Yahweh and the mode of inspiration as the manifestation and oracle revelation comes to him. Now he simply opens his ear to hear and his eyes to see. As he looks up, his gaze falls on the nation of Israel encamped in their orderly tribes. At this point he experiences another supernatural event: 'Balaam looked out and saw Israel encamped tribe by tribe, the Spirit of God came on him' (Num. 24.2). When the 'Spirit of God' (רוח אלהים) comes on Balaam, he is inspired to speak his third and fourth oracles. The coming of the Spirit of God on him indicates the difference in reception and inspiration from that of the first two oracles. The claim of Balaam at this juncture is that he 'hears the words of God', he 'sees a vision from the Almighty', he 'falls prostrate', his 'eyes are opened' (Num. 24.4, 16). Balaam now perceives the inspired 'word' (נאם) of prophecy.[103] He fully comprehends God's message, that is inspired by the Spirit rather than by technical means.[104]

---

103   With 376 occurrences in the OT, it is used for formulaic utterances of Yahweh 365 times. In this sense it 'emphasizes that the message of the prophets comes from God through whom their words are true and effectual'. Cf. H. Eising, 'נאם', TDOT, IX, p. 110.

104   The term 'seer' (חזה) is related to the word 'visionary' and 'prophet' and mainly indicates one of the functions of the prophet. Balaam becomes one who sees visions (Num. 24.4). The role of Balaam was to look into the future or into the unseen reality behind a situation for direction. The paradox of the Balaam episode is that the professional seer cannot perceive the reality of the situation, while the ass does, until God opens his eyes (Num. 22.31). The 'opening of the eyes' is something God must do and is what occurs subsequent to the coming of the Spirit of God on Balaam. Cf. A. Jepsen, 'חזה', TDOT, IV, p. 283.

Furthermore, Balaam shows humility in the presence of God in prostration yet fully engaged in the 'vision' (מחזה) of the 'Almighty' (שדי) through whom he receives the spiritual message (*Shaddai*; שדי). The terms indicate both spiritual perception of the vision as well as appreciation for the physical sight of Israel. His physical gaze sees the impressive tents and dwellings of Jacob and compares them to the palm-groves, gardens by a river, aloes, and cedars—all pleasant comparisons to the vision of Israel. Moreover, these gratifying images are pictured as productive plants with boughs full of moisture, roots full of water, indicating the future productivity of the nation.

A threatening note in the prophecy indicates that a king will arise in the nation above Agag (or Amalek who is Israel's most dreaded enemy—cf. Exod. 17.8-16), and their Kingdom will be exalted. These are not words or portents that the king of Moab wants to hear. The horns of the wild ox are a metaphor of power making Israel capable of devouring enemy nations. Like a crouching lion ready to take its prey, it is a dangerous thing to mount a challenge—Israel is capable of a violent response (crush bones; smash arrows). Finally, the Abrahamic promise is pronounced: 'Blessed are they who bless you; Accursed they who curse you!' (Num. 24.9b; cf. Gen. 12.1-3; 27.29).

24.10-14—Balak's Anger

This time Balak's rage against Balaam is fiercer. Balaam fails to curse as hired and instead pronounces blessings. Balaam is basically fired and sent home! Not only that but the promised reward is forfeited, and Balak claims that it is the Lord who keeps him from the reward! Balak's reaction of mounting anger is similar to Balaam's anger over his disobedient ass. The repetition of events in the narratives serve to emphasize Balaam's inability to see what his ass could see and Balak's inability to subvert Yahweh's promise of blessing to the chosen people. Even though his services seem to be terminated, Balaam responds in his characteristic, 'I told you so'. Even for gold and silver, he is kept from saying anything other than what the Lord instructs. Nevertheless, Balaam agrees to return to his people but has another warning to share.

24.15-19—Balaam's Fourth Oracle

Balaam has an additional word for Balak, which he affirms to be the divine truth about what will happen to the Moabites in the days to come. The affirmation is based on the clarity of the vision as well as the number of divine designations in the passage (cf. Num. 24.3-4 is repeated as the introduction) to oracle four. Three times he reiterates that the 'word' (נאם) comes from one who perceives clearly, who hears the words of God, has knowledge and sees a vision. In other words, what will transpire in the nations that stand in Israel's way has been clearly received through divine revelation and should be heeded. The terminology used indicates a heightened type of ecstatic reception and sense of inspiration.

> I see him, but not now; I behold him, but not near. A star will come out of Jacob; a scepter will rise out of Israel. He will crush the foreheads of Moab, the skulls of all the people of Sheth. Edom will be conquered; Seir, his enemy, will be conquered, but Israel will grow strong. A ruler will come out of Jacob and destroy the survivors of the city. (Num. 24.15–19)

This fourth oracle includes some positive and far-reaching prophecies for Israel. Balaam tries to vividly communicate the future portents of his 'vision' (מחזה): he sees an individual coming but the timing of his arrival is not yet. A 'star' (כוכב) will come out of Jacob and a 'scepter' (שבט) from Israel. The implication is that a ruler will come out of Israel with a symbol of authority to bring judgment on the nation's enemies. The first people to experience Israel's wrath are the Moabites who in fact are eager to curse Israel—now they will be crushed. Other enemies are added to those who will be conquered for various historical improprieties such as Edom, people of Sheth and Seir (cf. Gen. 25.23; 27.29). However, Israel will forge ahead in strength with the ruler from Jacob coming to mete out destruction. With this prophetic word that elevates Jacob and Israel but denounces Moab and others, Balak is rendered speechless. However, Balaam has a few more oracles to communicate—three brief ones which make a total of seven.

24.20–25—Three Brief Oracles and Balaam's Departure

The fifth message pertains to Amalek: 'Amalek was first among the nations, but their end will be utter destruction' (Num. 24.20). The classical prophets will include more extensive oracles against foreign nations for a variety of reasons—often because of their horrible treatment of Israel. Here Balaam states concise yet damning words. The context appears to be from his perch on Peor overlooking the valley below where he sees the Amalekites—their present circumstances appear to be positive as a 'leading' nation, but their future destiny is under threat.

According to the sixth pronouncement, the Kenites who seem secure in their place will also meet their demise at the hands of Ashur. It is not clear in what era this is to take place because some Kenites are a welcome part of Israel and related to the Midianites (cf. Num. 10.29). 'Your dwelling place is secure, your nest is set in a rock; yet you Kenites will be destroyed when Ashur takes you captive' (Num. 24.21–22).

In the seventh declaration, Balaam does not focus on a specific people but pronounces a more general statement. The meaning of the Hebrew and the referents are difficult to interpret: 'Alas! Who can live when God does this? Ships will come from the shores of Cyprus; they will subdue Ashur and Eber, but they too will come to ruin'. (Num. 24.23–24). The basic idea is that the survival of people groups ultimately lies in the hands of God. When invaders like those on ships from Cyprus come, they will be able to subdue people like Ashur and Eber, but their fate will also end in ruin. God's justice will prevail in the end.

With the record of seven oracles (four major and three minor) pronounced by Balaam, this part of his assignment is over. Both Balaam and Balak return to their places with neither one of them receiving the rewards they were anticipating. However, Balaam's new project will soon begin because his story is not over. The Balaam section is concluded in the traditional way: 'Then Balaam got up and returned home, and Balak went his own way'. It could be concluded that Balaam may be an impotent diviner when it comes to Israel. However, with his positive pronouncements for Israel's future, he turns out to be a profitable prophet.

Reflection and Response
Numbers 22–24: Yahweh's Blessing and Prophecy
Reflection

The Balaam section provides vital insights concerning physical and spiritual realities which may influence individuals and nations. The story illustrates typical ways that humans have devised in developing their culture and to address various challenges of life. To ward off evil and threats, several cultures have utilised functionaries who developed ideas and practices to manipulate invisible forces of disorder. These agents operate to bring about peace and productivity for their respective communities. It is apparent from the narratives and oracles in Numbers 22–24 that Balaam is a very talented individual whose divinatory craft has a wide-spread reputation and respect. From the rewards promised to him for his work it is evident that he is capable of conjuring up impressive positive results for people. As a functioning diviner, he knows and understands how to harness certain forces in the cosmos to affect the physical world, bringing either a curse or a blessing into reality. He does so through technical means, rituals and formulaic words. But he also understands that he is dependent on supernatural forces for divine insights or whatever gods he invokes for direction and action.

These three chapters make clear that Balaam is unable to curse the people of God. Balaam discovers that the God of the Israelites cannot be manipulated in the same way as the other forces he entreats. Moreover, he discovers that intended curses may fall back on those who desire to curse Israel. Balaam learns that he is sovereignly constrained to say only what God permits (cf. Num. 22.23; 23.12, 26; 24.13). The Abrahamic promises of blessing cannot be reversed through his typical divinatory practices and curses. Indeed, the curse would 'backfire' on those who curse Israel (Gen. 12.3). However, the narratives do not give Israel an unconditional state of blessing. In fact, they also remind the nation that spiritual, prophetic insight is crucial. Like Balaam's donkey they must have their eyes opened to the spiritual realm before them. The nation is dependent on the prophetic word of Yahweh to provide the way, the life, and the route to the land of promise. They are not to be reckless nor desirous of the path back to Egypt. Rather, they must trust Yahweh to lead them forward to the land of blessing, flowing with milk and honey. It is God's intention to bless Israel as he promises on oath, but they also must trust him and Moses to shepherd them to their destination.

Although Moses is not mentioned in the Balaam section, the theme of cursing and blessing will remind the reader of Moses' covenantal warnings. Customary for international treaties is a listing of blessings and curses that will come upon the participants for their obedience or disobedience to covenantal expectations (Deuteronomy 28). In the end, it will be the covenantal curses for disobedience that cause Israel's sufferings and not the manipulations of Balaam!

The Balaam section overwhelmingly reveals the sovereignty of Yahweh in every chapter. Yahweh is in control and directs the ways and words of the diviner who eventually experiences real prophetic inspiration. Yahweh tells the functionary when to go and what to say. Yahweh punishes the diviner for his erroneous craft and greedy motivations. He even sends his angel to confront Balaam and allows a donkey to speak sense to the functionary. Through all of these divinely orchestrated activities, Yahweh brings notable transformation in Balaam. He realizes early on in his quest that he will be impotent in changing Yahweh's blessing over Israel into the curse desired by Balak, Moab, and the Midianites. God even uses this wayward diviner and allows him to experience the Spirit of God who reveals impressive oracles. However, this does not mean that Balaam changes his evil ways and becomes a Yahwist. Numerous scriptures show that he proceeds in his evil motivations and finds another way to bring destructive teachings to the Israelites. For this he dies by the sword, but his legacy is inscribed in the scriptures as a warning to others not to follow in the ways of Balaam.

Balaam's experience reveals a comparison of divination with true prophetic functions. Whereas Moses will intercede for God's blessing and action in the nation, the diviner performs rituals. Whereas the blessings of Yahweh are spoken over the Israelites by the priest, the diviner uses altars and sacrifices to manipulate curses or blessings. Numbers 22–24 form a significant comparison with how true priests and prophets should function in bringing about the blessings of God. Aaron will administer the divine benediction and blessing as the High Priest. Moses will characteristically follow the instructions of Yahweh in every dimension, showing what true prophetic leadership is all about. He will fall prostrate, intercede, wait for the Lord at the Tent of Meeting, hear and heed the divine instructions, and speak the words of the Lord with authority.

Consequently, the Balaam accounts and oracles become one of the greatest affirmations in the Torah of God's intention to bless Israel. The episodes are placed before the second generational census to provide a foundation of confidence in the nation's final stretch to the land. The narratives offer similar encouragement for God's people in every generation, as they embark on new ventures of faith in partnership with the Lord.

Response

The human conundrum encountered in the narratives continues to have relevance for all people. How do individuals and nations achieve and experience blessing on earth? How is it that a diviner can also hear from Yahweh and speak oracles for him? How could Balaam use ritual sacrifices in his craft and still receive vision and utterance for both Balak and Israel? Although these ancient near eastern concepts are very common, they may seem like foreign, superstitious, or fictional ideas in contemporary settings. However, there are many societies and cultures in the world that have similar functionaries earning a living from divinatory practices. In fact, there are very powerful, wealthy, and reputable functionaries of this sort at work in greater dimensions than before in many parts of the world. The Balaam episodes serve as a warning of the counterfeit yet powerful reality of dabbling in the manipulation of unseen forces in the cosmos. They also provide elementary insights into the problem of discerning true and false prophets and prophecy.

The fact that these chapters form a vital part of Numbers indicates the importance of the content both theologically and spiritually. The warnings implicit in the Balaam narratives and in Deuteronomy 15 and 18 are still to be heeded today. The scriptures affirm the necessity of hearing the word of Yahweh and submitting to the divine will for his blessing. In the OT it is often the 'blessing' of God that brings about the positive effects of fertility, long life, prosperity, and security. From the creation narrative onward, it is evident that the ability of humankind to fulfil the commands of God depends on his blessing. For Adam and Eve to accomplish the divine mandates, they have to be under God's blessing. The commands: 'Be fruitful and increase in number; fill the earth and subdue it. Rule over the fish of the sea and the birds of the air and over every living creature that moves on the ground' (Gen. 1.28, 22; 5.2; 9.1), are impossible to discharge were it not for God's blessing. God enables humankind to fulfil the divinely imposed obligations through his conferral of blessing.

God is the source of both the blessing and the inspirational work of the Spirit (Num. 11.25–26; 24.2–4). Thus, the gift of fertility is given by God, who opens barren wombs (Gen. 17.16, 20; 22.17; 25.11; 28.3) and causes the massive population growth for Israel. God's blessing brings vitality, health, prosperity, and abundance to the people of God (Deut. 1.11; 7.13–15; 28.1–14). The blessing is tangible, indicating God's favour, which witnesses may observe (Isa. 51.2; 61.9), and know that the Lord is sovereign.

The lessons provided from the Balaam section are very clear. The blessing of nations and people is a divine prerogative. No rituals, formulaic curses, manipulative procedures can affect the purposes of the Lord. However, God is also faithful to warn Israel and to implement all of the covenant curses for persistent disobedience (Deut. 28.15–68). Blessings cannot be earned or secured by sacrificial means, positive speech, nor by visionary procurement. The scriptures provide ample instruction on how blessings are bestowed (Deut. 28.1–14; Psalm 1) and realized. 'But remember the Lord your God, for it is he who gives you the ability to produce wealth, and so confirms his covenant, which he swore to your ancestors, as it is today' (Deut. 8.18).

25.1–18—Israel's Religious Failure

The interpolation of Balaam's oracles is a masterful inclusion of essential content which explains certain backgrounds to Israel's historical experiences before the conquest period. The enigmatic and mysterious Balaam turns out to be a vessel of prophetic prediction, and in the course of his adventure from Pethor to Moab he learns much about Elohim and Yahweh. In the transformation of his personal advancement, Balaam ends up speaking dynamic words of revelation. Although Moses and Israel are passive campers in Numbers 22–24, the focus on Israel's destiny is an intense fixation for Balak and Balaam. When their manipulations are done, Israel continues to stand poised to reap the blessings which the Lord has prepared for them. However, the events that follow the Balaam section pose another serious conflict for the nation. With the clear revelatory action of Yahweh through Balaam's prophecy about the amazing destiny of Israel, and the divine affirmations to bless Israel, the last expectation is another reversion into rebellion and idolatrous practice. But this is what happens. Once again, key leaders become involved with tragic behaviours that bring drastic measures of punishment, death and plague.

Numbers 25 has a number of issues that have led to speculative views regarding three source traditions which are deemed to have been merged. One aspect of this has to do with the opening reference to Moabite women which then transitions to a focus on a Midianite woman in verse 6. Another assertion is that the placement of this narrative would be better with Numbers 31 where more analogous thematic development takes place. Additionally, commentators support various views with the intertextuality of the 'Baal of Peor' events that have similar elements of content but with different details (cf. Exod. 32.26–29; Num. 23.28; 31.16; Josh. 22.17; Deut. 4.3; Ps. 103.28; Hos. 9.10). While there may be good reasons for these assertions, the text as it stands provides insights into an important historical development in Israel's integration with the people groups of Canaan and their religious practices.[105] Moreover, the supportive traditions verify the importance of the events and details in the narrative record.

25.1–3—Another Apostacy

Israel is camping for some time in the area of Shittim (meaning acacia but an area with palm trees and resources), where they have a period with leisure time to interact with the locals. During this time of repose, the Israelite men began to fornicate with the Moabite women. The actual word for 'whoring' (זנה) is used in a form which implies that the Moabite women are actively enticing the Hebrew men.[106] This would align with the tradition that Balaam is influential in advising the women's behaviour: 'They were the ones who followed Balaam's advice and enticed the Israelites to be unfaithful to the LORD in the Peor incident, so that a plague struck the LORD's people' (Num. 31.15–16). The tradition indicates that Balaam's failure in securing curses on Israel does not stop him

---

105 The Ras Shamrah texts refer to Baal about 240 times in the solitary or compound form in reference to a god who is offered sacrifices and is generally known as the storm-god of the ancient Near East. Symbolized by the bull, Baal represents the fertility-god of Ugaritic religion. Baalism is worshipped in numerous locations by diverse people who have localized expressions of worship, thus the compound names which emphasize that Baal is the LORD of a local area. Thus, the Baal of Peor claims to be the god of the Moabite mountains (Num. 25.3; 32.38). The Baal cult at Ugarit includes four cultic festivals with a variety of sacrifices, rituals, and elaborate beliefs. Cf. J.C. de Moor, 'בעל', TDOT, II, pp. 182–192.

106 The verb is often used in contexts where the Baal cult is referenced and probably refers to sacral prostitution (cf. Judg. 8.33; Hos. 1.2). His association with fertility and weather features Baal as one who provides things that are necessary for life. Cf. M.J. Mulder, 'בעל', TDOT, II, p. 198.

from seeking the nation's downfall. Rather, he applies another tactic rooted in Israel's religious devotion to Yahweh and the moral conditions imposed on them. The implication of the actions taken by some of the Israelite men are that they inter-marry with the Moabites or take them as concubines.[107] Even more so, they participate with certain rituals of worship in the Baal of Peor cult.

Specifically, the Moabite women actively pursue Israelite men to participate in activities which blend sexual immorality with the religious cultic practices of Baalism.[108] A sacrificial meal is taken in honour of Baal and through participation in these rites, the Israelites 'worship' (וישתחוו), and actually 'prostrate' themselves before the 'god'. The attraction may be sexual but also involves a belief system. The pervasive beliefs of Baalism claim that Baal is the owner of the land and has exclusive power on its productivity. Sexual immorality includes rituals of sacrifice to Baal with sacrificial meals and prostration. For many Israelites, the temptation to Baalism and its claims are so strong that they submit to and 'yoke' (צמד) themselves to the 'Baal of Peor' (בעל פעור). The rites practiced by the people in this location of Peor are most likely similar to local expressions of Baalism in general. Intermarriage is a further consequence which makes allegiance to Yahweh and his religious requirements an impossibility. Apparently, the covenant with Yahweh and its requirements are more demanding than the rituals and practices of Baalism.

25.4–9—*The Judgment*

The context of this narrative indicates that the Baal of Peor apostasy exhibits certain parallels with the golden calf episode of Exodus 32. In a similar ritual of worshipping the golden calf, symbolic of Baal, the people fall into appalling behaviour and idolatry. In addition to divine punishment and violence meted out by the Levites, the Lord declares a promise of judgment: 'Now go, lead the people to the place I spoke of, and my angel will go before you. However, when the time comes for me to punish, I will punish them for their sin' (Exod. 32.34). There is an immediate judgment by plague, but the wrath of God will be kindled again in due course. This episode in chapter 25 appears to be the time for the prophetic punishment to be exacted: 'And the LORD's anger burned against

---

107 Levine, *Numbers 21–36*, p. 283.
108 As a divine name, Baal occurs 76 times in the OT and often with a local manifestation through the geographical location as in the Baal of Peor in Moab. The cult at Peor 'was characterized by sacral prostitution and by eating a sacrificial meal, by means of which an intimate relationship was established between the god and his worshippers'. Cf. Mulder, 'בעל', pp. 192–200.

them' (Num. 25.3). The consequences of Israel's persistent attraction and conversion to Baalism with its repulsive rituals of sympathetic magic, fertility, and immorality, are finally realized.

As 'prophesied' in Exodus 32, the punishment for another incident of idolatry is swift and drastic. Moses is instructed to execute (literally impale) the leaders and to expose their corpses before the Lord. The sentence of 'impaling' (יקע) suggests a slow state of exposure. This implies that the judgment is to be an expiation for the apostasy to turn away the wrath of the Lord. However, Moses delegates the execution of the leaders to the 'judges' (שפט) who are military personnel but mainly serve in judicial capacities to sort out the issues that arise between community members (cf. Exod. 18.21). The diminishing and delegating of Yahweh's instructions in this instance portrays Moses as limiting the death sentence to those who are guilty of the crime: 'Each of you must put to death those of your people who have yoked themselves to the Baal of Peor'. In this way Moses appears to act in a moderating capacity, but in an unusually different approach from his characteristic intercessory requests (cf. Num. 11.2; 12.13; 14.13–19; 16.22; 17.11; 21.7). He determines that only those who actively engage in the worship of Baal of Peor (a local land reference where Balaam also chooses to view Israel from the heights) are to be killed.

There is no report that the death sentences are actually carried out. Rather, the implication is that Phinehas (first mentioned in Exod. 6.25) intervenes in a flagrant public display of apostasy. One of the Israelite leaders of a Simeonite family, named Zimri son of Salu, engages with a Midianite woman, named Kozbi daughter of Zur, a tribal chief of a Midianite family. This example is an indicator of a growing trend in Israel where leaders begin to adopt the rituals associated with Baalism. It is not an isolated case of apostasy but an act of open rebellion since the leader brings the Midianite woman into the camp before Moses and all Israel where the community is weeping at the entrance to the Tent of Meeting. The gathering of the community at the Tent may indicate that the people are mourning the death of many by the plague. It may also suggest that not all are on the pathway to Baalism, and many are weeping for those who are going astray.

At this juncture, Phinehas quickly takes matters into his own hands. A number of implications must be conjectured at this point. The first is that Zimri is bringing Kozbi to his relatives in order to introduce his marital intentions. The tent that the couple enter is a *kubbah* (קבה), implying a 'marriage canopy' for the consummation of marriage. This tent is in apposition to the Tent of Meeting where Yahweh reveals himself. Incensed by the wanton act of apostasy in taking a foreign wife and aligning Israel with the Baal cult, Phinehas impales the two with a spear. The second implication is that a plague breaks out among the Israelites which causes them to gather with Moses at the Tent of Meeting. Before the action of Phinehas is taken, 24,000 Israelites die of the plague.[109]

Therefore, the narrative presents an unusual conflict. Yahweh's directive is apparently not heeded by Moses, so the Lord causes a plague to afflict many people. Probably the majority of those who die are the older members of the generation who are not permitted to enter the promised land (cf. Num. 26.64–65). In addition, Phinehas, full of 'passion' (קנא) as a Levitical guard of the sanctuary and all it represents, takes the initiative to mete out justice as a warning to Israel. For his zealous ardour for the affairs of God, he will be rewarded.

Interestingly, Moses marries Zipporah who is a Midianite (Exod. 2.21). However, her father Jethro is a priest of Midian who actually calls upon the name of Yahweh (Exod. 18.12) and is a positive influence for Moses. This may also explain Moses' reluctance to act harshly. The importance of this note is that many of the people groups in the region hold a variety of religious allegiances and although the Midianites become enemies of Israel, there are several semi-nomadic tribes that coexist together (cf. Gen. 25.2; Num. 31.8). Nevertheless, the implications and consequences of the Peor incident has lasting ramifications for Israel as Milgrom notes: 'Precisely because this was the first such Israelite encounter with the culture of Canaan and because the devastating plague was attributed to divine wrath, Baal-Peor came to be etched in the collective memory as a nadir in Israel's history (Deut. 4.3; Hos. 9.10; Ps. 106.28)'.[110]

25.10–18—A Covenant of Peace for Phinehas

With this turn of events, the Lord instructs Moses to communicate a significant reward for Phinehas. The grandson of Aaron who serves as the chief of the Levitical guards would now receive a 'covenant of peace' (ברית שלום).[111]

---

109   This devastating incident is another reminder of the divine judgment announced after Israel's failure to enter the promised land when afforded the opportunity.

As surely as I live, declares the LORD, I will do to you the very thing I heard you say: In this wilderness your bodies will fall—every one of you twenty years old or more who was counted in the census and who has grumbled against me. Not one of you will enter the land I swore with uplifted hand to make your home, except Caleb son of Jephunneh and Joshua son of Nun. As for your children that you said would be taken as plunder, I will bring them in to enjoy the land you have rejected. But as for you, your bodies will fall in this wilderness. Your children will be shepherds here for forty years, suffering for your unfaithfulness, until the last of your bodies lies in the wilderness. (Num. 14.28–33)

110   Milgrom, *Numbers*, p. 480; cf. pp. 476–480. Cf. F.M. Cross, *Canaanite Myth and Hebrew Epic* (Cambridge: Harvard University, 1973).

111   The noun 'shalom' (שלום) appears 237 times in the OT but mainly in the prophetic books with the concept of wholeness brought about by Yahweh. Cf. Stendebach, 'שלום', p. 28.

Furthermore, the implications of this covenant are not only 'peace', but it has 'everlasting' validity (cf. the 'covenant of salt' in Num. 18.19).[112] Due to the nation's propensity in breaking the covenantal obligations, the affirmation of the covenant to Phinehas is an important element here to validate the Lord's ongoing commitments for the next phase in the nation's history. It also signifies the necessity of bringing the leadership conflicts for the priesthood to an end. Although the term '*shalom*' is only referenced two times in Numbers, it points to the far-reaching elements of the Lord's blessings for the nation. In this context, the 'covenant of peace' is a reminder of the priest's role in pronouncing the divine blessing over the nation, and the desire for Yahweh to bring blessing and peace into reality (Num. 6.23–27; cf. Lev. 26.6–7).

Since Phinehas exemplifies the spirit of the Levitical guard to protect the sanctity of the Tent of Meeting, his action is acknowledged. Moreover, his 'zeal' (קנא) for upholding Yahwism and protecting encroachment from Baalism shows his perception for the inner requirement of the priesthood—passion for God and passion to bring blessing on the Israelite community (Num. 6.23–27). In fact, Phinehas's action turns Yahweh's wrath away from the people—his 'passion' for Yahweh, matches God's 'passion' (קנא) for the people. His act brings about expiation for Israel's sin: 'He and his descendants will have a covenant of a lasting priesthood, because he was zealous for the honour of his God and made atonement for the Israelites'. The reward is wide-ranging, and the descendants of Phinehas will serve in a dynastic priesthood.[113]

Finally, the summation addresses the reality of Israel's growing list of enemies. The killing of the Midianite leader's daughter would surely bring retribution. Moses is instructed to lead offensively to treat the Midianites as enemies and to kill them. Why? 'They treated you as enemies when they deceived you in the Peor incident involving their sister Kozbi, the daughter of a Midianite leader, the woman who was killed when the plague came as a result of that incident'. This may seem like an unusual way to end a major section in the book of Numbers! However, this episode sets the tone for a fresh response to Yahweh. Chapter 26 begins the final 10 chapters that make up the third major part where

---

112 Cf. Weinfeld, 'ברית', pp. 256–257. The covenant is a commitment confirmed by an oath which has binding validity for the partner (cf. Gen. 26.28; Exod. 19.8; Deut. 29.9 ff.) The term 'covenant' (ברית) appears 79 times in the Pentateuch, predominately in Genesis (26 times) and Deuteronomy (26 times; cf. Num. 10.33; 14.44; 18.19; 25.12–13). Although the covenant between Yahweh and Israel is an amazing treaty, the stipulations for obedience and loyalty were essential to avoid the curses that are promised for covenantal infidelity (Deut. 28.15–68).

113 Budd, *Numbers*, p. 280, notes the meaning is 'security of tenure' as translated in the NEB.

the new generation is poised for entry into the promised land. The incident at Baal Peor appears to validate the response of Yahweh to bring to fulfilment the decree that those who sinned at the Desert of Paran—an entry point to the land—would die in the wilderness. The key markers are the first census, the forty years of suffering and death in the wilderness, as well as the second census of those who will enter the land of promise.

Reflection and Response
Numbers 11–25: Severe Warnings before the Second Census
Reflection

The main theme in the second section of Numbers 11 to 25, presents examples of conflicts and challenges for Israel. However, they also illustrate problems that may commonly arise for leaders in contemporary ministry. The divine plan and vision are outlined and the conditions for achieving the goal are clear. However, the realization of the promises, require trust, faith, and compliance with the Lord's instructions. Promises are delayed and sometimes deferred. People get impatient and even unruly. Others believe they can lead better and may grasp ambitiously for power. Although the promised land is a gift, the timing for entry depends on the Lord. The Patriarchs faced similar tests as Abraham believed in the Lord but did not own the land. Jacob sought to enter the land but had to wrestle and submit before his ordeal was over and permission to proceed was granted (Gen. 32.22–32). Israel is tested in the wilderness to solidify a future in the promised land where rest in the presence of God becomes a reality.

Numbers 25 may be a harsh ending to this section but a necessary warning for a new generation. The only way forward to the promised land is through strict adherence to Yahweh's covenant and clear devotion to the Lord's ways. The events of the chapter bring to a climax the different conflicts that intensified to this point. All these narratives point out the crucial failures that could eventually lead to the curse that Balaam was unable to bring upon Israel.

Numbers 11 presented the nation's failure to trust God for provision. Combined with Numbers 12 the narratives present Israel's failure to trust the Lord for his leadership through Moses. The episode of the spies vividly portrays the failure to trust in Yahweh's protection and ability to gift the nation with a land and inheritance. Their fear and refusal to enter the land brought about the epic delay in the realization of rest within the covenantal borders. Consequences of the nation's rebellion and persistent failure caused the widespread grumbling and impatience which led to more intense rebellion with many leaders in Numbers 16–21. Such were the internal conflicts that afflicted the nation and their advancement to better days. Additionally, the Balaam narrative section reveals the external challenges to Israel's well-being through the cursing rituals of Balak and the diviner. These examples pose a steep mountain of challenge to overcome for the nation. As if that were not enough, the sin of many who attached themselves to the Baal of Peor, could have relegated the people to even more hardship and setbacks. It appears that apostasy and idolatry is a constant threat for the covenantal people.

The Numbers 25 episode highlights the absolute necessity for Israel's passionate commitment to Yahweh as Lord of the land, giver of life and blessing. The narrative emphasizes that the Baal of Peor can only bring death, not fertility nor life. The placement of the episode highlights the requirements of the Israelites to solidify their commitment to the Lord for a successful pilgrimage into the land of promise.

As sojourners in the land, Israel becomes acquainted with the religious beliefs of Baalism. Considered a local deity and the 'landowner', it is speculated that Baal as 'lord' controls the rain and therefore, the fructification of agricultural resources which are necessary for all life to flourish. Rituals associated with keeping Baal happy and beneficent include fertility rites. Ideas of sympathetic magic and intercourse are conceived to remind the deity to irrigate the land so that produce would grow. Thus, the appeal to Baalism is an enticement to some Israelites, including a few leaders. By engaging in sacrificial feasts followed by sexual acts and some intermarriage, they traded the blessings of Yahweh for the imaginary blessings of Baal. These activities would not be tolerated by Yahweh in Canaan.

Response

How can we apply the lessons of Numbers 11–25 in our contemporary contexts? In the historic reflection in Psalm 106, the details of the apostasy at Peor are affirmed as a warning to future generations:

> Then they despised the pleasant land;
>   they did not believe his promise.
> They grumbled in their tents
>   and did not obey the LORD.
> So he swore to them with uplifted hand
>   that he would make them fall in the wilderness,
> make their descendants fall among the nations
>   and scatter them throughout the lands.
> They yoked themselves to the Baal of Peor
>   and ate sacrifices offered to lifeless gods;
> they aroused the LORD's anger by their wicked deeds,
>   and a plague broke out among them.

> But Phinehas stood up and intervened,
>> and the plague was checked.
> This was credited to him as righteousness
>> for endless generations to come.
> By the waters of Meribah they angered the LORD,
>> and trouble came to Moses because of them;
> for they rebelled against the Spirit of God,
>> and rash words came from Moses' lips.
> They did not destroy the peoples
>> as the LORD had commanded them,
> but they mingled with the nations
>> and adopted their customs.
> They worshiped their idols,
>> which became a snare to them.
> They sacrificed their sons
>> and their daughters to false gods.
> They shed innocent blood,
>> the blood of their sons and daughters,
> whom they sacrificed to the idols of Canaan,
>> and the land was desecrated by their blood.
> They defiled themselves by what they did;
>> by their deeds they prostituted themselves. (Ps. 106.24–39)

The narratives and the Psalmist call for daily appreciation of the Lord's provisions and blessings. They affirm the benefits of covenantal obedience and passion for the kingdom of God and his ways. Compliance with the Spirit of God and his guidance brings great reward and successful leadership results for the people of God.

PART 2

*The Second Generation Anticipates
Entry into the Land of Promise
(Numbers 26–36)*

∴

26.1–32.42—From Moab to Canaan: Preparing to Receive Their 'Inheritance'

The third major section of Numbers re-focuses the nation on matters pertaining to a new horizon where entry into the promised land by a new generation of Israelites is imminent. While the death of a generation in the wilderness is an ominous reminder for the nation of a very difficult and unforgettable season in Israel's history, the second census provides a positive way forward. The census provides a renewed vision for the nation, of a land that is dreamed of but never realized until the brink of a new day. These eleven chapters include a variety of materials which are focalized on the preparations required for land acquisition. Leadership matters and transitions, certain legal provisions for women, tribal land allocations, cultic requirements with Levitical provisions plus a summation of the overall wilderness itinerary are recorded.

With the positive view forward, the realization of a bleak four decades of death in the wilderness verifies the resolve of Yahweh to not permit a rebellious, cantankerous generation of people into a new place where a solid foundation must be built for worship and life. Deaths from plagues and judgments will subside and new life will begin. Former slaves will experience a new freedom and life. The census listing identifies leaders and the strong young men over twenty who will be involved in land acquisition and land allocation. Another feature of the census is the historical reach back to the sons of Jacob and their wives who become the main clan members in Israel. The detailed list from Genesis is partially reiterated again in Exod. 6.14–28 which presents the family representatives who are to leave Egypt for the promised land. In Exodus 6 the focus is on the Levites, including the notice that Levi and Amran live 137 years and Kohath 133. Genesis 26 appears to be used for Numbers 26 but includes some divergences in a few name references. The following record sets the context for a comparison with the Numbers census list.

> Then Jacob left Beersheba, and Israel's sons took their father Jacob and their children and their wives in the carts that Pharaoh had sent to transport him. So Jacob and all his offspring went to Egypt, taking with them their livestock and the possessions they had acquired in Canaan. Jacob brought with him to Egypt his sons and grandsons and his daughters and granddaughters—all his offspring. These are the names of the sons of Israel (Jacob and his descendants) who went to Egypt: Reuben the first-

born of Jacob. The sons of Reuben: Hanok, Pallu, Hezron and Karmi. The sons of Simeon: Jemuel, Jamin, Ohad, Jakin, Zohar and Shaul the son of a Canaanite woman. The sons of Levi: Gershon, Kohath and Merari. The sons of Judah: Er, Onan, Shelah, Perez and Zerah (but Er and Onan had died in the land of Canaan). The sons of Perez: Hezron and Hamul. The sons of Issachar: Tola, Puah, Jashub and Shimron. The sons of Zebulun: Sered, Elon and Jahleel. These were the sons Leah bore to Jacob in Paddan Aram, besides his daughter Dinah. These sons and daughters of his were thirty-three in all. The sons of Gad: Zephon, Haggi, Shuni, Ezbon, Eri, Arodi and Areli. The sons of Asher: Imnah, Ishvah, Ishvi and Beriah. Their sister was Serah. The sons of Beriah: Heber and Malkiel. These were the children born to Jacob by Zilpah, whom Laban had given to his daughter Leah—sixteen in all. The sons of Jacob's wife Rachel: Joseph and Benjamin. In Egypt, Manasseh and Ephraim were born to Joseph by Asenath daughter of Potiphera, priest of On. The sons of Benjamin: Bela, Beker, Ashbel, Gera, Naaman, Ehi, Rosh, Muppim, Huppim and Ard. These were the sons of Rachel who were born to Jacob—fourteen in all. The son of Dan: Hushim. The sons of Naphtali: Jahziel, Guni, Jezer and Shillem. These were the sons born to Jacob by Bilhah, whom Laban had given to his daughter Rachel—seven in all. All those who went to Egypt with Jacob—those who were his direct descendants, not counting his sons' wives—numbered sixty-six persons. With the two sons who had been born to Joseph in Egypt, the members of Jacob's family, which went to Egypt, were seventy in all. (Gen. 26.5–27)

These are the foundational members that will flourish in Egypt and become the group of Hebrews that eventually leave for the promised land.

26.1–65—Second Generation Census

26.1–51—*The Census*

After the plague, the Lord instructs Moses and Eleazar to conduct another census beginning with the men over twenty years of age who are fit for military conscription. This instruction is carried out in the plains of Moab by the Jordan across from Jericho. When completed, the census undertaking tabulates an impressive force of 601,730 men.

The following table presents the tribe members and clans which derive from the sons of Jacob through the blessings of Yahweh for the military services that are required for the conquest of the land. A few differences in the census num-

26.1–32.42—FROM MOAB TO CANAAN

TABLE 8   The Israelites by clan representatives who depart from Egypt

Tribe	Clans	1st Census	2nd Census	Difference
Reuben, Israel's firstborn son	Hanokite; Palluite; Hezronite; Karmite	46,500	43,730	Less 2,770
Simeon	Nemuelite; Jaminite; Jakinite; Zerahite; Shaulite	59,300	22,200	Less 37,100
Gad	Zephonite; Haggite; Shunite; Oznite; Erite; Arodite; Arelite	45,650	40,500	Less 5,150
Judah	Shelanite; Perezite; Zerahite; Sons of Perez including Hezronite & Hamulite	74,600	76,500	Plus 1,900
Issachar	Tolaite; Puite; Jashubite; Shimronite	54,400	64,300	Plus 9,900
Zebulun	Seredite; Elonite; Jahleelite	57,400	60,500	Plus 3,100
Manasseh, of Joseph	Makirite [Makir is father of Gilead]; Gileadite [6 clans]	32,200	52,700	Plus 20,500
Ephraim, of Joseph	Shuthelahite; Bekerite; Tahanite; Eranite	40,500	32,500	Less 8,000
Benjamin	Belaite; Ashbelite; Ahiramite; Shuphamite; Huphamite; Ardite; Naamanite	35,400	45,600	Plus 10,200
Dan	Shuhamite	62,700	64,400	Plus 1,700
Asher	Imnite; Ishvite; Beriite; Beriah;	41,500	53,400	Plus 11,900
Naphtali	Jahzeelite; Gunite; Jezerite; Shillemite	53,400	45,400	Less 8,000
TOTALS		603,550	601,730	Less 1820

bers are evident and several explanatory notes are made in the census lists which will be commented on below.

The explanatory comments added into the census list are important historical notices that will have significance for the future land allocations which are made by Joshua. The first comment under Reuben identifies the son of Pallu, father to Eliab whose sons are Nemuel, Dathan, and Abiram. This comment serves to remind the community of the rebellious actions of Dathan and Abiram who revolted against Moses, Aaron and the Lord. In the judgment which killed the perpetrators in the sinkhole, along with 250 others by fire, the incident is a memorable warning to restrain similar insubordination. However, the episode does not kill all the progeny in Korah's lineage. The Korahite remnant continue to not only exist, but they become influential servants in Israel's cultic ministry (Num. 26.8–11; cf. Psalms 42; 44–49; 84–85; 87).

Another note concerns two sons of Judah named Er and Onan, who die in Canaan. They are included in the Genesis 26 listing and their demise is noted in both census lists (Num. 26.19). Also notable is that verses 28 to 34 provide more detail than the other clan notices and deserve special mention. In Genesis 26.20 it is recorded that when Joseph lives in Egypt, he fathers Manasseh and Ephraim with Asenath daughter of Potiphera, priest of On. Manasseh now takes seventh place among the clans:

> The descendants of Manasseh: through Makir, the Makirite clan (Makir was the father of Gilead); through Gilead, the Gileadite clan. These were the descendants of Gilead: through Iezer, the Iezerite clan; through Helek, the Helekite clan; through Asriel, the Asrielite clan; through Shechem, the Shechemite clan; through Shemida, the Shemidaite clan; through Hepher, the Hepherite clan. (Zelophehad son of Hepher had no sons; he had only daughters, whose names were Mahlah, Noah, Hoglah, Milkah, and Tirzah.). These were the clans of Manasseh; those numbered were 52,700. (Num. 26.29–34)[1]

Several generations are presented here. Milgrom references the Samaria ostraca records which mention respective districts near Samaria that include the names Abiezer, Asriel, Helek, Shechem, and Shmida which align with some of the clan names. The implication is that the Samaria ostraca and the Manasseh clan names, indicate the assimilation of Canaanite clans into the nation. 'The fact that five of Manasseh's six clans and two of Zelophehad's daughters are names of erstwhile Canaanite districts, coupled with the fact that Tirzah, another daughter, as well as Shechem are erstwhile Canaanite city-states, points to a sizeable Canaanite element in Manasseh's population'.[2] Special mention of Zelophehad's five daughters also introduces an important

---

[1] The biggest changes in census numbers are for Simeon and Manasseh. Milgrom, *Numbers*, p. 220, observes that,
> The major changes are the precipitous decline in Simeon and the sizable increase in Manasseh, perhaps reflecting the historical situation of the settlements: Simeon was soon absorbed by Judah (cf. Judg. 1.3; Josh. 19.1), whereas Manasseh expanded beyond its settled territory (Josh. 17.11, 16) and dominated political events during the judgeships of two of its sons, Gideon and Abimelech. (Judges 6–9; cf. 12.1–6)

[2] Milgrom, *Numbers*, p. 224.

theme which is followed up with additional commentary due to the fact that only sons are typically allocated land inheritance. This proves to be a difficult family and cultural perspective that is addressed in Numbers 27. The matter is resolved with further detail and legal interpretation in ch. 36—the concluding narrative of Numbers! The inclusion of the females in the record is an important measure in what is commonly referred to as a patriarchal culture which typically neglects and subordinates the position of women. Furthermore, in Asher's clan list, his daughter Serah is also mentioned.

In tallying up the census numbers, the total number of the men of Israel is 601,730.

26.52–56—Land Allotments

After the census record is completed, the Lord gives further instructions to Moses concerning the second major purpose for the census undertaking. The focus is on the process of an equitable way of 'allocating' (חלק) or dividing parcels of land for each tribe when the nation enters Canaan. Also, some tribal allotments are made on the Transjordanian side as recorded later in Josh. 13.15–32. As the 'owner of the land', Yahweh provides property as an 'inheritance' for each clan and family.[3] The size and place will be determined in part from the census numbers and population of each group. Larger groups receive more in order to facilitate each clan's needs.

The actual process is further supplemented in chapter 34 where Moses is provided with the land boundaries of Canaan which will be 'inherited' (נחל). There, Moses commands the Israelites:

> Assign this land by lot as an inheritance. The LORD has ordered that it be given to the nine and a half tribes, because the families of the tribe of Reuben, the tribe of Gad and the half-tribe of Manasseh have received their inheritance. These two and a half tribes have received their inheritance east of the Jordan across from Jericho, toward the sunrise. (Num. 34.13–15)

Accordingly, the determination of the actual land parcels is to be discovered by 'lot' (גורל; cf. Num. 33.54; 34.13; 36.2–3). This procedure allows for some of the leaders to see the outcome, which is believed to be predetermined by God. Typically, the casting of lots includes prayer. It may be similar to the use of the

---

3 Land inheritances are highly valued in families and were to be kept for descendants. It is referred to five times in the chapter (Num. 26.53, 54 [2 times], 56, 62).

Urim and Thummim used by priests (Exod. 28.30; cf. 1 Sam. 10.20–21; Acts 1.23–26) but is considered to be an impartial way of apportioning the land. The Urim is referred to only once in Numbers in the sense of decision making for battle and land apportioning. 'He is to stand before Eleazar the priest, who will obtain decisions for him by inquiring of the Urim before the Lord. At his command he and the entire community of the Israelites will go out, and at his command they will come in' (Num. 27.21). As instructed, Joshua implements the use of the lot in the detailed land allocations (Joshua 14–19). In this way each clan receives their land from Yahweh and not from Moses or other leaders who could be accused of misappropriation of property.

26.57-62—*Census for the Levites*

Finally, the focus of attention returns to the Levites who are also counted and recorded according to their clan affiliation. The first census list from Numbers 3 tabulates the number of Levites at 22,000 with the spotlight on the main families of Gershon, Kohath and Merari.

Special mention is made of Gershon's son Libni and the Libnite clan. The reiteration of Moses' and Aaron's lineage is a reflection on the Levitical commitment of these two brothers who faithfully lead Israel to this point in their national development. Their parents are Amram (Kohath lineage) and Jochebed (Levi lineage) who give birth to Aaron, Moses and Miriam during their Egyptian residency. A further reminder explains the current positions of Eleazar and Ithamar who take the place of elder brothers Nadab and Abihu who are killed for offering unauthorized fire before the Lord (cf. Num. 3.1–4).[4] Not only does this comment affirm the Aaronides authority through Eleazar, but it reminds the Levites of the strict requirements of their sacred service. Of Kohath's sons, the Hebronite clan is recorded as well as the Korahite clan which stems from Izhar (Exod. 6.21). Of Merari, the Mahlite and Mushite clans are cited. This census record is added to further emphasize that the Levitical order continues to be ready, strong, and committed for the next phase in Israel's pilgrimage to the land of promise. Although their numbers are not large, the second census indicates some growth, with all the male Levites a month old or more numbering 23,000. Again, the distinction is made between the Levites and other Israelites because they receive no land inheritance as property (cf. Num. 35.1–8).

---

4 The notice of Nadab and Abihu's transgression is reiterated for emphasis and warning: 'But Nadab and Abihu died by the will of the LORD, when they offered alien fire before the LORD in the wilderness of Sinai; and they left no sons. So it was Eleazar and Ithamar who served as priests in the lifetime of their father Aaron' (Num. 3.4; JPS).

26.63–65—Summation

The final census summation verifies that a whole generation of people die in the wilderness. It is a significant marker in the form of an obituary notice which registers the fulfilment of Yahweh's decree that they would die in the wilderness for their rebellion and failure to move forward in faith. Moses and Eleazar the priest are responsible for the second census that occurs on the plains of Moab. The census verifies that none of the current generation are among those counted forty years prior by Moses and Aaron in the Desert of Sinai. However, the men of faith who have the vision for entering the land of promise thirty-eight years prior, namely Caleb son of Jephunneh and Joshua son of Nun, are still alive to lead the nation to their inheritance.

27.1–23—Land Issues and Leadership Transitions

27.1–11—Inheritance Regulations

In the second census the daughters of Zelophehad are introduced due to the fact that their father had no sons. He is the son of Hepher and belongs to the clans of Manasseh son of Joseph. There seems to be a certain amount of prestige attached to the sons of Joseph—perhaps in honour of what his role as vice-regent in Egypt confers on Israel. This man of character and wisdom is used of God to provide bread not only for Israel but for many nations during a severe famine (cf. Gen. 47.13–27). The daughter's names are Mahlah, Noah, Hoglah, Milkah, and Tirzah (Num. 27.1) and are repeated three times in Numbers (cf. 26.33; 36.11). As noted in the census comments the daughter's names are also the names of towns on the west side of the Jordan. These women are bold and bring their petition to Moses and other leaders in a clear and concise manner: 'Our father died in the wilderness. He was not among Korah's followers, who banded together against the LORD, but he died for his own sin and left no sons. Why should our father's name disappear from his clan because he had no son? Give us property among our father's relatives'. The presentation of the daughters reflects an impressive understanding of judicial process. The sons of Joseph grew up in the international context of Egypt and acquired a keen sense of cultural and diplomatic skill.

Here the daughters make a public appeal before Moses, Eleazar, leaders and the community at the Tent of Meeting. Their appeal has to do with the death of their father who has no sons. The girls make it clear that he was not involved in the Korah rebellion but died as a consequence of unbelief and Yahweh's judgment on the generation. The implication of his death and the laws of 'inheritance' (נחל) meant that the name of Zelophehad would be withdrawn from the family lineage since there was no male inheritor. Inheritance laws are essential to confer family property rights among heirs for the well-being of family relationships and tribal concerns.[5]

Their request is warranted but requires legislative insight from the Lord. The appeal to Moses for a 'possession among our father's brothers' is brought to Yahweh and receives the following, detailed verdict, and instructions: The women are accurate in their presentation of the matters and their perception of justice. Therefore, in cases where there is no male heir, the inheritance of land and belongings transfers to the daughter. If there is no daughter, then the inheritance transfers to the man's brother. In a case where there are no brothers, the property is given to the nearest relative. This resolution is then made a case law which becomes an ordinance and practice for the nation to apply. The daughters of Zelophehad receive an inheritance in order to maintain the family since their father had no male heir. However, this type of ruling is 'subject to the condition that they must marry within their father's tribe, in order to prevent the family estate from falling into the hands of a different clan' (cf. Num. 36.1–9).[6]

This episode is an example of how the laws that are revealed to Moses by Yahweh over time are applied as cases arise to bring order, justice, and equity to a young nation who are called to be a kingdom of priests for the nations. Cultural approaches to societal issues like inheritance rites have a variety of methods that are applied but Israel added a whole new way to address them. The whole process of Mosaic revelation with the instruction of Yahweh provides an unmatched system for equitable judgments. The Pentateuch's focus on land allocation features Yahweh as the landowner with the ultimate authority to distribute property for clans and family use—to work the land and produce what is needed (cf. Gen. 2.15). Furthermore, it is the Lord who apportions land for the nations and determines the times and extent of their habitation.

27.12–14—Moses' Final Days

This section provides an intimate insight into the nature of Yahweh's relationship with Moses. The Pentateuch records an epic narrative about the prophet's life and leadership and now reveals how Moses approaches the end of his days. As evident in Moses' birth story, call narrative and the wilderness episodes, Yahweh's presence is always near the prophet. His close relationship with the Lord

---

5   Inheritance is a primary focus in this text with six occurrences (Num. 27.7 (twice), 8, 9, 10, 11). Typically, the land is handed down to sons but here the daughters are given legal rights to inherit family property. The loss of land from the family and clan is so serious that marriages outside of the clan are restricted (cf. Num. 26.2–4). Cf. E. Lipiński, 'נחל', p. 326.

6   Lipiński, 'נחל', pp. 324–326.

during his latter forty years in leadership is an answer to Moses' plea for the divine presence to remain with the nation during their trek (cf. Exodus 33).

> Then Moses said to him, 'If your Presence does not go with us, do not send us up from here. How will anyone know that you are pleased with me and with your people unless you go with us? What else will distinguish me and your people from all the other people on the face of the earth?' And the LORD said to Moses, 'I will do the very thing you have asked, because I am pleased with you and I know you by name'. (Exod. 33.15-17)

As in his life, so also at his imminent demise, the Lord is near and informs Moses of his impending death (cf. Amos 3.7). With the metaphoric phrase, 'you too will be gathered to your people', Moses knows the end is drawing near. Although he is one hundred and twenty years of age when he dies, he is still instructed by Yahweh to climb a mountain in the Abarim range so that he can survey the land promised to the Israelites (cf. Deut. 34.7).[7] Whereas Abraham traversed and lived in the land by faith, Moses would only view the land from an elevated perch, by faith. However, the Lord allows Moses to have a marvellous panoramic view of the promised land from a mountain vista:

> Then Moses climbed Mount Nebo from the plains of Moab to the top of Pisgah, across from Jericho. There the LORD showed him the whole land—from Gilead to Dan, all of Naphtali, the territory of Ephraim and Manasseh, all the land of Judah as far as the Mediterranean Sea, the Negev and the whole region from the Valley of Jericho, the City of Palms, as far as Zoar. (Deut. 34.1-3)

Moses is reminded of the reason he will not enter the land—both he and Aaron exceeded the Lord's instructions in the Desert of Zin (at Meribah in Kadesh) where they did not honour explicit commands and so dishonoured the Holy One. They failed to honour or treat Yahweh with respect before the community. This incident is a serious infraction in his leadership career with consequences

---

7 Talmudic scholar L. Ginzberg provides intriguing insights into the last days of Moses' life and activities in preparation for his death. Although these legends embellish some of the biblical details, the narratives illustrate Moses' epic character, prayer life, and prophetic leadership. The stories are often told in synagogues and make for valuable reading. Additionally, the concern and care of Yahweh for his chosen prophet at the end of his life is nicely portrayed in the account where 'God Kisses Moses' Soul'. L. Ginzberg, *Legends of the Bible* (Old Saybrook, CT: Konecky & Konecky, 1956), pp. 500-502; Cf. pp. 488-499.

that come to a final determination. The punishment of not being permitted to enter the promised land is difficult for Moses to accept and Yahweh continually reminds Moses of this reality. He will not enter the promised land. He will die in the wilderness along with the generation of those who left Egypt (Num. 14.30; 20.12, 24; 26.65; 27.13; Deut. 1.35–37; 3.23–27; 31.1–3; 32.52; 34.4). The number of times Yahweh affirms he will not enter the land is impressive. Although Moses is able to intercede on behalf of Israel and achieve positive resolutions from the Lord, he is not able to plead his case in this regard, as his summation reveals:

> And I pleaded with the LORD at that time, saying, 'O Lord GOD, you have only begun to show your servant your greatness and your mighty hand. For what god is there in heaven or on earth who can do such works and mighty acts as yours? Please let me go over and see the good land beyond the Jordan, that good hill country and Lebanon'. But the LORD was angry with me because of you and would not listen to me. And the LORD said to me, 'Enough from you; do not speak to me of this matter again. Go up to the top of Pisgah and lift up your eyes westward and northward and southward and eastward, and look at it with your eyes, for you shall not go over this Jordan.' (Deut. 3.23–27)

In the parallel account of Moses' death, the Lord affirms that the promised land which is covenanted to the Patriarchs will soon be realized by the Israelites. As the faithful servant of the Lord who cares for the nation and witnesses the burial of a whole generation, he is buried by Yahweh in Moab, in the valley opposite Beth Peor. When he finally is laid to rest at the age of 120, the nation grieves for 30 days with weeping and mourning (cf. Deut. 34.4–8).[8]

---

8 With the variations in Moses' death reports, and perhaps a dearth of detail, the rabbis have written and refined several *midrashim* regarding the last days of his life. Some of them propose extensive arguing with God regarding his end with pleas for entry into the land of promise. Additionally, there are legends about God coming down to take the soul of Moses with angels who assist with the death preparations of linens and the bier.

> As the angel of death was afraid to take his soul, God Himself, accompanied by Gabriel, Michael, and Zagziel, the former teacher of Moses, descended to get it. Moses blessed the people, begged their forgiveness for any injuries he might have done them, and took leave of them with the assurance that he would see them again at the resurrection of the dead. Gabriel arranged the couch, Michael spread a silken cover over it, and Zagziel put a silken pillow under Moses' head. At God's command Moses crossed his hands over his breast and closed his eyes, and God took his soul away with a kiss. Then heaven and earth and the starry world began to weep for Moses. (Midr. Peṭirat Mosheh, *l.c.*; Yalḳ., Deut. 940; Deut. R. xi. 6; cf. 'Moses' death', in *The Jewish Encyclopedia*)

In both the Numbers and Deuteronomy accounts, the aged prophet is still able to climb a mountain in the Abarim range to survey the promised land from a peak on Mount Nebo. At the age of one hundred and twenty he has impressive vitality and eyesight (Deut. 34.7). When Moses indicates that he is no longer able to lead the nation (Deut. 31.2), he acknowledges that his leadership role is coming to an end as informed by the Lord (Num. 27.13). Although some commentators view this to mean that Moses is too frail to continue, the heroic summation of his life affirms that Yahweh provides the strength Moses needs for his prophetic leadership until the wilderness generation has finished its course. About the same time as Moses completes his forty-year epic leadership marathon![9] The reality of Moses' impending demise leads to the important subject of transition. Who is to lead the nation during the next phase of their journey?

27.15-17—*Moses' Leadership Succession Prayer*

In anticipation of his impending demise, Moses shows his true character by petitioning Yahweh for a successor: 'May the LORD, the God who gives breath to all living things, appoint someone over this community to go out and come in before them, one who will lead them out and bring them in, so the LORD's people will not be like sheep without a shepherd' (Num. 27.16–17). Moses' first inclination is to honour the Lord as the giver of life. Just as God breathes life into Adam, so he is the author of breath to all living creatures (cf. Num. 16.22; Gen. 2.7; 6.17). Within this context Moses is also recognizing the Lord as the one who will take his breath away. Moreover, he acknowledges that Israel requires stable leadership for the next phase of the journey and conquest of the promised land. The idiom used for 'going out' (יצא) and 'coming in' (בוא) refers to the military leadership role which the next leader will need to be proficient in. The metaphor of 'shepherd' (רעה) exemplifies the care and guidance which will also be required for the next phase of the nation's expedition. These primary elements will be attended to in Yahweh's instructions. Interestingly, the announced death of Moses does not occur in this episode but is left pending. Moses has more work to do before the end described in Deuteronomy 34.

---

9   Coats, G.W. 'Legendary Motifs in the Moses Death Reports', in D.L. Christensen, *A Song of Power and the Power of Song: Essays on the Book of Deuteronomy* (Winona Lake, IN: Eisenbrauns, 1993), pp. 181-194. Leadership transitions are extremely important and carefully dictated by the LORD as evident from the conflict narratives suggesting ambitious power grabs. This is apparent with transitions in the priesthood as well as with prophets (cf. Aaron to Eleazar; Eli to Samuel; Elijah to Elisha, etc.).

27.18–21—Joshua's Commissioning

The text provides the thematic thesis for a programmatic and paradigmatic leadership transfer. It begins by confirming the selection of Joshua and continues with instructions for the formal act of designation by Moses' hand. This is followed with the public commission and conferral of authority which verifies Joshua's tremendous responsibilities in Israel.

> So the LORD said to Moses, 'Take Joshua son of Nun, a man in whom is the spirit of leadership, and lay your hand on him. Have him stand before Eleazar the priest and the entire assembly and commission him in their presence. Give him some of your authority so the whole Israelite community will obey him. He is to stand before Eleazar the priest, who will obtain decisions for him by inquiring of the Urim before the LORD. At his command he and the entire community of the Israelites will go out, and at his command they will come in.'

The designated leader is Joshua son of Nun who exhibits spiritual devotion, military prowess, boldness and courage. The choice of Joshua is not surprising since he is Moses' aide and constant supporter. To lead the armies of Israel against the foes which terrified the ten spies will not be easy. Joshua prepares for this role in the battle against the Amalekites (Exod. 17.9–16). He attends to the needs of Moses and is present on many occasions when others are excluded (cf. Exod. 24.13–14). Whenever dangers or threats are evident, Joshua is present to raise an alarm (Exod. 32.17; Num. 11.28). Only he and Caleb stand against the ten spies who are afraid to move forward in faith, thereby earning the right to eventually enter the land that they scouted (Num. 14.6–9). The image of Joshua presented here indicates his tenacity in following Moses to learn as much as possible about leadership. However, the record of Moses as the exemplary leader and prophet par excellence puts any succession plan at risk. To come out of Moses' shadow to take the lead at a most dangerous period in the nation's history was a huge mountain to climb. Therefore, the narratives present Joshua in his own stature and competence. He is not called a prophet but is depicted as a competent charismatic leader with several prophet type competencies.[10] Additionally, Joshua's spirituality and love for the presence of

---

10 Cf. J. Blenkinsopp, *A History of Prophecy in Israel* (Philadelphia: Westminster Press, 1983), p. 51. Cf. Hildebrandt, *An Old Testament Theology of the Spirit of God*, pp. 108–109. Cf. Oeste who also shows how "The coda to Joshua's career (24.28–32) compares him with Moses in three respects: (1) Joshua's lifespan (110 years); 2) Burial in the land, and (3)

Yahweh is affirmed in his lingering at the Tent of Meeting—even after Moses went back to the camp (Exod. 33.11). Moreover, it is Joshua who is concerned about the prophetic activities of Eldad and Medad. When Joshua hears about the two elders who remain in the camp and are prophesying, he views it as a potential threat to Moses' leadership, and a potential impingement on his authority. Joshua faithfully sought to protect the best interests of Moses and the nation (Num. 11.24–30).

In addition to these formative experiences and practical responses of Joshua, Yahweh verifies that Joshua has 'the spirit of leadership' (NIV), or more accurately, 'a man in whom is the Spirit' (ESV).[11] It is not clear when this endowment of 'Spirit' is given to Joshua, but this designation generally signifies that he has leadership skills to implement the divine purposes that the Lord has for Israel.[12] An appropriate inference is that Joshua is included in the Numbers 11 event when the Spirit on Moses is shared with the 70 elders. The bestowal of the 'Spirit' (רוח) of leadership is something only Yahweh can provide. The account of Moses' 'Spirit' shared with the seventy elders reveals a fundamental requirement for leadership positions in Israel.[13] It is through the animating power

---

attribution of the title 'servant of Yahweh'". G. Oeste, 'The Shaping of a Prophet: Joshua in the Deuteronomistic History', in M.J. Boda & L.M. Wray Beal (eds.), *Prophets, Prophecy, and Ancient Israelite Historiography* (Winona Lake, IN: Eisenbrauns, 2013), pp. 23–41. Ginzberg's narrative account of Joshua's succession considers Joshua a prophet, reflecting Talmudic perspectives (*Legends of the Bible*, p. 488). Cf. Josh. 7.3 and 24.2, where Joshua uses the prophetic messenger formula 'thus says Yahweh'.

11 The Hebrew 'רוח' occurs 38 times in the Pentateuch and in certain contexts is translated as the 'Spirit' of God. Typically, רוח refers to wind, breath or the animating spirit of life in humankind. Numerous references to the 'Spirit' occur to indicate the LORD's animating power for leadership positions and prophecy. Cf. S. Tengström, 'רוח', *TDOT*, XIII, p. 372.

12 Levine surmises that the 'spirit' reference could be an abbreviation for the 'Spirit of Yahweh' with the same intent as in other charismatic transfer episodes, as in 'the potent spirit alighting upon or clothing a hero (Judg. 3.10; 11.29; 13.25)' (cf. Levine, *Numbers 21–36*, p. 350). However, the text does not include 'Yahweh', so the emphasis is on the skill and wisdom imparted (cf. Deut. 34.9) and needed for the role. Milgrom summarizes 4 potential interpretations and concludes that the 'spirit' referent probably refers to the endowed talent attested by his military success or the courage he so often exemplified (cf. Exod. 17.9–13; Num. 14.6–10; 26.65; Josh. 2.11; 5.1). Milgrom, *Numbers*, p. 235.

13 The Numbers 11 account is more dramatic, with the elders gathered around the Tent of Meeting. Yahweh appears in a cloud, speaks with Moses, and then 'withdraws' (אצל) a portion of the Spirit (רוח) that is on Moses. With the Spirit 'deposited' on the elders and 'resting' (נוח) on them, the elders spontaneously begin 'prophesying' (ויתנבאו). Although Joshua is present, there is no verification that he too prophesied. However, his presence with the leaders surely solidified his leadership prowess before the community and the elders.

of the Spirit that Moses is able to carry the burden of leadership. Therefore, it is expected that Joshua would need the same power to fulfil his leadership assignment. This is the logical place for Joshua to be enabled for a new level of leadership authority and practical skill. His recognition is noted after this episode when Moses prophetically changes his name from Hoshea son of Nun to 'Joshua' (יהושע), the theophoric 'Yehoshua' ('Yahweh is salvation'). This name change indicates not only the considerable interaction and experiences he has with Moses, but the respect Joshua had earned (Num. 13.16; cf. Exod. 17.9–13; 24.18; 32.17; 33.11; Num. 11.28). His new name also infers the salvation of the nation during the period of conquest and habitation of the promised land.

A further endorsement of the succession plan is Moses' hand of blessing on Joshua. With the verification that Joshua is the selected leader, Moses is instructed to lay his hand upon him, designating the Lord's choice and conferring some of Moses' authority on the successor.[14] All this is a public event before the community with Eleazar the priest officiating the transfer of responsibility to Joshua. In a parallel account in Deuteronomy, Moses gives a public endorsement of Joshua as his successor and charges him to facilitate Israel's conquest of the land. 'Be strong and courageous, for you must go with this people into the land that the LORD swore to their ancestors to give them, and you must divide it among them as their inheritance. The LORD himself goes before you and will be with you; he will never leave you nor forsake you. Do not be afraid; do not be discouraged' (Deut. 31.7–8). Joshua also has a private commissioning event at Yahweh's behest with Moses:

> The LORD said to Moses, 'Now the day of your death is near. Call Joshua and present yourselves at the tent of meeting, where I will commission him'. So Moses and Joshua came and presented themselves at the tent of meeting. Then the LORD appeared at the tent in a pillar of cloud, and the cloud stood over the entrance to the tent. (Deut. 31.14–15)

Furthermore, as in the case of Moses, the Lord promises to remain with him in the task of taking the land. 'The LORD gave this command to Joshua son of Nun: "Be strong and courageous, for you will bring the Israelites into the land

---

14 Both Moses and Joshua are leaders with immense tasks. While both leaders have individual strengths, the endowment of the Spirit is essential in order to fulfill their distinctive leadership roles. The crux of their responsibilities is to benefit the people of God who are like sheep without a shepherd. The Mosaic prayer for God to care in providing authorized leadership is answered: Joshua has the Spirit of Leadership and will take Israel into the land of promise.

I promised them on oath, and I myself will be with you"' (Deut. 31.23).[15] With the public commission, Moses is instructed to give Joshua some authority, literally 'majesty' (הוד). This infers the public endorsement of Joshua featuring Yahweh's authorization before the community so that they will indeed support the Lord's choice. The use of the term majesty (הוד) 'appears to be a transmission of demonstrable power, sufficient to elicit obedience from the congregation'.[16]

Joshua will work in tandem with the priest for the directions obtained from Yahweh and will lead the nation in accordance with military protocols. Joshua will consult Eleazar's directions when it comes to the conquest. The Urim was a device used by the priest that would provide specific guidance to the military on when to go to battle and when to retreat. In the military functions and land allocation duties, Joshua will lead differently from Moses who has more direct communication with Yahweh. The Urim is only mentioned here in Numbers where it refers to 'oracle stones' that the priest carries for decision making. According to Exodus 28, the stones are carried in a leather apron with a square pouch and worn over the breast (cf. Exod. 28.15–30). Other verses indicate that the breast piece also holds the 12 precious stones representing the tribes (Exod. 28.17–28; 39.10–21). The symbolic meaning of the 'breast piece' (חשׁן) (sacred pouch of the High Priest designed to hold the Urim and Thummim) comes to signify the presentation of the 12 tribes before the Lord over the priest's heart. 'The central element of the high priest's regalia thus functions as a visible symbol of the intercessory role of its bearer'.[17]

27.22–23—*Moses Publicly Lays Hands on Joshua*

Finally, the summation indicates Moses' fulfilment of Yahweh's commands to invest Joshua with authority to lead Israel (cf. Deut. 31.14–15, 23). 'Moses did as the LORD commanded him. He took Joshua and had him stand before Eleazar the priest and the whole assembly. Then he laid his hands on him and commissioned him, as the LORD instructed through Moses'. While several *midrashim* surmise how difficult it is for Moses to relinquish his leadership role and power, none of that is evident in the honourable commissioning of his successor. Moses lays his hands on Joshua before Eleazar and the whole Israelite commu-

---

15   G. Oeste, 'The Shaping of a Prophet: Joshua in the Deuteronomistic History', p. 28.
16   Cf. L.D. Hawk, 'Joshua', in T.D. Alexander & D.W. Baker (eds.), *Dictionary of the Old Testament: Pentateuch* (Downers Grove, IL: InterVarsity Press, 2003), p. 479 (hereafter abbreviated as DOTP). Another implication of the text for Hawk is the 'occasion for defining the relationship between charismatic and institutional authority'.
17   Cf. W. Dommershausen, 'חשׁן', *TDOT*, V, pp. 260–261.

nity to officially signify the one who would lead Israel like a shepherd. Moses is a humble leader to the end who has trained his aide and effectively prepared him for Yahweh's service.

One of the leadership motifs which elevates the status of Moses over all other leaders is the level of authority he carries due to the Spirit which empowers him to an extraordinary extent. It is not the spirit of Moses that exudes such authority but the Spirit of Yahweh who determines the extent and power in which divine authority is bestowed. For Joshua, the spirit of leadership will enable him to fulfil the divine plan that Yahweh has prepared for his people.

Reflection and Response
Numbers 26–27: Second Chances and Transitions in Life
Reflection

These two chapters feature a new beginning and season of anticipation for Israel. The covenantal promises of the Lord are nearing fruition and 'spring' is in the air. The mustering of a new generation of leaders is set in place and the people only know about the servitude in Egypt through the narration of their parents. Talk of a promised land after decades in the wilderness must have seemed like a dream. But the promises of the Lord are firm and inspire faith to prepare for a fresh new phase.

The wilderness themes of pilgrimage and testing surely give way to thoughts of settlement. The people are poised to move forward to a land they could call their own, where they could build, grow, worship, and develop. However, the new destination is not a vacation. Entry into a land inhabited by others requires covenantal obedience, trust in new leaders, plus risky military procedures. The land is a gift from Yahweh the landowner, but it will be a challenge to obtain their inheritance. The fact that Zelophehad's daughters will also inherit property affirms that the land allocations will be equitably distributed by leaders with Yahweh's involvement.

Another watershed moment remains before the nation. Their great shepherd, intercessor and leader will soon pass into the afterlife, just like their priest Aaron did. New leaders are chosen and have to be trusted. However, the leadership transitions are carefully orchestrated by Yahweh to provide a principled and orderly transition of power. As Yahweh is with Moses so he will also be with Joshua. In the transition of leadership, the extraordinary calibre of Moses is observed in his prayer for the Lord's choice to be confirmed. He does not pick his own successor but intercedes for God's will to be done.

An analysis of the events surrounding the lives of Moses and Joshua, the Scriptures present an incredibly successful leadership transfer. Moses affirms and supports his successor publicly and privately as does Yahweh. In the Deuteronomistic history, additional evidence of this is apparent as Joshua's leadership experience soon mirrors that of Moses in many typological dimensions. Both leaders send out spies for scouting missions, both lead the people through 'water' with miraculous intervention by Yahweh. Both witness military victories provided by the Lord and set up places of remembrance for celebration (the Passover). They allocate lands and show their care in applying the instructions of Yahweh for the nation. Both are effective intercessors, lead in covenantal commitments, and give incredible farewell exhortations that reflect the calibre of their leadership legacies. In all these characteristics, the spirit of leadership exhibited by Joshua reflects a seasoned, mature servant of the Lord. He lives almost as long as Moses and earns the same title of servant as his predecessor. 'After these things, Joshua son of Nun, the servant of the LORD, died at the age of a hundred and ten. And they buried him in the land of his inheritance, at Timnath Serah in the hill country of Ephraim, north of Mount Gaash' (Josh. 24.29–30; cf. Num. 12.8).[18] The transition of responsibilities from Moses to Joshua exemplifies positive leadership attitudes and characteristics. Other transitions in the OT are also instructive: Eli to Samuel, Saul to David, and Elijah to Elisha. However, the transition from Moses to Joshua is the succession par excellence.

Response

The wilderness events and leadership transfers are full of life lessons and a reminder that transitions, change, and death are inevitable realities. The important things to remember are attitudinal and include setting the right priorities. What really is important in life? How do we seek first the kingdom of God when there are so many temporal challenges in this life? Traditionally, Psalm 90 is considered as Moses' wise reflection on life. Firstly, he acknowledges that God is eternal, but also everlasting, accessible, and available. As Creator, he has made all things and provides his people with a dwelling place, shelter, gifts of land, produce and blessings.

Secondly, he reminds humans of their frailty, their many limitations and that they ultimately return to dust. In comparison to eternity, life on earth is short, and constrained. Like grass the body withers and dies. When young and healthy, life may be full of vigour and optimistic with few worries. Humans tend to be tenacious, productive, and bursting with plans. Then like the flowers in Israel which quickly fade in the heat, people wear out, become frail and tired. In the

---

18   Oeste, 'The Shaping of a Prophet: Joshua in the Deuteronomistic History', p. 30.

end, all pass through the valley of the shadow of death into a different reality. Another Psalm echoes this reality: 'Show me, LORD, my life's end and the number of my days; let me know how fleeting my life is. You have made my days a mere handbreadth; the span of my years is as nothing before you. Everyone is but a breath, even those who seem secure' (Ps. 39.4–5).

Thirdly, the prophet exhorts observation with wise application: 'Teach us to number our days, that we may gain a heart of wisdom' (Ps. 90.12; the superscription for Psalm 90 is 'A prayer of Moses, the man of God'). In the light of this, we are challenged to make our time on earth count. Moses is very realistic when he recounts the trials and difficulties experienced on earth. Yet, he serves Yahweh to the end of his days. Although life on earth may be shorter than Moses' 120 years and Joshua's 110, years, every person is exhorted to make the most of their time on earth, using God given skills to benefit people and serve God. We are exhorted to trust in the Lord and his wisdom to navigate life and its challenges.

Learning from those who went before and applying the lessons learned from faithful servants, will make us more effective, able to implement positive development in our family, church, synagogue and places of work. This is one of the great lessons we learn from Joshua—the intentional servant of Moses who was a faithful disciple and rose to every challenge. In the end, he like Moses, is lauded as the servant of the Lord. He exhibited tenacity in learning from Moses and Yahweh. He exhibited courage, faith and diligence. Moses concludes Psalm 90 with an exemplary prayer: 'May the favour of the LORD our God rest on us; establish the work of our hands for us—yes, establish the work of our hands' (Ps. 90.17).

28.1–29.40—Offerings and Sacrifices

With the anticipated entry into the promised land finally before them, Israel is reminded of the cultic duties that are an essential element in the nation's covenant with Yahweh. Redemption from Egypt is never to be forgotten. In the past the people served a hard task master and were forced to attend to the projects of Egypt. In the future they would serve Yahweh by attending to the agricultural and livestock needs of Israel along with the sacrificial obligations of the cultus. Just as Adam is placed in the garden of Eden to cultivate and worship, so too is Israel expected to till the soil and worship the Lord according to an ordered cultic calendar. They are to be a kingdom of priests and a holy nation (Exod. 19.6). From the beginning of time, Yahweh is considered to be the provider of the blessing that ensures productive, fertile land so that the people could enjoy the abundance of agricultural produce. In return the people would show their gratitude by offering a portion of the proceeds to Yahweh in acknowledgement of his beneficence. To accomplish this effectively, in a regulated and appropriate manner, Yahweh provides the instructions for the giving of gifts. In chapters 28–29, the offerings are listed along with details for their administration, including the timing, frequency, quantity, and amounts.

Due to the importance of the cultic requirements and calendar, the details presented in Numbers 28–29 are based upon earlier specifications presented in Exodus, Leviticus, as well as in Numbers (Numbers 9; 15; cf. Exod. 23.14–17; 29.38–43; 34.18–26; Leviticus 23). The purpose of the offerings is summarized in Leviticus:

> These are the LORD's appointed festivals, which you are to proclaim as sacred assemblies for bringing food offerings to the LORD—the burnt offerings and grain offerings, sacrifices and drink offerings required for each day. These offerings are in addition to those for the LORD's Sabbaths and in addition to your gifts and whatever you have vowed and all the freewill offerings you give to the LORD. (Lev. 23.37–38)

The additional details that are presented in Num. 28.1–15 are focused on the daily worship rituals that are to be performed at the Tent of Meeting. The annual calendar which Israel is to follow is primarily to begin when the promised land is inherited (Lev. 23.9; Num. 15.2).[19] The importance of adherence to the daily offerings is highlighted in verse 2 with the command that Israel must attend to the regular offering of the required products. The offerings belong to Yahweh who takes pleasure in their aroma and presentation.

Although the offerings listed in Numbers 28–29 are detailed and specific, they are not in the form of a cultic calendar but assume the schedule of dates, days and festivals that are recorded in Exodus and Leviticus. Furthermore, the catalogue of offerings in these two chapters does not always specify the actual name of the festival. Rather, they are presented according to specific days and months of the year with the assumption that the major festival in question is self-evident. According to the Pentateuch, Israel as a community is instructed to observe three annual feasts or 'festivals' (חגג) at specific times of the year.

---

19   Several chronological markers, dates, and events in the Pentateuch have some variations in their references. The divergences are due to the extensive periods of time through which the festivals are practiced in Israel. Slight adjustments are made in the transmission of instructions and their application during different historical eras (cf. Van Goudoever, *Biblical Calendars*, pp. 54–61).

These are the Feast of Unleavened Bread which begins with the Passover. The Feast of Harvest or Weeks comes at the end of the wheat harvest. Lastly, the Feast of 'Ingathering' (אסיף) or Booths comes at the end of the fruit and grape harvest (Exod. 23.14–17; 34.23; cf. Deut. 16.16). These periods of celebration are connected to seasons and the agricultural cycle, beginning with the full moon in spring and ending with the autumn harvests.

The implication for the cultus requirements is that the presence of Yahweh among the Israelites is dependent on their attendance to the detailed stipulations of the sacrificial system. However, the apparent excessive demands of the cultus with its numerous animal, grain, oil, and wine emoluments, highlight the incredible beneficence of Yahweh in providing everything Israel requires for life in the land. Israel gives what the Lord provides! The core ingredients are summarized here with further commentary below.

TABLE 9A Offerings and sacrifices

Name & scheduled offering	Main references	Required products	Time & instruction	Purpose
Burnt; 'fire' (אשה) Offering (קרבן)	Num. 28.1, 3, 4, 8; Exod. 29.38–43	2 lambs	Each day; 1 per morning; 1 per twilight	Food offering with aroma for Yahweh
Grain 'offering' (מנחה); 'food' (לחם)	Num. 28.1, 5	(מנחה סלת) grain/finest flour; olive oil	Each day with lamb	Thanksgiving; Gratitude to God
Libation (נסך)	Num. 28.7–8	Fermented drink	Each day with lamb	Appreciation for provision

TABLE 9B Additional offerings and sacrifices

Name & scheduled offering	Main references	Required products	Time & instruction	Purpose
Sabbath Offering [in addition to daily burnt] (אשה)	Num. 28.9–10; Exod. 29.38–43	2, 1-year-old lambs; grain of fine flour with oil	Each Sabbath day;	Remembering Sabbath day
Monthly Offering; 1st day of month	Num. 28.11–15	2 young bulls; 1 ram; 7 male lambs; grain, flour & oil; Wine libations occur with each bull, ram & lamb	At each new moon; Burnt Sacrifices are made together with each animal	Marks the beginning of month; pleasing aroma for Yahweh.
Monthly Offering	Num. 28.15	1 male goat	Presented to the Lord	For a sin offering

TABLE 9B Additional offerings and sacrifices (cont.)

Name & scheduled offering	Main references	Required products	Time & instruction	Purpose
The Passover	Num. 28.16–25; cf. Num. 9.2–14	2 young bulls; 1 ram; 7 male lambs; grain, flour & oil; Wine libations occur with each bull, ram & lamb; 1 male goat	On 14th day the first month; 1st and 7th day is a sacred day with no work	The Lord's Passover; Special offerings over and above daily sacrifices; The goat is for an atoning sin offering.
Passover (פסח) Festival (חג)	Num. 28.17, 25	Daily offerings	On 15th day the first month; Eat bread without yeast for 7 days; 7th day ends Passover with a sacred assembly	Festive occasion
Feast of Weeks	Num. 28.26–31	2 young bulls; 1 ram; 7 male lambs; grain, flour & oil; Wine libations occur with each bull, ram & lamb; 1 male goat	On day of Firstfruits, new grain offerings are given with a sacred assembly	Pleasing aroma; Appreciation for produce; Atonement
Feast of Trumpets	Num. 29.1–6	1 young bull; 1 ram; 7 male lambs; grain, flour & oil; 1 male goat	On 1st day of 7th month, sound the trumpets; sacrifices; sin offering	Offerings are made to the Lord; a pleasing aroma
Sacrifice (זבח)	Num. 7.17–88 (13×); 15.3–8	Cf. Num. 7 & 15	Cf. Num. 7 & 15	Festival (מועד) Freewill (נדבה)
Grain offering (מנחה)	Num. 28.5	(מנחה סלת) grain/finest flour; olive oil	Each day with lamb	Thanksgiving; Gratitude to God
Libation (נסך)	Num. 28.7–8	Fermented drink	Each day with lamb	Appreciation for provision

28.1–8—The Daily Offerings

The instructions for the daily and 'regular' (תמיד) regimen of 'offerings' (קרבן) are an essential requirement which Moses relays to the Israelites. Daily offerings are foundational sacrifices, brought to Yahweh all year round—each and every day. The two main sacrifices fall under the category of 'burnt offerings' (עלה) and public sacred festivities where animal 'sacrifices' (זבח), grains and libations are ritually prepared and offered. Typical sacrifices involve animals but in Numbers 15 additional food items are incorporated. For most animal sacrifices the entire corpse is consumed by 'fire' (אש).[20] Sacrifices that are ignited

---

20 Kellermann, 'עלה', p. 99 (referred to 286 times in the OT).

by fire include animals, grains and wine. The additional festival offerings which occur thirty days a year, as well as the Sabbath offerings, are supplementary to the daily requirements. On special festival celebrations, including the New Moon, Unleavened Bread, Feast of Weeks, New Year, Day of Atonement, and the Days of Sukkot, the required sacrificial lambs are seven and fourteen. In fact, the numbers seven (19 times) and fourteen (9 out of 12 times) are featured prominently in these two chapters to symbolically affirm the completion of Yahweh's promises of entry into the promised land which also may signify the theological concept of 'rest' in the land.[21]

Specified offerings must be made at the appointed time and are stated to bring a pleasant aroma to Yahweh. The food offerings must be without defect—the best of the flock. The timing is also mandated as morning and evening. The grain offerings amount to about two litres and are stipulated to be of the finest flour. The oil mixed with the flour amounts to about one litre of pressed olive oil.[22] This daily offering is not new but is instituted at Mount Sinai: 'For the generations to come this burnt offering is to be made regularly at the entrance to the tent of meeting before the LORD. There I will meet you and speak to you; there also I will meet with the Israelites, and the place will be consecrated by my glory' (Exod. 29.42–43).

Furthermore, the sacrifices require an accompanying drink offering which may be wine but the fermented or 'strong drink' (שכר; *sakar*) is fortified and given as a libation at the sanctuary. The recurring phrase indicates the value of the sacrifice: 'This is a food offering, an aroma pleasing to the LORD'. However, the pleasing aroma and food for Yahweh are understood as anthropomorphic descriptions.

28.9-10—*Sabbath Offerings*

Every seventh day is marked with twice the daily offerings which are presented after the daily sacrifices. The 'Sabbath' (שבת) day is only referred to three times

---

[21] As stated earlier, over 300 occurrences of seven, seventh, seventy are used in the OT, often with metaphoric import. In some form, 'seven' (שבע) occurs approximately 65 times in Numbers.

[22] Regarding the specified measurements, a dry measure of an *ephah* equals a half bushel or 4 gallons; A *hin* of oil or wine is about 3.5 quarts or 3.9 litres; cf. G.L. Archer, 'The Metrology of the Old Testament', in Frank E. Gaebelein (ed.), *The Expositor's Bible Commentary: Introductory Articles* (Grand Rapids, MI: Zondervan, 1979), p. 378. According to Budd the exact measures are difficult to translate into modern equivalents. 'It may be 7.5 pints (4.5 litres) of flour and 3 pints (1.8 litres) each of oil and wine'. Cf. Budd, *Numbers*, p. 168. These are the same quantities used in Numbers 28–29.

in Numbers (cf. Num. 15.32). However, from descriptions in Exodus (16 times) and Leviticus (25 times) the importance of the seventh day is foundational to Israel's weekly cycle of work, rest and worship. Its main significance from Exod. 20.8–11 is as a day of rest and reflection on the Creator's creation, rest, and holiness. The Sabbath day is holy and blessed by Yahweh. By implication, Israel offers sacrifices which acknowledge the divine blessings of work and provision throughout the week. They are free to rest, recline and reflect on the greatness of Yahweh's character and accomplishments. The concise summation in Leviticus is expanded on in Exodus and Deuteronomy: 'There are six days when you may work, but the seventh day is a day of sabbath rest, a day of sacred assembly. You are not to do any work; wherever you live, it is a sabbath to the LORD' (Lev. 23.1). The Sabbath day is so sacred that the penalty exacted on the Sabbath breaker in Numbers 15 is death.

The emphasis in Exodus is on the holy character of the Sabbath day which is rooted in the creation event:

> Remember the Sabbath day by keeping it holy. Six days you shall labor and do all your work, but the seventh day is a sabbath to the LORD your God. On it you shall not do any work, neither you, nor your son or daughter, nor your male or female servant, nor your animals, nor any foreigner residing in your towns. For in six days the LORD made the heavens and the earth, the sea, and all that is in them, but he rested on the seventh day. Therefore, the LORD blessed the Sabbath day and made it holy. (Exod. 20.8–11)

A cessation of work is commanded so that a day of rest may be enjoyed by all. In the extended version of the Sabbath command in Deut. 5.15, an additional component of redemption reflection is featured: 'Remember that you were slaves in Egypt and that the LORD your God brought you out of there with a mighty hand and an outstretched arm. Therefore, the LORD your God has commanded you to observe the Sabbath day'. From the various details regarding the Sabbath, it is evident that the day is a special provision of the Lord for the well-being of individuals and the community. It legislates a period of respite so that people can be free from the regular concerns of life to reflect on earthly, spiritual, and eternal matters.

28.11–15—*The Monthly Offerings*

Every month is marked by the sighting of the 'new moon' (חדש), signaling the first of the month as a regular celebration. On the first of every month the burnt offerings are presented along with all the required sacrifices (cf. Num. 15. 2–12). These are considerable offerings and may include ideas of sacrifice for protection at the beginning of a new month.²³ Additionally, a purification offering of a male goat to Yahweh is made, as a public act for the cleansing of any sins or infractions that may have defiled the sanctuary. Overall, the New Moon marker launches a fresh monthly cycle to celebrate Yahweh's faithful provisions and sovereignty. References to this celebration occur often to indicate the importance of the new moon (1 Sam. 20.5; 2 Kgs 4.23; Isa. 1.13; Amos 8.5; Hos. 13).

28.16–25—*The Passover and Festival of Unleavened Bread*

Instructions regarding the 'Passover' (פסח) celebration are communicated by Moses to Israel in Lev. 23.5–8:

> The LORD's Passover begins at twilight on the fourteenth day of the first month. On the fifteenth day of that month the LORD's Festival of Unleavened Bread begins; for seven days you must eat bread made without yeast. On the first day hold a sacred assembly and do no regular work. For seven days present a food offering to the LORD. And on the seventh day hold a sacred assembly and do no regular work.

Based on this directive, Numbers 9 provides further insights and emphasizes the Passover seven times in Num. 9.2–14 (also cf. Num. 26.16; 33.3).²⁴ The Passover event celebrates the great deliverance of the Hebrews from their enslavement in Egypt and provides a foundation for the nation's existence, hope, and constitution. Initially the Passover is a family-oriented event to commemorate the exodus from Egypt and protection of the firstborns in Israel. Israel is to observe the Passover event according to the precise time and instructions which are given in Exodus 12 when Israel is still under the bondage of the Egyptians. The Passover event would be celebrated in the first month of Israel's year—the month of Nisan.²⁵ The Passover is not a separate annual

---

23 Budd cites Snaith who claims that the 'association of the goat with the purification offering with this celebration goes back to times when protection was sought against demons who were supposed to be operative in the dark days of the new moon' (Cf. Budd, *Numbers*, p. 316).

24 Scholars have offered many interpretations of the Passover rite and the actual meaning of the term (cf. E. Otto, 'פסח', *TDOT*, XII, pp. 7–8), but the historical connection between the events surrounding the occasion and its cultic observances rooted in Exod. 12.13–27 as described here continue to be understood as primary concepts for the Passover celebration. The septenary emphasis on the Passover appears to highlight the thematic connection between creation and redemption which flows throughout the OT.

25 There are three records of Passover celebrations from Exodus to Joshua. The first one is after the exodus event (Exodus 12); the second is in the wilderness as noted in Numbers 9

festival but marks the beginning of the Feast of 'Unleavened' (מצה) Bread (cf. Ezek. 45.21–22).

In Numbers 28 Israel is instructed to hold a sacred assembly on the Passover which marks the beginning of a seven day 'festival' (חג) which is held at the sanctuary (cf. Exod. 12.29–30; פסח *pesach*) and features the sacrifice of the lamb. The prohibition for work is qualified as occupational or 'laborious' work and not complete cessation as on the Sabbath, for the first day (Passover) or on the last day of the festival. For seven days of celebration the people eat bread without yeast and offer the required burnt offerings, lambs, and goat for atonement (as indicated in the table above).

28.26–31—*The Feast of Weeks*

This festival is referred to as 'weeks' (שבוע) for the seven days of celebration but is also called the 'harvest' (קציר) festival in Exod. 23.16 (cf. Exod. 34.22). The background details for the festival are presented in Lev. 23.9–14 which feature the lasting and extensive requirement of this ordinance:

> When you enter the land I am going to give you and you reap its harvest, bring to the priest a sheaf of the first grain you harvest. He is to wave the sheaf before the LORD so it will be accepted on your behalf; the priest is to wave it on the day after the Sabbath. On the day you wave the sheaf, you must sacrifice as a burnt offering to the LORD a lamb a year old without defect, together with its grain offering of two-tenths of an ephah of the finest flour mixed with olive oil—a food offering presented to the LORD, a pleasing aroma—and its drink offering of a quarter of a *hin* of wine. You must not eat any bread, or roasted or new grain, until the very day you bring this offering to your God. This is to be a lasting ordinance for the generations to come, wherever you live.

The festival is initiated on the day of first fruits to celebrate the great day for beginning the wheat harvest. In Leviticus, specific instructions are given for the first fruits of grain which would be the barley harvest. According to the instructions in Lev. 23.15–16, the wave offering of the grain sheaf begins a countdown of fifty days to the wheat harvest (thus 7 weeks; in the Septuagint it is referred to as Pentecost). The sacrifices include the presentation of two loaves of bread

---

and the third is in Joshua after the people enter into the promised land (Josh. 5.10–12). The annual commemoration provides the historical context for what God had done thereby instilling hope for the nation in what God would do through his provision, guidance, and protection. Cf. Armerding, 'Festivals and Feasts', pp. 300–313.

made from the finest flour baked with yeast which is a wave offering before the Lord. Additionally, Lev. 23.18–21 stipulates they must:

> Present with this bread seven male lambs, each a year old and without defect, one young bull and two rams. They will be a burnt offering to the LORD, together with their grain offerings and drink offerings—a food offering, an aroma pleasing to the LORD. Then sacrifice one male goat for a sin offering and two lambs, each a year old, for a fellowship offering. The priest is to wave the two lambs before the LORD as a wave offering, together with the bread of the first fruits. They are a sacred offering to the LORD for the priest. On that same day you are to proclaim a sacred assembly and do no regular work. This is to be a lasting ordinance for the generations to come, wherever you live.

In Exodus the feast celebrates the grain harvest with the produce from crops that the Israelites planted themselves on their own fields (Exod. 23.16).

In Deuteronomy Moses affirms that freewill offerings should also be considered in proportion to the blessings that the Israelites could anticipate and acknowledge. The Mosaic exhortation provides another image of hope for the nation who will receive their promised inheritance: 'And rejoice before the LORD your God at the place he will choose as a dwelling for his Name—you, your sons and daughters, your male and female servants, the Levites in your towns, and the foreigners, the fatherless and the widows living among you. Remember that you were slaves in Egypt, and follow carefully these decrees' (Deut. 16.9–12).

29.1–7—*Annual Congregation in the Seventh Month*

The seventh month of the calendar year in Israel is special as it inaugurates the beginning of the agricultural year. It also is a marker for the sabbatical cycle that matches the lunar cycle of 'new moon' (חדש) as well as the beginning of the New Year (*Rosh Hashanah*). Here and in Leviticus the celebration is heralded with trumpet blasts to signal the sabbath and a gathering. 'On the first day of the seventh month you are to have a day of sabbath rest, a sacred assembly commemorated with trumpet blasts. Do no regular work, but present a food offering to the LORD' (Lev. 23.24–25). It is an auspicious day of celebration devoid of work. The offering of one young bull, one ram and seven male lambs are prescribed along with the grain offering. A male goat is also sacrificed to make atonement for sin.

There is an emphasis made throughout the chapter that the offerings must be made as 'specified' (Num. 29.6, 18, 21, 24, 27, 30, 33, 37). Usually the term means 'judgment or ordinance' (משפט) so it is a constant reminder of the meticulous attendance to the offerings and observances prescribed by the Lord. The chapter ends with the characteristic summation that Moses faithfully delivers all the instructions to Israel that the Lord commands of him.

29.8–11—Day of Atonement

Another special day in the seventh month occurs on the tenth day with a sacred gathering of the people. The specific mention of *'Yom Kippur'* (יום כפר) occurs in Lev. 23.27–28; 25.9, but not in the Numbers text. However, this appears to be the day referred to here with the annual purification of the sanctuary conducted by the priests according to Leviticus 16. The day is a solemn occasion characterized by individual acts of self-denial, penitence, fasting and bringing the required offerings. Serious consequences are warned for those who do not comply:

> Those who do not deny themselves on that day must be cut off from their people. I will destroy from among their people anyone who does any work on that day. You shall do no work at all. This is to be a lasting ordinance for the generations to come, wherever you live. It is a day of sabbath rest for you, and you must deny yourselves. From the evening of the ninth day of the month until the following evening you are to observe your sabbath. (Lev. 23.29–32)

The offerings for the day include the regular as well as the additional:

> Present as an aroma pleasing to the LORD a burnt offering of one young bull, one ram and seven male lambs a year old, all without defect. With the bull offer a grain offering of three-tenths of an ephah of the finest flour mixed with oil; with the ram, two-tenths; and with each of the seven lambs, one-tenth. Include one male goat as a sin offering, in addition to the sin offering for atonement and the regular burnt offering with its grain offering, and their drink offerings. (Num. 29.9–11)

Atonement for the Most Holy Place, for the Tent of Meeting, the altar, the priest and for all the people is made once a year to purge sanctuary and community of their sins (Lev. 16.33–34).[26] With strict compliance of the requirements, atonement is accomplished for the people and the sanctuary is purged of desecration.

---

26   Cf. Milgrom, *Numbers*, pp. 246–247.

29.12–34—Week Three in the Seventh Month

This celebration begins on the fifteenth day of the seventh month and is a sacred convocation that lasts seven days, with a concluding benediction on the eighth day. In Exodus the festival is called the Feast of Ingathering (Exod. 23.16; 34.22) and marks the beginning of the grape harvest. In Leviticus, the festival is referred to as the Feast of 'Booths' (סכות) or Tabernacles, which depicts a crude kind of shelter that reflects the historical phase of wilderness wanderings and their nomadic ordeal. Although the celebration has both an agricultural and an historical referent, it also provides hope in a future consummation of life in a new context like the promised land. The basic procedures for the festival are described in Lev. 23.34–36:

> On the fifteenth day of the seventh month the LORD's Festival of Tabernacles begins, and it lasts for seven days. The first day is a sacred assembly; do no regular work. For seven days present food offerings to the LORD, and on the eighth day hold a sacred assembly and present a food offering to the LORD. It is the closing special assembly; do no regular work.

Although the festivities last one week, there is a concluding 'solemn' (עצרה) gathering on the eighth day. The whole period is marked with joy, rest, and a camp-ground atmosphere with genuine celebration. Reflection on the redemption from Egypt forms a new anticipation for Yahweh's future acts of redemption for Israel. Details for this festival are presented in Leviticus and are a lasting ordinance for all generations in Israel. The annual celebration begins on the fifteenth day of the seventh month and last seven days. The first and concluding day is observed as a sabbath day of rest. Celebrations include the waving of branches from palm, willow, and other leafy trees, with much expressive rejoicing before the Lord. An additional feature of the festival requires the erecting of temporary shelters which serve as a reminder of the exodus conditions (cf. Lev. 23.39–43). The celebration brings a dramatic, sensory, and symbolic experience to the participants for a memorable connection to Israel's history.

The hard work of harvesting is concluded with the pilgrimage to observe the festival. The prescribed offerings for the first day include burnt offerings of thirteen young bulls, two rams and fourteen male lambs a year old, with grain, oil, and a goat sin offering. For each of the following seven days there are similar prescribed sacrifices according to this paradigm:

> On the second day offer twelve young bulls, two rams and fourteen male lambs a year old, all without defect. With the bulls, rams, and lambs, offer their grain offerings and drink offerings according to the number spec-

ified. Include one male goat as a sin offering, in addition to the regular burnt offering with its grain offering, and their drink offerings. (Num. 29.17–19)

However, beginning with thirteen young bulls on day one, there is one less bull sacrificed each day so that on day seven, seven bulls are sacrificed (cf. Num. 29.13–38).

29.35-40—*Final Day Offerings and Summation*
The eighth day marks the final day for another sacred assembly with a lower number of animal offerings.

On the eighth day hold a closing special assembly and do no regular work. Present as an aroma pleasing to the LORD a food offering consisting of a burnt offering of one bull, one ram and seven male lambs a year old, all without defect. With the bull, the ram and the lambs, offer their grain offerings and drink offerings according to the number specified. Include one male goat as a sin offering, in addition to the regular burnt offering with its grain offering and drink offering. (Num. 29.35–38)

It is a fitting conclusion to the annual event which acknowledges Yahweh's faithful covenantal promises of redemption and abundant living in the land of promise.

Finally, the summation reflects on the preceding directives and reminds the worshippers to make good on their sacred vows and intentions to bring gifts: 'In addition to what you vow and your freewill offerings, offer these to the LORD at your appointed festivals: your burnt offerings, grain offerings, drink offerings and fellowship offerings'. This exhortation reminds the community that the sacrificial system is not just a number of rituals with calendar festival events. It includes the private decisions of worshippers to be faithful in their personal relationship with Yahweh to fulfil promises and stay true to their intentions. Regarding the religious use of making a vow or promise, there often are personal circumstances that motivate the individual to take the oath and make the personal sacrifices: 'An oath is a solemn promise to a deity to perform a certain act if the deity acts in a certain way. It is thus a prayer demanding emphatically that God act'.[27] Vows and promises are to be carefully considered before their declaration.

---

27 Cf. Kaiser, 'נדר', p. 244.

The summation affirms Moses' role in faithfully communicating the instructions for the Israelite's offering requirements (Num. 29.40).[28]

30.1–16—Making Vows

30.1–2—A Man's Word

The instructions which Moses communicates end with the assumption that individuals would make vows to the Lord along with giving their offerings and sacrifices. Within the context, the vows are to be differentiated from the Nazirite vows which have more extreme requirements (cf. Num. 6.1–21). The function of a community vow is illustrated in Numbers 21 when the nation fears an attack from the Canaanite king of Arad.[29] In this instance the Lord hears their vow and intervenes in the distressing situation. Nevertheless, vows are not to be entered into lightly or without due concern since the implications of breaking a vow are significant. This is the main focus in Numbers 30 where the undertaking of a personal vow is described and regulated. Reference to the term 'vow' (נדר) occurs 13 times from verse 2 to 14, in the context of human relationships where a person makes a pledge along with an invocation for divine involvement.

Moses addresses the tribal leaders of Israel who have responsibilities in overseeing the life and societal affairs of their people. The assumption in the directives given implies the close social bonds within family, tribe, and extended community—even concerning the personal spiritual commitments of individuals. In the first instance, the man is cautioned regarding the undertaking of a 'vow' (נדר) or swearing by an 'oath' (שבע), due to the binding 'obligations' (אטר) of such a pledge [cf. in Num. 30.2–10, to 'bind' (10 times) with a 'pledge' (11 times)]. By undertaking a solemn oath before Yahweh, the man commits to certain activities or acts of abstinence—usually to obtain divine intervention in some sphere of life.[30] The spoken pledge becomes a bond which holds the

---

28 In the Masoretic text Num. 29.40 is the first verse in ch. 30 (30.1).

29 Note the example in Numbers 21: 'Then Israel made this vow to the Lord: If you will deliver these people into our hands, we will totally destroy their cities. The Lord listened to Israel's plea and gave the Canaanites over to them. They completely destroyed them and their towns; so the place was named Hormah' (Num. 21.2–3).

30 'A special form is the unconditional self-imposed obligation that binds the person making the vow to a particular way of life for a period of time or perpetually' (Kaiser, 'נדר', pp. 244, 254). Kaiser and others assert that the Numbers 30 instructions are perhaps postexilic casuistry, but the wilderness context and close proximity of family life make the examples of vows an early and understandable issue.

person liable for keeping and fulfilling the undertaking. The quantity of times these terms are repeated in the chapter emphasize the importance of fulfilling all pronounced obligations. 'To swear in the Old Testament was to give one's sacred unbreakable word in testimony that the one swearing would faithfully perform some promised deed, or that he would faithfully refrain from some evil act' (cf. Gen. 21.22–23).[31]

Invoking such a commitment must be carefully weighed so that the spoken vow along with its commitments will not be broken. What is spoken and pledged, must be fulfilled. In Deut. 23.21–23 the importance of fulfilling a vow is made clear:

> If you make a vow to the LORD your God, do not be slow to pay it, for the LORD your God will certainly demand it of you and you will be guilty of sin. But if you refrain from making a vow, you will not be guilty. Whatever your lips utter you must be sure to do, because you made your vow freely to the LORD your God with your own mouth.

A man's word is a pledge and when spoken as a commitment made to the Lord, it is considered a binding, votive offering. In other words, it is better not to make a vow unless it is carefully considered, necessary, and spiritually beneficial. Failure of fulfilling commitments and vows could have negative consequences.

30.3–5—A Woman's Pledge

A vow contemplated by a woman has even greater implications. In the instance presented, the vow may be affected by the cultural status of the woman as well as the pledge made to the Lord. According to the case, when the woman lives under the protection of the father, in Hebrew culture, the father is regarded as the leader and overseer of all who dwell in the home. The father is responsible for the well-being and security of the household.

The implication here is that even if some vows may be considered private spiritual matters, the effects of the vow may impact more people than the person making the vow. While it is possible that individuals make private personal vows that no one knows about, the actual carrying out of a vow could be observed in people's actions. Therefore, some pledges might be more expansive and affect not only the woman, but the whole household. In this case, the father claims the right to determine whether the vow is appropriate or

---

31 Cf. V.P. Hamilton, 'שׁבע', *TWOT*, II, pp. 899–901. The action "to swear" occurs 184 times in the OT. Taking an "oath" (30 references) serves to verify innocence, affirm action, solemnize peace treaties, pledge loyalty or renewal of spiritual devotion.

unacceptable—whether it is personal or has wider community implications. When a vow is reckoned as personal, and perhaps beneficial for the woman, the vow may be ignored—the woman becomes responsible for her pledge. If deemed inappropriate, the father may forbid the undertaking. In this case the woman is freed from the obligation and potential consequences. Not only so, but in such a case the woman is totally released from the vow—literally, 'forgiven' (סלח) for making the rash, unsuitable or impactful pledge.

30.6–16—A Married Woman's Vow

In a similar instance where the woman is married and makes a vow, her husband has the authority to intervene. The first example refers to vows made before marriage but continue to be in effect after the marriage is consummated. In this instance the husband is permitted to address any promises made by the bride which has implications for the newly wedded couple. The husband is authorized to nullify any previously made promises which are deemed to have a negative effect on the recently inaugurated home. Reasons for this have to do with culture as well as divine directive.

In the marriage arrangement, the father has transferred the responsibilities of care for the daughter to the husband who now fills the role of overseer in the home. In Hebrew culture the marriage vows not only transfer responsibilities to the man but also transition the man and woman into a sacred relationship whereby the two become one. They no longer have an independent existence but now forge their lives together. There is a mutual interdependence that has implications for most elements of marital life. In the case of a vow taken before the marriage, it is anticipated that the woman would declare her pledge—especially if it has ramifications for the husband. In the case of a rash promise, the husband also has the authority to nullify the promise for the well-being of the woman and the home. She would be released and forgiven for her promise. Although certain elements of culture and family structure are evident in this ruling, the importance of the supplicatory offerings are clarified.

The principle is different for a woman who is independent due to being widowed or divorced. Such a person is responsible for any vow or promise made to the Lord. The same implications stated above on taking care not to make rash or careless promises are implicit for the independent woman—she is responsible for words spoken which are binding.

In the final instance given for the woman living with her husband who makes a vow or obligates herself by a pledge under oath, the regulations are similar to those noted above. For appropriate promises made to the Lord within justifiable circumstances, the husband will let them stand. However, for those vows made which include promises of abstinence and oaths that impinge on family matters, the husband is empowered to nullify them. Tardiness in doing so will make the husband responsible for any consequences that arise from the vows that are made and not cancelled in time.

In summation, the regulations regarding the undertaking of vows, oaths and promises are an important reminder to the family and community of the power of words which affect not only the individual but the larger social fabric. They concern family relationships which are foundational to the nation. Moreover, when the worshipper invokes the Lord into personal or family situations by making requests and promises in return for divine intervention, the vows made are binding. Once verbalized privately or publicly, the oath has effectual power that anticipates commitment and fulfilment.

Reflection and Response
Numbers 28–30: Spiritual Discipline and Personal Responsibility for Words

Reflection

The sacrificial system is a regulated and demanding system that requires daily devotion, sacrifice and compliance. In these chapters the narrator provides meticulous details concerning the products and procedures for bringing gifts to Yahweh during daily and annual administration. The worshipper is encouraged to follow through with sacrificial intentions which provide a sense of peace and vitality in spiritual life. The overall objective is to maintain a vibrant relationship with God and neighbour. The appropriate role of making promises and giving offerings is expressed by the Psalmist: 'I will come to your temple with burnt offerings and fulfil my vows to you—vows my lips promised and my mouth spoke when I was in trouble. I will sacrifice fat animals to you and an offering of rams; I will offer bulls and goats' (Ps. 66.13–15).

It is within the divine and community relationships that the taking of vows, commitments, and oaths are addressed. Individuals are frequently warned in the scriptures to be careful with their words and promises. Failure to follow through with stated commitments brings negative consequences in relationships. In such matters the example of the Lord who made covenantal promises to the patriarchs is to be followed. Several texts affirm the Lord's unequivocal promise to bring Israel into their inheritance of land—with an oath: 'After the LORD brings you into the land of the Canaanites and gives it to you, as he promised on oath to you and your ancestors' (Exod. 13.11; 33.1; cf. Num. 11.12; 14.16, 23). The Psalmist affirms that the Lord is trustworthy in all he promises and faithful in all he does (Ps. 145.13b). Alternatively, the Lord's declaration that those who were twenty years old or more when they came up out of Egypt will not enter the land was also upheld (Num. 32.10–12). This is also affirmed by the

Psalmist: 'For forty years I was angry with that generation; I said, 'They are a people whose hearts go astray, and they have not known my ways'. So I declared on oath in my anger, 'They shall never enter my rest'. (Ps. 95.10–11). As God is faithful to bring judgment on a generation as promised, so too is he faithful to bring the people into the promised land, and increase their numbers, as he swore on oath (Deut. 6.13–23; 8.1; 13.17; 19.8; 26.15).

Those who fail to keep their commitments and vows fall into the category of the wicked who cannot be trusted. 'Not a word from their mouth can be trusted; their heart is filled with malice. Their throat is an open grave; with their tongues they tell lies' (Ps. 5.9; Cf. Pss. 36.3; 59.12). But the righteous are those who maintain their integrity and keep their words (Prov. 11.3). The tenor of OT teaching affirms the value of speaking truth and fulfilling vows—even when they are private reflections known only by the Lord. 'May these words of my mouth and this meditation of my heart be pleasing in your sight, LORD, my Rock and my Redeemer' (Ps. 19.4). An example of promise and fulfilment is presented in Numbers 32 where the Gadites and Reubenites make some far-reaching commitments for the nation. Moses concludes his exhortation with these warnings: 'But if you fail to do this, you will be sinning against the LORD; and you may be sure that your sin will find you out. Build cities for your women and children, and pens for your flocks, but do what you have promised' (32.23–24).

Response

The ninth commandment warns individuals not to speak falsehood or lies (שקר) against anyone (Exod. 20.13; Deut. 5.17). Consistent truth telling is foundational for character formation and fortifies a person's reputation with integrity. Vows, oaths, and words are meaningful. Those who make promises that are trustworthy and fulfilled, are considered faithful and dependable. In contemporary contexts the truth has become very difficult to find. In an era where propaganda, conspiracies and falsehood is trending, the truth is a valuable currency to apprehend and embrace. For this reason, the stipulations for making vows are rigorous. Vows are not to be made flippantly or frequently. They are to be carefully considered and meaningful with total intentionality to implement them. Vows made to the Lord with specific terms must be carried out as stated or they may render a person guilty of sin. The words of a vow or oath are optional but once vocalized, they are very consequential (Deut. 23.21–23). These principles are affirmed in the teachings of Jesus who raises the bar in his application for the disciples: 'Again, you have heard that it was said to the people long ago, 'Do not break your oath, but fulfil to the LORD the vows you have made'. But I tell you, do not swear an oath at all: either by heaven, for it is God's throne; or by the earth, for it is his footstool; or by Jerusalem, for it is the city of the Great King. And do not swear by your head, for you cannot make even one hair white or black. All you need to say is simply 'Yes' or 'No'; anything beyond this comes from the evil one' (Mt. 5.33–36).

There are many contemporary contexts where vow making and oath taking are applicable. How are we doing with marriage vows before God and witnesses? How are things in the world of business where oral agreements and signed contracts stipulate commitments? According to the legal systems there is a back log of claims and disputes even among brothers and sisters for broken commitments. What about the oath of office which so many prominent politicians have made publicly with their hand on the Bible? What about work commitments, contracts, promises and service? Right down to the domestic sphere, our words and promises have incredible force and power when they are followed through and implemented. Promises made to a spouse, children, fellow workers and employers are remembered. Keeping them and implementing them consistently builds trust and a positive reputation. Alternatively, a broken trust or an unfulfilled promise becomes a relational barrier that is difficult to mend.

31.1–54—Vengeance on the Midianites

The chapter opens with a solemn instruction for Moses who is informed that he has one final commission to fulfil. He is directed to take vengeance on the Midianites, presumably for the incidents and behaviour presented in Numbers 25. In that episode, severe judgment is to be meted out on the Moabites and Midianites by Moses as instructed by the Lord. Moses must take action in order to avert the wrath of Yahweh on Israel. 'Take all the leaders of these people, kill them and expose them in broad daylight before the LORD, so that the LORD's fierce anger may turn away from Israel' (Num. 25.4). However, the punishment on the enemies of Israel is not implemented and additional action is expected of Moses: 'The LORD said to Moses, "Treat the Midianites as enemies and kill them. They treated you as enemies when they deceived you in the Peor incident involving their sister Kozbi, the daughter of a Midianite leader, the woman who was killed when the plague came as a result of that incident."' (Num. 25.16–18). Not only are these difficult matters for Moses to settle, but after he fulfils the instructions, he is notified that he too will be 'gathered to his people'. His leadership duties are coming to an end and he will finally enter his eternal reward.

The details of the chapter are difficult for many commentators to reconcile. They point out several incongruencies and historical problems. Some of the key matters identified by Gray include that the Midianite men are not annihilated as claimed (Num. 31.7) but continue to live according to Judges 6–8. Furthermore, it seems incredulous that the Israelites do not lose any men in battle (Num. 31.49). Additionally, the amount of plunder taken by Israel from the enemy appears to be excessive. Finally, Joshua, the new leader is nowhere to be seen in the narration, but Phineas is featured as a key leader in the battle.[32]

Nevertheless, there are several commentators who discern the antiquity of the text and view the account as containing 'a verifiable historical nucleus'. Although, Milgrom states that the quantitative data and spoil is not to be taken literally and that some details seem to be embellished, he agrees that 'the assembled evidence clearly points to the historic reality that Midian was the most powerful and menacing enemy that Israel had to encounter during its migration to Canaan'.[33] He also points out that there is much authentic ancient detail in the narrative as noted by Eissfeldt; there is evidence that during the Mosaic period, Midian probably enjoyed a protectorate over the whole Transjordanian region, and only those Midianites in Moses' vicinity were decimated, while several other groups continued to live in different regions. The Midianites were strong enough to provide refuge to people like Moses, and the Midianite people were at home in the entire wilderness region (Cf. Num. 10.29–32; Exod. 2.15–16; 3.1; 4.19).[34]

The reality is that Israel is transgressing on the property of many diverse people groups who obviously view the nation of migrants as a powerful threat. In the course of living in close proximity to these people, many things occur which bring resentment and hatred between groups. It so happens that the Moabites and Midianites conduct themselves inappropriately and according to Yahweh's estimation, deserve judgment. Moses is commissioned to bring justice.

31.1–6—Carrying out Yahweh's Sentence

As instructed, Moses prepares to carry out the Lord's instructions concerning the Midianites who bring great harm to Israel. Rather than vengeance, the term implies a 'vindication' (נקם) for harm done, and although the judgments are severe, they are the consequences for the people's wrong behaviour.[35] To bring

---

32 Gray, *Numbers*, p. 418.
33 Milgrom, *Numbers*, p. 491; cf. Excursus 67 and 68, pp. 490–492.
34 Cf. Milgrom, *Numbers*, p. 490.
35 The term occurs about 36 times in verbal forms indicating the idea of avenging the innocent from wrongs perpetrated against them. In this passage it is Yahweh who directs the avenging procedure by armed men because of the Midianite's role in causing Israel to desecrate the covenant stipulations. Cf. E. Lipiński, 'נקם', *TDOT*, X, pp. 1–9.

about the punishing sentences, Moses instructs the people to assemble men for a military campaign.

They are to prepare for a battle which will not only teach the Midianites a lesson but will punish them. Israel assembles twelve divisions of men representing all twelve tribes in equal numbers amounting to a total of 12,000. They are prepared to enter battle (מלחמה) with Phinehas son of Eleazar, representing the priesthood.[36] His presence is notable for his actions taken in Num. 25.7-13. There he intervenes to bring an end to the seduction of the Israelites by the Midian women. He takes with him some sacred utensils, which are not specified, as well as the trumpets for signaling. Use of the trumpets includes the signal for battle which also signifies a call for divine intervention: 'When you go into battle in your own land against an enemy who is oppressing you, sound a blast on the trumpets. Then you will be remembered by the Lord your God and rescued from your enemies' (Num. 10.9). His presence with the military men provides courage and confidence in the heat of the battle, but the main function is probably to deliver guidance as needed. The frequent references to the battle in this chapter signal a new reality for Israel going forward. In order to take possession of their inheritance, they will have to fight for it.

31.7-12—Death and Plunder

The initial results of the campaign indicate a resounding defeat of the Midianites, with all the men in that battle killed. Some of the prominent victims are named and included Evi, Rekem, Zur (the father of Kozbi; cf. Num. 25.15), Hur and Reba—the five kings of Midian. An additional but notable victim is Balaam son of Beor, who is killed with the sword. His presence with the Midianites indicates some kind of affiliation with them, possibly as a functionary to bring direction or even curses upon the invaders.

Additionally, the Israelites capture the Midianite women and children along with all the Midianite herds, flocks and goods as plunder. In their wake they leave a trail of destruction by burning the Midianite towns and settlements to the ground. Finally, with the spoils of the battle in their possession, the 12,000 men return to the Israelite encampment on the plains of Moab, by the Jordan across from Jericho. Believing that they accomplish all that is required of them, they present the plunder and captives to Moses and Eleazar the priest and the Israelite community.

---

36   Of the 13 times that 'battle' (מלחמה) is mentioned in Numbers it occurs 8 times in ch. 31 (Num. 31.4, 5, 6, 14, 21, 27, 28, 36). It is also used in the war with the King of Og in the battle of Edrei (Num. 21.33).

31.13–18—Breach of Instruction and Punishment

The reception of the military occurs outside of the camp due to the defilement caused in battle. The men probably did not anticipate the anger of Moses due to the victory that is in hand. The main reason for his wrath is the captive women whom Moses alleges are the ones who enticed the Israelites to be unfaithful. They are guilty of leading Israel into the episode of apostacy at Baal-Peor. Moses also implicates Balaam for being the one who instigates the whole plot which leads to the serious plague outbreak that kills 24,000 Israelites (Num. 25.9). The judgment to follow is harsh as Moses demands the killing of all the boys, and all the non-virgin women. Other girls are to be spared.

Typically, this kind of judgment would come under the 'ban' or law of destruction which would be made before the battle (cf. Num. 21.2–3). In this case the harsh judgments seem to be due to the nature of the apostasy and the dangerous precedent it sets in Israel's relationships with the inhabitants. Covenantal requirements are to be maintained in order for the community to be blessed and sanctified for the Lord's purposes. The Israelites are warned against the adoption of religious ideas and practices which go against the covenant, sanctuary and commands of Yahweh. This may even include instructions against inter-marriage (cf. Deut. 7.2–6; 20.10–18), and specifically against the teachings and cultic practices of foreign cultures.[37]

31.19–24—Ceremonial Cleansing

The returning army with captives and plunder are considered defiled and must undergo the purification rites (cf. Numbers 19). This includes segregation for seven days followed by the cleansing rituals. People are purified through the administration of the cleansing water on the third and seventh day of the week of isolation. To be effective, the 'cleansing water' must be the specially prepared solution which includes the ash of the red heifer, cedar wood, hyssop and scarlet wood (Num. 19.5–6). All materials, including clothing and every product made with leather, goat hair, and wood, are purified by the appropriate washing rituals. These strict measures are set in place before any of the people, animals and products may be permitted inside of the camp.

---

37 This is the main intention of the law of the 'ban' (חרם) and threat of religious contamination:

> However, in the cities of the nations the Lord your God is giving you as an inheritance, do not leave alive anything that breathes. Completely destroy them—the Hittites, Amorites, Canaanites, Perizzites, Hivites and Jebusites—as the Lord your God has commanded you. Otherwise, they will teach you to follow all the detestable things they do in worshiping their gods, and you will sin against the Lord your God. (Deut. 20.16–18)

Additional procedures are required for the purification of any metal products that are taken in the plunder, which would include the enemies' weapons. All metal materials including those that can withstand heat without melting must be purified with fire (gold, silver, bronze, iron, tin, lead, etc.). Moreover, the metals must be sprinkled with the cleansing water to finalize the process. Weaker metals are just washed in water. All these rituals are performed by the seventh day of segregation which then provides the way back into the camp and community life.

31.25–47—*Allocating the Plunder*

The allotment of the plunder is superintended and directed by the Lord. Moses and Eleazar with community heads are to take an inventory of all the people and creatures that are captured so that an equitable distribution could be made. Specific instructions are given for the allocation of goods for the soldiers as well as the community members. Additionally, a portion of the soldier's rewards are to be donated as a tribute for Yahweh and given to Eleazar (including people, cattle, donkeys, and sheep). From the community member's allocation, a portion of their rewards are donated to the Levites for their work in caring for the Tabernacle (considered a tribute, gift, or levy).

The amount of goods that are taken from the Midianites is staggering. An accounting of the plunder remaining from the spoils that the soldiers took includes 675,000 sheep, 72,000 cattle, 61,000 donkeys and 32,000 women who have never slept with a man. In tabulating the half share of the soldier's goods, the remaining products include 337,500 sheep (with 675 as the Lord's tribute), 36,000 cattle (with 72 as tribute), 30,500 donkeys (with 61 as tribute), and 16,000 people (with a tribute of 32). All of these tributes are presented to Eleazar the priest. The amounts given to community members total 337,500 sheep, 36,000 cattle, 30,500 donkeys, and 16,000 people. The tribute given to the Levites includes one out of every fifty people and animals. With the stunning amount of plunder taken by the Israelites, it presents another source of supplies that are needed for the daily regimen of sacrifice.

31.48–54—*Impressive Results*

When the battle is over and the spoils of war are assessed, the military leaders also tabulate the numbers of the remaining army. The amazing realization is that no soldiers are missing in the ranks! As an indication of gratitude, the leaders make an 'offering' (קרבן) of many valuable gold metal ornaments (armlets, bracelets, signet rings, earrings, and necklaces). In their estimation, the offerings are to serve as an 'expiation or atonement' (כפר). The motivation and purpose of the offering for 'atonement' is not clear. It could be done to cover for the counting of the soldiers (cf. Exod. 30.12), or for taking plunder from dead corpses.[38] However, the magnitude of their donations indicates an honourable desire to cover any action of wrongdoing on their part. The total weight of the metal amounts to approximately 600 pounds (16,750 shekels).

Judging from the acceptance of the gold spoils of war by Moses and Eleazar the priest, the soldier's gifts are viewed as admirable and acceptable to cover any transgressions. The fact that the gold is brought into the Tent of Meeting as a 'memorial or reminder' (זכרון) of the battle, indicates the importance of the event. Typically, such metal ornaments would be melted down to be crafted into appropriate vessels for use—especially if they are used in the sanctuary. In this case, Milgrom claims that 'Moses and Eleazar convert the gold into vessels for the sanctuary as a permanent reminder to the Lord on behalf of Israel'.[39]

32.1–42—Land Allocations

With a few victories behind them the Israelites begin to build their confidence in the attainment of their own property. The content of Numbers 32 is focused on the Transjordanian lands that are taken by Israel according to Num. 21.21–35 (cf. Deut. 3.3–7).[40] Battles are won against the Amorite King Sihon and Og, the King of Bashan. Interestingly, the land on the eastern side of the Jordan is not part of the promised land domain.[41] However, it is the obstinance of the kings and their refusal to allow Israel safe passage through the territory, that brings about the battle leading to an amazing victory (cf. Deut. 2.24–37). This victory provides the new generation with a renewed assurance that Yahweh is fighting for the nation. His promises of land inheritance are true and could soon be realized.

---

38 Cf. Milgrom, *Numbers*, p. 264–265; and Excursus 68, pp. 491–492.
39 Cf. Milgrom, *Numbers*, p. 264.
40 Some commentators prefer to refer to the land on the western side of the Jordan as 'Cisjordan'—literally the Latin term for the land on the other side of the river.
41 Although the Transjordanian land is good for grazing cattle, it technically is outside of the 'promised land' which is specially designated for Israel. It is usually described with amazing characteristics. 'As Yahweh's inheritance, the land has exuberant epithets. It is the good land (Exod. 3.8; Num. 14.7; Deut. 1.25) an expression that combines fruitfulness, wealth, beauty,—in short, the fulness of blessing'; (cf. Ottosson, 'ארץ', p. 403). It has paradisiacal characteristics as the abundantly blessed, glorious land, flowing with milk and honey (Num. 13.27; Deut. 6.3; 11.9).

32.1-5—A Special Request from the Reubenites and Gadites

With enemies vanquished, Israel has considerable time to enjoy camping in the Transjordan regions. They are able to see for themselves the productivity of the land and its adequate resources of water, agriculture, produce and pasture lands. Apparently, all kinds of fruit orchards, vineyards, and grazing lands are available. It is not surprising then, that some of the people begin to picture what life could be like in the regions of Jazer and Gilead—the areas which are north and south of the Jabbok river. However, the request remains unique in that it falls outside of the territory considered the promised land. In reference to Canaan (cf. Num. 32.30-32), there is special theological significance implied but the area is not always clearly defined. Its greatest extent is referred to in the expression 'from the river of Egypt to the Euphrates' but most often in the general sense of 'the land of the Canaanites' (Num. 34.2). Nevertheless, the theological truth that all the land belongs to Yahweh and is his 'heritage' to give, is confirmed. He owns it, rules over it, and allocates it according to his determination.

The Reubenites and Gadites, take the initiative to approach Moses, Eleazar and community leaders to make a request. Major decisions such as land allocations are subject to the judgment of tribal representatives and also the priest Eleazar who holds the Urim for decision making (typically in contexts of battle and land allocations; cf. Num. 27.21).[42] Also notable in this chapter is that the references to Reuben and Gad in the first verse are inverted to place Gad first. This occurs seven times in the chapter which has several septenary references (cf. Num. 32.2-37).

These two tribes possess large herds and flocks and need substantial grazing land for the animals—land which they are presently enjoying. Their pitch to the leaders sounds diplomatic and has a theological element to it. They contend that the Lord subdued that land and therefore it should be available for their use. In part this is true because Yahweh as warrior is typically involved in Israel's victories in a variety of ways (cf. Exodus 15; Deut. 2.24-25). But their request is extravagant in asking for several towns to be distributed to them. They ask for Ataroth, Dibon, Jazer, Nimrah, Heshbon, Elealeh, Sebam, Nebo, and Beon. Their appeal is well thought out and concludes with a diplomatic note: 'If we have found favor in your eyes', they said, 'let this land be given to

---

42 Although Reuben lost his right of primogeniture, it appears that he wants to take the 'first portion' (Num. 32.1-5). The leaders act as referees. 'Although economic considerations led to division of the land on the basis of the number of people in each tribe (Num. 26.53-56; 33.54), it was ultimately done by lot which determined the נחל of each individual tribe'. Cf. Lipiński, 'נחל', p. 324.

your servants as our possession. Do not make us cross the Jordan'. The appeal to not 'cross' (עבר) the Jordan, is reiterated seven times for emphasis, as is the appeal to hold the land as their 'possession' (אחזה) (cf. Num. 32.5–32).[43] The purpose of these septenary repetitions is to feature elements in the carefully laid out literary structure. These elements highlight the major implications for Israel regarding the land allocations that will be made in Canaan. With the Gadites and Reubenites remaining in the Transjordan, more land will be available to the other tribes, in accordance with the covenantal disbursements.

32.6-15—*Moses Fears Another Reversion*

As the primary leader, Moses responds to the request in a rather harsh way which interrupts their presentation. His questions imply that he jumps to conclusions that may not be warranted. His assumption is that they do not want to participate in the necessary battles that are to be organized for the conquest of Canaan. He assumes that their request to remain in the Transjordan will discourage the other tribes to move forward in their quest to the promised land. He alleges that their actions are comparable to the first generation of spies who also disheartened the people from entering the land. Moses compares the negotiation of the Gadites and the Reubenites with the Israelite rebellion at Kadesh Barnea. He indicates his fear that their appeal may bring about another devastating judgment as experienced by the generation of the exodus. He reminds them of the Lord's response of anger and the resolution that they will not receive their inheritance. The key issues in that episode are the lack of a wholehearted commitment to the Lord's provision of land and the deficiency in trust for Yahweh to bring them into the promised land. It is that very bleak event that causes the Lord to declare his judgments which Moses repeats to reinforce his prophetic warning: 'The LORD's anger burned against Israel and he made them wander in the wilderness forty years, until the whole generation of those who had done evil in his sight was gone' (Num. 32.13). However, Moses

---

43   Milgrom observes that five key terms bind the focalization of the chapter together with important motifs and septenary emphases. The first one concerns the order of names for Gad and Reuben. Gad is mentioned first seven times (Num. 32.2, 6, 25, 29, 31, 33, 34–37). The second concerns the possession of property as 'hold or share' (אחזה; Num. 32.5, 8, 19, 22, 29, 32). Thirdly, the references to crossing over (עבר) the Jordan (Num. 32.5, 7, 21, 27, 29, 30, 32). Fourthly, their request to be selected or be picked as 'shock troops' (חלץ) who are prepared for 'battle' (מלחמה; Num. 32.17, 20, 21, 27, 29, 30, 32). And finally, to be considered 'before the LORD' (לפני יהוה; Num. 32.20, 32, 33 [twice], 27, 29, 32). Cf. Milgrom, *Numbers*, p. 492.

also reminds them of the two spies who did follow the Lord wholeheartedly and who consequently live to see and dwell in the land of promise—Caleb and Joshua.

Finally, Moses launches into what he really thinks! They are a 'brood of sinners', implying that they are just like their rebellious fathers. He warns them that if they continue with their plans, the anger of the Lord will be even greater than at the Kadesh-Barnea episode. In fact, he reasons that the Lord may sentence them to another round in the wilderness which could lead them to destruction.

32.16–27—Negotiations

Diplomatically, the Reubenites and Gadites patiently wait for Moses' allegations and warnings to subside before beginning their carefully considered proposals. They admit that they definitely would like to build their cities and homes for family and animals in the Transjordanian regions. However, they insist that they will not shirk their responsibilities among the Israelites. They will indeed arm themselves for the 'battles' (מלחמה; cf. Num. 32.17, 20, 27, 29) which lie ahead. In fact, they will take the front lines in the wars to come and escort their fellow tribesmen to the places that Yahweh is preparing for them. In this role they pledge to serve as the 'shock troops' (חלץ; referenced seven times in Num. 32.17–32), prepared and ready for battle. While they are away with Israel's armies, their families will be tucked away in fortified cities for protection from enemies.

Finally, they make some far-reaching commitments. They will not return to rest in their new homes until all of the Israelites are in possession of their 'inheritance' (נחלה; Num. 32.18, 19)—their allocated 'properties' (אחזה; cf. Num. 32. 5, 8, 19, 22, 29, 32 [twice]). Furthermore, they are willing to give up any properties to which they are entitled to with the Israelites in the promised land west of the Jordan river. They will instead be satisfied with homes and life on the east side of the Jordan.

With these magnanimous assurances and commitments, Moses has a change of heart. Realizing the implications of the situation and with clearer comprehension, he presents some terms for an agreement. If the two tribes will arm themselves for the battles to come and march with the Israelites across the Jordan to the land they must conquer, then an arrangement may be considered. However, their obligations will not be finalized until all the enemies of Yahweh are driven out of their habitations. When all the land is subdued and the Israelites have their own settlements, then they will be released to return to the Transjordan towns and their homes. At that time, these properties will be considered their inheritance before the Lord.

The terms of the agreement, however, are conditional. If they follow through with the stated arrangements, all will be well; and blessings will be realized. If they fail in their commitments, however, then Moses' initial allegation that they are a brood of sinners would be proven! Failure of compliance with the promises will amount to sin against the Lord with consequences. With these conditions made clear, Moses instructs them to go ahead with their plans to build cities for their families and pens for their livestock. He also leaves them with the warning to honour their spoken words.

Based on these terms, the Gadites and Reubenites reiterate their commitments and affirm their desire to be servants. They will honour Moses' directives. Their families will remain in secure settlements in Gilead while all the men fit for battle will cross over the Jordan together with the Israelite armies to fight for the promised land 'before the Lord' (לפני יהוה). This final septenary reference 'before the Lord', affirms their dependence on Yahweh as the one who will lead in the battles ahead (cf. Num. 32.20, 32, 33 [twice], 27, 29, 32). With this affirmation they are basically agreeing to be in the vanguard of the army when it is deployed for the conquest.[44]

32.28-32—*Finalizing the Appeal*

Due to Moses' initial response to the Gadites and Reubenite proposition, he is now prepared to endorse the proposal before the leaders. In fact, he gives orders about them to Eleazar the priest, to Joshua son of Nun, and to the family heads of the Israelite tribes, indicating that if they follow through with their commitments, they will be rewarded. Gilead must become their inheritance. This public notification confirms the resolution, leaving the responsibility for compliance with the two tribes. It also registers the decision with the leaders for the land allocations to be made after the conquest.

In turn, the Gadites and Reubenites confirm that their promises will be honoured. They will serve as 'shock-troops' (חלץ; armed for battle) when the nation enters Canaan. For this service, they anticipate receiving their 'inherited property' (אחזה) on the east side of the Jordan (cf. Num. 32. 5, 8, 19, 22, 29, 32, twice).

32.33-38—*Land Inheritance in the Transjordan*

Based on the negotiated agreement, Moses makes several preliminary land allocations. In fact, he gives more towns for the tribes to rebuild and inhabit than they initially ask for. Furthermore, he includes the half-tribe of Manasseh son

---

44   Cf. Milgrom, *Numbers*, p. 271.

of Joseph in the allotments. Firstly, the Gadites and the Reubenites are assigned the former lands of the kingdom of Sihon king of the Amorites and the kingdom of Og king of Bashan—the whole land with its cities and the territory around them. With the approvals given based on the conditions, the tribes begin to develop the Transjordan regions as follows:

> The Gadites built up Dibon, Ataroth, Aroer, Atroth Shophan, Jazer, Jogbehah, Beth Nimrah and Beth Haran as fortified cities, and built pens for their flocks. And the Reubenites rebuilt Heshbon, Elealeh and Kiriathaim, as well as Nebo and Baal Meon (these names were changed) and Sibmah. They gave names to the cities they rebuilt. (Num. 32.34–38)

This summation provides a positive and encouraging perspective on the inheritance of property and the tenacity of the people in rebuilding, occupying, and settling into their new habitations.

The whole issue with land assignment in the Transjordan does cause considerable discussion among commentators. Levine analyses the materials in Numbers 21 and 32 concerning the legitimacy of the Transjordanian Israelite communities, asserting in part, 'It is conceived as a special dispensation to the tribes involved, who were really supposed to cross the Jordan and settle in Canaan proper, but were excused from doing so by Moses under the terms of a negotiation granting them territories in Transjordan'.[45] This episode presents Moses with considerable power to make decisions that fall outside of the original plan for land allocation. It also indicates that the idea for settlement in the Transjordan comes from the tribes rather than the initial divine plan for Canaan. Milgrom presents the implications for this in a unique way: 'The nine and one-half remaining tribes will receive their land by lot (33.54), whereas the Transjordanian tribes have their land "assigned", that is by Moses, not by God. God as it were, will have nothing to do with the settling of Transjordan.'[46] However, Moses appears to make the best of a difficult situation by allowing the assignment for Reuben, Gad and Manasseh.

---

45 Levine, *Numbers 21–36*, p. 494; cf. pp. 477–494. Levine, p. 478, views Numbers 32 as performing a pivotal literary function in that,
> It carries forward the historiographic chain that began in Numbers 21, by focusing on an issue prominent in the writings of the Deuteronomist (Deuteronomy 3), namely, the legitimacy of the Transjordanian tribes of Reuben, Gad and half tribe of Manasseh. Concern with such legitimacy remains a prominent theme in the Book of Joshua.

46 Milgrom, *Numbers*, p. 274 and pp. 494–496.

32.39-42—Manasseh

The reference to descendants of Manasseh and their inclusion in the Transjordan region is obscure.[47] The note inserted here seems out of place, however, as a descendant of Joseph the Manassehites have strong tribal representation. From the first census of 32,200 men to the second census of 52,700 their growth is substantial (cf. Num. 26.29-33). The intention of the notice serves to explain how half of the Manasseh tribe ends up settling in the Transjordan while the rest of the tribe decides to settle in Canaan with the other Israelite tribes.

The inclusion appears to be made due to the military prowess of the Makirites who drive the Amorites out of Gilead. Based on this initiative Moses makes a similar allocation as he does for the other two tribes and permits the descendants of Manasseh to settle there. Other descendants also capture settlements and rename them after themselves. Jair's towns become Havvoth Jair, and Nobah, who captures Kenath calls it Nobah after himself.

---

47   Later records show that the Makirites were settled in Canaan (Josh. 17.14-18).

33.1–56—A Synopsis of the Wilderness Expedition

Throughout the book of Numbers, locations and places are documented where important events occur in Israel's epic journey. Some of these toponyms are now brought together with additional details to register the account of key places where Israel camps. Although the main purpose of the synopsis is to catalogue the route of Israel's trek and encampments, a number of historical events are also alluded to from the Exodus account.[1] The itinerary begins with Israel's departure from Rameses, Egypt and ends with the nation's arrival in the plains of Moab. Although the itinerary synopsis is structured in three sections, the forty-year journey is mainly focused on the first two years after the Exodus event (Num. 1–10.11) and on the last year where the nation prepares to enter Canaan (Numbers 21–36). This focalization indicates that the preparations for the trek to Canaan are paramount. However, the journey is thwarted by the rebellious incidents that occur which leads to the meandering in the wilderness until the new generation is poised for entry into the promised land.

The Pentateuch records include information about certain routes that are used by people and the writers did their best to record the names which were known at the time of the wilderness journeys. Although there are significant variations in the names of itinerary places recorded in Numbers 21, 33 and in Deuteronomy 1–3, it is the writer's purview to record the names as known and to omit other names for whatever reason. According to the itinerary the journey takes them along routes or roads that are eventually named and run south to north along the Jordan. This includes the 'Way of the Wilderness of Edom', the route through the 'Wilderness of Moab' and also, the 'King's Highway'.

The itinerary shows the faithfulness of Yahweh in leading Israel out of Egypt towards the land of promise. It catalogues the extensive forty-year period of time through which they marched in the wilderness. The record verifies the judgment of God on the nation for their disobedience and failures. Moreover, it registers the reliability of Yahweh in leading, providing, protecting, and preparing Israel for the entry and acquisition of the promised land.

---

[1] Challenges arise when comparing other notices of the journey which may indicate variations in place names. Instances which appear to be discrepancies are evident in Exod. 12.37; 13.20; 17.1; 19.2; Num. 10.12; 21.10–11; 22.1. Moreover, some of the information in Exod. 13.17–18; 15.22, 27; 16.1; 19.1–2; Num. 10.33; 20.1,22; 21.4, 33, along with notes on the Transjordan sites add to the complexity.

Due to the complexity of the Pentateuchal records, commentators have chosen to refer to Numbers 33 as a composite of references that are gleaned from different traditions and documents. Levine, and others indicate that the primary source is Priestly and for the most part follows the Exodus tradition.[2] However, commentators also acknowledge the influence of other traditions and the Deuteronomist in the final compilation which explains why different routes appear to be evident (cf. Deuteronomy 1–3; Judges 11). While some of the observations made offer insightful readings in the passages noted above, the overall assumptions do not explain why names in lists are different or missing. Milgrom asserts that 'it is more logical to assume that since so many names in Numbers 33 are unattested anywhere else, it represents the master list for the other sources'.[3] It is a unified authentic itinerary in a style comparable to other ancient Near Eastern military itineraries which record military exploits. Therefore, the assumption that the itinerary is a legitimate reflective summary of the forty-year wilderness trek, is in order. Some comments on variations will be noted below.

33.1–2—Moses' Records

The record of Israel's pilgrimage from Egypt to the plains of Moab is catalogued for the nation. The primary leaders for the epic journey are Moses and Aaron. It is Moses who is instructed to 'record' (כתב) the stages of the trek. This is one of the clear instances verifying Moses' writing ability (cf. Exod. 24.4). It is more than probable that records are kept during the wilderness excursion which become a source of the details chronicled in this travel log. While Moses is the capable and initial recorder of the itinerary, additional notes are added in due course to finalize the list.

The phases of the journey are presented in three main sections and make reference to a total of forty-two places. The first segment begins with Rameses (cf. Gen. 47.11; Exod. 1.11; 12.37) and ends in the wilderness of Sinai (Num. 33.5–15).

---

2 Levine, *Numbers 21–36*, p. 511. He goes on to summarize that
   The difference between the JE and the priestly historiographers, except for the authors and compilers of Numbers 33, is that the priestly authors had the Israelites migrate in Sinai for thirty-eight years before arriving at Kadesh. From that point on, however the priestly route also had the Israelites circumvent Edom and Moab. In contrast, Numbers 33 has the Israelites marching to the Gulf of Elath before repairing to Kadesh, and it then charts their continuing route northward through Edom and Moab via Dibon-Gad, north of the Arnon, to the Plains of Moab (Num. 33.40–49).

3 Milgrom, *Numbers*, p. 497.

The second phase takes them from the wilderness of Sinai to the wilderness of Zin at Kadesh (Num. 33.16–36). The third segment brings them to the plains of Moab along the Jordan, across from Jericho (Num. 33.37–49). According to the first verse the Israelites walked 'troop by troop' signifying a military formation in a disciplined procession (cf. Num. 1.3; 10.14–28).[4]

33.3–15—Departing Egypt

The epic journey by faith finally begins after the confrontational struggle of Moses with Pharaoh. The Israelites depart from Rameses on the fifteenth day of the first month, the day after they celebrated the Passover (cf. Exod. 12.1–16). The Exodus record claims that Israel leaves Egypt and 'marched out defiantly in full view of all the Egyptians, who were burying all their firstborn, whom the LORD had struck down among them; for the LORD had brought judgment on their gods'. In Exod. 12.36 the Egyptians also give the departing people gifts and plunder as they exit the land of oppression. Furthermore, the confrontation between Moses and Pharaoh may be the visible battle, but in reality, it is the Lord who brings judgment on Egypt and on their false gods. The first three places mentioned in the list are located in Egypt (Num. 33.5-7), and once they pass through the sea they enter the wilderness of Sinai.

Israel's first stop is 'Sukkoth' (סכות) and then onward to Etham, on the edge of the desert. In Exod. 13.20-22, the text provides further detail in showing how Yahweh is guiding the nation on their journey: 'After leaving Sukkoth they camped at Etham on the edge of the desert. By day the LORD went ahead of them in a pillar of cloud to guide them on their way and by night in a pillar of fire to give them light, so that they could travel by day or night. Neither the pillar of cloud by day nor the pillar of fire by night left its place in front of the people'. The name of the place characterizes the type of 'booths' for lodging they use in their encampments.

After leaving Etham, their trek takes them in a southern direction toward Pi Hahiroth, to the east of Baal Zephon, where they camp near Migdol. According to Exodus 14, it is at this location that the Pharaoh is once again determined to pursue and stop the Israelite exodus. The itinerary continues without any explication on the great deliverance other than the fact they leave Pi Hahiroth and pass through the sea into the desert. Milgrom notes that the detail regarding the next three-day excursion in the Desert of Etham, which brings them to

---

4 Milgrom, *Numbers*, p. 277.

Marah (Bitter Spring), is the only reference to time travelled. He indicates that it may underline the pledge that Israel makes to Pharaoh to only take a three-day trip for worship (cf. Exod. 3.18; 15.22–23).[5]

After Marah they stop at Elim where they are fortified with water and food. The oasis has twelve springs and seventy palm trees, where they camp. Continuing southward after Elim they camp by the Red Sea and then proceed to the Desert of Sin. According to Exodus 16, a crisis arises between Elim and Sinai due to the lack of food supply. The timing of the incident is noted as the fifteenth day of the second month after they had come out of Egypt. There, Yahweh provides 'bread from heaven' as well as quail.

Another crisis develops as they continue from the Desert of Sin and camp at Dophkah, then Alush, and finally at Rephidim, where there is insufficient water for the people to drink. After Rephidim, they finally camp in the Desert of Sinai. Keeping true to the intention of mainly cataloguing the place names, the incidents of Exodus 17 are not mentioned here. The lack of water instigates another instance of grumbling among the people who mourn the departure from Egypt which brings the wilderness trials upon them. It is at the rock of Horeb that Moses strikes the rock, which provides water and which is renamed Massah and Meribah to commemorate the incident of testing and quarrelling before Yahweh (Exod. 17.7).

The actual location of Mount Sinai is disputed on several grounds, with commentators speculating that it is anywhere from the middle of the peninsula (called Jebel Sin Bisher) to the southernmost region (called Jebel Musa).[6] According to Exod. 3.18, the intended destination is a three-day journey from Egypt and eleven days from Kadesh-Barnea (cf. Deut. 1.2). A more detailed comment is made in Exod. 19.1-2: 'On the first day of the third month after the Israelites left Egypt—on that very day—they came to the Desert of Sinai. After they set out from Rephidim, they entered the Desert of Sinai, and Israel camped there in the desert in front of the mountain'. A primary reason for the Jebel Sin Bisher location is that it can be reached in the period of time indicated in Exodus. The most southern location would take more than three days to reach but is also an eleven-day march to reach Kadesh.[7] It is probable that Israel is encamped in this location for about eleven months.

---

[5] Milgrom, *Numbers*, p. 279.
[6] Mount Sinai, also referred to as Mount Horeb (Exod. 3.2; Deut. 1.2; 1 Kgs 8.9; Mal. 4.4; etc.), continues to be a difficult place to locate with accuracy. This is a characteristic of some biblical places perhaps due to the human propensity to make shrines and turn holy places into sites of pilgrimage or veneration.
[7] Milgrom, *Numbers*, p. 281. Also, cf. Allen, *Numbers*, pp. 986–988.

33.16–36—Sites of Wandering

In this segment there are several places which are not mentioned in other records and due to the antiquity of the places and locations in the wilderness, the actual sites cannot be located on a map (verse 18 to 29 toponyms are not listed in other locations). However, this section marks an important phase of wandering in the wilderness of Sinai and eventually ends up in Kadesh. According to Deut. 1.19 this is a particularly difficult wilderness terrain with few resources. Historically this trek begins in conflict and will end in an even more severe conflict at Kadesh.

The nation leaves the Desert of Sinai and camps at Kibroth Hattaavah. According to Num. 11.34–35, this is the place of conflict where people desire meat and are severely punished for their recalcitrance. It is also from Kadesh where the 12 spies enter Canaan and then return to decry instructions for a military incursion back into the land. The itinerary presents these places which are assumed to be in the wilderness of Sinai, recorded with this stylistic repetition.

> They left Kibroth Hattaavah and camped at Hazeroth.
> They left Hazeroth and camped at Rithmah.
> They left Rithmah and camped at Rimmon Perez.
> They left Rimmon Perez and camped at Libnah.
> They left Libnah and camped at Rissah.
> They left Rissah and camped at Kehelathah.
> They left Kehelathah and camped at Mount Shepher.
> They left Mount Shepher and camped at Haradah.
> They left Haradah and camped at Makheloth.
> They left Makheloth and camped at Tahath.
> They left Tahath and camped at Terah.
> They left Terah and camped at Mithkah.
> They left Mithkah and camped at Hashmonah.
> They left Hashmonah and camped at Moseroth.
> They left Moseroth and camped at Bene Jaakan.
> They left Bene Jaakan and camped at Hor Haggidgad.
> They left Hor Haggidgad and camped at Jotbathah.
> They left Jotbathah and camped at Abronah.
> They left Abronah and camped at Ezion Geber.
> They left Ezion Geber and camped at Kadesh, in the Desert of Zin.

These are the purported, some-what mysterious, locations through which Israel journeys until they come to the more familiar territory of Kadesh where the incident with the twelve spies occurs (cf. Num. 13.26). 'Kadesh' (קדש) is literally the 'sanctuary or holy place' (cf. Num. 13.21; 20.1; 27.14; 34.3) where many watershed events happen for Israel. Miriam died at Kadesh (Num. 20.1). It is the venue where the spies lead the nation in their refusal to enter the promised land. It is probably the central location where much of their 38 years in the wilderness is spent (cf. Deut. 2.14).[8]

33.37–49—From Mount Hor to the Abarim Mountains

From the Desert of Zin, the journey continues from Kadesh until they arrive at Mount Hor. Israel sets up camp at this location on the edge of Edom. During this section of travel through various sites, a number of historical events occur. It is probable that former place names changed or are referred to with more than one toponym, making some locations obscure. The first event concerns the death of Aaron which is described in Num. 20.22–29 and briefly referenced here in 33.38. It is at Mount Hor where the Lord informs Moses of Aaron's impending death. Aaron will 'be gathered to his people' and will not live to see the land promised to the Israelites. It is here that the succession of the priesthood is also conferred to Aaron's son Eleazar. When Moses and Eleazar come down from the mountain without Aaron, the community mourns his demise for thirty days.

Numbers 20 and 33 are in agreement that Aaron dies on Mount Hor. However, Deut. 10.6–7 claims it is at Moserah (cf. Num. 33.30).[9] The timing of Aaron's death is noted along with the additional note in Num. 33.37–39 concerning the age of Aaron at his death:

> They left Kadesh and camped at Mount Hor, on the border of Edom. At the LORD's command Aaron the priest went up Mount Hor, where he died on the first day of the fifth month of the fortieth year after the Israelites came out of Egypt. Aaron was a hundred and twenty-three years old when he died on Mount Hor. (cf. Exod. 7.7)

---

8 Allen, *Numbers*, p. 988. Although Kadesh is mentioned often as a very important base for Israel, the general location of the site is difficult to verify. Cf. Milgrom, *Numbers*, p. 281.

9 It is possible that Moserah/Moseroth may be an alternate name for Mount Hor (cf. Ashley, *Numbers*, p. 630).

The second event noted here refers to the events reported in Numbers 21.[10] However, the brief itinerary citation: 'The Canaanite king of Arad, who lived in the Negev of Canaan, heard that the Israelites were coming', omits the gravity of what happens:

> When the Canaanite king of Arad, who lived in the Negev, heard that Israel was coming along the road to Atharim, he attacked the Israelites and captured some of them. Then Israel made this vow to the LORD: 'If you will deliver these people into our hands, we will totally destroy their cities'. The LORD listened to Israel's plea and gave the Canaanites over to them. They completely destroyed them and their towns; so the place was named Hormah. (Num. 21.1–3)

'Hormah' (חרמה) signifies that it is devoted for destruction but the actual location of the place remains obscure. After this the nation marches from Mount Hor onwards through these places.

> They left Mount Hor and camped at Zalmonah.
> They left Zalmonah and camped at Punon.
> They left Punon and camped at Oboth.
> They left Oboth and camped at Iye Abarim, on the border of Moab.
> They left Iye Abarim and camped at Dibon Gad.
> They left Dibon Gad and camped at Almon Diblathaim.
> They left Almon Diblathaim and camped in the mountains of Abarim, near Nebo.

Finally, they left the mountains of Abarim and camped on the plains of Moab by the Jordan across from Jericho. There on the plains of Moab they camped along the Jordan from Beth Jeshimoth to Abel Shittim.

---

10 As noted in Numbers 20–21 there are other itinerary notices that are part of Israel's journey narrative. The prominent mention of Kadesh is notable in Num. 20.14 and 16 (cf. Deut. 1.46; Judg. 11.16–17). The narrative continues to register the main trek locations through the land of Edom (Num. 21.4), on the east of Moab (Num. 21.11), to the Zared Stream and Arnon River (Num. 21.12–13). Finally, the battle against Sihon the Amorite king leads to the war at Jahaz where Israel defeats him and takes the land from the Arnon to the Jabbok. The war with Sihon is situated within the context of a journey through the Transjordan, which is mentioned in several itineraries. This victory led to the capture of the Amorite cities including Heshbon and all its surrounding settlements.

This purported itinerary covers forty-years of life in the wilderness for the Israelites. The synopsis includes their departure from Egypt and assumes the death of a generation. The nation's attention is refocused on the promised inheritance of Yahweh. The 'inheritance' (נחלה; possession; property; share) of the promised land becomes the focal point for the new generation. It is mentioned 34 times in Numbers with most of the references (22) occurring after Chapter 26. This repetition elevates the anticipation which the nation is realizing as they are on the borders of the promised land. Furthermore, the list of places reminds the nation of their long and extensive journey.

> Each stopping place is a witness not only to the leadership of Moses (who is about to die; cf. Num. 27.12–23), but also to the mighty grace of God who led the people on, in spite of it all, toward the promised land. The motif of the 'journey of life' is a powerful one in the Bible, and it is helpful, at points throughout the journey, but especially toward its end, to look back and reflect.[11]

33.50–56—Poised for Conquest

Israel is finally positioned on the plains of Moab by the Jordan across from Jericho. Moses is once again commissioned to instruct the Israelites to prepare for a military strike. This agenda has been on the back burner for thirty-eight years after the promised land is explored by the twelve spies. Their surveillance of the land is to prepare them for possession of Canaan but their abdication of faith in Yahweh brings about judgment and delay. Fear of the intimidating inhabitants keeps them from their incursion at that time. Now Moses instructs a new generation with a similar reminder from Yahweh's instruction given in Num. 26.52–56:

> The LORD said to Moses, 'The land is to be allotted to them as an inheritance based on the number of names. To a larger group give a larger inheritance, and to a smaller group a smaller one; each is to receive its inheritance according to the number of those listed. Be sure that the land is distributed by lot. What each group inherits will be according to the names for its ancestral tribe. Each inheritance is to be distributed by lot among the larger and smaller groups.'

---

11 Ashley, *Numbers*, p. 627.

Due to the circumstances in Chapter 32, the instructions mainly pertain to nine tribal allotments. This situation brings about a change in how the allocations will be made. However, the main emphasis in these verses is the divine declaration of judgment on the inhabitants of Canaan—they are to be totally eradicated from the land. Although the inheritance lies before them, Israel is to be an instrument of judgment on the idolatrous inhabitants who have defiled the property of Yahweh. The instructions are clear with two distinctive elements. The first one is dispossession and the destruction of false religion: 'When you cross the Jordan into Canaan, drive out all the inhabitants of the land before you. Destroy all their carved images and their cast idols, and demolish all their high places'. The religious practices of the Canaanites are incompatible with the monotheistic beliefs of Israel and Yahwism. Covenantal requirements call for no other gods and no images nor high places.

The second is the ownership and allocation of the land: 'Take possession of the land and settle in it, for I have given you the land to possess. Distribute the land by lot, according to your clans. To a larger group give a larger inheritance, and to a smaller group a smaller one. Whatever falls to them by lot will be theirs. Distribute it according to your ancestral tribes'. Finally, the equitable inheritance of land is in view and each tribe can look forward to receiving a place to call home. The distribution of property will be according to lots as well as the size of tribal groups. However, failure to complete the task as instructed by Yahweh will have severe consequences. Just like the curse in Genesis 3 where thorns and thistles will impede the work of Adam, so too the inhabitants that remain will become very difficult to manage and will bring trouble on the land through their idolatry.

The consequences are spelled out in Yahweh's declaration to establish Israel's borders and remove the inhabitants that live there. Israel is warned not to make a covenant with the people nor to allow them to continue living among them due to their foreign worship practices (cf. Exod. 23.31–33). Further consequences are indicated in the conclusion of the chapter to elevate the exhortation: 'But if you do not drive out the inhabitants of the land, those you allow to remain will become barbs in your eyes and thorns in your sides. They will give you trouble in the land where you will live. And then I will do to you what I plan to do to them' (Num. 33.55–56). The implication is that the religious practices of the Canaanites will continue to be a threat to the covenantal requirements of Yahweh. This message is a recurrent one in the OT and the promises of the Lord for idolatry are rooted in the ultimate covenant curses as presented in Deut. 28.64–68. The threat of idolatrous practices is a reality for each generation and the events of Numbers 25 at Baal Peor illustrate the propensity to Baalism. Moses' final Deuteronomic exhortation highlights the danger of false worship practices and alliances:

You yourselves know how we lived in Egypt and how we passed through the countries on the way here. You saw among them their detestable images and idols of wood and stone, of silver and gold. Make sure there is no man or woman, clan or tribe among you today whose heart turns away from the LORD our God to go and worship the gods of those nations; make sure there is no root among you that produces such bitter poison. (Deut. 29.16–18)

34.1–36.13—Anticipation of the Promised Land

After cataloguing the places where Israel has sojourned, the narrative turns to a description of the covenantal property that Israel is to inherit. The promise of land is a vital component of the Abrahamic and Mosaic covenant (Gen. 12.1–3; 13.14–17; 15.7–21; Exodus 6). The assurance that Yahweh will bring Israel to their own place of rest is engrained in their national vision. The promise is both extensive and enduring. 'The whole land of Canaan, where you are now an alien, I will give as an everlasting possession to you and your descendants after you; and I will be their God' (Gen. 17.8). It is this vision that motivates the nation to keep moving forward even though many obstacles and seasons of despair emerge to quell their faith.[1] With the promised land before them and a journey of forty years behind them, the anticipation is palpable. Although forty years must have felt like a lifetime, it is only a fraction of history in comparison to the 400 years of time that Israel expended in Egypt!

The Israelites hang on to the oath sworn by Yahweh that someday they will inhabit their own land 'flowing with milk and honey'. The Lord affirms his promise to bring Israel into their inheritance of land with an oath: 'After the LORD brings you into the land of the Canaanites and gives it to you, as he promised on oath to you and your ancestors' (Exod. 13.11; 33.1; cf. Num. 11.12; 14.16, 23). Alternatively, those who rebelled against the Lord's instructions to enter the land will not see it (Num. 32.10–12; cf. Ps. 95.10–11). As God is faithful to bring judgment on a generation as promised, so too is he faithful to bring the people into the promised land and increase their numbers, as he swore on oath (Deut. 6.13–23; 8.1; 13.17; 19.8; 26.15).

For this reason, reminders and assurances from Yahweh are frequent in the Pentateuch. The realization of the land is integral to the nature of the divine name and the covenantal agreement: 'God also said to Moses, "I am the LORD. I appeared to Abraham, to Isaac and to Jacob as God Almighty, but by my name the LORD I did not make myself fully known to them. I also established my covenant with them to give them the land of Canaan, where they resided as foreigners"' (Exod. 6.2–4; cf. 6.8). Even though 400 years went by, the affirmation of land inheritance is a constant refrain in Yahweh's promises to Israel (as noted above). Even though the rebellion and conflicts with threatening inhabitants made the provision unlikely, the Lord keeps his promises to the nation.

---

1 Canaan as the 'promised land' is referred to 19 times in Numbers. It is typically described with excellent characteristics which include adequate resources of water and produce (cf. Exod. 3.8; Num. 13.37; 14.7; Deut. 1.25; 6.3; 11.9; cf. Ottosson, 'ארץ', p. 403).

34.1–15—The Covenantal Borders

Once again, the Lord instructs Moses to address the Israelites regarding their prospective entry into the land of Canaan. Israel is finally ready to encounter the vista of their new dwelling place. A fresh affirmation is given which is similar to previous verifications: 'When you enter the land to which I am taking you' (Num. 15.2). The instruction attests the divine intention to bring the Israelites 'home'—it is no longer 'if' they will enter the land but 'when'. Even so Israel is to consider themselves as a guest of Yahweh in the land which is sacred. The land occupied by the Canaanites will be allocated as an 'inheritance' (נחל) to Israel.

> Thus the gift of this (נחל) inheritance to Israel is represented as the fulfilment of the promise to the patriarchs (Exod. 32.13; Ps. 105.8–11; Ezek. 47.14; 1 Chron. 16.15–18); the extermination of the Canaanite population becomes the means whereby Yahweh has his people take possession of the נחל (Exod. 23.30; Deut. 4.38; 20.16; Pss. 47.4 ff.; 78.55; 135.10–12; 136.17–22).[2]

The assertion of Yahweh is now followed by the contours of the actual 'boundaries' (גבולה) of the gift of land.[3]

On the southern side, the border includes some of the Desert of Zin along the border of Edom. The southern boundary begins from the southern end of the Sea of 'Salt' (מלח; the Dead Sea), crosses over to the south of Scorpion Pass (ascent of Akrabbim), goes on to a portion of Zin and south to Kadesh Barnea (between the Negev and Sinai). This area is known for its copper mines. The property line goes on to Hazar Addar and over to Azmon. The Kadesh Barnea area on the western side is the 'richest and most centrally located springs of

---

2 Lipiński, 'נחל', p. 329. The inheritance of land is referred to 5 times in the chapter.
3 In reading this chapter with the toponyms as recorded, it becomes evident that some of the place names are not known and it is difficult to precisely locate them on maps. Additionally, further details on the stated borders are presented in Joshua 15. According to Milgrom the borders coincide with the boundaries of the Egyptian province of Canaan during the 15th to 13th centuries and may never have been fully occupied during Israel's occupation of the land (Milgrom, *Numbers*, p. 284; cf. Num. 13.21; Josh. 13.2–5). Furthermore, the Egyptian boundaries also ended at the Jordan as the eastern border of Egyptian Canaan (cf. Milgrom, *Numbers*, p. 501). Ultimately, the borders defined in Numbers 34 are realistic in comparison to other texts which make reference to the Euphrates and the Nile (cf. Gen. 15.18; Exod. 23.31; Deut. 1.7; 11.23; Josh. 1.4).

the southern edge of Negev and continued to the Mediterranean coast at the 'Brook of Egypt', the Wad-el-Arish that naturally divides Egypt from Palestine'.[4] The western boundary included the coast of the 'Great' (גדול) Sea (the Mediterranean Sea).

The northern boundary begins at the Mediterranean Sea to Mount Hor, then to Lebo Hamath, to Zedad, Ziphron and finally ends at Hazar Enan. This northern area is probably just past Byblos and bordered on the edge of the desert. The Mount Hor noted here is a northern location (one of the summits of Lebanon, north of Byblos) and different from the southern Mount where Aaron passed away (cf. Num. 20.22–29; 33.38).

The eastern boundary includes the border from Hazar Enan to Shepham, which continues down from Shepham to Riblah on the east side of Ain and goes along the slopes east of the Sea of Galilee. Some of the sites mentioned here are not known but the 'northeastern border passed the edge of the desert to include Bashan and at least part of Hauran, to descent southwest ward to the Sea of Galilee, the Yarmuk valley, and the Jordan'. From there the boundary goes down along the Jordan to end at the Dead Sea.[5]

These are the boundaries of the generous gift of land provided by Yahweh the landowner. It must be noted that the borders listed here are general geographic areas which are mentioned in a variety of texts but difficult to locate on contemporary maps. Commentators and historians continue to grapple with the geographic uncertainty, but the overall area of Canaan and the key locations of the promised land are for the most part reported.

These instructions for Moses are an update from Num. 26.52–56 since the Reubenites, Gadites and half of the Mannasehites are given their allocations in the Transjordan regions (cf. Numbers 32). According to the initial plan, the actual land allocations are to take into consideration the number of names in the census. Groups sizes are also a factor, and the final distribution is to be determined by 'lot' for each ancestral tribe (Num. 26.52–56).

---

4 Houston refers to Num. 34.1–12 as 'one of the most interesting geographical documents of the Bible' with its delineation of the boundaries for Israel. Cf. Houston, 'The Geographical Setting of the Bible', pp. 92–93.

5 Houston, 'The Geographical Setting of the Bible', pp. 93, goes on to note that 'This territory was never fully Israel's, however, for even in the time of David, the land of Canaan never passed north of Sidon, and included Gilead that was excluded in the conquest period. From other Egyptian evidence, however, it appears that this description of Israel fits accurately into the context of the thirteenth century B.C.'

34.16–29—Leaders for Land Allocations

The Lord instructs Moses to prepare for the equitable distribution of land to tribal representatives through appointed leaders. The occasion marks another memorable turn of events signifying the end of one generation and transition of leadership to the new generation. The older generation of the exodus are gone, and the new one is stepping forward to take over and show a fresh response to Yahweh's direction. Moses will soon depart from the scene as narrated in Numbers 27. Aaron is dead and Joshua will lead the nation with Eleazar the priest. Together they will be responsible for the conquest of Canaan and land disbursement.

Since land allocations were already made for the families of Reuben, Gad and the half-tribe of Manasseh (cf. Num. 32.14–15) on the east side of the Jordan, they are not included in the list of leaders involved in land allocation. Furthermore, the territories allocated to Israel do not include the land east of the Jordan where the Reubenites, Gadites and Manassehites were resident (cf. Numbers 32). This notice affirms the resolutions arrived at in the confrontational episode with Moses and results in larger tracts of land made available to the remaining tribes.

It is evident from the many lists and recorded names in Numbers, that Yahweh and Moses value individuals. They are more than just names. They are leaders who represent their people and are responsible for many lives. The importance of structure, leadership, and community involvement in land issues is apparent in the records kept for posterity. Additionally, land ownership is a powerful gift with many implications for community, prosperity and long-term inheritance.[6] Allocations must be made equitably and with divine participation through the lot (cf. Num. 26.52–56).

Yahweh selects the overseers for the task as Eleazar the priest and Joshua son of Nun. Several of the names are theophoric and describe a characteristic which the parents believe to be desirable.[7] Other leaders are appointed from each tribe to help with inheritance allocation, including.

> Caleb ('Dog') son of Jephunneh (perhaps 'He Makes Clear'), from the tribe of Judah;

---

6 Cf. Ottosson, 'ארץ', pp. 393–405.

7 The name meanings are suggested by Allen who notes that the interpretation is not always clear and perhaps speculative. Nevertheless, they do indicate a developing emphasis on the theophoric element that reflects growing trust in Elohim for their future. Cf. Allen, *Numbers*, pp. 997–998.

Shemuel ('His Name is God') son of Ammihud ('My Kinsman is Majesty'), from the tribe of Simeon;

Elidad ('God loves') son of Kislon ('Confidence'), from the tribe of Benjamin;

Bukki (perhaps 'Proven') son of Jogli ('Led Away'), the leader from the tribe of Dan;

Hanniel ('Grace of God') son of Ephod ('Ephod'), the leader from the tribe of Manasseh son of Joseph;

Kemuel ('God Establishes') son of Shiphtan ('Judgment'), the leader from the tribe of Ephraim son of Joseph;

Elizaphan ('My God Protects') son of Parnak (unknown), the leader from the tribe of Zebulun;

Paltiel ('My Deliverance is God') son of Azzan ('Mighty'), the leader from the tribe of Issachar;

Ahihud ('My Brother is Majesty') son of Shelomi ('My Peace'), the leader from the tribe of Asher;

Pedahel ('God Ransoms') son of Ammihud ('My Kinsman is Majesty'), the leader from the tribe of Naphtali.

The importance of the property allocations in an equitable fashion cannot be emphasized enough. For this reason, the Lord is involved in the appointment of leaders and personnel to ensure that things are conducted fairly and with integrity. Inheritance laws are essential to confer family property among heirs for the well-being of family relationships and tribal concerns. As adequately illustrated in Numbers 27 and 36, the daughters of Zelophehad also receive an inheritance in order to maintain the family since their father has no male heir 'subject to the condition that they must marry within their father's tribe, in order to prevent the family estate from falling into the hands of a different clan' (Num. 36.1–9).[8]

35.1-5—The Levitical Towns

The importance of land, justice and equitable tribal allocation, continues to be forefront with the legal instructions given in Numbers 35. As is procedurally considered after other tribal details are looked after in Numbers, attention turns to the needs of the Levites as well as to those who may need refuge. From

---

8 Lipiński, 'נחל', p. 324.

the position of the plains of Moab by the Jordan across from Jericho, Moses receives further instructions for the Israelites to give the Levites towns to live in from the 'inheritance' (נחל) that the Israelites will soon possess.

The people are instructed to assign towns for the Levites to live in. These are to be apportioned from the properties that the Israelite's inherit. According to Numbers 18.23 the Levites would forego receiving agricultural land as property. The theological explanation is that 'Yahweh was their inheritance' (Num. 18.20; cf. Deut. 10.9; 18.2; Josh. 13.33). Instead of specific land allocations, they receive the tithes and portions of sacrifices. Now they are assigned Levitical 'towns' (עיר) that belong to individual tribes (Num. 35.2–8; Josh. 21.13).[9] It is not clear when the allocations begin to be made but the family heads of the Levites follow up the 'promise' by approaching Eleazar and Joshua when they are at Shiloh in Canaan (Josh. 21.1–3). The generous provision of towns with homes include 'pasture' (מגרש; or open, common land) for their livestock needs.

The notion of Levites receiving 'Levitical cities' has caused much dialogue for scholars since it appears to go against the concept that Yahweh is their inheritance (Num. 18.20).[10] Budd points out that the Deuteronomic tradition claims that the Levites are distributed among the other tribes and do not have their own territories. This appears to be the sentiment in Deuteronomy: 'The Levitical priests—indeed, the whole tribe of Levi—are to have no allotment or inheritance with Israel. They shall live on the food offerings presented to the LORD, for that is their inheritance. They shall have no inheritance among their fellow Israelites; the LORD is their inheritance, as he promised them' (Deut. 18.1–2; 3–6). Furthermore, Budd concludes that the idea of Levitical cities occurs only in 'late texts' like in Ezek. 48.13–22 where the Levites have a 'slice of land apportioned to them' for their habitation.[11] Additionally, forty-eight towns for the Levites appears to be a high number and even the size of

---

9   The allocation of Levitical cities appears to be another generous grant by Yahweh in recognition of the sacrifices and responsibilities they had for the cultic ministry (Num. 3.12; 8.10, 16). Their roles in protecting, carrying, and erecting the Tabernacle according to Yahweh's direction (Num. 1.47–54) carried significant risks. By replacing the 'firstborn' (בכור) of other tribes so that the firstborn sons could serve their family needs (Exod. 4.22; 13.12–13; 29.9, 44; 40.15), the Levites gave up their individual freedoms. These realities have implications for the provisions that are described in this chapter.

10 'The assignment of the Levitical cities totally contradicts the so-called "Levitical law" that the Levites are to own no property. Thus, the notion of Levitical cities seems to be an idealized embodiment of idealized claims, a purely utopian scheme dating from a later period' (Kellermann, 'לוי', p. 494).

11 Cf. Budd, *Numbers*, p. 371; (cf. Lev. 25.32–24; Josh. 14.4; 21; 1 Chron. 13.2, 2 Chron. 31.15–19).

pastureland connected to each city seems expansive. This dispute has not been settled and historical factors which are evident behind the materials transmitted over several centuries makes it difficult to be clear on what actually is given. However, the initial purpose of the town allocations is to ensure the welfare of the Levitical families. They may not have received 'title deeds' for the properties but are given secure places to live and work for the well-being of the nation. Details of the allotments to the descendants of the Kohathites, Gershonites, and Merarites are specified and verified in Josh. 21.1–42. The tribes which give the towns along with the numbers are clearly documented there (cf. 1 Chron. 6.54–81). 'The towns of the Levites in the territory held by the Israelites were forty-eight in all, together with their pasturelands. Each of these towns had pasturelands surrounding it; this was true for all these towns' (Josh. 21.41–42).

35.6-15—Designated Towns of Refuge

Just as provisions are made for the Levites, attention turns to those who may need refuge and justice. For this purpose, six towns are reserved for those who have committed an unpremeditated killing and need a hearing. The connection of this provision appears to be the service and ministry element of the Levitical heritage. They are tasked with the custody of the refuge seeker until an impartial judicial decision is made.

With this specification on the use of six towns, it is left to the Israelites to determine which specific towns are designated for refuge. Three towns are to be in Canaan with another three in the Transjordan territory. The number of towns to be allocated are in proportion to the inheritance of each tribe: 'Take many towns from a tribe that has many, but few from one that has few'. The purpose of the six towns is to facilitate a place of refuge for an individual who fears retribution until the authorities can consider the story and evidence of a case. The occurrence of the term for asylum (מקלט) as a place of refuge for the person who has committed murder, is limited (cf. Numbers 35; Joshua 20 and 1 Chronicles 6), but the intention is clear.[12] Offenders who kill someone may flee to such a city for asylum and be protected from avengers until the facts of a case are determined. Both Israelites and foreigners are entitled to use the provision when unfortunate accidents occur. Whether a killing is accidental or premeditated the procedural instructions are the same. The asylum seeker flees

---

12   R. Schmid, 'מקלט', *TDOT*, VII, pp. 552–556.

to the town of refuge and pleas for protection at the city gate. The authorized elders function in the role of adjudicators at the city gate where the perpetrator is interviewed. Asylum seekers are then provided with protective custody until the final verdict is made. The whole community is involved in hearing the trial and making the judgment (Num. 35.12).

A number of examples are presented that give insights to the kind of incidents which cause death and what the penalties are. These are similar to case laws documented in Exodus 21 which describe incidents that require care, justice and judgment. An analysis of motive is at the core of the procedures that are stipulated. 'Anyone who strikes a person with a fatal blow is to be put to death. However, if it is not done intentionally, but God lets it happen, they are to flee to a place I will designate. But if anyone schemes and kills someone deliberately, that person is to be taken from my altar and put to death' (Exod. 21.12–14). This case deals with homicide but recognizes that not all killings are premeditated or intentional. For accidental actions resulting in death, the responsible person can flee to a place of refuge at the Tabernacle altar and seek asylum. By grabbing the altar the individual appeals to the divine will for clemency. This example sets the precedent for cities of refuge located in various tribal centres for accessibility.

The wrongdoer will then be protected by the community from the 'avenger' (גאל) of blood who will act on behalf of the family to find justice or vengeance (cf. Num. 35.12, 19, 21, 24–25, 27). Ultimately, the avenger's role is to bring about a return to some form of order in the family that is affected by the death of their relative. Order and justice is essential since murder brings a curse on the land which is the result of evil perpetrated on others. However, when the community determines the guilt of a murderer, the avenger of blood is authorized to carry out the death sentence.

Although these provisions are made for circumstances that involve death, the ideal situation is to avoid such tragedy. To remediate such situations, the law declares 'you shall not kill'. Furthermore, Num. 35.33–34 specifies restraint and presents consequences for the shedding of blood: 'Do not pollute the land where you are. Bloodshed pollutes the land, and atonement cannot be made for the land on which blood has been shed, except by the blood of the one who shed it. Do not defile the land where you live and where I dwell, for I, the LORD, dwell among the Israelites'.[13] The killing of Abel by his brother Cain illustrates

---

13 The issue of land defilement due to improper living and rejection of commands is documented in Lev. 18.25–28:
> Do not defile yourselves in any of these ways, because this is how the nations that I am going to drive out before you became defiled. Even the land was defiled; so I punished

this case. The blood of the innocent brother seeps into the ground and cries out for justice. Until justice is found, the ground is cursed, affecting societal conditions as well as the fertility of the land.

> The LORD said, 'What have you done? Listen! Your brother's blood cries out to me from the ground. Now you are under a curse and driven from the ground, which opened its mouth to receive your brother's blood from your hand. When you work the ground, it will no longer yield its crops for you. You will be a restless wanderer on the earth.' (cf. Gen. 4.10–12)

Furthermore, the law seeks to bring an end to a spike in killing when vengeance becomes the prime motivator to find and deal with the offender. This human tendency is illustrated in the example provided in Deut. 19.1–13 where an accidental death occurs. For this kind of situation, the place of refuge becomes an important place of sanctuary.

Provision of refuge in Israel is based on justice, whereas in the ancient Near East, most cultures function on the basis of blood vengeance leading to vengeance. Milgrom describes the process developed in Israel which modifies the typical practices.

> 1. Only the guilty party is involved; thus, no other member of his family may be slain. 2. Guilt is determined by the slayer's intention: the involuntary homicide is not put to death. 3. No ransom is acceptable in place of the death of the murder. 4. The verdict of deliberate or involuntary homicide is made by the state and not by the bereaved kinsman, and to this end asylum cities for the homicide are established. 5. His trial is by a national tribunal and not by the kinsmen of either party. 6. The deliberate homicide is executed by the *go'el*, and the involuntary homicide is banished from to the asylum until the death of the High Priest.[14]

Additionally, the right of asylum is provided only for unpremeditated killing.

---

it for its sin, and the land vomited out its inhabitants. But you must keep my decrees and my laws. The native-born and the foreigners residing among you must not do any of these detestable things, for all these things were done by the people who lived in the land before you, and the land became defiled. And if you defile the land, it will vomit you out as it vomited out the nations that were before you.

14   Milgrom, *Numbers*, p. 291.

35.16–29—Premeditated Murder

In cases where murder is the result of anger leading to actions which bring about the death of a person, the consequences are more severe. A number of instances are described to illustrate how to determine deliberate and involuntary murder. If a perpetrator takes up and uses lethal weapons, the onus is on such a person to prove their innocence. Both motivational words and implements are examined for a judicious determination. The examples are clear.

Using an iron, a stone or a wooden object to strike a human being implies anger, motive and intent. Such a person receives the death sentence which is to be carried out by the avenger of blood who is authorized to put the murderer to death—in other words the avenger becomes the executioner for the state which authorizes the capital punishment. The same fate is authorized for those who in a state of premeditated anger or enmity cause the death of a person by throwing, shoving, or hitting someone. Their actions, motives, and rage are evidence of their malice aforethought which brings about the death. Once again, the avenger of blood is authorized to implement capital punishment on the guilty party. These are six examples of uncontrolled resentment that develop into a Cain style action resulting in the death of an innocent person which must be avenged judiciously. Rather than viewing capital punishment as vindictive, the law is valuating every individual's right to life.[15] The law calls for restraint and self-control. The notion is illustrated in Yahweh's caution to Cain who is warned: 'But if you do not do what is right, sin is crouching at your door; it desires to have you, but you must master it' (Gen. 4.7).

The law also provides cases where accidental death results from an individual's actions. That is, in examples where a shove, a tossed implement or a dropped stone causes death but is unintentional, the details of the case are to be heard. The offender flees to the city of refuge where the assembly hears the case to determine whether there is enmity, motive, or malicious intent. This testimony is also informed by the avenger who is given opportunity to provide witness. When an incident is proven accidental, the assembly reserves the right to a determination. Protection is provided in a city of refuge until the death of the high priest.

> As the High Priest atones for Israel's sins through his cultic service in his lifetime (Exod. 28.36; Lev. 16.16, 21), so he atones for homicide through his death. Since the blood of the slain, although spilled accidentally, cannot

---

15   Cf. D. Patrick, *Old Testament Law* (Atlanta: John Knox Press, 1985), pp. 70–74, 256–257.

be avenged through the death of the slayer, it is ransomed through the death of the High Priest, which releases all homicides from their cities of refuge.[16]

Underlining the effectiveness of this atonement, the High Priest is anointed with the holy oil (Lev. 21.10), making his service effectual even with death. However, even with the accidental death of a person, the consequences of the offender's actions remain upon them. They are warned that departure from the city of refuge is not permitted. The family loss of a loved one is not soon forgotten and if the offender leaves the place of asylum, they take their own life into their hands—the avenger of blood is permitted to take life without guilt.

35.30-34—Legal Summation

In case the preceding instructions are not clear enough, the importance of the laws concerning the death of individuals is highlighted in a summation. These additional laws serve as an appendix to illustrate and emphasize the value of human life. They reinforce the function and importance of the places of asylum until individual cases of killing may be heard. The force of law is for the Israelite nation wherever they live (even if not near a city of refuge). The law stipulates capital punishment for those proven guilty. 'Anyone who kills a person is to be put to death as a murderer only on the testimony of witnesses. But no one is to be put to death on the testimony of only one witness'. For the death sentence to be carried out, evidence proving the murderer's guilt must be presented along with the testimony of more than one witness (cf. Exod. 21.12–13; Deut. 19.1–13).

Furthermore, the death sentence must be carried out in order to satisfy the judicial process where guilt has been established. 'Do not accept a ransom for the life of a murderer, who deserves to die. They are to be put to death'. A convicted murderer deserves the death sentence which provides the victim's family with a level of justice. In such cases, there is no recourse for the payment of a 'ransom' (כפר), which would free the murderer. This term in the *piel* form infers the meaning to wipe off, clear, clean and to expiate the actual deed. In other words, any offer of a ransom to free the guilty party would be consider a bribe. This code is strengthened with an additional command which reinforces the in-acceptability of a ransom payment from those who made it into a place of refuge. Such a person is no longer free to live in their own land with family as

---

16 Milgrom, *Numbers*, p. 294.

if nothing happened—until the death of the high priest. This only applies to those who have been exonerated of premeditated murder and upon the death of the high priest, an amnesty could be declared (cf. Lev. 8.12; 21.10). This unique allowance has to do with the priest who is anointed with sacred oil of 'unction' (Exod. 30.25–31) that has an atoning effect.[17]

As noted above, the importance of human life is reiterated with the valuation of 'blood' (דם) which is essential for life. It leads to the concept that spilt blood which seeps into the ground actually 'defiles' (חנף) the land and must be cleansed of the wrongdoing which caused it. Until justice is found, the blood cries out for vengeance. Levine notes the implication: 'The notion that the land and its inhabitants are linked to each other, so that human behaviour defiles the land as well as the people, and leads to exile and loss of the land, is basic to several biblical sources'.[18] Thus, the land which is defiled through the killing of the innocent remains polluted until it is 'expiated' (כפר; purged; atoned for), through the judicial reconciliation process. This is where the actions of the avenger of blood come into play. The wrongdoer is protected by the community from the 'avenger' (גאל) of blood whose role is to avenge the relative's life (cf. Num. 35.12, 19, 21, 24–25, 27). The avenger serves to restore the family's dignity by avenging the death and stopping acts of vengeance in the community. When the community determines the guilt of a murderer, the avenger of blood is authorized to carry out the death sentence.

The need for justice and order is developed in several laws which are designed to uphold the right of all living people to their life. This concept is fundamental in the Pentateuch and runs through the case laws like a thread. In Exodus the *lex talionis* stipulates that certain actions are to be avenged by reciprocal actions: 'But if there is serious injury, you are to take life for life, eye for eye, tooth for tooth, hand for hand, foot for foot, burn for burn, wound for wound, bruise for bruise' (Exod. 21.23–24). Similarly in Leviticus: 'Anyone who takes the life of a human being is to be put to death. Anyone who takes the life of someone's animal must make restitution—life for life. Anyone who injures their neighbour is to be injured in the same manner: fracture for fracture, eye for eye, tooth for tooth. The one who has inflicted the injury must suffer the same injury. Whoever kills an animal must make restitution, but whoever kills a human being is to be put to death. You are to have the same law for the foreigner and the native-born. I am the LORD your God' (Lev. 24.17–21; cf. Deut. 19.21). Of course, this appears to be cruel justice on the surface, but the underlying

---

17   Levine, *Numbers 21–36*, pp. 558–559.
18   Levine, *Numbers 21–36*, p. 560.

intention is to uphold the value of life and every individual's right to existence, security, and protection. The law is to restrain acts of violence and that which causes societal damage. The provision of the towns of refuge provides a judicial system to uphold life and order within the community.

Reflection and Response
Numbers 33–35: The Promise of Land
Reflection

History continues to display how vital land issues are in the middle east where conflict regarding land allocation is ongoing—especially in Israel. As world populations continue to rise and land shortages are evident due to urbanization, climate change, land hoarding and migration, the value of land ownership is at extraordinary highs.

Every human dreams about a place of comfort and security that they can call home during their earthly wanderings. Scripture begins with this theme where creatures and humans inhabit a veritable paradise—a habitat free from danger, suffering, and deprivations. The Garden of Eden presents the idyllic place of sanctuary where Adam and Eve had meaningful work as well as deep spiritual vitality in their relationship with God. They enjoyed all that life could afford as well as physical and visual pleasures in creation. Extraordinary wildlife was in the garden and Adam as the first zoologist, got to name them! However, life in the garden was conditional. The failure of their one simple test ushered them into another reality on earth outside of the paradisical garden. Two observations may be drawn. The first is that the Lord cares for his people and desires to allocate a place where they can live, develop culture, and serve. The second is that life in the assigned land must be lived with due concern for God's identity, ways, and restrictions. Otherwise, entry into the land is withheld, limited, or restricted. Furthermore, life outside of the garden is often fraught with danger, insecurity, and conflicts as nations jostle for position and dominion.

The book of Numbers affirms that the Lord had a specific place carved out for Israel. The boundaries are carefully described, which indicates that God determines the boundaries and placements of people. The Apostle Paul affirms this reality in his Mars Hill sermon:

> Rather, he himself gives everyone life and breath and everything else. From one man he made all the nations, that they should inhabit the whole earth; and he marked out their appointed times in history and the boundaries of their lands. God did this so that they would seek him and perhaps reach out for him and find him, though he is not far from any one of us. For in him we live and move and have our being. (Acts 17.25b–28a)

The sovereignty of God is reflected in his creation of all humanity. His provision of land and his sustaining care is evident in his blessing so that humanity will reach out and acknowledge him.

For Israel, the vista of land was always held before the people as a dream to be realised. It is an allocation by the Lord in accordance with his promise. However, it proved to be like a mirage for most generations. But it was a real place that had expectations for reaching it and inhabiting it. The land required faith for entry, trust and military strength for retention, and the Lord's blessing of inheritance. After the conquest of Canaan by Joshua and Israel, the Lord's promises of land were realized and verified:

> So the LORD gave Israel all the land he had sworn to give their ancestors, and they took possession of it and settled there. The LORD gave them rest on every side, just as he had sworn to their ancestors. Not one of their enemies withstood them; the LORD gave all their enemies into their hands. Not one of all the LORD's good promises to Israel failed; everyone was fulfilled. (Josh. 21.43–45)

Response

Although land is an obviously desirable commodity for life and security on earth, it is not something that is available to all 8 billion people plus currently on the planet. In fact, real estate has become an elusive luxury for most people. Of course, secure and comfortable places are available for rent; but far too many people today suffer in refugee camps, 'caravan treks', or migrant situations and are forced to survive in desperate environments. These are unfortunate realities for people and believers must seek ways of alleviating the stress and trauma of those in poor living conditions. Israel was commissioned to offer help and access to their community, to foreigners, aliens, widows and orphans. Additionally, the attitude of Abraham is to be replicated. Although he believed in the promise of land, at the end of his life he only owned a burial plot for Sarah.

> By faith Abraham, when called to go to a place he would later receive as his inheritance, obeyed and went, even though he did not know where he was going. By faith he made his home in the promised land like a stranger in a foreign country; he lived in tents, as did Isaac and Jacob, who were heirs with him of the same promise. For he was looking forward to the city with foundations, whose architect and builder is God. (Heb. 11.8–10)

Abraham believed God but he had his sights set on a future reality in the presence of God. He believed that the blessings of eternal life with God far outweighed the luxuries of life on earth.

Sometimes humans must set down roots and live in accommodations that may not be great, but they provide shelter, refuge, and a place to serve. Planet earth is not the final destination. All people are pilgrims on the road leading up to the city of God. Purpose and meaning for life are found in serving God—not in earthly materials or property that will pass away. Jesus' teachings on earthly belongings are applicable for every generation of believers: 'But store up for yourselves treasures in heaven, where moths and vermin do not destroy, and where thieves do not break in and steal. For where your treasure is, there your heart will be also' (Mt. 6.20–21). Heaven is the goal. Possessions are to be invested in things that have eternal value. Trust and focus on kingdom work and values is what matters most. 'So do not worry, saying, 'What shall we eat?' or 'What shall we drink?' or 'What shall we wear?' For the pagans run after all these things, and your heavenly Father knows that you need them. But seek first his kingdom and his righteousness, and all these things will be given to you as well' (Mt. 6.29–31).

36.1-4—Inheritance Security

The book of Numbers ends with a unique cultural and domestic problem that requires the legislative interpretation of Moses. Although it seems like an odd and sudden way to end the book, it is a fitting example which solidifies Moses' integral role in giving and interpreting the law in Israel. The prophet is faithful to the end in leading, serving and providing wise application of the Lord's instructions. Moses would not enter the promised land but is vitally involved in the land allotments and laws which secure the tribal property allocations. Furthermore, the chapter bookends the third and final section of Numbers with the grand theme of land inheritance. In fact, the land inheritance motif is focalized with a total of 17 references to 'inheritance' (נחלה) in 9 verses.[19]

---

19   The land allocations as an inheritance to families and tribes is focalized in the second half of Numbers to raise the hopes of a generation that a place of rest would soon be realized. In its verbal forms, 'inheritance' (נחלה) occurs 59 times, and as a noun 220 times in the OT. Supervision of the land distribution is done by Moses, with assistance from priests and tribal leaders. The importance of the inheritance of land is evident in the more than 40 occurrences in Numbers as a vital component of the covenantal promises. Cf. Lipiński, 'נחל', pp. 319–335.

The chapter wraps up this final part of Numbers 26–36 with a focus on the judicial way that land inheritance issues will be settled in Israel with leaders and Yahweh's authorization. Numbers 36 finalizes an inheritance issue for the daughters of Zelophehad which was introduced in Numbers 27 with further stipulations.

A concern arises when Zelophehad, a grandson of Gilead dies, leaving no male heir in the family. The problem was common with cultural practices in the patriarchal context of the ancient Near East pertaining to land inheritance. Upon the death of a father, inheritance laws stipulated that the male heir is to receive family possessions, including land. Although a unique way to end the book, it raises a potentially typical problem that has major implications for people at various times and requires special provision and justice. Not only is this another case where cultural practice adversely affects the women, but it reveals a forward-looking perspective and confidence that land allotments will soon to be made. The example also shows how Hebrew culture rises above the typical ancient Near Eastern procedures and the 'patriarchal' demeaning of women.

The case in question is a further response to the incident in Chapter 27 where the daughters of Zelophehad, the son of Hepher brought their situation to Moses. The daughter's lineage is documented to trace Zelophehad through Hepher, the son of Gilead, the son of Machir, the son of Manasseh, of the families of Manasseh, all the way back to Joseph. Zelophehad is blessed with five daughters but has no sons. Not only is the plight of the women featured, but their names are recorded as Mahlah, Tirzah, Hoglah, Milcah, and Noah. Surprisingly, their names are recorded several times to affirm the importance of their situation (Num. 26.33; 27.1; 36.11, and Josh. 17.3).

Whereas in Numbers 27 the daughters made a direct public appeal before Moses, Eleazar, leaders and the community at the tent of meeting, here it is the family heads in Gilead's clan who address Moses, and community leaders. In the first resolution the matter dealt with the death of Zelophehad and the implication of the 'inheritance' (נחלה) laws. According to custom, the name of Zelophehad would be withdrawn from the family lineage and the property would be lost from the family estate. When Moses sought clarification from the Lord, the matter is resolved with the inheritance rights transferred to the daughters. Other potential cases are also noted to ensure that inherited property would remain within family and clan ownership. Resolutions made become an ordinance and practice to be implemented in the nation (cf. Numbers 27).

Although the basic resolution is dealt with publicly and appropriately, there are further implications that are addressed in Numbers 36. Here it is the leaders of the family of the sons of Gilead, the son of Machir, the son of Manasseh, of the families of the sons of Joseph, who approach Moses and other tribal leaders concerning significant details of inheritance law. The question concerns the implications on inheritance when a woman marries into another tribe. The hypothetical situation is posed that if they marry men from other Israelite tribes, their inheritance would be transferred over into the tribe they become a part of. The cultural practice would cause the loss of the ancestral inheritance from the clan. This transfer of the inheritance would be ratified during the Year of Jubilee with the implication that any rights to their inherited property would be gone forever. The tribal lands would be transferred to another tribe.

36.5–12—Marriage

With this potential dilemma presented to Moses, he interprets the law with the Lord's authorization ('at the Lord's command') that the daughters of Zelophehad are permitted to marry a person of choice as long as they are within their tribal family:

> No inheritance in Israel is to pass from one tribe to another, for every Israelite shall keep the tribal inheritance of their ancestors. Every daughter who inherits land in any Israelite tribe must marry someone in her father's tribal clan, so that every Israelite will possess the inheritance of their ancestors. No inheritance may pass from one tribe to another, for each Israelite tribe is to keep the land it inherits. (Num. 36.7–9)

This stipulation mandates that ownership of the inheritance is essential and secure in order to protect the nation from inter-tribal conflicts. The legacy of the family name and estate would continue, and the inherited land would be ensured.

The wise daughters of Zelophedad accept Moses' ruling and 'did as the Lord commanded Moses'. The five women named Mahlah, Tirzah, Hoglah, Milcah, and Noah, married within the clans of the descendants of Manasseh. Consequently, their inheritance remained with the tribe of the family of their father. Moreover, they set an example for the Israelites and are honoured for their foresight and tenacity by the repeated mention of their names in the scriptures. The example highlights the worldview of community centred cultures which emphasize the well-being of the clan over the individual rights and desires of the person.

36.13—The Reliable Leadership of Moses

The concluding statement in Numbers affirms the faithfulness of Moses in transmitting the instructions of the Lord to the Israelites. The 'commandments' (מצוה) and the 'ordinances' (משפט) encapsulates the content of what Moses received. The verse sums up the fulfilment of Moses' prophetic ministry in communicating the words of Yahweh to the Israelites. Specifically, the reference indicates that this refers to the regulations Moses received on the plains of Moab by the Jordan across from Jericho. However, it aligns with other summary statements that affirm Moses' faithful prophetic work over his forty-year ministry.

The 'commandments' (מצוה) and the 'ordinances' (משפט) of Yahweh given through Moses are to be implemented and followed for the well-being of the nation. In numerous summation statements, Moses' compliance in the transmission of the Lord's commands are confirmed and the instructions given are noted as accomplished by Israel or leaders or individuals (cf. Num. 36.10). 'The Israelites did all this just as the LORD commanded (צוה) Moses'. This is a notable theme throughout Moses' epic leadership assignment in the book of Numbers, but also in the Pentateuch (cf. Num. 1.19, 54; 2.33–34; 3.51; 4.49; 8.3, 20–22; 10.13; 15.36; 17.26; 20.27; 26.4; 27.22–23).[20]

The regulations are authoritative as delivered through Moses for Israel's legislative system.[21] The example presented in the concluding chapter illustrates the implementation of divine edicts. The book of Numbers employs the term (מצוה) seventy-one times and concludes the book with the refrain 'at the Lord's command', emphasizing that the work of Moses in communicating Yahweh's instructions is fulfilled (Num. 36.2, 5–6, 10, 13). Other terms in the OT are also employed to convey the legal notions of divine authority which required that the rules, ordinances, statutes, and commands given through Moses are to be made public and obeyed because they are authoritative.[22]

---

20 This is a characteristic feature in the Pentateuch where the word or commands of the Lord are transmitted through Moses with the expectation that the Israelites (leaders and individuals) will hear and obey them. The phrase is typically 'as the LORD commanded' (צוה) in the *piel* form (Exodus 48 times; Leviticus 24 times; Numbers 29 times; Deuteronomy 33 times; and also in Joshua 36 times).

21 These two terms occur often to communicate the authority of the Lord in revealing his instructions for Israel. The commandments of Yahweh are necessary for instruction and the ability for Israel to live life skillfully in the promised land. The 'judgments' (משפט) of the Lord indicate the legal ordinances which are to be implemented for the well-being of the nation to bring order in society.

22 Cf. Ringgren, 'מצוה', pp. 505–507.

Finally, the noted location on the plains of Moab will eventually be the place of Moses' demise (Deut. 34.8). The Israelites arrived at this place according to Num. 22.1 and from that time, Moses received the instructions that brought the nation to the frontier of the promised land (cf. Num. 26.3, 63; 31.2; 35.1). The reference probably refers to the laws the Lord transmitted to Moses from Num. 22.1 onwards which according to Milgrom may 'include the regular public sacrifices (chaps. 28–29), the division of the land (26.52–56), the law of succession in inheritance (27.1–11; 36), the leadership succession both religious (chap. 25) and civil (27.12–23), a woman's vows and oaths (chap. 30), the division of the spoils (chap. 31), and the laws of homicide (35.9–34)'.[23] Additionally and finally, the regulations concerning inheritance and marriage for the daughters of Zelophedad.

Lastly, it will be from these plains of Moab, that the Lord allows Moses to survey the panorama of the land:

> Then Moses climbed Mount Nebo from the plains of Moab to the top of Pisgah, across from Jericho. There the LORD showed him the whole land—from Gilead to Dan, all of Naphtali, the territory of Ephraim and Manasseh, all the land of Judah as far as the Mediterranean Sea, the Negev and the whole region from the Valley of Jericho, the City of Palms, as far as Zoar. (Deut. 34.1–3)

Reflection and Response
Numbers 26–36: Anticipating the Inheritance
Reflection

The ending of Numbers seems abrupt and unusual, but the import of the last section highlights the positioning of the nation for the period of conquest. The nation is on the precipice of inheriting their incredible property. The vista before the people must have been breathtaking. The preview of Canaan affirmed the good intentions of the Lord to bring them to the place that was promised—a land flowing with milk and honey. After forty years in the wilderness, the anticipation of finally entering the land must have seemed like a dream.

It may also seem paradoxical that Moses, the distinguished leader, was not permitted to enter the land although he asked Yahweh for this concession (Deut. 3.23–27). Nevertheless, Moses was the faithful prophet who delivered all the commands and ordinances that the Lord communicated to him through

---

23   Cf. Milgrom, *Numbers*, p. 299.

the many ordeals, conflicts, and circumstances that arose in the wilderness. His main ministry was done. He was allowed to witness many miraculous events with divinely orchestrated provisions. He witnessed several divine judgments and saw an extraordinary amount of death. But to his last breath Moses served the Lord and people by speaking the words of Yahweh to Israel. He was instrumental in delivering the Torah to countless generations. He used his shepherding skills to care for and lead the Israelites to the promised land. On multiple occasions Moses interceded on behalf of the people and was heard by the Lord.

Although Moses was not permitted to enter Canaan proper, he was able to see the divine promise from a distance. His selfless desire for the Israelites was for them to receive their inheritance. However, perhaps one of his greatest desires for Israel was that all the people would be prophets and receive the Spirit (Num. 11.29). It appears that his desire was that all people would experience what he did when the Spirit rested upon him for service. Moreover, he may have wanted others to have access to the Lord's presence as he did when he spent time with the Lord and heard words of instruction. He desired for Israel to hear directly from the Lord so that they could implement the word of life and live skilfully in the land. It was the presence of the Lord, and obedience to the commands that would ultimately provide the nation with a blessed life in the promised land.

Response

In the light if Israel's epic journey and experience in the wilderness, several questions arise. Why do the promises of God seem to take forever to be realized? Was there not an easier way for him to make his purposes known? Why were there so many judgments and hardships along the way? Was the intense suffering necessary and did a whole generation have to pass away in the wilderness? Does the Lord continue to take prolonged periods of time to implement his purposes? The Psalmist often lamented 'How long oh Lord'? It appears that many positive things in life take time, processing, aging, maturing, refining, and preparing. Even the discipline of the Lord brings about positive consequences for those who listen, learn, repent, and abide.

In recent memory, waves of the Covid-19 pandemic and its effects had ongoing effects and restrictions for people which may provide a measure of what the wilderness experience was like. The limitations on simple freedoms, travel and resources continue to have a powerful effect on people. Many still refuse to believe the scientific reports and the need for government restrictions. And yet the suffering and devastation continues around the globe as a variety of conditions and plagues are experienced. No doubt the challenges for humanity will continue to develop as history moves forward to the consummation. But we hope for the promised land—a better place for rest, renewal, freedom, and blessing.

The primary and recurring theme in Numbers is leadership. As the problems and issues that affect humanity continue to grow around the globe (floods, drought, war, migration, displacement, etc.), the need for Godly, wise, and authoritative leadership has never been greater. Many principles, values, and practices are presented in Numbers to assist leaders in their roles as shepherds. Blessed are the people who have leaders that apply them for the well-being of families, clans, and nations.

Select Bibliography

Commentaries

Allen, Ronald B., *Numbers* (Expositor's Bible Commentary, Vol. 2; Grand Rapids, MI: Zondervan Publishing House, 1990).

Ashley, Timothy R., *The Book of Numbers* (NICOT; Grand Rapids, MI: Eerdmans, 1993).

Brown, Raymond, *The Message of Numbers* (Downers Grove, IL: InterVarsity Press, 2002).

Budd, Philip J., *Numbers: Word Biblical Commentary* (Waco: Word Books Publisher, 1984).

Childs, Brevard S., *The Book of Exodus: A Critical, Theological Commentary* (Old Testament Library; Philadelphia: The Westminster Press, 1974).

Coats, George W. and Knierim Rolf P., *Numbers: Forms of Old Testament Literature* (Grand Rapids, MI: Eerdmans, 2005).

Dozeman, Thomas B., *The Book of Numbers* (The New Interpreter's Bible, Vol. 2; Nashville: Abingdon Press, 1998).

Gray George B., *A Critical and Exegetical Commentary on Numbers* (ICC; Edinburgh: T & T Clark, 1903).

Keil, C.F. & F. Delitzsch, *Biblical Commentary on the Old Testament: The Pentateuch*. Vol. 3. (Trans. J. Martin; Grand Rapids, MI: Eerdmans, n.d.).

Levine, Baruch A., *Numbers 1–20: A New Translation with Introduction and Commentary* (Anchor Bible; New York: Doubleday, 1993).

Levine, Baruch A., *Numbers 21–36: A New Translation with Introduction and Commentary* (Anchor Bible; New York: Doubleday, 2000).

Milgrom, Jacob, *Leviticus 1–16: A New Translation with Introduction and Commentary* (Anchor Bible; New York: Doubleday, 1991).

Milgrom, Jacob, *Numbers: The JPS Torah Commentary* (Philadelphia, PA: The Jewish Publication Society, 1990).

Sarna, Nahum M., *Exodus: The JPS Torah Commentary* (Philadelphia, PA: The Jewish Publication Society, 1991).

Tigay, Jeffrey H., *Deuteronomy: The JPS Torah Commentary* (Philadelphia, PA: The Jewish Publication Society, 1996).

Wenham, Gordon J., *Numbers: An Introduction and Commentary* (TOTC; Downers Grove, IL: InterVarsity Press, 1981).

Other Works

Alexander, Desmond T. & Baker, David W. (eds.), *Dictionary of the Old Testament: Pentateuch* (Downers Grove, IL: InterVarsity Press, 2003).

Alter, Robert, *The Art of Biblical Narrative* (New York: Basic, 1981).

Boda, Mark J., & Lissa M. Wray Beal (eds.), *Prophets, Prophecy and Ancient Israelite Historiography* (Winona Lake, IN: Eisenbrauns, 2013).

Botterweck, Johannes G., and Helmer Ringgren (eds.), *Theological Dictionary of the Old Testament* (Vols. 1–6; Grand Rapids, MI: Eerdmans, 1974–1990).

Botterweck, Johannes G., Helmer Ringgren, Heinz-Josef Fabry (eds.), *Theological Dictionary of the Old Testament* (Vols. 7–15; Grand Rapids, MI: Eerdmans, 1995–2006).

Childs, Brevard S., *Introduction to the Old Testament as Scripture* (Philadelphia: Fortress Press, 1979).

Clines, David J.A., *The Theme of the Pentateuch* (Sheffield: JSOT Press, 1986).

Eichrodt, Walther, *Theology of the Old Testament* (Vol. 1; translated by J.A. Baker; Philadelphia: The Westminster Press, 1961).

Fishbane, Michael, *Biblical Interpretation in Ancient Israel* (Clarendon Press, Oxford, 1985).

Hildebrandt, Wilf, *An Old Testament Theology of the Spirit of God* (Peabody: Hendrickson Publishers, 1995).

Hymes, David C., 'Heroic Leadership in the Wilderness, Part 1'. *Asian Journal of Pentecostal Studies* 9.2 (2006), pp. 295–318.

Hymes, David C., 'Heroic Leadership in the Wilderness, Part 2'. *Asian Journal of Pentecostal Studies* 10.1 (2007), pp. 3–23.

Hymes, David C., 'Numbers 11: A Pentecostal Perspective'. *Asian Journal of Pentecostal Studies* 13.2 (2010), pp. 257–281.

Kitchen, Kenneth A., *On the Reliability of the Old Testament* (Grand Rapids, MI: Eerdmans, 2003).

Levison, John R., *Filled with the Spirit* (Grand Rapids, MI: Eerdmans, 2009).

Levison, John R., 'Prophecy in Ancient Israel: The Case of the Ecstatic Elders', *Catholic Biblical Quarterly* 65.4 (2003), pp. 503–521.

Rendtorff, Rolf, *Canon and Theology: Overtures to an Old Testament Theology* (Minneapolis: Fortress Press, 1993).

Sanders, James A., *Torah and Canon* (Philadelphia: Fortress Press, 1972).

Index of Modern Authors

Alexander, T.D. 34*n*44
Allen, R.B. 3, 3*n*5, 5*n*8, 7*n*14, 25*n*31, 68*n*10, 80*n*34, 179*n*36, 316*n*7, 318*n*8, 326*n*7
Alter, R. 195*n*49, 198*n*52, 241*n*86, 245*n*96
Archer, G.L. 288*n*22
Armerding, C.E. 128*n*62, 291*n*25
Ashley, T. 3, 143*n*3, 243*n*93, 318*n*9, 320*n*11
Averbach, R.E. 114*n*54

Beyse, K.M. 247*n*101
Boda, M.J. 39*n*55
Boshoff, W. 35*n*44
Budd, P.J. 200*n*55, 261*n*113, 288*n*22, 290*n*23, 328*n*11

Cazelles, H. 33, 34*n*42
Childs, B.S. 34*n*43, 37*n*52, 38*nn*53–54
Christensen, D.L. 34*n*41
Clines, D.J.A 17, 17*n*19, 18*n*21, 21*n*24
Coats, G.W. 27*n*34, 28*n*34, 277*n*9
Conrad, J. 147*n*9
Cross, F.M. 260*n*110

De Moor, J.C. 257*n*105
Dommershausen, W. 85*nn*29–30, 210*n*62, 281*n*17
Dumbrell, W.J. 7*n*14, 57*n*72

Eichrodt, W. 18*n*22, 226*n*75
Eising, H. 250*n*103

Fabry, H.J. 33, 34*n*42, 94*n*39, 204*n*58, 223*n*72, 224*n*72, 229*nn*77–78, 231*n*79
Freedman, D.N. 130*n*64, 131*n*66, 144*n*5
Fuhs, H.F. 159*n*19, 241*n*85

Gese, H. 39*n*57
Ginzberg, L. 275*n*7
Gray, G. 3, 3*n*4, 13*n*16, 164*n*26, 302*n*32

Hamilton, V.P. 297*n*31
Harper, L. 87*n*32
Hawk, L.D. 281*n*16
Hildebrandt, W. 51*nn*64–65, 54*n*68, 143*n*4, 147*n*9

Houston, J.M. 47*n*62, 325*nn*4–5
Hymes, D. 3, 3*n*6, 5*n*8, 45*n*61, 164*n*25

Jepsen, A. 241*n*85, 250*n*104

Kaiser, W.C. 18*n*21, 102*n*42, 104*nn*47–48, 177*n*35, 295*n*27
Keener, C.S. 2*n*1
Kellermann, D. 64*n*1, 70*n*14, 71*n*16, 87*n*33, 122*n*59, 87*n*40, 287*n*20, 328*n*10
Kitchen, K.A. 23, 24*n*27, 25*n*29, 32, 33*n*40, 36, 36*n*49
Knierim, R. 22*n*25
Koch, K. 64*n*1, 72*n*17
Kornfeld, W. 89*n*36, 92*n*38, 199*n*53

Lang, B. 121*n*58, 189*n*42, 203*n*56
Lee, B. 38, 39*n*56
Levine, B. 3, 3*n*4, 43*n*60, 80, 80*n*23, 129*n*63, 139*n*74, 174*n*33, 197*n*51, 203*n*57, 222*n*71, 239*n*83, 242*n*88, 258*n*107, 279*n*12, 311*n*45, 314*n*2, 334*nn*17–18
Levison, J.R. 146*n*8, 148*n*11, 149*n*12, *n*14
Levy, D. 65*n*5, 68*n*12
Lipiński, E. 214*n*66, 274*nn*5–6, 302*n*34, 307*n*42, 324*n*2, 327*n*8, 337*n*19
Lundbom, J.R. 144*n*6

Martin, L.R. 149*n*13
Mayer, G. 104*n*46
Milgrom, J. 3, 3*n*1, 5*n*8, 7, 7*nn*12–13, 18*n*20, 27*n*33, 65*n*5, 68*n*12, 76*n*18, 80*n*25, 84*n*27, 87*n*32, 98, 99*n*41, 120*n*57, 136*n*71, 139*n*74, 143*n*2, 152*n*17, 159, 159*n*20, 163*n*24, 169*n*30, 188*n*41, 190, 190*n*43, 195, 195*n*48, 205, 205*n*59, 208, 208*n*60, 211*n*63, 214*n*67, 215*n*68, 225, 225*n*73–74, 228*n*76, 234, 234*n*81, 249*n*102, 260, 260*n*110, 270, 270*nn*1–2, 279*n*12, 293*n*26, 302, 302*nn*33–34, 306, 306*nn*38–39, 308*n*43, 310*n*44, 311, 311*n*46, 314–315, 314*n*3, 315*n*4, 316*n*5*n*7, 318*n*8, 324*n*3, 331, 331*n*14, 333*n*16, 341, 341*n*23
Miller, P.D. 34*n*41, 159*n*22
Mulder, M.J. 257*n*106, 258*n*108

Niehr, H.   66n8, 68n11

Oeste, G.   279n10, 281n15, 283n18
Olsen, D.T.   7n14, 21n24
Otto, E.   126n61, 290n24
Ottosson, M.   20n23, 167n29, 170n31, 306n41, 323n1, 326n6

Patrick, D.   332n15
Preus, H.D.   181n38

Rashi, R.   76, 76n18, 79n22
Ringgren, H.   84n28, 89n36, 94n40, 159n21, 193n47, 199n53, 209n61, 340n22

Sanders, J.A.   31n38, 33n41, 35nnn46–48, 36, 36n50, 38n54
Sarna, N.M.   29n36, 43n59, 48n63, 52n66, 132n69, 176n34
Scharbert, J.   55nn69–70, 56n71, 102nn43–44, 242n87n89
Schmid, R.   329n12

Seybold, K.   86n31
Simion-Yofre, S.   71n15, 134n70
Stendebach, F.J.   109n49, 111n53, 260n111

Talmon, S.   14, 14n17, 15, 15n18, 64n3, 65n4
Taylor, D.J.   196n50
Tengström, S.   51n63, 147n10, 279n11
Tigay, J.H.   31n39, 38n55, 170n31
Tsevat, M.   90n37

Van Goudoever, J.   126n60, 285n19

Waltke, B.   38, 38n55
Watts, J.W.   13n15, 37n51, 192n45
Weinfeld, M.   103n45, 117n56, 131n67, 136n72, 182n39, 213n65, 261n112
Whybray, R.N.   28n35, 34n44
Wright, D.P.   215n68
Würthwein, E.   6n10

Zobel, H.J.   77n19

Index of Scriptures

Genesis
1	45	22.11–17	226n75, 256
1.3–4	119	22.17–18	248
1.21	231	23	169n30
1.22–28	54, 166, 256	23.4	187
2.7–15	57, 274, 277	23.17–20	20, 81
3	98, 174, 321	24.3–7	20n23, 154, 167n28
3.14–15	230	25.2	260
3.19	105	25.11, 12–19	54, 84n26, 256
4.7, 10–12	331–332	25.23	252
5.1, 2	54, 84n26, 256	26	19, 267, 270
6.4	172	26.1, 3 f., 24	19, 20n23, 100, 167n28
6.9	84n26	26.5–27	268
6.17	277	26.20	270
8.1	152	26.28	103, 136, 213n65, 261n112
9.1	54, 256	27.29	251–252
10.1	84n26	27.46	154
11.10, 27	84n26	28.1–9	154, 256
11.30	19	28.3, 13–15	19, 20n23, 54, 167n28
12	19	28.14	248
12.1–3, 12–50	18, 251, 323	29.31–30.24	68, 70
12.1–10	18–20, 20n23, 21, 47	31.11	226n75
12.3	18–20, 248, 254	32.22–23	262
12.6–9	167n28, 169	32.45	226
13.8	47	33.18	21
13.14–17	18, 20, 20n23, 21, 167n28, 323	34.25–26	70
13.16	248	35.12, 18	21, 68, 167n28
14	109	35.22–26	66
14.1–12, 13	47, 187	36	171
15.1 ff.	157, 161	36.1, 9	84n26
15.3–5, 6	15, 19, 81, 169	36.11, 15, 42	171
15.4 f., 17–21	18, 20–21, 167n28, 170, 323	36.30	213
15.18	324n3	37.2	84n26
16.7, 9–11	226n75	39.9	100
17.1–11, 36	18–19, 20n23, 42	40.5–8	243
17.4–8	81, 167n28, 323	41.1–8	243
17.16, 20	54, 256	41.51–52	68
18.10–11, 16–21	19, 157	44.4, 15	243
20	19	46.27	19
20	12.1–9, 13.17, 23.17–20, 20n23	47.11, 13–27	273, 314
20.6–7	100, 157	48.4, 8–10	20n23, 77, 167n28
21.22–23	297	49	78
22	49	49.3–4, 10	197, 205
22.1–19, 31–33	18–19, 47, 54, 256	49.5–7, 8–12	70, 77
		49.16–21, 22–26	21, 78
		50.20	249
		50.22–26	20n23, 22, 167n28

Exodus

1.5, 7	80
1.7, 9, 12, 20	19
1.11	314
1.19–20	80
2.1–10	23, 70
2.4–10, 21	154, 260
2.15–16	302
2.18–22, 24	19, 136, 136n71
2.23–25	144
3	24
3.1–4	157, 226n75, 302
3.2–6, 11–12	24, 316n6
3.5	42
3.8	21, 170n31, 323n1
3.10	19, 24
3.11–4.17	155
3.12, 18	19, 95, 316
3.16–18	13, 27, 146, 162
3.22	187
4.1–3, 20	205
4.1–10	24, 160, 230
4.14, 22	19, 70, 83, 143n5
4.15–16	84
4.18–26	136, 302
4.22, 23	95, 328n9
5.19–23	235
6	267
6.2–6, 8	19, 323
6.6 ff., 14–28	19, 267, 272
6.16–19, 25	84n26, 259
7–11	179
7.1–7	84, 157, 236, 318
7.4, 16	19, 95
7.8–12, 20	205, 224
8.1, 10–13	19, 224, 231
9.1, 9	19, 71
9.23	205
10.3	19
10.3–26	95
11.4–7	87, 122
12	81, 126, 212n64
12.1–16, 29–36	127, 315
12.12–29	87n33, 126n61
12.13–27	290n24–25
12.15–19	190
12.21	27, 146, 162
12.29–31	95, 291
12.35–38	48, 70, 79, 79n22, 130, 172
12.37–38, 41	15, 144, 313n1, 314
13.1–2	87, 87n33, 122
13.11–16	87n33, 151, 176, 299, 323
13.12–13	70, 83, 212, 328
13.15–18	212n64, 235
13.17–14.31	41, 49, 52, 131, 313n1
13.20–22	41, 315
14	13
14.10–12	49, 143, 179, 235
14.13–18, 31	25, 224
14.19	131n65, 226, 226n75
14.20–24	53, 131, 152
15.1–27	49, 139, 236
15.2	20
15.20–24	64, 154, 155, 179, 316
16	152
16.1–3, 13–15	50, 64n4, 143, 179, 236
16.4	49, 235
16.8, 12	20
16.11–35	81, 145, 179
17	145
17.1–9	48, 50, 179, 205, 223, 316
17.1–17	224–225, 235–236, 279n12
17.7–16	20, 109, 168, 251, 278
17.9–14	29, 30, 280
18	136
18.9–12	48, 136, 260
18.15–18	40
18.20–23, 27	137, 259
19.1–2	313n1, 316
19.3–24	32, 42, 71
19.5–6	44, 47, 87, 248, 284
19.8	103n45, 107, 136, 194, 213n65, 261n112
19.9–11	150
19.12–25	20, 52, 132–133, 208
20.4–6	75, 103, 177
20.8–11, 13	191, 290, 300
20.18–26	32, 40, 157
20.20–23	226n75
20.22–23.33	30n37, 138
21.12–14, 24	32, 330, 333–334
23.14–17	127, 285–286, 291–292, 294
23.25–30	42, 324
23.31–33	321, 324n3
24	85, 146
24.1–9, 12–18	32, 131, 147, 168
24.3–4, 27–28	29, 30, 30n36, 314

INDEX OF SCRIPTURES

Exodus (*cont.*)
24.10–14	20, 213, 278
24.19–20	212
25.4	92
25.8–9	64, 72*n*17, 114, 158
25.12–15	138
25.22, 25–26	53, 118
25.31–41	119
26.1–6	72*n*17, 94
27.8	158
27.20–21	118
28	84, 114
28.1–4	199
28.1, 40–43	85–86
28.17	76
28.15–30, 36	87, 272, 281, 332
29	84, 114
29.7	86
29.9, 44	70, 83, 328
29.27–28	211
29.38–43	118, 285–286, 288
30	114
30.7–10	118, 220
30.11–13	79*n*22, 157, 306
30.22–33, 38	86, 190, 334
31	50
31.1–11	114, 279–280, 306*n*41
31.12–17	191
32–34	159
32–33.23	32, 74
32.1–35	179, 257–258, 324
32.4, 11–14	20, 21, 145, 159, 175
32.7–10	50, 175
32.10–19	144*n*5, 278, 280
32.10, 31–34	27
32.25–29	71, 79*n*22, 83–84
33.1, 3, 17	124, 168, 299, 323
33.13, 15–17	27, 141, 272
33.7–11	72*n*17, 118, 168, 174
33.11–20	110, 111
34.1–9	30*n*37, 32, 176
34.10–11	178
34.4, 27–29	29, 31
34.14–16	103, 154, 193
34.18–26	127, 285–286, 291, 294
35	50
35.30–39	114
37	81
37.29	86
38.21	71
38.26	70, 79, 80–81
39.10–21	281
39.32–43	114
40.1–35	114, 118, 125
40.9–15	70, 86, 328
40.34–38	22, 41–42, 52–53, 131, 209

Leviticus
1, 2, 6	188
1.1, 4	120, 125
1.3–9	217
1.14–15	221
3.2, 9	120, 212
2.3, 12	210–211
2.13	213
2.14 f.	117*n*56
4.1–23	188, 217
4.15	120
4.25	211
4.27–35	220
5	220
5.8	221
5.1–6, 15	220
6.1–11	185, 220
7.1–6	211
7.3–16	212
7.30	211
7.11–34	5, 185, 190
8.1–5	120, 125
8.10–36	84, 86, 334
9.1	125
9.5, 8–24	84, 87, 107, 120, 131
9.21	211
10.1–3	85, 201, 204
10.8–11	209
13.1–8	96
14.2–7	217*n*69
15.29–34	97, 220
16.2	201, 204
16.3–28	217, 332
16.33–34	293
18.4–5	99
18.25–28	330*m*13
19	212
19.23–25	88
19.1, 10, 33–34	48, 187
19.26	243*n*92

Leviticus (*cont.*)

20.3–18	190
20.27	243n92
21.1–3, 14	105, 154, 221
21.10	333–334
23	212
23.1–8	126, 289, 290
23.9, 10–11	212, 285
23.9–16, 18–25	291–292
23.14–41	193, 285, 293
23.34–36, 39–43	294
23.22	48, 187
24.1–9	93, 119
24.10–23	32, 191, 334
25.6, 9	187, 293
25.32–34	328n11
26	193n46
26.6–12	19, 103n45, 109, 261
26.3–46	20, 23, 220
27.28	211
27.30–34	23, 214

Numbers

1	25n30, 41
1.1	14, 79n22
1.1–10.10	21
1.2	64n6, 68n11
1.3	315
1.4	64n6, 68n11
1.4–16	134
1.5–16	66, 77
1.16	64n6
1.19	73, 340
1.20–21	69
1.20–46	84, 204, 224n72
1.44–47	68, 79, 81
1.47–54	66, 54, 83, 196, 328n9
1.49	64n6
1.50–53	64, 71n16, 92, 134, 136, 138
1.51	25n30, 72, 90
1.51–53	25n29, 41, 54, 83, 124
1.53	87, 196
1.54	73, 340
2.1–31	134
2.2	76n18
2.3–31	204, 224n72
2.32	81
2.33–34	73, 79, 340

3.1	84n26
3.2–50	212n64
3.1–4	85–86, 272, 272n4
3.5–10	70, 83, 122
3.7	122
3.10	72, 90
3.11	25, 41
3.11–13	121, 124, 212n64
3.12	70, 83, 87n33, 121
3.12–13	91
3.12–16	328n9
3.13	90n37
3.16	90, 199
3.32	227
3.38–39	72, 90
3.40–51	90
3.44–45	91, 121
3.46–51	91, 213
3.51	73, 90, 340
4	41, 122
4.2	64n2, 123
4.5	71n15, 72, 134
4.15–49	145, 190
4.16	86, 227
4.17–20	25, 41, 124
4.22	64n2
4.23–24	94, 123
4.30	94, 123
4.33–43	94n40
4.37, 41	90
4.45–46	90, 94
4.49	73, 340
5	25, 41
5.1–5	215
5.6–12	100, 220
5.11–31	100
5.18–19	102
5.22–27	102
6.1–21	299
6.6–12	215
6.10	85
6.21	106
6.22–27	25, 41, 55, 124, 240
6.23–27	108, 261
6.24–27	44, 56, 100
7	287
7.1	86n31
7.1–3	125
7.2	64n6, 68n11

INDEX OF SCRIPTURES

Numbers (*cont.*)

Reference	Pages
7.10	68*n*11
7.10–83	134
7.12–88	68, 77, 125, 287
7.84–89	117*n*7
7.89	25, 41, 71*n*15, 72, 124, 134
8	213
8.3–22	73, 340
8.4	119, 158
8.5	125
8.10	70, 83
8.11–15	120
8.14	121
8.16	70, 83
8.17	90*n*37, 212*n*64
8.19	121
8.24–26	86, 94*n*40
9	135
9.1–3	125
9.2–14	126, 287, 290
9.4–5	126, 216
9.8–23	130
9.11–19	126, 216
9.13	190
9.17	41
9.15	134, 136
9.15–23	41, 52, 131–132
9.22	42, 126
10	135
10.1–7	134
10.1–10	135, 191, 302
10.11–12	14, 21, 70, 126, 313*n*1
10.13	73, 340
10.14–28	77, 204, 315
10.29	21, 23, 252, 302
10.33	261, 313*n*1
10.33–36	81, 136, 182*n*39, 213*n*65
11.1	14, 143
11.1–3	50, 152, 236
11.2	27
11.2–9	144
11.2–21	145, 145*n*7, 152
11.4–34	21, 50, 143, 179, 228, 236
11.5	48
11.7	26
11.12	146, 299, 323
11.13	21
11.16–29	72, 143, 147
11.17	161
11.18–23	48, 143, 152
11.21	69, 79, 81
11.21–23	148
11.25	45–46, 48, 50, 53, 131*n*68, 162
11.24–30	143, 256, 279
11.26–29	21, 147*n*10, 148
11.28–29	168, 280, 342
11.31–34	98
11.33	109, 143, 182
11.34–35	6, 317
12	21, 72
12.5	156
12.1–5	143
12.3	27
12.5	132, 201, 203
12.6–8	28, 45, 159, 162, 283
12.13	27, 259
13	21, 50
13.16	283
13.21	64, 318, 324*n*3
13.23	221
13.25–26	170, 222, 318
13.27–28	50, 237, 306*n*41
13.32–37	21, 323*n*1
14	21
14.1–4	143, 179, 180, 228
14.3–4	48, 50, 237
14.5	173, 223
14.6–7	164, 170*n*31, 306*n*41, 323*n*1
14.7–9	173, 278–279
14.10–20	124, 174
14.11–12	109, 164
14.12	48
14.12–23	27, 177, 237
14.13–20	27, 174, 259
14.14–27	132, 224*n*72
14.16	21, 64, 146
14.18	144
14.20–23	50, 53
14.20–29	180
14.23–24	21, 146, 164
14.26–35	164, 180, 260*n*109
14.30	21, 276
14.29–37	6, 181*n*38
14.33	100, 103
14.35	181
14.37	182

Numbers (cont.)

Reference	Pages
14.44	136, 139, 182n38, 213n65, 261n112
15	287
15.1–2	186, 285, 324
15.2–12	287–288
15.4–5	186
15.17–19	186, 191, 221
15.30–31	190
15.20–40	130, 186, 189, 191
15.20–21	211
15.27–29	217
15.32–36	69, 289, 340
15.36	73
15.39	103
15.40–41	194
16	21, 196, 215
16.3–38	198
16.4–45	173, 205, 223
16.5–40	198
16.9	70
16.13–38	200
16.22	27, 172, 201, 211–212, 259, 277
16.33	190, 202
16.35	6
16.39–40	203
16.45–47	173, 203
16.48–50	181n38, 182, 216
17	196, 215
17.2–3	31
17.4–10	134, 136
17.6–7	143
17.10–13	198, 200, 204, 259
17.17	68
17.21	68
17.25	224
17.26	73, 340
18	196
18.1	213
18.2	136, 198
18.3	190, 209
18.4	94n40
18.3–32	206–212, 212n64, 214
18.7	90
18.8–31	91, 201, 211
18.12	189
18.15–17	91
18.19	136, 182n39, 213, 213n65, 261
18.20–23	122, 191, 328
18.25	213
18.44	94n40
19.2–21	216–217, 227
19.5–6	304
19.10–13	130, 190–1
19.13–20	190, 218
20	21, 73, 213
20.1–13	64, 143, 222
20.1	6, 98, 313n1, 318
20.5–6	48, 173, 228
20.8–11	205, 223
20.11–24	224, 276
20.17–21	226, 228
20.22–29	6, 85, 98, 313n1, 318, 325
20.27	73, 340
21	21
21.1–3	182, 304, 319, 341
21.2–3	104, 296n29
21.4–14	64, 313n1, 319n10
21.5	48, 143, 228
21.6, 7	27, 182
21.10–14	31, 313n1
21.10–35	231–233, 303n36, 306
22	21, 73, 241
22.1–2, 4	240, 313n1
22.5–7	241, 242, 259
22.6–17	242n87
22.18	244n94
22.21–35	245n95, 246, 246n98
22.23–27	245, 254
22.31	250 n104
23.1–29	247
23.7	242, 247n101
23.8–27	242n87
23.9, 21	241
23.12	254
23.18–26	248, 254
23.23	241
23.28	257
24	241n85
24.1–4	241, 250 n104, 251, 256
24.2–15	241, 247n101, 250
24.4, 16–17	158, 241n85
24.9	242n87, 251
24.13–22	205, 252, 254
24.23–24	253
25.1–3	181n37, 257n105, 259

Numbers (cont.)

25.4	301
25.8–10	98
25.7–18	181n38, 301
25.15	303
25.9	6, 182, 304
25.10–13	109n50
25.12–13	136, 182n39, 213, 261n112
26.1	181n38
26.3–63	235, 341
26.2–4	73, 274n5, 340
26.10	182
26.16	290
26.29–33	312
26.33	273, 338
26.51–56	70, 320, 325
26.53–62	213n66, 271n3, 307n42
26.57–61	153, 152n18
26.63–65	180, 182, 260, 276
26.64–65	97
26.65	6, 98, 279n12
26.19–81	270, 326
27.1, 2	68, 69, 273, 338, 341
27.3, 12	6, 182
27.7–11	213n66, 274n5
27.12–23	320, 341
27.13–14	64, 276–277
27.16–17	57, 143, 162, 277
27.15–21	16, 135
27.16–17	45, 151
27.21	85, 272, 307
27.22–23	73, 120, 340
28	341
28.1–15	285–286
28.16–31	126, 287
29	341
29.1–6	287
29.6–37	290
29.9–11	293
29.13–40	295–296, 296n28
30	104
30.2–10	296
31	14, 341
31.2	341
31.4–36	302n36
31.5	14
31.7–20	6, 239, 260, 302
31.11	146
31.12–13	68, 235
31.15–16	100, 181n38, 257
31.23	217
31.49	302
32	306
32.2–37	307–309
32.10–12	299, 323
32.14–15	326
32.20–32	310
32.34–38	257n105, 311
33.1–53	51, 237
33.2	29, 31
33.5–15	314–315
33.3–4	7, 126, 290
33.16–40	315
33.30–39	222, 235, 318
33.40–49	234, 314
33.50–54	15, 271, 307n42
33.55–56	321
34.1–3	170, 307, 318, 325n14
34.7–9	169
34.8–19	204
34.13–15	271
34.18–23	224n72
35	69
35.1	235, 341
35.1–8	213, 272, 273, 328
35.12–34	330, 334, 341
36	341
36.1–9	327, 339
36.2–13	200n54, 271, 338, 340
36.10	73
36.13	23, 234–235

Deuteronomy

1–3	313–314
1.2	316, 316n6
1.6–3.29	51, 237
1.7	324n3
1.8	21
1.11	256
1.10 ff.	18, 49, 54, 146
1.19	235, 317
1.22–45	165, 166
1.25	170n31, 306n41, 323n1
1.34–37	159, 166n22, 276
1.46	222, 319n10
2.3–6	227
2.14–16	14, 222, 318
2.24–37	306–307

Deuteronomy (cont.)

3	311n45
3.1–11	324, 324n80
3.3–7	306, 328
3.23–27	159, 276, 341
4.1	21
4.3	257, 260
4.5, 14	159
4.38	324
5.9, 10	103, 178
5.15	289
5.17	300
5.22–27	30n37, 38, 157
5.23–29	25, 38
5.31	159
6.1	159
6.3–23	21, 300, 306n41, 323
7.2–6	47, 304
7.8, 13–15	21, 54, 256
7.9	178
7.18–23	81
8.1	300, 323
8.18	256
8.25	81
9.7–29	159, 165
9.28	21
10.6–9	71, 83, 318, 328
10.10–11	159
11.6	202
11.9	170, 306n41
11.23	324n3
12	31n38
13.17	300, 323
14.29	48
14.23–26	91
15	255
16.2–7	128
16.9–12	286, 292
16.16	127, 286
16.5–7	129
18	27, 38, 255
18.9–12	243n92, 328
18.14–22	38, 202
18.15–18	25, 27, 157, 159
18.18–19	26, 162
19	38
19.1–13	331, 333
19.8	300, 323
19.21	32, 334
20.10–18	304
20.16–18	304n37, 324
21.1–21	147n9
21.15–17	88, 214n66
23.4–5	239n83
23.21–23	297, 300
24.1–3	32
24.14–22	48
24.16	177n35
25.5–10	147n9
26	31n38
26.15	300, 323
27.29	48
28	21, 55, 183, 193n46, 254
28.1–14	54, 256
28.15–68	56, 240, 256, 261n112
28.64–68	321
29	21
29.9 ff.	103n45, 136, 213n65, 261n112
29.16–18	322
31.1–3, 19, 22	31, 276–277
31.7–15	280
31.9–13, 22–30	30n36, 38, 48, 281
32	31
32.44–47	31
32.5–12, 48–52	6, 276
33	313
33.10	220
34	22, 27, 277
34.1–3, 8	275, 341
34.4–8	159, 276–277
34.7	28n33, 275
34.9	279n12
34.10–12	26, 157, 159, 162

Joshua

1.1–15	159, 184
1.4	324n3
2.11	279n12
3.4–6	139
5.1	279n12
5.10–12	126, 129, 291
6.6–7	139
7.3	279n10
8.31–32	31
13.2–5	324n3
13.15–33	271, 328

INDEX OF SCRIPTURES

Joshua (*cont.*)

13.22	239n82, 241
14.4	328n11
14.5 ff.	171
14.6–11	173
17.3	338
17, 11, 16	270n1
17.14–18	312n47
19.1	270n1
21	328n11
21.1–13	328
21.1–45	329, 336
22.2–5	159
22.17	257
23.6	31
24.2	279n10
24.9, 10	55, 239n82
24.29–30	283

Judges

1.3	270
1.16	137
3.10	279
6–9	270
8.33	257n106
11	314
11.16–17	319n10
11.29	279
13.25	279

1 Samuel

10.20–21	24n28, 272
20.5	290

1 Kings

2.3	31
8.9	316
19.16–21	24n28

2 Kings

4.23	290
14.6	31
17.17	243
23.25	31

1 Chronicles

6.57–81	329
13.2	328n11
16.15–18	324

2 Chronicles

23.18	31n39
31.15–19	328n11
34.16	31n39

Ezra

3.2	31n39
7.6	31n39

Nehemiah

1.7–9	31n39
9.12	41
13.1	31n39
13.2	239n82

Psalms

5.9	300
9.4, 5	74, 300
19.8–10	193n46
23	16
36.3	300
39.4–5	284
47.4	324
59.12	300
66.13–15	299
68	1
69.28	74
78	1
78.17 ff.	51, 152, 237
90.12, 17	284
95	1
95.7–11	51, 237, 300, 323
99.7	41
103.28	257
105.8–11	324
105.40	152
106	1
106.24–39	27, 260, 264
145.13b	299

Proverbs

11.3	300
16.33	243

Isaiah

1.13	290
5.1–7	170
6	24n28
51.2	256

Isaiah (*cont.*)
61.9	256
63.9	226
63.11–14	161n23
42–61	24n27

Jeremiah
1	24n28
7.25	38
27.9	243n92
29.8	243n92

Ezekiel
1–3	24n28
13.6–9	243n60
16.8	103
20	1
23	103, 243n92
38.17	38
42.1–2	126n60
45.21–22	291
47.14	324
48.13–22	328

Daniel
1.17	243n91
2.1–11	243n91
9.1, 13	31n38

Hosea
1.2	257
4.13–15	103
9.10	257, 260
12.13	26
13	290

Joel
2.28–30	151
3.1–2	147n10

Amos
3.7	275
8.5	290

Micah
3.6 f.	243n92
6.5	279n82

Zechariah
10.2	243n92

Malachi
4.4	26, 316n6
2.10–16	103

Matthew
5.33–35	301
6.20–21	337
6.29–31	337
17.3	26
18.15–20	207

Mark
9.4	26
10.5	31
12.19–27	31

Luke
2.22	31n39
9.30	26
24.44	31n39

John
1.45	31n39

Acts
1.23–26	272
2.1–4	2
7	32
7.20–44	23, 23n26
8.15–19	2
10.44–46	2
17.25b–28a	335
19.1–7	2

1 Corinthians
10.1–11	51, 237
10.1–6	16, 141

2 Timothy
2.24–26	207

Hebrews
3.15–19	51
11.8–10	336
11.23–28	23

INDEX OF SCRIPTURES

2 Peter
2.15   239n82

Jude
1.11   239n82

Revelation
2.14   239n82

Index of Subjects

Aaron   240x, 5, *passim*
Aaronides   31, 44, 46, 83–87, 93–94, 109n50, 204, 206, 209–210, 272
Abraham   18–21, 42, 47, 49, 54, 63, 124, 138, 143, 157–158, 161, 167, 167n28, 168–170, 174–175, 187, 230, 262, 275, 323, 336–337
Administration   43, 45, 161, 285, 299, 304
Altar(s)   3, 42, 47, 85–86, 88, 93–94, 107, 113, 115, 115n55, 116–117, 118–119, 125, 169, 201–203, 210, 212, 220, 239, 247–249, 255, 293, 330
Ambition(s)   100, 163, 194–197, 199, 206–207, 235
Ancestral   15, 31, 65–66, 78, 204, 320–321, 325, 339
Anger   23n26, 26–27, 109n50, 143, 143n5, 152, 159–160, 165–166, 175–177, 179, 200, 203, 224, 236, 245, 251, 263, 300–301, 304, 308–309, 332
Anointed   54, 85–86, 114, 117, 333–334
Anointing   40, 86, 86n31, 93, 114–115
Ark   25n29, 30, 41, 49, 71–72, 89, 92–93, 118, 124, 134, 136, 138–139, 140, 142, 168, 182, 205–206
Atonement   25n29, 41, 54, 70, 99, 105, 118, 121, 121n58, 124, 138, 189, 189n42, 191, 220, 261, 287, 288, 291–293, 305, 330, 333
Audience   13, 13n15, 15–16, 36–37, 85, 248
Authority   28n33–34, 29, 32, 37, 37n50, 38, 38n52, 39, 44, 120, 146, 149–150, 151, 162–163, 193, 193n46, 198, 200–202, 205–206, 208–209, 230, 235, 237–238, 252, 255, 272, 274, 278–279, 282, 298, 340, 340n21
Authorized   42, 46, 53, 66, 72, 90, 149–151, 161–162, 205, 207, 229, 280n14, 298, 330, 332, 334
Authorship   29, 32, 34, 37–39, 155, 195

Baal   103, 181n38, 246, 257, 257n105, 258–260, 262–263, 303–304, 311, 315, 321
Balaam   6, 49, 55–56, 111, 158, 195, 231, 234, 238, 239, 239nn82–83, 240–241, 241n85, 242–257, 259, 262, 303–304, 331
Balak   111, 239–249, 251–256, 263

Battle(s)   14, 20, 41, 48, 55, 65, 73, 79, 132–133, 139, 171, 180, 182, 228, 232–234, 240, 242, 272, 278, 281, 302–310, 315, 319n10
Bless   19, 21, 44, 55, 55n69, 56, 102, 108, 111, 205, 231, 235, 240, 242, 242n89, 248, 249–251, 254–256
Blessing(s)   1, 7, 18–19, 23, 25n29, 40–43, 44, 47–49, 53–57, 65, 71–72, 75, 77, 77n19, 78, 78n21, 79–80, 84, 91, 101–102, 106–107, 107n111, 113–114, 124, 128–129, 137–138, 151, 156, 159, 170, 183, 186, 193–194, 197, 206–207, 210n62, 212, 232, 237, 239–240, 242, 248, 249, 251, 253–256, 261, 263–264, 268, 280, 283–284, 289, 292, 306n41, 310, 336–337, 343
Blood   23, 86, 97–98, 118, 127, 154, 198, 211–212, 216–217, 217n69, 220, 248–249, 264, 330–333, 334
Burden   26, 94, 113, 124, 142–143, 143n4, 145–146, 146n8, 147–149, 149n14, 150–151, 161–163, 194, 209, 214, 280

Caleb   6, 21, 48–50, 98, 138, 144n6, 164, 166–168, 171–174, 179–183, 237, 260n109, 273, 278, 309, 326
Camp(ed)   155x, 13, *passim*
Canaan   1, 13, 15, 19, 21, 23, 31, 47–48, 55, 82, 108, 124, 129, 144n5, 164, 167, 169–170, 171, 174, 180, 183, 238, 257, 260, 263–264, 267–268, 270–271, 302, 307–308, 310–312, 312n47, 313, 317, 319–321, 323–324, 323n1, 324n3, 325–326, 328–329, 336, 341–342
Canaanite(s)   20, 48, 169, 170–171, 178, 180, 182, 185, 200, 228, 238, 260n110, 268, 270, 296, 299, 304, 307, 319, 321, 323–324
Census   4–7, 14–15, 53, 63, 65, 65n6, 66, 68–69, 70, 70n13, 71–73, 75–79, 79n22, 80, 80n24, 83, 88, 91, 94–95, 98, 116, 125, 153, 180, 182, 255, 260n109, 262, 267–268, 269, 270–273, 312, 325
Ceremonial   96, 105, 112, 119, 120, 123, 212–213, 217n69, 218–219, 304
Charismatic   24, 45n60, 53, 57n71, 149n13, 161, 278, 279n12, 281n16

INDEX OF SUBJECTS

Clan(s)   5, 15, 24, 44, 46, 65–66, 68n11, 69–70, 76–79, 80–81, 88–89, 92, 122, 133, 153n18, 171, 197, 202, 267–269, 270–273, 274n5, 321–322, 327, 338–339, 343

Cloud   14, 16, 41–43, 52–53, 71–72, 114, 118, 125–126, 130, 130n64, 131, 131n65–68, 132, 134–135, 138–141, 142, 148, 150, 156–157, 174–176, 203, 226n75, 279n13, 280, 315

Command   13, 26, 30–31, 90, 138, 147, 165, 178, 182, 190–191, 193, 201, 222, 225, 244, 248, 272, 276n8, 278, 280, 285, 289, 318, 333, 339–340

Commands   22, 25, 52–53, 56, 118, 123, 130, 137–138, 178, 186, 188–189, 190, 192, 192n45, 193, 193n46, 194, 209, 234, 244–245, 271, 275, 281, 293, 304, 330n13, 340–342, 340n20

Commandment(s)   29, 30n36, 31–32, 37n50, 99, 138, 177, 191–192, 192n45, 193, 340, 340n21

Communication   4, 25n29, 26, 28n33, 32, 39, 40–42, 45, 72–73, 108, 111, 118, 123–124, 138, 146–147, 155–159, 162, 186, 243, 244n94, 247n99, 281, 243n91

Community   4, 6, 16, 28, 37–38, 44–46, 48, 63–65, 68–69, 72, 74–75, 81, 85, 87, 90, 95, 97–99, 101–102, 104, 107–109, 111–4, 120, 122–124, 127–135, 139, 141, 143, 147, 150–151, 160, 162, 170, 172, 173–175, 181–185, 187–192, 194, 196–199, 201–207, 215–219, 221–224, 227–228, 232, 235, 240, 259, 261, 269, 272–273, 275, 277, 278–281, 285, 289, 293, 295–296, 298–299, 303–307, 318, 326, 330, 334–336, 338–339

Composition   3, 3n7, 22n25, 29, 33, 34n43, 35–38

Conflict(s)   1, 16, 19, 28, 37, 40, 46–47, 56, 75, 99, 100–101, 109, 111, 122, 139, 142, 145, 152–153, 162–163, 179, 194–197, 198, 200, 202, 214, 223–224, 226, 236–238, 256, 260–262, 277, 317, 323, 335, 339, 342

Conquest   15, 17n20, 22, 48, 72, 108–109, 170, 172, 174, 184, 194, 233, 256, 268, 277, 280–281, 308, 310, 320, 325n5, 326, 336, 341

Consecration   71, 84, 84n28, 86n31, 87, 89n36, 92, 103, 105, 106–107, 114–115, 118–119, 122, 199n53, 209, 220

Counted   6, 21, 53, 69, 70n13, 79, 79n22, 83, 88–90, 153, 180, 182, 192, 248, 260, 272–273

Covenant   14, 18n22, 19, 21–22, 24–25, 29, 30, 31–32, 39, 41, 43, 47, 48–49, 52, 54–57, 63, 71, 71n15, 72, 79, 81, 83, 85, 92, 103n45, 106, 109n50, 118, 124, 134, 136, 138, 140, 142–143, 166, 169, 175, 178, 182, 186, 191, 193, 194, 196, 205–206, 210, 213, 220, 240, 242, 248, 256, 258, 260–261, 260n112, 262, 284, 302, 304, 321, 323

Covenantal   5, 14, 17n20, 18, 18n20, 19–23, 28–29, 32, 39, 40, 42–44, 47, 49, 50, 52, 54–55, 63–65, 71, 71n15, 73, 75, 81–82, 84, 94, 100, 103, 103n45, 107, 111, 126, 130, 133–134, 136, 162, 164–166, 168–169, 175–178, 181, 183, 193–194, 213, 213n65, 220, 226, 240, 248, 254, 261–264, 282–283, 295, 299, 304, 308, 321, 323–324, 337

Cultus   1, 3, 22, 44, 46, 53, 55, 72, 24, 85, 89n36, 92n38, 93, 115, 117, 117n56, 121, 154, 162, 185–187, 188, 199, 208–210, 240, 247, 284, 286

Curse(s)   16, 21, 23, 46, 57, 100–101, 102, 111, 113, 180–181, 183, 191, 197, 230, 240, 242, 242n89, 247, 249, 249n102, 250–254, 255–257, 261–262, 303, 321

Dead   97, 98, 105, 179, 181–182, 190, 202–203, 205, 216, 219, 222, 232, 235, 243n92, 276, 306, 324–325, 326

Death   6–7, 16, 22–23, 27, 46, 72, 87, 90, 94, 97–99, 101, 105, 112, 122, 147, 159, 162, 166, 172, 176–177, 181, 181n38, 182, 190–192, 194, 200, 203–206, 208–209, 214–216, 217–219, 221–222, 227, 229–230, 235, 238, 247, 257, 259, 262–263, 267, 273, 275n7, 276, 276n8, 277, 280, 283–284, 289, 303, 318, 330–334, 338, 342

Dedication   84, 103–104, 106, 115–117, 120, 126n60, 185, 211, 213

Defiled   96, 98, 105, 121, 215, 219, 264, 290, 304, 321, 330n13, 331, 334

Defilement   44, 95–96, 98, 102, 129, 160, 202, 204, 215–219, 220, 304, 330n13

INDEX OF SUBJECTS

Desert   13–14, 40, 64, 64n3, 98, 125, 140, 109, 179–180, 182, 184, 222–223, 262, 273, 275, 315–318, 324–325

Devotion   43, 70, 83–84, 87, 106–107, 112–113, 178, 180, 188, 220–221, 258, 262, 278, 299, 297n31

Died   14–15, 50, 97, 153n18, 171, 201, 222, 237, 268, 272n4, 273, 283, 318

Die(s)   6, 40, 97–98, 145, 157, 172, 177n35, 181–182, 191, 206, 219, 221, 223, 228–229, 236, 238, 247–248, 254, 260, 262, 270, 273, 275–276, 283, 318, 320, 333, 338

Divine   1, 7, 16, 18–19, 21, 24, 28–29, 32, 34, 37–44, 46, 48, 51–57, 64–66, 68, 71–73, 77, 29n22, 81, 83–86, 90, 92, 95, 100–101, 106, 108–111, 113, 130–132, 135–136, 138–140, 143–144, 147–148, 150–152, 156–162, 164, 166, 170, 173–174, 178, 180, 182–183, 185, 190, 193–194, 198, 202, 204–205, 208, 220–221, 223–224, 226–227, 236–239, 241, 243–245, 247, 249–253, 255–256, 258, 260–262, 275, 279, 282, 289, 296, 298–299, 303, 311, 321, 323–324, 326, 330, 340, 342

Diviner(s)   111, 238–239, 243, 244–249, 253–255, 263

Documentation   32–33, 38–39, 69, 73, 75, 135, 164

Document(s)   1, 2, 4, 6–7, 16–17, 29–30, 32, 34, 35n44, 36, 38, 38n53, 39, 333, 71n15, 73–75, 134, 151, 164, 314, 325n4

Dream(s)   21, 28, 140, 142, 157–158, 243, 243nn91–92, 279, 282, 335–336, 341

Eden   49, 53, 124, 139, 168, 180, 230, 246n97, 284, 335

Egypt   1, 5, 13–15, 19–21, 23–26, 31–32, 39, 42, 47–48, 50, 52, 63–64, 70–71, 79–80, 84, 87, 90, 95, 108, 110, 112, 121–122, 125–128, 130–131, 135–136, 139, 140, 143–144, 148, 153, 155–156, 158, 161, 163, 165–167, 169–170, 172, 175–177, 179, 181, 185, 187, 194, 200, 204–205, 222–224, 226, 228–230, 235–238, 240–242, 248–250, 254, 267–270, 273, 276, 282, 284, 289–290, 292, 294, 299, 307, 313–316, 318, 320, 322–323, 325

Elders   27, 30, 44, 46, 53, 111, 120, 131n68, 137, 146–153, 161–163, 194, 223, 235, 241, 243, 279, 330

Evil   16, 68n10, 105, 121, 141, 166, 166n27, 168, 175, 207, 240, 248, 253–254, 297, 301, 308, 330

Exodus   193x, 6, *passim*

Family   5, 19–20, 23–24, 47, 65, 65n6, 66, 66n7, 67–70, 74–75, 78–79, 81, 83–84, 84n26, 85, 88, 91, 96, 100, 105, 112–113, 122, 125, 127, 138, 145, 152–153, 155, 178, 185, 190, 195, 197–198, 202, 204, 212, 215, 219–220, 224, 237, 259, 267–268, 271, 274, 284, 290, 296, 298–299, 309–310, 327–328, 330–331, 333, 338–339

Firstborn(s)   13, 23n26, 69–70, 80–84, 87, 87n33, 88, 90, 90n37, 91, 112, 119, 121–122, 127, 136, 178, 212–213, 218, 269, 290, 315, 328n9

Food   1, 6, 16, 21, 42, 49–50, 57, 80, 95, 129, 141–144, 146n8, 147–148, 153, 163, 180, 186–189, 218–221, 227–228, 235–237, 285–292, 294–295, 316, 328, 330

Foreigner(s)   30, 47–48, 130, 138, 144, 144n6, 177, 187–188, 218, 292, 323, 329, 331, 336

Furnishings   54, 71–72, 83, 86–87, 89–90, 92–94, 114–116, 118–119, 134, 199, 208–209, 219

Generation(s)   1, 5–7, 14–17, 21, 35, 37–38, 40, 49, 73, 75, 82, 97–98, 164, 166, 175–178, 180–182, 184–185, 189, 191–192, 204, 214, 216, 222, 224, 227, 231, 238, 255, 260, 262–264, 267–268, 270, 276–277, 282, 288, 291–294, 300, 306, 308, 313, 320–331, 323, 326–327, 336, 342

Gift(s)   4, 20, 44, 54, 67, 93, 106, 115–117, 121–122, 166–167, 172–173, 176, 180, 183–185, 189, 210–211, 221, 233, 235, 256, 262, 285, 282–283, 295, 299, 305–306, 324–326

Glory   22, 42–43, 50, 52, 80, 107, 110, 114, 118, 131, 135, 140, 174, 176, 179, 201, 221, 223, 237, 288

God   620x, 1, *passim*

Guidance   19, 40–41, 45–46, 51–52, 56, 64, 101, 127, 129–132, 135, 139–141, 147, 160,

INDEX OF SUBJECTS 363

Guidance (*cont.*) 162, 181, 184, 191, 208, 240, 264, 277, 281, 291, 303, 358

Hardships 143, 162, 155–156, 180, 235–236
Historical 2–4, 26n31, 27–28, 28n34, 29, 33–34, 34n43, 35–37, 64–65, 67, 70, 73, 75, 77, 125–127, 164, 170, 175, 194, 226, 232–233, 247, 249, 252, 256–257, 267, 269–270, 285n19, 290–291, 294, 301–302, 313, 318, 329
History 1, 15–16, 22n25, 26, 28n34, 29, 33, 36–39, 43n58, 48, 65–66, 73–75, 84–85, 90n37, 109, 112–113, 126, 195, 209, 226–227, 241, 260–261, 267, 278–279, 281, 283, 294, 323, 335, 343
Holiness 23, 42–43, 48, 51, 54, 63, 72, 85, 87, 92, 94, 98, 104, 191–192, 198–199, 201, 208, 218, 220, 225, 289

Inheritance 14–15, 22–23, 28, 47–48, 50, 55, 63, 88, 108, 138, 141, 167, 170–173, 175, 178, 180, 184, 195, 200, 200n54, 213–214, 237, 262, 267, 271–274, 280, 282–283, 292, 299, 303–304, 306, 308–311, 320–321, 323–324, 326–329, 336–339, 341–342
Inspiration 2, 4, 17, 32, 37, 37n50, 39, 46, 51, 154, 163, 247n101, 250, 252, 254
Intercede(s) 27, 50, 124, 145, 158–160, 165, 175, 176n34, 201, 203, 254–255, 276, 282, 342
Intercession 27, 110, 124, 144, 144n5, 156–157, 163n24, 164, 166, 173, 175, 177, 179, 183, 185, 199, 201, 206, 229
Intervention(s) 37, 43, 83, 109n50, 126, 142, 148, 161, 174–175, 178, 205, 208, 226, 228–229, 229n77, 246, 283, 296, 299, 303
Israel 8 25x, 4, *passim*
Israelites 204x, 6, *passim*
Itinerary 7, 13–14, 29, 31–32, 47, 125, 135, 139, 140, 144, 169, 174, 180, 182, 222, 231–232, 234, 267, 313–315, 317, 319, 319n104, 320

Jethro 24, 48, 136–137, 144n6, 147, 154, 171, 260
Joshua 133x, 6, *passim*

Journey 1–2, 5, 13, 15, 22, 31–32, 39, 41, 43, 47, 52–53, 55, 63–64, 71–72, 74, 77, 81, 107–108, 110–111, 114, 116, 125, 127, 130–132, 134–135, 137–142, 144–146, 179–180, 222, 225–227, 234, 235–236, 245, 277, 313–316, 318, 319n10, 320, 322, 342
Judah 36, 67–69, 77, 77n19, 116, 134, 167–168, 171, 173, 268–270, 275, 326, 341
Judgment 6, 13, 21, 25, 27, 36, 40, 46, 49–51, 54, 71, 83, 97, 110, 112, 119, 127, 131, 142–144, 146, 148, 150, 152, 159, 163–166, 172, 175–176, 179–180, 184, 190–191, 196, 198–199, 201–203, 207–208, 214, 223–225, 227–228, 235–238, 252, 258–260, 269, 273, 293, 300–302, 304, 307–308, 313, 315, 320–321, 323, 327, 330
Justice 37, 178, 191, 237, 253, 260, 274, 302, 327, 329, 330–331, 333–334, 338

Kadesh 7, 33, 170, 179, 222, 225, 238, 275, 308–309, 314n2, 315–319, 324
Kingdom 20, 28, 46–47, 57n71, 71, 83, 128, 151, 166, 184–185, 212n64, 234, 234n80, 239, 240, 248–251, 264, 274, 283–284, 311, 337

Lampstand 89, 93, 118, 119, 158
Land 640x, 1, *passim*
Law(s) 7–8, 14, 17, 23–24, 25n29, 26–31, 31nn38–39, 32–33, 37–39, 41, 43, 52, 83, 85, 90, 92, 99, 106, 118, 124–125, 129–130, 138, 144, 159, 162, 166, 176, 186, 188–189, 190, 192, 196, 205, 215–216, 273–274, 304, 304n37, 328n10, 330–335, 333–334, 337–338, 341
Leaders 312x, 23, *passim*
Leadership 277x, 1, *passim*
Levites 30, 42–44, 46, 53–54, 66, 70–73, 75, 77, 79, 83–92, 95, 103, 106, 112–113, 115–116, 118–123, 125, 134, 153n18, 162, 182, 190, 194, 196–197, 199, 208–210, 213–215, 221, 258, 267, 272, 292, 305, 327–329
Life 2, 15–16, 22–26, 28–29, 33, 36–38, 41–44, 46, 48–49, 53–54, 57, 65, 69–70, 74–75, 82–83, 85–87, 92, 95, 97–99, 102–104, 108, 110, 112–113, 119, 125, 129–130, 139, 141–143, 153, 155–156, 161–163, 166, 183–185, 194, 201, 205–206, 208, 212, 215,

Life (*cont.*)   218, 220–222, 227, 230, 232, 235–237, 239–240, 242, 247, 253–255, 257, 263, 267, 274–275, 275n7, 276n8, 277, 279n11, 282–284, 286, 289, 294, 296, 296n30, 298–299, 305, 307, 309, 320, 332, 333–337, 340n21, 342
Literary   3, 6–7, 33–35, 38, 195–196, 216, 308, 311

Manna   20, 49–50, 129, 144–145, 179, 236
Marriage   48, 75, 100, 102, 103n45, 136, 154, 156, 259, 298, 301, 304, 339, 341
Message(s)   148, 151n15, 157–158, 202, 204, 242–243, 246–247, 250n103, 251–252, 321
Midian   24, 136–137, 154–156, 161, 181, 241, 243, 260, 302–303
Midianite(s)   6, 14, 48, 240, 252, 254, 257, 259–261, 301–303, 305, 135, 154
Military   21, 25, 44, 46, 53, 63, 65–66, 68, 68n11, 69, 71, 75, 77n19, 78, 80–81, 87, 95, 132, 154, 161–162, 168–169, 172–174, 183, 235, 241, 268, 277–279, 281–283, 303–305, 312, 314–315, 317, 320, 336
Milk and Honey   47, 50, 170, 170n31, 173, 184, 200, 237, 254, 306, 323, 341
Miraculous   25, 51, 81, 83, 142, 148, 161, 175, 205, 208, 224–225, 230, 236, 283, 342
Miriam   6, 45n60, 98, 132, 153, 533m18, 154–157, 159–160, 163, 194, 222, 227, 231, 238, 272, 318
Moab   7, 15n13, 15, 31, 182, 231–235, 238, 240–243, 245–246, 249, 251–252, 254, 256, 258n108, 268, 273, 275–276, 303, 313, 314, 314n2, 315, 319, 319n10, 320, 328, 340–341
Mosaic   3n7, 14, 29, 32–34, 37, 39, 43, 54, 155, 159, 175, 186, 274, 280, 292, 302, 323
Moses   1065x, 1, *passim*
Mount Sinai   5, 13–14, 22, 24, 26, 30, 32, 41, 43, 47, 50, 52, 63, 71–72, 72n17, 79, 84, 113, 119, 123–125, 129, 132–134, 136, 138–139, 142, 157, 162, 165–166, 174, 176, 179, 191, 208, 222, 288, 316, 316n6

Name(s)   191x, 4, *passim*
Nation(s)   387x, 1, *passim*
Nazirite   103–107, 113, 296
Number(s)   759x, 1, *passim*

Oil   86, 86n31, 93, 100, 105, 115–116, 118–120, 187–188, 210–212, 214, 286–288, 288n22, 291, 293–294, 333–334
Oracle(s)   32, 56, 85, 239, 241n85, 247, 247n101, 248–256, 281
Order(ly)   1, 5, 13, 20, 28, 32, 35, 44–46, 48, 52–54, 65–66, 72–76, 78–79, 81–82, 88, 91–92, 101, 103, 109, 111, 113, 115–116, 127, 131, 134–136, 142, 149, n14, 162, 167, 169, 178, 190, 192, 193n46, 203n57, 208, 210, 214–216, 217n69, 220–221, 226, 231, 237, 243, 247, 250, 259, 271–272, 274, 280, 282, 301, 303–304, 308n43, 314, 327, 330, 333–335, 339–340
Ordinance(s)   20, 187, 191–193, 193n46, 213–214, 219, 274, 291–294, 338, 340–341
Offering(s)   306x, 6, *passim*
Organization   13, 40, 43n58, 44, 65, 75, 82, 125–126

Paran   14, 64, 134, 160, 167, 170, 179, 234, 262
Passover   13, 23n26, 87, 125–130, 283, 286, 287, 290–291
Patriarchal   19, 20, 23, 21–22, 65–66, 75, 78, 81, 100–101, 142, 153–154, 160–161, 176
Patriarchs   18–20, 66, 75, 82, 84, 170, 262, 276, 299, 324
Peace   44, 49, 56–57, 68, 108–109, 109n50, 111, 133, 206, 213n65, 220, 253, 260–261, 297n31, 299, 327
Pentateuch   1, 3, 7, 13, 17–18, 21–22, 26–28, 32, 34, 36–37, 39–40, 42, 46, 49, 51, 54, 68, 70–71, 82, 84n26, 86, 94, 103, 108–109, 121, 126, 130–131, 136, 143n5, 147n10, 156–157, 157, 160, 168, 186, 190, 192n45, 207, 239, 261n112, 274, 279n11, 281, 285n19, 313, 322, 334, 340, 340n20
People   696x, 1, *passim*
Phineas   109, 264, 303, 259–261
Pillar   41, 52–53, 71, 72n17, 130–131, 131nn65–66, 132, 141, 156, 175, 226, 280, 315
Plague(s)   1, 6, 16, 50, 54, 70, 82, 98, 121, 127, 152, 174–176, 179, 181, 181n38, 203–204, 207–208, 215–216, 229, 236–238, 257–261, 263–264, 267–268, 301, 304, 342
Political   77, 197–198, 235–236, 239–240, 270n1

INDEX OF SUBJECTS 365

Population(s)   1, 22, 42, 46, 55, 68, 70, 75, 79, 81–82, 95, 145, 148, 168, 171, 216, 241, 241n86, 248, 256, 270–271, 324–325
Power   1, 25, 27n33, 43, 46, 52–53, 55, 64, 78, 102, 112, 122, 139, 147–148, 150, 157, 161, 163, 175–176, 177, 180, 197–198, 200, 204–207, 224–225, 232, 235, 238, 242, 249, 251, 258, 262, 77n9, 279–282, 299, 301, 311, 334
Prayer(s)   4, 7, 27, 44–45, 50, 56, 104, 106, 111, 128, 151, 159, 162, 175, 192, 206, 212, 221, 229, 271, 275n7, 277, 28n14, 282, 284, 295
Presence   5, 15, 18n20, 20, 24–25, 32, 39, 40–45, 48, 51–53, 55, 63–64, 71–72, 79n22, 83, 85–86, 93, 95, 97, 105, 107–108, 110–111, 111n52, 112, 114, 118–119, 130–132, 135–141, 142, 147–148, 150–151, 157, 159, 161–162, 171–174, 176, 182, 201, 203, 208, 210, 223, 226, 245, 251, 262, 274–275, 278–279, 286, 303, 337, 342
Priest(s)   250x, 26, *passim*
Priestly   3, 25, 34–36, 44, 55–56, 76, 84–86, 89n36, 100, 120, 133, 155–156, 164, 164n26, 182, 195, 197, 199, 201–203, 205–206, 209–210, 210n62, 213, 215, 217, 227, 239, 240, 314, 314n2
Promised   198x, 14, *passim*
Promise(s)   5, 15, 17n20, 18, 18n21, 19–23, 31, 34n43, 40–41, 48, 52–55, 63–64, 66, 71, 80n24, 81–82, 104, 107, 109–111, 118, 127–128, 133, 137–138, 142–143, 145, 148, 151, 155, 160, 162, 165–167, 169–170, 173, 176–178, 181, 185, 189, 224–226, 228, 235, 237, 244, 248–249, 282, 288, 298–301, 306, 309–310, 313, 321, 323–324, 328, 335–336, 342
Prophet(s)   24–29, 30, 33–34, 38, 38n55, 39, 44, 51, 55–56, 64, 84, 86, 102–103, 111, 123, 130, 135, 140, 146–149, 150–151, 154–155, 157–163, 201–202, 204–210, 225, 238–240, 241n84, 244, 250n104, 252–253, 255, 274–275, 277–289, 281, 283–284, 337, 341–342
Prophetic   1, 24–28, 32, 37n50, 38–39, 40–41, 43n58, 45–46, 51, 53, 56–57, 79, 109n51, 111, 123, 135, 140–144, 146–147, 147n10, 148–150, 153–158, 160–162, 163–164, 175, 181–183, 185, 194, 201–202, 225, 230–231, 239, 241n85, 247, 252, 254–255, 258, 260, 275n7, 277, 279, 308, 340
Providence   7, 23, 40, 45, 74, 162, 185, 215, 221
Providential   67, 78n21, 80, 109, 154
Purification   44, 87, 116–117, 119–121, 125, 188, 190, 211, 215–217, 217n69, 218, 220, 290, 290n23, 293, 304–305
Purity   84, 96, 98, 101, 209, 215, 217, 305

Quail   2n2, 20, 50, 146, 152, 179, 236, 316

Rebellion   21, 42, 56, 109, 124, 142–143, 143n5, 165, 172–173, 175–179, 181, 183, 190, 194–195, 196n50, 197–198, 201–202, 206, 208, 220, 224, 227, 238, 256, 259, 262, 273, 308, 323
Rebellious   27, 64, 124, 165–166, 174, 198–199, 201, 267, 269, 309, 313
Record(s)   5–6, 13–16, 22–23, 26, 29, 31n37, 32–33, 53, 67–68, 71n15, 73–74, 79–82, 92, 107, 124, 134, 136, 140, 155–156, 197, 221, 237, 239, 253, 257, 267, 271–272, 278, 313–315
Recorded   1, 4–5, 13, 35, 37, 63, 69–70, 54–55, 79, 81, 90, 107, 111, 115, 124–125, 130, 137, 165, 167, 182, 186–187, 190, 196, 209–220, 222–223, 232, 234, 267, 270–272, 285, 313, 317, 324, 326, 338
Reconciliation   121, 178, 189, 203, 215, 220, 334
Reconnaissance   163, 167, 182, 194
Redemption   42, 87n33, 90–91, 127, 213, 284, 289, 290n24, 294–295
Resource(s)   1, 3, 16, 21, 33, 42, 49, 56, 64, 80, 82–83, 97, 115, 129, 140, 142, 146–147, 150, 152, 160, 162, 167, 171, 183, 211, 220, 228, 232, 241, 257, 263, 307, 317, 323n1, 342
Responsibility   44–45, 72, 74–75, 77, 83, 85–86, 88–89, 91, 94, 107, 112, 119, 122, 125, 142, 151, 153, 162–163, 187, 196, 199, 207–210, 212n64, 213, 216, 220, 278, 280n14, 283, 296, 298, 309, 328n9
Restitution   99, 220, 334
Revelation   19–20, 23, 25, 28, 32, 37–40, 42–43, 52, 64, 94, 114, 119, 124, 131, 140, 149n14, 157–159, 161, 174, 176, 179, 194,

Revelation (*cont.*)   208, 239*n*84, 241, 241*n*85, 250, 252, 256, 274
Reverence   24, 43, 54, 72, 95, 112–113, 193*n*46, 207, 210
Rite(s)   88, 97, 119–120, 122, 125, 126*n*61, 154, 213*n*65, 219–221, 258, 263, 274, 290, 290*n*24, 304
Ritual(s)   20, 84, 100–102, 104–106, 115, 117, 119–121, 127–128, 185, 187, 189–190, 193, 211, 213, 215–218, 220–221, 243, 246–247, 249, 253–259, 262–263, 285, 295, 304–305

Sacred   1, 15, 17, 24, 30, 42–43, 46, 54, 63–64, 71–73, 75–76, 83–90, 92*n*38, 93–97, 100, 103–104, 106, 112–116, 118–120, 120, 134, 138, 162, 166, 187, 191, 193, 196, 199, 202–203, 205, 207–210, 214–216, 221, 272, 281, 285, 287, 289–295, 297–298, 303, 324
Sacrifice(s)   1, 5, 20, 42–44, 54, 72, 84–85, 89*n*36, 91, 97, 99, 101, 104–107, 114–117, 117*n*56, 118, 120–122, 128, 133, 137, 169, 185–190, 193, 203, 206, 209–210, 212–213, 218, 220–221, 238–239, 241, 243, 246–247, 249, 255, 257–258, 263, 284–289, 291–292, 294–296, 299, 305, 328, 328*n*9, 341
Sanctified   42, 52, 63, 86, 92*n*38, 95, 103, 132, 191, 199, 209, 304
Sanctuary   22, 25, 42–43, 53–54, 63–64, 71–72, 75–76, 78, 83, 85–87, 89, 89*n*36, 90–93, 95, 112–114, 116–117, 119–122, 158, 190, 205–206, 208, 211, 219–220, 260, 288, 290–291, 293, 304, 306, 318, 331, 335
Scripture(s)   2, 17–18, 23, 26, 29, 21*n*38, 33–34, 36–38, 45, 49, 51, 53–54, 83, 101, 123–125, 153, 158, 170, 207, 221, 237, 239, 247, 254–256, 282, 335, 339
Security   1, 46, 54, 56, 83, 87, 108, 140, 187, 194, 209, 228, 240–241, 243, 255, 261, 297, 335–337
Seer(s)   56, 158, 241*n*85, 244*n*94, 250*n*104, 238–239, 239*n*83
Septenary   71, 216, 290*n*24, 307–308, 308*n*43, 310
Service(s)   2*n*2, 53, 55–56, 70–71, 73, 83–84, 87, 90–91, 93–95, 94*n*40, 112–114, 119–122, 125, 127–128, 148, 156, 159–160, 162, 183, 199, 203, 205, 209–211, 213, 215, 239–241, 272, 282, 301, 210, 329, 332–333, 342, 249, 251, 268
Serving   112, 174, 193, 199, 227, 239, 246, 337
Seven(th)   107x, 30, *passim*
Seventy   19, 46, 53, 70, 80, 116–117, 131*n*68, 146–147, 150, 161, 163, 193–194, 247*n*100, 268, 279, 288*n*21, 316, 340
Shepherd(s)   16, 23, 45, 53, 78*n*21, 125, 135, 139–140, 143*n*1, 145, 148, 161*n*23, 162, 181–182, 205–206, 225, 254, 260*n*109, 277, 280, 282, 343
Song   7, 27, 31, 34, 49, 139, 154, 231–232, 236, 249, 277
Speak(s)   15, 25, 25*n*29, 26, 28, 32, 38*n*52, 40, 41, 45, 47, 56, 63, 75, 84, 107, 110, 118, 123–125, 131, 146, 148, 150, 152, 155, 157–159, 162, 175, 206, 223–225, 236, 238–240, 244*n*94, 246, 248, 250, 254–255, 276, 279*n*13, 288, 300
Spoke   4, 13, 25, 25*n*29, 27, 39, 40–41, 45, 53, 63, 124–125, 131*n*68, 150, 155, 201, 258, 299
Spoken   55–56, 102, 107, 111, 128, 153, 155, 181, 194, 202, 242, 247, 296–298, 310
Spokesman   84, 149, 153, 155–157, 204
Spies   6, 21, 48, 50, 167, 172, 182–183, 186, 226, 233, 236, 262, 278, 283, 308–309, 317–318, 320
Spirit(s)   2*nn*1–2, 26, 51, 53, 57, 57*n*71, 86, 100, 111, 125, 131*n*68, 141, 147, 147*n*10, 148, 149–151, 153, 160–161, 163, 180, 194, 237, 243, 250, 256, 279, 279*nnn*11–13, 280, 282–283, 342
Spirit of God   2, 40, 45–46, 51, 51*n*63–64, 53–54, 57, 114, 141, 147, 147*n*10, 148, 250, 254, 261*n*23, 264, 278*n*10, 279*nn*11–12
Spirit of Leadership   57, 151, 278–279, 280*n*14, 282–283
Spiritual   2, 16–17, 23*n*26, 39, 56, 83, 95, 102–104, 106, 113, 119, 139, 141, 160, 162, 177, 187, 190, 219–201, 235, 241, 241*n*86, 245, 251, 253–254, 278, 289, 296–297, 299, 335
Staff   31, 77*n*19, 127, 204–206, 223–224, 224*n*72, 230–232, 238, 245

INDEX OF SUBJECTS

Tabernacle   196x, 13, *passim*
Tent of Meeting   13, 25, 32, 41–42, 43, 52, 63–64, 70, 72, 72n17, 75–77, 81, 88–89, 94, 94n40, 105–107, 108, 114, 118, 120–121, 123–124, 131, 133, 148–149, 150–153, 157, 161, 174, 200, 203, 205, 210, 214–217, 223–224, 238, 255, 259–261, 273, 279, 279n13, 280, 285, 288, 293, 306, 338
Test(ed)   14, 16, 19, 25, 31, 40–41, 49–51, 65, 81, 100, 102, 124, 168–170, 179, 199–201, 204–205, 223, 228, 230, 235–237, 237, 262, 282, 316, 335
Theological   1–4, 16, 22, 33–34, 41, 47, 51, 57n71, 64, 66, 81, 92, 149, 152, 154, 170, 192, 195, 213, 231, 233, 237, 239, 249, 288, 307, 328
Torah   3n3, 6n11, 13, 16–18, 29–30, 31n37, 33, 35n45–47, 36, 38–39, 43n59, 64–65, 74, 84, 90n37, 98, 118, 123, 126, 138, 140, 149n13, 190, 192, 192n45, 221, 255, 342
Tribe(s)   160x, 4, *passim*
Trumpet(s)   31, 40, 71, 132–135, 138, 140, 287, 292, 303

Vengeance   301–302, 330–331, 334
Visionary   28, 149n14, 151, 158, 241n85, 250n104, 256
Vision(s)   28, 46, 68, 75, 151, 157–158, 162–163, 180, 183, 185–186, 241, 241n85, 247n101, 250–252, 250n104, 255, 262, 267, 273, 323
Vow(s)   103–107, 113, 173, 187–188, 228, 295–299, 300–301, 319, 341

Wandering   1, 14–15, 40, 49, 56, 65, 83, 130, 181, 222, 226, 228, 235, 294, 317, 335
War   1, 47–48, 65, 69, 82, 133, 139, 172, 227, 232, 303, 305–306
Warning(s)   1, 14–15, 40, 49, 56, 65, 83, 181, 222, 226, 228, 235, 294, 317, 335
Water   1, 20, 31, 42, 49–50, 57, 64, 80, 87, 100–102, 120, 128, 147, 171, 179–180, 216–217, 217n69, 218–219, 221–228, 232, 235–238, 250–252, 283, 304–305, 307, 316, 323
Wilderness   243x, 1, *passim*
Word(s)   2–6, 16, 19, 25–26, 28–32, 37–38, 40–41, 44, 47, 52, 55, 64–65, 73–74, 82–83, 85, 102, 104–107, 110, 120–121, 123–125, 134, 141, 143, 148, 155, 157–159, 161–163, 174, 181–183, 185, 188–190, 195, 198, 202, 204, 207, 210, 219, 225, 236, 242–243, 244, 240–241, 246–250, 264, 296–297, 298–301, 310, 332–333, 340, 342
Worship   1, 13, 19–20, 24, 40, 42–43, 43n58, 51, 53, 55, 57, 63, 72, 74, 85, 90, 93, 95, 107, 114–115, 117, 132, 165, 177, 185–187, 194, 210, 216, 221, 249, 257n105, 258–259, 267, 282, 284–285, 289, 316, 321, 322
Wrath   27, 72, 90, 109, 119, 143, 143n5, 165–166, 177, 196, 203, 203n57, 206, 210, 229, 245, 252, 258–261, 301, 304

Yahweh   767x, 5, *passim*

Printed in the United States
by Baker & Taylor Publisher Services